Supervisor's Survival Kit

Eleventh Edition

Cliff Goodwin, Ed.D.
Daniel B. Griffith, J.D., SPHR

PEARSON
Prentice
Hall

Upper Saddle River, New Jersey
Columbus, Ohio

Library of Congress Cataloging-in-Publication Data

Goodwin, Cliff, 1948–
    Supervisor's survival kit / Clifford R. Goodwin, Daniel B. Griffith.—11th ed.
        p. cm.—(NetEffect series)
    Includes index.
    ISBN-13: 978-0-13-239698-1
    ISBN-10: 0-13-239698-X
    1. Supervision of employees.   2. Personnel management.   I. Griffith, Dan (Daniel B.)   II. Title.
    HF5549.12.G66 2008
    658.3'02—dc22   2008029177

Editor in Chief: Vernon Anthony
Acquisitions Editor: Gary Bauer
Editorial Assistant: Megan Heintz
Production Coordination: Anupam Mukherjee/Aptara
Project Manager: ChristinaTaylor
Senior Operations Supervisor: Pat Tonneman
Art Director: Diane Ernsberger
Cover Designer: Kellyn Donnelly
Cover art/image/photo[s]: iStock
Director of Marketing: David Gesell
Marketing Manager: Leigh Ann Sims
Marketing Assistant: Les Roberts
Copyeditor: Mercedes L Heston

This book was set in Minion by Aptara®, Inc. It was printed and bound by Edwards Brothers Company.
The cover was printed by Coral Graphics.

Pearson Prentice Hall™ is a trademark of Pearson Education, Inc.
Pearson® is a registered trademark of Pearson plc
Prentice Hall® is a registered trademark of Pearson Education, Inc.

Pearson Education Ltd.   Pearson Education Australia Pty, Limited
Pearson Education Singapore, Pte. Ltd   Pearson Education North Asia, Ltd.
Pearson Education Canada, Ltd.   Pearson Educación de Mexico, S.A. de C.V.
Pearson Education—Japan   Pearson Education Malaysia, Pte. Ltd.
                                                        Pearson Education, Upper Saddle River, New Jersey

                                                        10 9 8 7 6 5
                                                        ISBN-10:   0-13-239698-X
                                                        ISBN-13: 978-0-13-239698-1

Contents

About This Book

The managerial responsibilities of today's supervisor continue to evolve as companies compete in today's fast-moving business environment. To be successful, front-line managers must possess a diverse set of technical, human relations, and conceptual skills. They need to develop a repertoire of skilled behaviors in each of these areas to deal with the challenges presented in the workplace. Challenges include dealing with an increasingly diverse work force, empowering employees, encouraging teamwork, hiring and firing, training and enhancing employee performance, ensuring health and safety, and improving productivity and quality. These are just some of the important tasks supervisors are asked to manage.

It is often the case that an employer will promote an outstanding employee to the position of supervisor. Unfortunately, the skills recognized and rewarded by a promotion to supervisor are not always the same ones needed to be an effective supervisor. New supervisors must be developed and trained by their employer in order to survive and thrive in their new managerial role. This book was written for the purpose of developing the skills of these new or prospective supervisors.

Supervisor's Survival Kit has enjoyed a great deal of success. Since the original edition, nearly a million readers have benefited from this brief, to-the-point, practical book. One of its strengths is that this book works effectively in a variety of training and development situations. It is sufficiently comprehensive and substantive to be used as a text for a formal college course, yet organized tightly enough to meet the constraints of an in-service seminar delivered by training professionals within their organization. Using this book will help develop a sound fundamental foundation on which an employee can build a rewarding career as a supervisor and leader. Feedback from long-time users of this book testifies to the fact that students enjoy learning from the cases and participating in the role-playing activities.

Putting theory into practice is the strongest feature of this new edition. The text focuses on the learner as an active participant and partner in the learning process. There are a variety of experiential exercises including case studies, role-playing activities, short vignettes, self-assessments, and personal growth exercises that help make the principles in the text come alive for students. These experientially designed exercises actively engage students in authentic learning experiences that connect theory with practice and help develop their critical thinking skills.

The book has been revised to be even more learner friendly and comprehensive. One significant change that long-time users will notice is that materials formerly included in the Participant's Guide are now incorporated into the text, thereby dispensing with the need to purchase a separate Participant's Guide. The Instructor's Manual continues to provide excellent information on how to use the text for teaching a course. It is also an excellent resource to the independent learner who wants to improve his or her supervisory skills without taking a formal course or workshop.

Another change for the eleventh edition is the addition of a co-author, Daniel B. Griffith, who has joined Cliff Goodwin to prepare this text. The authors wish to thank long-time users of this text for their suggestions on how it could be improved. At their request, much of the pertinent information and style of presentation from the previous edition have been kept to preserve the integrity of the text. This new edition, while improved, maintains the overall effectiveness and comprehensiveness of previous editions. Among the most significant changes from the prior edition are:

- The **Role Profiles for Cases** at the end of the book has been revised and updated. New profiles have been added while a few familiar profiles are no longer included in the hypothetical organization. We hope previous users will not miss these familiar characters for long as they become acquainted with new characters. The main purpose for this update is to create a story line that focuses more on team-based approaches to management rather than hierarchical management structures.

- An additional discussion on **competencies** has been added to Chapter 1 (Should You Be a Supervisor?) to broaden the understanding of what supervisors must know and apply in today's modern organization as they develop technical, human relations, and conceptual competence.

- A model for **analyzing performance gaps** and **identifying performance barriers and solutions** has been added to Chapter 4 (Achieving Productivity Through People).

- The information from the former chapter concerning "Five Irreplaceable Foundations" has been incorporated into Chapter 5 (The Supervisor-Employee Relationship).

- New information has been added to Chapter 7 (Quality Control and Continuous Improvement) regarding various **quality methodologies** and tools a supervisor can use to initiate **quick, simple process improvement measures** with her team.

- An expanded discussion on **diverse work teams** and how to work with new employees who join the team is included in Chapter 8 (The Effective Work Team).

- New information concerning **behavioral interviewing**, steps for conducting **reference and background checks** prior to job offer, and an **overview of the laws and regulations** affecting the employment relationship has been added to Chapter 11 (Staffing).

- Chapter 14 has been retitled from "The Formal Appraisal" to "Managing Performance," and new information has been added to reflect the broader **scope and purpose of the performance management process** than simply conducting the formal evaluation.

- Chapter 20 (Converting Change into Opportunity) has been revised to provide **updated information regarding business, society, and economic changes affecting the workplace** and additional information on **assisting employees to deal with change.**

- As noted, material formerly in the Participant's Manual such as **true-false questions, application exercises, self assessments,** and **personal growth exercises** has been added to the text. In addition, new features have been added such as **performance checklists** and a **"to learn more" section** that provides additional resources readers can consult.

About the Authors

Professor Goodwin has been on the faculty of the Purdue School of Engineering and Technology for the past twenty-five years. His primary teaching emphasis is in the area of supervisory skill development. He has conducted research, authored articles, and presented seminars on a wide variety of supervision- and management-related topics. In addition to his university work, Professor Goodwin has acted as a consultant to numerous businesses throughout Indiana. Prior to his university appointment, he was in management in the automotive manufacturing industry. Professor Goodwin holds degrees from Purdue University and Ball State University in management and industrial training areas. He completed his Doctorate of Adult Education at Indiana University.

Mr. Griffith is an adjunct faculty member of the Purdue School of Engineering and Technology at Indiana University–Purdue University Indianapolis (IUPUI), where he teaches courses in leadership and conflict management. He is also Manager of Training and Organization Development at IUPUI. His primary responsibilities include providing training and development in the areas of supervisory, employee, and leadership skills development; legal compliance; conflict management; diversity; and communications. He also has a background in mediation and is a mediator in the Indiana legal system. Prior to his present work and teaching roles, he worked for the state of Indiana as an attorney for the state's civil rights agency and as an attorney and administrative law judge for the state's transportation department. Mr. Griffith holds a Bachelor of Arts degree in English from DePauw University and a Doctorate of Jurisprudence from Indiana University School of Law–Indianapolis.

Professor Goodwin and Mr. Griffith are also co-authors of *The Conflict Survival Kit: Tools for Resolving Conflict at Work,* also published by Pearson Education, Inc.

Introduction

Someday, if it hasn't happened already, you may become a supervisor and be responsible for the productivity of others. Should it happen, your life will change.

Will you be ready for your new responsibilities? Will you earn the respect of those who work for you? Will those who promoted you be pleased with your work? The answers lie in how you go about motivating, supporting, guiding, and building relationships with those you supervise; the kind of working climate you create; the quality of the decisions you make; the skill you demonstrate in handling a wide variety of human problems; the way you manage your time and set priorities; your ability to mold employees from different cultures into a team; and the amount of leadership you put into your supervisory style.

Common sense will help you somewhat in becoming a good supervisor, but to make a really successful transition you need the kind of help this book provides. It is both a classroom text and an on-the-job guide for the "instant" supervisor who has not had the advantage of formal preparation. It can help make your move into management graceful, rewarding, and permanent, as well as help you provide the foundation for moving into even more challenging management roles in the future.

At the end of each chapter, you will find either a case study or a role play designed to involve you in a realistic management problem. The case studies can be used for discussion, written assignments, or self-instruction. Suggested answers are provided in the back of the book. The role-plays are intended primarily for use in the classroom or seminar. A role-play can be played in fifty minutes or less; specific instructions are provided for each game. Role-plays can also be used as traditional case studies.

Cases are built around nine different roles that are profiled in detail in the back of the book. Please become acquainted with each character before reading any of the cases or playing any of the role-plays.

In addition to case studies and role-plays, the following content is also at the end of each chapter: (1) self-assessment and application exercises that help you react to authentic situations and provide a limited substitute in the event you miss class time in which the chapter is discussed; (2) self-test true–false questions that enable you to check your comprehension and retention and measure your learning progress without instructor assistance; and (3) personal growth exercises that help you integrate what you have learned from the text to your personal life.

The authors recommend that you make a contract with yourself to complete these exercises and to analyze the cases on your own if you do not have the opportunity to discuss them or engage in role-plays in a course or seminar. Why? The answer is simple—what you learn from the text will be *reinforced*, which means that you will *retain* what you learn longer. You are also more apt to apply what you learn to a job, either now or in the future. Finally, if you are already a supervisor, you immediately become more professional by demonstrating immediate positive behavior change as the result of applying what you've learned to real-world situations. This will enhance your career progress.

We wish you well as you study this text and put theory into practice and increase your confidence and effectiveness as a supervisor. Enjoy the journey.

GETTING INTO SUPERVISION

"Whatever you can do, or dream to do, begin it."

GOETHE

chapter **one**

SHOULD YOU BE
A SUPERVISOR?

"Nothing noble is done without risk."

Andre Gide

Improving Productivity
Leading Teams
Communicating Effectively
Managing Conflict
Improving Performance
Managing Time
Benefiting from Change

PERFORMANCE COMPETENCIES

After you have finished reading this chapter, you should be able to:

- List a minimum of six characteristics of an effective supervisor

- Explain six advantages to being in management

- Describe the skills and competencies needed at the front-line supervisory, middle, and upper levels of management

P atti drove home from her job with a financial institution feeling both elated and troubled. After less than two years with the firm, she had been offered a promotion to a supervisory role. Should she accept it?

Manuel has been happy as a short-order chef for three years. Yesterday he was offered a position as night manager at a substantial increase in pay. Should he accept the challenge?

Gerald was surprised when he was invited to apply for a management position with his electronics firm. Should he leave his highly paid, satisfying, skilled position for the headaches of management?

Clarice reentered the labor market in the health care industry at the age of forty-three. After less than six months, she has been invited into management. Should she make the move?

George has been encouraged to start thinking about a supervisory role with his national supermarket chain. Should he leave the security of his union for the problems of management?

The decision to make the transition into management is difficult and serious. When your opportunity comes, you should weigh both the advantages and the disadvantages. Would you be happier as an employee with fewer responsibilities? Which would mean more to you—the personal satisfaction of being a specialist, or the status that comes from being a leader? Some people would never consider becoming supervisors, as shown by the following comments:

> As a supervisor, you are squeezed between a rock and a hard place. You have to please management and at the same time keep your employees happy. It's an impossible situation. No, thanks.

> I've seen too many burned-out supervisors to want the impossible headaches of a supervisor for a few more dollars each week.

I'd rather be happy without the pressure and additional income, and my family agrees with me.

I'm a skilled person who takes pride in and receives pleasure from doing my specialized job well. Why should I abandon a skill it took me years to develop? I consider myself to be an excellent technical person, but after taking a management seminar I could tell that being a supervisor would never be in my comfort zone.

MANAGEMENT DEFINED

The definition of management is getting things done within an organization through other people. It means guiding people's efforts toward organizational objectives; it means inspiring, communicating, planning, organizing, controlling, and evaluating; it means setting goals and moving employees toward them. Management is leadership.

Obviously, management is not for everyone. Most employees in all classifications are wise to remain non-managers, especially when they do not have the temperament or personality for successful careers as supervisors. Make no mistake—there is tremendous value and need for specialists and individual performers who do not aspire to larger leadership roles in their organizations. Being a manager is neither better nor worse than being a specialist, nor should it confer any superior status in contrast to the specialist. Being a manager means added work pressures, leadership responsibilities, and the continuous development of specific skill sets and competencies not typically expected of specialists. Although there are rewards to being a manager, there are also significant challenges.

How about you? Should you seriously consider a permanent career in management? Would it satisfy your personal needs and values? Would you achieve greater self-fulfillment? Would you be successful? To help you think it through, try answering the ten questions in the following checklist.

CHECKLIST FOR PROSPECTIVE SUPERVISORS

	Yes	No
1. Do you consider yourself a highly ambitious person?	❏	❏
2. Do you sincerely like and have patience with people?	❏	❏
3. Do you like solving problems that don't have just one correct answer?	❏	❏
4. Are the financial rewards you may receive worth the added work pressures you will experience?	❏	❏
5. Is seeing that others do a job well more important to you than taking pride in doing the job yourself?	❏	❏
6. Would you enjoy learning about psychology and human behavior?	❏	❏
7. Would you be happier with more responsibility?	❏	❏
8. Would you rather work with problems involving human relationships than with mechanical, computational, creative, clerical, or similar problems?	❏	❏
9. Do you desire an opportunity to demonstrate your leadership ability?	❏	❏
10. Do you desire the freedom to do your own planning rather than being told what to do?	❏	❏

Total Number: _____ Yes _____ No

If your total number of yes answers exceeds your no answers, you probably make an excellent candidate for a supervisory position.

This checklist is intended to start you thinking, not to tell you definitively whether you should become a supervisor.

If most of your answers are yes, it appears that the role of supervisor might be attractive and comfortable for you. If, however, you gave more no than yes answers, it appears (at least at this stage of your life) that you should proceed with caution. Such a checklist also helps by pointing out that many important factors are involved in such a decision. Following are five factors that should receive your special attention:

- *How deep is your need for the status and recognition that comes from being a manager?* Some people have a strong drive for positions that confer status and authority, while others gain their self-esteem from the intrinsic value of their individual contributions. There is nothing inherently wrong with this drive for status and recognition from others, because it can be one important motivator that drives leaders to assume increasingly responsible positions within their organizations. However, it also means you will likely be more intensely scrutinized. With this status comes accountability for the performance of others, for which you will be evaluated as well. If you are unwilling to pay the price that this additional status confers or if your self-esteem needs can be more readily met through your daily work activities and working relationships with your co-workers, you might be happier as a non-supervisor.

- *How important are people to you?*   Most jobs require some contact with people, but the job of supervisor requires much more than most. You must be a personnel director, counselor, teacher, and practical psychologist at the same time. You must learn to work constructively with and accept people who irritate, frustrate, disappoint, and hurt you. You must develop your interpersonal or "people" skills. Active listening and use of correct grammar in written and spoken communication are examples of these skills. You must familiarize yourself with employment laws and regulations, such as those pertaining to anti-discrimination, sexual harassment, family and medical leave, and worker's compensation, which require you to treat all employees in a consistent and equitable manner. You must be receptive to assist new employees from diversified cultures. You must have a great deal of patience, perception, and compassion. In other words, you must like people—all kinds of people. You can't fake it. Yet, if people are truly important to you, building lasting relationships with those you supervise can be highly rewarding.

- *Do you consider yourself a good planner?*   Are you an organizer? Supervisors must prepare and implement plans. They must spend quiet periods reorganizing their departments. They must think ahead. If you prefer to leave planning to others, you may not be happy as a supervisor.

- *How willing are you to relinquish control of daily work tasks and rely on others to complete assignments?*   One mistake that new supervisors often make is they continue to perform essentially as they did as specialists who are responsible only for their own work activities. Although becoming a supervisor doesn't mean you won't retain some of these responsibilities, you are now responsible for ensuring that others perform these tasks so you can focus on broader activities involving planning, organizing, and directing others. Some managers lack the skill and, more importantly, the willingness to delegate these day-to-day activities to others. If you don't want to let go of these activities, you will probably be happier as a non-supervisor.

- *Do you have leadership potential?*   A supervisor, department manager, or crew chief is, more than anything else, a leader. He or she must set the tempo, provide the inspiration, and sometimes nurse the employees along, while at other times exercise harsh discipline and hand out constructive feedback. It is a constant balancing act designed to keep the team spirit of the department alive. Although some people seem to have natural leadership ability, most managers have had to develop their skills through training, experience, and reflection on their experiences. Don't worry about whether you have been able to demonstrate your leadership yet—it's the desire that counts. If you believe that you have the potential, look ahead with confidence to your role as a supervisor. Opportunities to demonstrate your leadership come later.

ADVANTAGES OF BEING IN MANAGEMENT

If you have never been a leader, it may be difficult to predict how you will react or perform in a management role. If you have the slightest interest in finding out what your chances are, why not try? Start preparing now and accept the first opportunity that presents itself. Following are some advantages to consider:

1. *Opportunities abound.*   Approximately one out of every nine employee positions is a supervisory or management one so there must be room for you. The police officer who is on a beat can prepare to become a sergeant. The registered nurse can plan to become a superintendent. The factory worker can aspire to become a supervisor. The young person at McDonald's can set the goal of becoming its CEO. The opportunity to move up is nearly always present in those who are willing to plan ahead and prepare. Effective leaders are more able to move to another organization, thus creating the opportunity for advancement.

2. *Becoming a supervisor is often the best way to achieve a better-than-average income quickly if you don't have a technical skill or a professional specialty.* Specialists are paid well for their expertise, which they gained through education, on-the-job training and work experiences, and the attainment of specific licenses and certifications required for their field. If you have a general educational background and do not have a trade, specialized skill, or professional or semiprofessional license or certificate, you should consider becoming a supervisor. The opportunities, especially in service organizations, are excellent.

3. *Supervisors can learn more because of the greater opportunity to participate in company training.* They can attend more classes, read more, and associate with experts. In fact, supervisors must continue to improve and grow with the company. Organizations experience many changes that require their employees to learn new skills. Along with technical training that supervisors or managers get, they are often given the opportunity to attend seminars on leadership, team dynamics, or in technical areas like inventory control, production planning, or quality assurance. Employees may be able to find a little niche where they can hide, but supervisors cannot. The Bigger Pot Principle applies here. If you believe your personal growth is restricted as an employee, moving into supervision would be like transplanting a plant to a bigger pot where greater root growth is possible in many directions.

4. *Supervisors almost always know what is happening within the organization.* As part of the management team, they attend meetings, receive more written communications, and are often consulted by leaders in upper-level positions. They interact with other departments and deal with a wide variety of challenges.

5. *Supervisors are in an ideal position to contribute to the welfare of others.* As managers, supervisors can go to bat for the employees they supervise. The supervisor is the employee's link to policymakers in the organization. The process of meeting the special needs of employees often begins with the supervisor.

6. *Supervisors are more mobile than workers.* Front-line supervisors usually find it easier to locate a new job should their firm downsize, right size, or simply shut its doors and go out of business. This is because they generally gain additional knowledge and experience over their non-supervisory counterparts and they have demonstrated leadership capability that can be applied to new situations.

DISADVANTAGES OF BEING IN MANAGEMENT

In addition to the many advantages in becoming a manager, a few of the disadvantages are listed next. Think about them before making a final commitment.

1. *Problem employees can be difficult.*   As an employee, you have already noticed that some co-workers have unusual behavior patterns that cause problems for their supervisors. Handling confrontations, working with grievances, and doing corrective interviews can be traumatic for some people. Supervisors often find themselves in the middle of complex human problems that seem to have no possible solution.

2. *Expect to be more alone as a supervisor.*   Successful supervisors—even team leaders—must isolate themselves to some extent from the employees they supervise. This challenge can be especially difficult for new supervisors who have been promoted to lead their former peers. It can be difficult to be a supervisor and a close friend at the same time. You must frequently back away when you might prefer to be a part of the group. You may be asked to withhold confidential information from your employees until an official announcement is made. As a member of the management team, you may be perceived as being one of "them" and not one of "us" by your employees. You might feel this isolation most when you make an unpopular decision and the people you supervise let you know you are on opposite sides. It is an unreasonable expectation to think that you can please everyone all the time.

3. *You may not receive constant reinforcement from your supervisor.*   People in management usually treat other managers differently from the way supervisors treat their employees. As a supervisor, you are expected to support and protect your employees at all times. You must give them day-to-day security and constant personal attention. Do not, however, expect this same treatment from your supervisor. Because you are a manager, you are expected to be stronger, so your supervisor may not feel the same need to reinforce you. He or she will take it for granted that you will provide your own personal confidence and self-motivation and will deal more openly and directly with you.

4. *You may have to change your behavior more than you expect.*   Becoming a supervisor for the first time may become one of the most important things to happen to you in your lifetime. It can be a bigger transition than people expect. In becoming a supervisor, you lay your career and reputation on the line; if you fail, your adjustment to a lower level can be brutally difficult and often impossible. The change requires realigning your thinking because your whole approach to your career must be different. Your daily routine, your human relationships, and your self-concept may have to change. Underestimating the degree of change you might have to make could cause you to fail as a supervisor.

5. *A position as a supervisor could mean longer hours without overtime pay.* Although many workers are paid on an hourly basis and entitled to overtime pay (usually time and a half of their regular hourly pay) pursuant to the Fair Labor Standards Act, many supervisory positions are paid on a salary basis for which overtime rules do not apply. As a salaried professional, you may be expected to do work outside the standard 40-hour workweek. Often, a supervisor's schedule is so tight during the regular working day, assisting staff, addressing employee concerns, and meeting

with other managers, that he or she might not have time to plan and perform other management functions during the regular business day. This may mean taking extra work home, which in turn cuts into family time. Such is the price for those who wish to lead.

6. *High-productivity and high-quality standards are more important today than they were in the past.*   Your challenge is to gain higher-quality standards and greater production with fewer people. These demands increase the pressure on supervisors to learn new technology and approaches in workflow and job design.

7. *Your skills as a supervisor may need to be developed.*   Often, the best and most capable technician may be given a promotion to supervisor. Even though technical skills are important, other skills are needed too. As mentioned earlier, you need interpersonal skills, such as people and leadership skills, as well as time-management skills.

THE PRESSURES OF MANAGEMENT

The promises and the pitfalls of management are many. However, is there any truth in the belief that becoming a manager is a sure way to get an ulcer? A first-class ticket to a heart attack? A one-way passage to a nervous breakdown? Not really.

This frequently expressed fear—that becoming a manager is injurious to one's physical and mental health because of excessive pressures—is a myth. Management people, in general, are as healthy as those not in management. The supervisor can learn to deal with organizational pressures just as the politician must deal with public pressures. Certainly, the job may tax your nervous system a little more than some other kinds of work, and the emotional and mental strain may be greater in some careers than in others. Every job has its own special demands. The solution, of course, is to handle the job without letting it become too much of a strain. Special

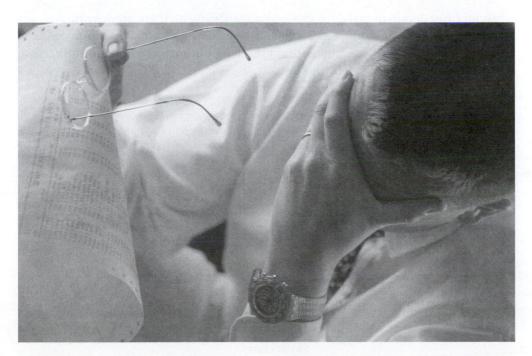

courses teach strategies for dealing with stress. Some individuals who are highly self-motivated apply pressure to themselves by setting difficult goals that force them to live up to their potential. Properly controlled, stress increases productivity.

Let's look at an example of one individual who wanted the challenge and involvement of a supervisory role. Hank recently accepted an opportunity to become a supervisor.

> I admit that I have many fears about becoming a supervisor. I've never thought of myself as a natural leader and have never really had an opportunity to work under pressure. But I've got to cross over the line sometime or I'll never know whether I can make it. I might as well start now and find out what it's like. I realize the days ahead will be the most critical of my career, even though I will supervise only four people at first.
>
> I see the whole thing as a sort of laboratory experiment. I'll be able to try out all the principles and techniques of good supervision, and if they work well with four people now, they should work well with four hundred people later. It's my first chance to test my ability as a leader. I feel somewhat like a young senator on his first trip to the capitol. I've won the election, but now I must prove to myself that I can survive.

Hank is approaching his new assignment with an excellent attitude. He has assessed his personal desire to be a supervisor, his potential as a leader, and his drive to succeed, and has decided it is worth the time and investment. He is also going into his first role as a supervisor with his eyes wide open, knowing it won't be easy, but viewing it as an opportunity to learn, grow, and test himself. Like Hank, if you have engaged in similar self-assessments and determined that supervision is for you, you will likely find that the challenges and rewards far outweigh the pressures and stress you will face.

THE SKILL SETS AND COMPETENCIES YOU MUST DEVELOP IN YOUR NEW SUPERVISORY ROLE

Should you decide to make the move into management, there are specific skill sets and competencies you must develop and continue to develop as you progress in your career through the management ranks. Depending on your specific role and your relative position within your organization's hierarchy, the extent to which specific skill sets and competencies are needed will vary.

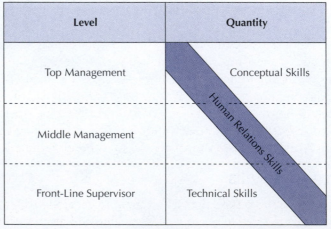

Skills chart

The chart on page 10 shows the levels of management (front-line, middle, and upper) and the type of skills needed or used at each level. The three skills sets are technical, human relations, and conceptual.[1] Notice that at the supervisory level, technical skills are used the most. The amount of technical and conceptual skills one uses at each level of management changes. Supervisors use their technical skills most often, with some conceptual skills. Upper management, however, uses a smaller portion of technical skills but a larger portion of conceptual skills. For example, when an effective engineer gets promoted to supervisor, he uses his technical skills a great deal of the time to guide and direct the efforts of his direct reports. He also is expected to use human relations skills in dealing with his employees. When he moves to middle management, he is expected to use less technical and more conceptual skills than he did at the supervisory level. When he reaches upper management, he is expected to use a great deal more conceptual skills and fewer technical skills. Again, he continues to use the same amount of human relations skills.

After being in upper management for years, it is conceivable that a CEO who came up through the management ranks from engineering may no longer be a qualified engineer, because he has not had to continue to use or develop his technical engineering skills and relies instead on qualified front-line and middle managers to ensure that a technically competent workforce is maintained. He must instead use more of his human relations and conceptual skills. Conceptual skills are essential for establishing the overall direction of the organization that front-line and middle managers, along with staff, fulfill through their day-to-day activities. While the CEO uses his human relations skills in equal proportion as he progresses through the supervisory-, middle-, or upper-management ranks, he presumably hones them more sharply as he advances in order to respond to and manage the increasingly complex human relations challenges that typically accompany the CEO role. Consider, however, the CEO who fails to understand the importance of continued development in the human relations realm. There are ample stories of leaders who are respected within their industry for their vision and technical expertise, but who fail to inspire trust and loyalty among employees because of their inability to develop competence in this critical area. Clearly, a supervisor who wishes to advance within managerial ranks must never undervalue the importance of developing human relations skills.

Technical Skills

The supervisory ranks are often filled with technically skilled workers possessing a strong work ethic. These characteristics are normally the ones that got the employee promoted to supervision in the first place. The supervisor must possess sound technical, job-related skills that are developed on the job, by completing an apprenticeship in a skilled trade, or by completing a two-year associate degree or four-year bachelor's degree in a specific technical area. Technical skills are important because the supervisor is often required to make decisions, answer questions, train, or guide and direct the work of her followers. The supervisor often must be trusted to be a technically qualified resource to his or her employees. The chart shows the relative need for these skills as the supervisor moves into middle and upper management.

Human Relations Skills

Human relations skills are those skills that are required to get along with other people. These are commonly referred to as *people skills* and include, among others, interpersonal communication, knowing how to lead others, giving and receiving feedback, coaching, relating to others, empathizing, managing conflict, negotiating, influencing others, and maintaining motivational environments. Highly qualified technical people who are promoted because of their technical expertise often struggle as supervisors because they do not possess these skills. They have not learned what it takes to get along with their employees. If you are promoted to supervision based on your technical expertise and work ethic, you should invest your time and energy into learning and developing your human relations skills. Even if you are a naturally talented "people person," you may need to further develop that talent by studying human relations. There are many books and courses available on this topic.

Conceptual Skills

Justice, fairness, the difference between right and wrong, legitimacy, truth, equal opportunity, and valuing and appreciating diversity are examples of *human conceptualizations*—that is, their definitions are not universally defined because they do not exist in nature as a tangible object, but are in our minds as concepts. *Concepts* are very important in that they form the foundation of our beliefs and values. They may be only slightly different or perhaps substantially different for one person or group than for another. The executive often defines these types of concepts for the company they lead. His or her meanings of these concepts influence greatly the decisions made and thus the company's direction. Upper-level managers must possess sound conceptual skills. We expect our executive-level managers to know the difference between right and wrong and be ethical and fair with their employees, customers, and community.

There are also problems and challenges of a conceptual nature that executives must solve. Dealing with change, growth, and decline; creating new markets; outsourcing; investing money; and dealing with local, national, and international politics are a few of the conceptual problems facing the modern executive. Unfortunately, there are no universal solutions to most conceptual problems they face, but only approaches that the executive may adopt and use. As a result, executives must learn from their successes and failures as they go. To learn, they must be open to new ideas. Learning often requires skill handling ambiguity and uncertainty. Executives set the example for their employees. They must be able to conceptualize a vision for their company and guide their organization to the realization of that vision.

ADDITIONAL SKILL SETS AND COMPETENCIES

A few specific skill sets and competencies have been identified in recent years that, although part of the technical, conceptual, and human-relations framework, have received special attention among employers and, therefore, require your attention to develop. These additional skill sets and competencies include the following:

1. *Emotional intelligence.*   Emotional intelligence encompasses an individual's capacity to manage his or her emotions and harness them appropriately to guide behavior and thinking to enhance performance and achieve better results. It also covers an individual's ability to respond appropriately to the emotions of others without overreaction in order to minimize escalation and ideally to help others manage their emotions better. Someone who demonstrates emotional intelligence possesses self-awareness regarding his or her

moods and emotions and their impact on performance, empathy toward the moods and emotions of others, understanding of how others react to your emotions and behaviors, and self-regulation of behavior to respond appropriately rather than impulsively to given situations.

2. *Social intelligence.*   Social intelligence involves the ability to determine the appropriate requirements for leadership for particular situations and to respond accordingly. It includes social perceptiveness to understand the needs, problems, and opportunities of the team, group, or organization and the relative working relationships, characteristics, and traits of members and collective capabilities that enhance the leader's ability to influence change. It also includes the ability to vary behavior to accommodate team and organization relationships and the social situation at hand.

3. *Political savvy.*   Political savvy involves the ability to recognize and take advantage of the unwritten and unspoken rules, norms, roles, and channels people use to get things done within the organization.

4. *Systems thinking.*   Systems thinking involves the knowledge and understanding of how various organizational components such as processes, systems, policies, decision making, relationships among teams and individuals, and the work of individual performers interrelate, and how change in one component impacts other components. Systems thinking requires an understanding of these interrelationships and has impacts at the organizational, process, and job and performer levels.

5. *Continuous learning.*   Continuous learning involves the ability to introspectively analyze the processes and efforts engaged in while working, consider ways to improve, and apply new learning for future situations, in a continuous cycle of improvement. It also involves the ability and willingness to modify behavior and change assumptions and beliefs based on new experiences.

6. *Managing diversity.*   Managing diversity includes understanding how the differences and similarities reflected in the workforce can be used to strategic advantage to achieve synergy and better results. It involves valuing diversity and respect among and between teams and individuals, as well as accepting the challenges that result based on differences among people and their perspectives and managing them rather than avoiding or minimizing their importance. It also involves incorporating diversity values in every component of organizational work, life, function, and systems rather than viewing diversity as an isolated subset of activities.

PERFORMANCE **CHECKLIST**

1. Management is leadership. It involves getting things done within an organization through other people. It means guiding their efforts toward organizational objectives, inspiring them, communicating, planning, organizing, controlling, and evaluating. It means setting goals and moving employees toward those goals.

2. Management may be for you if you have leadership potential, feel a deep need for the status and recognition that comes with being a manager, like people, and are a good planner, willing to relinquish day-to-day work activities to others and direct their work instead.

3. There are many advantages to being in management, including the abundance of opportunities available, income potential, opportunities for training and development, upward mobility, and the opportunity to contribute to the well-being of others.

4. There are, however, disadvantages, including the difficulties of working with problem employees, occasional feelings of loneliness with limited opportunities to receive reinforcement from upper management, long hours with little or no extra pay, the pressure of producing high-quality work, and the necessity to change your behaviors and develop appropriate skills in order to become effective in the supervisory role.

5. The competencies that a supervisor must develop can be categorized into three areas: technical, human relations, and conceptual. Front-line supervisors are relied on and must use their technical skills on a daily basis, whereas they are expected to use conceptual skills less. Upper management uses conceptual skills more often and technical skills infrequently. However, the need to use and continually develop human-relations skills remains constant, regardless of one's role and rank within an organization's management structure.

6. In addition to the skill sets and competencies reflected in the technical, human-relations, and conceptual frameworks, a few specific skill sets and competencies have been given increasing attention among employers and, therefore, demand the supervisor's attention to develop. These include emotional intelligence, social intelligence, political savvy, systems thinking, continuous learning, and managing diversity.

TEST **YOURSELF**

For each statement below, check true or false.

True   False

____   ____   1. People with general educational backgrounds but no technical skills should seriously consider a role in management.

____   ____   2. Beginning supervisors can count on constant support and reinforcement from their superiors.

____   ____   3. Supervision is basically getting things done through others.

____   ____   4. Little behavioral change is required in making the transition into supervision.

____   ____   5. The most successful supervisors are those that become close friends with their employees.

____   ____   6. The skill set needed to manage diversity requires the supervisor to seek to avoid or minimize differences so that employees can work productively together.

____   ____   7. Those who do not have previous leadership experience tend to become poor supervisors.

____   ____   8. Developing your interpersonal and people skills is a must as a supervisor, regardless of the level of responsibility in the organization.

____   ____   9. The process of meeting the special needs of employees often begins with the employee.

____   ____   10. The company promotes you to supervisor because of your background and skills; therefore, furthering your development is not necessary.

Turn to the back of the book to check your answers.

Total Correct ____

DISCUSSION **QUESTIONS**

1. For you, right now, based on the challenges, advantages, and disadvantages described in this chapter, is the price of becoming a supervisor too high to pay?

2. Should a college student who does not have specific clerical, mechanical, technical, or professional skills take courses in management? Defend your answer.

3. From your personal experience as an employee, what percentage of supervisors would you say are truly professional? How would you differentiate between supervisors who are professional and supervisors who are not?

4. Describe the job of your supervisor. As you do so, ask yourself whether the rewards justify the sacrifices.

5. How accurate do you think your score is on the Checklist for Prospective Supervisors? Do you believe it provides you an objective perspective of whether supervision is right for you?

6. Describe the three skill areas for management. Discuss your management's strengths and weaknesses in relation to these skills.

CASE: CHOICE

Please turn to the back of this book and become acquainted with the roles of Bill, Ricardo, Renee, and Marty before analyzing this case.

Bill must fill a vacant supervisory spot and is considering both Renee and Marty, who have applied. He asked Ricardo for advice on this decision and to get back to him soon on his recommendation. Ricardo must, therefore, choose one of his employees to recommend for promotion. Ricardo is ambivalent about whom to recommend. He knows that Renee believes she is entitled to the promotion because she leads the department in personal productivity. She is the better choice on the basis of educational background and mental ability, but Ricardo is not sure that other employees will respond well to her assertive ways and high demands. Renee's relationships with others are not as good as Marty's.

Ricardo also knows that Marty believes he is ready to make the move. Marty has paid his dues, his ability is sufficiently high, and he might be more sensitive to the needs of employees. Ricardo must consider one additional factor: Renee seems to have more personal confidence than Marty.

No matter what happens, Ricardo knows he will have a human relations problem with the employee not selected. Even so, he wants credit from Bill for recommending the most successful candidate and wants to choose wisely.

Ricardo comes to you for your advice. Base your choice on the preceding information and your interpretation of the roles of Renee and Marty (as described in the back of the book). If you were Ricardo, how would you proceed? On what factors would you base your decision? What process would you follow? What information will you need to make your choice? What information is missing that would help you make a more informed choice? Would you recommend either at this point in favor of looking at other candidates (either internally or externally)? You know you will be expected to justify your recommendation to Bill and to the one (or both) you do not recommend.

Do you feel qualified to make such a decision? Is Bill using this situation as an opportunity to test your skills in leadership? If so, can you identify your leadership skills?

Turn to the back of book to compare your thoughts to those of the authors.

LEADERSHIP POTENTIAL SCALE

Supervisors are both managers and leaders. Once you become comfortable with your supervisory role, you may want to add more and more leadership to your management style. If you have not (up to now) had the opportunity to demonstrate your leadership talents, you may have more potential than you think. This scale is designed to help you evaluate just how much potential you possess.

Circle the number that indicates where you fall in the scale from 1 to 10. After you have finished, total your scores in the space provided.

If you rated yourself 80 or higher, it appears that you have both the desire and the potential to be an excellent leader. If you rated yourself between 50 and 80, you may need more desire and confidence in yourself, but you seem to have the potential to become a highly successful leader. If you rated yourself less than 50, you probably are not ready for a leadership role at this stage of your life. See the authors' comments in the back of this book.

I can develop the talent and confidence to be an excellent speaker in front of groups.	10 9 8 7 6 5 4 3 2 1	I could never develop the confidence to speak in front of groups.
I have the capacity to build and maintain productive relationships with workers under my supervision.	10 9 8 7 6 5 4 3 2 1	I'm a loner. I do not want the responsibility of building relationships with others.

I intend to take full advantage of all opportunities to develop my leadership qualities.	10 9 8 7 6 5 4 3 2 1	I do not intend to seek a leadership role or to develop my leadership skills.
I can develop the skill of motivating others. I would provide an outstanding example.	10 9 8 7 6 5 4 3 2 1	I could never develop the skill of motivating others. I would be a poor example to follow.
I can be patient and understanding with others.	10 9 8 7 6 5 4 3 2 1	I have no patience with others and could not develop it.
I could learn to be good at disciplining those under me—even to the point of terminating a worker after repeated violations.	10 9 8 7 6 5 4 3 2 1	It would tear me up to discipline a worker under my supervision; I'm much too kind and sensitive.
I can make tough decisions.	10 9 8 7 6 5 4 3 2 1	I do not want decision-making responsibilities.
It would not bother me to isolate myself and maintain a strong discipline line between workers and me.	10 9 8 7 6 5 4 3 2 1	I have a great need to be liked; I want to be one of the gang.
I would make an outstanding member of a "management team."	10 9 8 7 6 5 4 3 2 1	I would be a weak member of a "management team."
In time, I would be a superior leader— better than anyone I have known.	10 9 8 7 6 5 4 3 2 1	My leadership potential is so low it is not worth developing.

Total Score _____

PERSONAL GROWTH **EXERCISE**

Interview a supervisor who you know and ask about the challenges and rewards of being a supervisor. Ask for any advice he or she would give or lessons learned that would benefit you in your decision whether to pursue a supervisory role.

TO LEARN **MORE**

To learn more about the specific competencies and managerial behaviors that supervisors must develop, refer to the following references:

Goleman, Daniel. *Emotional Intelligence.* New York: Bantam Books, 1995.

Goleman, Daniel. *Working with Emotional Intelligence.* New York: Bantam Books, 1998.

Goleman, Daniel, Richard Boyatzis, and Annie McKee. *Primal Leadership: Learning to Lead with Emotional Intelligence.* Boston: Harvard Business School Press, 2004.

Senge, Peter M. *The Fifth Discipline: The Art and Practice of the Learning Organization.* New York: Currency Doubleday, 1990.

Thomas, R. Roosevelt, Jr. *Beyond Race and Gender: Unleashing the Power of Your Total Work Force by Managing Diversity.* New York: AMACOM, 1991.

Thomas, R. Roosevelt, Jr. *Redefining Diversity.* New York: AMACOM, 1996.

Weisinger, Hendrie. *Emotional Intelligence at Work.* San Francisco: Jossey-Bass, 1998.

Yukl, Gary. *Leadership in Organizations,* 6th ed. Upper Saddle River, NJ: Pearson Education, 2006.

NOTE

1. Katz, Roger L. 1974, "Skills of an effective administrator," *Harvard Business Review* September–October: 90–102.

chapter **two**

MAKING THE TRANSITION

"Leadership, like swimming, cannot be learned by reading about it."
Henry Mintzberg

Improving Productivity
Leading Teams
Communicating Effectively
Managing Conflict
Improving Performance
Managing Time
Benefiting from Change

Last year, Marsha was a quiet and unassertive computer operator; today, she is an efficient office manager. Last year, Craig was a graduate student doing research; today, he is supervising the work of a dozen employees. Marsha and Craig have successfully made one of the most difficult transitions of their lives. Last year, they were responsible only for their own work—today, they are leaders directing the work of others. Could this transition happen to you?

Many individuals move into their first supervisory position from a nonsupervisory job within the same organization. Your move into supervision may likely take this path. You may move up within the same department or be transferred from another section. Either way, you have a challenging experience ahead of you. To help you explore this transition, let's look at two contrasting examples and what they tell us about the need for preparation.

Harry and Lynn, who just completed such a transition, are the same age and have similar personal goals and track records. They became supervisors for the same organization at almost the same time. Their appointments, however, occurred under quite different circumstances.

Because Harry knew about his promotion three months in advance, he was able to prepare for his new responsibilities by taking a supervision course at a nearby college, doing some reading about management, and working closely as an understudy to the person he was to replace. This preparation was designed to guarantee a smooth transition for both Harry and the organization. Lynn, however, was a regular employee one day and a supervisor the next. Unlike Harry, who was groomed for his new role, Lynn became an instant supervisor, with almost no opportunity to prepare.

PERFORMANCE COMPETENCIES

After you have finished reading this chapter, you should be able to:

- Write a specific step-by-step plan outlining your successful transition from the role of an employee to that of a supervisor in the same department

- Describe how to introduce change gradually

- Describe five initial goals for a supervisor

- Describe three major differences between the mechanical and biological realms and their relevance to how supervisors should manage

Why did Lynn not receive the same training and preparation time as Harry? The answer is simple: Management cannot always predict supervisory vacancies caused by resignations, transfers, and promotions. Sudden growth sometimes causes the demand for supervisors to be greater than the supply. As a result, management is often forced to fill slots quickly. Every day remarks like the following are being made somewhere:

> I realize, Palmer, that you've been with us for only three months and haven't had supervisory experience, but because of an emergency situation, we want you to take over the department tomorrow morning.

> It may come as a shock, Susan, because we haven't had a chance to groom you as a team leader, but we'd rather give you the opportunity than to bring in an outsider.

> Remember when you came to work, Sam, and you said you wanted to be a supervisor within a year? Well, you've made it ahead of schedule. Drop by my office later, and we'll talk about salary and other details.

No matter what your age, education, or experience, you cannot predict what opportunities will occur in the future. You cannot anticipate when your supervisor will leave or when some other supervisory opening will occur. Even in periods of recession, when some firms cut back, an opportunity may surface. In some organizations, if you have not previously demonstrated an interest and some level of understanding about the role of supervision, such as would be obtained through taking management courses or participating in an in-house pre-supervision preparation training program, you will be passed over for such an opportunity in favor of someone who is better prepared. In other organizations, such as where Harry and Lynn work, the chance to become a supervisor occurs virtually overnight, although the likelihood of success is greater for someone in Harry's situation than Lynn's. Whatever the case, when the opportunity comes, the more you prepare yourself and can demonstrate that you are ready to take on increased responsibility, the more likely you are to be considered and the more smooth your transition will be. The time to prepare is now.

YOUR FIRST STEP AS A SUPERVISOR

When you move into your first management role, keep your eyes open and get the lay of the land as quickly as possible. Every position of leadership responsibility entails certain unwritten agreements or ground rules of operation.

- Are you about to encounter some sensitive human relations situations you need to know about in advance?
- Will you be inheriting a problem employee?
- Do any special legal or safety precautions require your attention?
- Does your leadership style differ significantly from that of your predecessor?
- Should you be apprised of some informal reports or unusual protocol?
- Do you know how to handle an incident of employee theft or a problem of sexual harassment?

You hope answers to such questions come automatically from your new superior either before or shortly after you make your transition—but do not depend on it. You may have to uncover the problems and dig up some answers on your own. Some new supervisors make a list of questions similar to those just given so that they can get answers in advance and avoid unnecessary initial mistakes.

Even if you do an outstanding job of learning which hurdles to jump and which to avoid, the position likely holds other pitfalls to guard against. It is one thing to learn theory and prepare for management, but it is quite another to put that knowledge into practice. No matter how much formal preparation you receive in advance, your first few weeks are critical. Seek to begin on the right foot.

BECOMING A GOOD SUPERVISOR IS NOT A PIECE OF CAKE

Making the move from an individual performer to a supervisor is a difficult passage involving behavioral changes on your part and adjustments on the part of those who work for you. If you underestimate the challenge, you will not live up to your own expectations, let alone those of your superiors.

At the outset, a new supervisor is well advised to not overestimate the true level of power, authority, and control he or she truly has to get things done. In today's work world, the traditional concepts of hierarchical, command and control management structures are giving way to more team-based approaches. The view of the supervisor as "boss" is giving way to one where the supervisor is more of a "team leader" or "team facilitator" who supports processes that maximize opportunities for the generation of ideas and solutions based on team participation and input rather than decision making and direction giving that comes solely from management. If you have been a part of these team approaches in previous positions, your transition to supervision may come more easily for you. If not, understand that although you are, in fact, still the boss, your effectiveness comes more from working with your team members in an interdependent fashion and garnering their trust and commitment than from relying on your authority, power, or status to force compliance and cooperation.

HOW TO SURVIVE YOUR FIRST FEW WEEKS AS A MANAGER

To help you survive during your first few weeks as a supervisor, try the suggestions presented in the following pages. They can help make the difference between a sound, easy transition and a needlessly difficult one that will cause you problems before you can show your real ability. They may get you through the crucial period when people's reactions to you may be the most critical.

Use Your New Power in a Sensitive Manner

You may think it cannot happen to you, but sudden authority has a strange way of inflating your feelings of self-importance without your being aware that it is happening. Guard against this danger by neutralizing your new power with a strong dose of humility. Keep reminding yourself that you are basically the same person you were before you became a supervisor. You must now succeed through the efforts of others, but you do not want to abuse your new authority and create hostility in those who must now look to you for leadership.

Be Patient with Yourself

Your first days as a supervisor may be hectic. You will likely face paperwork and deadlines you did not expect, meetings that gobble up your time, and problems you did not anticipate. At the same time, you may become impatient because you want to try new things right away. Relax. Back away. Try taking the long view. You may wish to confide in a fellow supervisor or with your supervisor. Support from others you trust can help you deal effectively with change.

Decide to Be a Professional

The only way you will be happy as a supervisor is to satisfy your belief that you are effective. Personal pride comes only after you feel comfortable with your new role—not before. Recognition from both your employees and superiors shows that you have achieved your goal.

Stay in Close Contact with All Employees

The temptation to please management by increasing productivity may cause you to be less sensitive to the people in your department and their problems. This insensitivity is a serious mistake. Despite all your pressing new responsibilities, it is important that you take time to make personal and positive contacts with each employee in the department during your first few weeks as their supervisor, regardless of whether you were promoted from within the department or were brought in from outside. These contacts can be accomplished through brief stand-up conversations, coffee-break talks, or invitations to talk things over. How you meet with employees and the frequency in which you meet depends on the number of employees, the time available, and other circumstances. The purpose of each contact is to let each person know that you appreciate her or him as an individual. It is your responsibility to initiate the contact and build the relationship while encouraging employees to get in contact with you as needs arise.

Make Changes Gradually

Sudden change scares many people. Unless management demands immediate changes, it is best to get used to the way the department operates before introducing major innovations. When you are ready to make changes, explain them to the people who will be affected by them. And remember, people are more motivated to make changes when they have been involved in the planning of the change.

Ron has been in his new assignment for one week now and is very anxious to make some much-needed changes to his department. He is new to this particular building, although he has worked for the company at another location for three years. He has been very successful at fixing problem areas and this certainly is one of them. It is one of the worst performing departments in the entire company. His analysis tells him there are a few problem employees; however, the majority of his direct reports are good employees who want to be productive. The department has had three different supervisors in the last two years and, for the most part, serious quality and productivity problems have been ignored.

He sees many ways to improve the performance of the department, but experience has taught him that because he is new, he should move slowly first. He learned that employees are more motivated to carry out changes that they have had a part in planning. Their participation in identifying changes and planning them (with his guidance) will also improve the flow of communication throughout the department, thus helping to make the changes successful.

Ron called a meeting with his three group leaders, during which he shares his vision and plans for the department. He is quick to point out that they will be involved in the planning of all changes.

After the meeting, two of his group leaders came to his office to thank him for having the meeting and assured him that they were very willing to give their support and input. They said how happy they were to finally have the opportunity to participate in helping the department improve.

Watch the Up Side—Protect the Down Side

Naturally, you want to satisfy your superiors during your first few weeks because you must earn their support. In doing so, however, be sure to protect those who work in your department. Do not pass on to your people the sudden pressures you feel from above. You must act as a buffer and keep your frustrations and disappointments to yourself if you are to keep a smoothly operating and productive department. Your job is to make the work of those in your department easier, not harder.

Save Some Planning Time

The hustle and bustle of being a new supervisor may cause you to spin your wheels and try to operate without a plan. You may spend too much time moving in one direction and not enough in another. You might solve one problem only to discover that a problem having a much higher priority has been neglected. Take the time to think and plan. Evaluate yourself and your performance on a day-to-day basis. If you cannot find any time for planning while you are on the job, do it at home.

Redefine Your Workplace Friendships

It is possible that some of your close on-the-job friends may try to capitalize on a previous personal relationship now that you are a supervisor—in other words, they may seek preferential treatment. Do not permit this manipulation. Your first responsibility as a supervisor is to keep all relationships with your people fair and equal. If you violate this principle at the beginning, you may jeopardize the respect and confidence you receive from others.

Adopt New Standards of Integrity

Previous co-workers with whom you have mature friendships will recognize your new responsibilities and will not expect favoritism. These friendships can continue to be close, although both parties may need to redefine their agreements and expend additional energy to keep them in balance. As you adjust to these situations, new standards of integrity on your part may be necessary. Such matters as confidentiality (keeping management matters to yourself), self-control, and personal adherence to company rules come into play.

Let Your Employees Help You

Some of your employees may know more about your department than you do. How can you handle this situation? By all means, go to them with questions. Ask their advice and accept it. Involve them in as many decisions as possible, especially those decisions that affect them personally. You need their help, especially at the beginning.

Adopt a Learning Attitude

Once you become a supervisor, do not become so preoccupied with pleasing everyone that you neglect your education. Do not hesitate to ask necessary questions of your superiors, fellow supervisors, and knowledgeable employees; continue to read and study this book (it is most helpful after you become a supervisor); and enroll in any available outside courses that can offer important direction to your success. For example, if you discover that your new role is putting extra demands on you in a specific area such as data processing, then study these skills on the outside while you are performing inside. It is widely accepted among educators that when you can apply what you learn immediately, you are motivated to learn faster, cover more material, and understand it better. Once you are a supervisor, your learning should accelerate, not decline. To be an effective supervisor, you must first be an effective human being. Lifelong learning is necessary in our modern world. Take the opportunity to learn new skills when you can. Do not become obsolete.

Balance Home and Career

New supervisors have two important reasons for learning more about how to balance home and career. One is to improve immediately their own "balancing act" so that they can survive as supervisors; the other is so that they will be in a position to teach and counsel their employees to do the same later on. With more single parents in the workplace, the need for such training has increased dramatically. Following are four tips to assist you in getting started:

1. Apply the same management techniques you learn in this book to do a better job of leading your family. Remember that home can be a good and safe place to practice newly acquired techniques of leadership.

2. Demonstrate to your employees and superiors that you know how to balance home and career by not jeopardizing one for the other. Stresses at work can cause stress at home, and vice versa. It can be difficult sometimes to keep one from spilling over into the other.

3. Use your weekends to catch up on home responsibilities and enjoy a few leisure activities so that you arrive in the office on Monday morning fresh and organized.

4. Arrive ahead of your staff so that you have some quiet time to plan your daily activities.

When you first become a supervisor, be careful not to create more problems than you solve. Move in with confidence and enthusiasm, but keep your eyes open and do not destroy previous relationships instead of building new ones. Create a climate of excitement, but do not sacrifice your long-range goals for immediate gains. Remember that it is easier to win popularity than to achieve respect. The management ladder has many rungs; if you do not make a smooth transition to the first one, you may never climb the others.

INITIAL GOALS AS A SUPERVISOR

More than ever, it is a time to read and listen. The new supervisor should attempt to accomplish the following during the first few weeks:

1. *Maintain productivity.*   Try to keep the productivity and efficiency of the department at previous levels, with some improvement if possible.

2. *Build relationships with employees.*   Redefine and start building a new and strong relationship with each employee. Get to know your people. Introduce yourself. Let them get to know you. Self-disclosure can help employees see you as a person, not just as a supervisor.

3. *Build relationships with peers.*   Keep in mind that fellow supervisors can often assist you in making your transition.

4. *Think like management.*   Make some progress in the direction of becoming a solid member of the management team. Start the process by thinking like a manager, not like an employee. Do not fall into the trap of criticizing management openly to your employees. Work as a member of management to correct problems, and do so with a spirit of unity and teamwork.

5. *Ask questions and learn.*   Begin with the premise that the people doing the work know more about how things are done, and why things are done in certain ways, than you do. Inquire about their jobs and work processes without feeling you have to immediately fix things. Once you are assured you have the full picture, you will avoid implementing premature changes that may backfire. Assess now; make changes later.

6. *Stay positive.*   No matter how you feel on the inside, stay positive and appear confident on the outside.

Later, you can attempt to accomplish more dramatic results. If the first steps have been successful, your future goals are attainable. The willingness of your followers to follow you rests on your track record. Success begets success. The way you pace yourself during the first few weeks determines to a large degree your long-range success or failure. Let's look at an example of what to avoid.

After two years of waiting, Ron finally became a supervisor with the Acme Discount Stores. He was given a clothing department with seven full-time employees. He began with great enthusiasm, stirring up the employees, making changes on the run, and generally applying the new-broom technique. Predictably, the immediate results were gratifying. Sales jumped and management was pleased. Ron was the new hero around the store. In a few weeks, however, some problems slowly became evident. First came some rumbles from the employees. Next came the resignation of one long-time employee, followed soon after by another. Finally, sales dropped drastically, and management's enthusiasm for Ron changed to discouragement. They soon realized he had committed the cardinal management sin: He had sacrificed the relationships between himself and the people in his department in order to make a big show with immediate results. He had taken the short view instead of the long one, and the price both Ron and the company paid was high.

PHILOSOPHY OF LEADERSHIP

Supervisors are leaders. Your effectiveness as a supervisor is determined by your leadership philosophy. Your philosophy consists primarily of your beliefs and values, and it guides and directs your decisions, behaviors, expectations, and assumptions.

The extent to which your philosophy is founded on sound principles must be considered. With this in mind, let's examine some basic truths about the nature of leadership by examining the characteristics of two separate realms of existence, each quite different from the other. Your philosophy of leadership is based to a great extent on your understanding of these differences and how you manage each. The two realms are called the *mechanical realm* and the *biological realm.*

The Mechanical Realm. Clocks belong to the mechanical realm, as do all mechanisms. It is very likely, given the proper training, tools, equipment, and time, that you could build a clock. Building a clock is not impossible; in fact, it is not very hard at all. The clock is a mechanism, a piece of machinery. We know how it works and how its parts interrelate to keep time. We can take it apart and put it together again.

We do not so much motivate our clock as we make it move. The clock's motivation (if it can be called that) is external to itself. The clock moves because we wind its spring or place a battery in it. The clock cannot move itself. This we know.

Science provides laws of mechanics and formulas that explain the clockwork's design, and when built correctly, it keeps accurate time regardless of where it happens to be. Like most mechanisms, the clock is easily mastered and understood. It is by no means a mysterious thing. Like the clock, the tools, equipment, machines, mechanisms, structures, systems, and other assets for which you are responsible for managing in your work setting belong in the mechanical realm. If you can move or manipulate it and explain its inner functions, however complex, then it relates to the mechanical realm. In contrast, there is one vital asset for which you are responsible to manage that does not belong in this realm—people.

The Biological Realm. Like people, oranges belong in the biological realm. Can you build an orange? What kind of training, tools, equipment, and time would the task require? This may seem like a silly question, because, as we know, no one can "build" an orange. We know that oranges are grown, not made. We must take a seed, put it in the right soil, and provide the proper conditions. Then we must wait. The seed germinates, grows into a tree, and bears its fruit. From seed, to tree, to orange, takes years. We might take credit for growing juicy and delicious oranges, but in reality, we did not "motivate" the orange to grow. Its motivation lies within itself. It decides. Our most learned scientists agree that they are ignorant of what motivates oranges to grow.

At most, we provide the environment suitable for its growth. We do not understand the motivation within the orange. If your life depended on the production of one orange, how many seeds would you plant? Probably as many seeds as you can get your hands on. The mystery of growth is inherent to things belonging in the biological realm; the realm in which the orange certainly belongs, the realm of all living things. Unlike the clock, and like the orange, people belong in the biological realm. This is the one critical asset for which you have responsibility that is hugely different from all others that belong in the mechanical realm. It is important, therefore, that you fully understand and appreciate this difference, as it will significantly influence your leadership philosophy.

Obviously, a person is more complex, more mysterious than our orange. Leadership is about people. People are the most fascinating of all creatures, and understanding their motivation is complex. It is not, however, impossible. How do we grow a person? Where do we start? What are the tools and equipment needed, and how much time does it take? What conditions assist in the growth of a person? If we want delicious oranges, we trim and prune the tree. How do you trim and prune your son or daughter, or an employee you manage? What do you leave on and prune off? If you cannot know what motivates an orange to grow, how can you possibly know how to motivate your son or daughter, or any other person, to grow? When we wish to understand people, we certainly immerse ourselves in the realm of the mysterious and the marvelous. Internally motivated, ever-changing, and uncertain probabilities define the boundaries of this realm. We cannot understand the workings of the human by taking one apart and studying its individual pieces. Scientists have all but given up that research approach.

Your boss might tell you to "Get out there and motivate your employees." Your boss may say that the organization should "run like clockwork," or be a "tight ship." Such expectations represent mechanical realm–type thinking. These expectations and metaphors do not relate to people. Rather than thinking of organizations as clocks and ships, it may prove useful to think of them as **gardens and grounds.** Just as a gardener maintains an environment for growth, so should the leader of any organization.

Sadly, many times our leaders create the type of environment where you feel motivated to work in opposition to the goals of the organization.

Characteristic Differences Between the Mechanical and Biological Realms

The following list of words or metaphors helps us identify and understand the differences between the two realms. As you examine and consider the opposing pairs of words found in each realm, you begin to comprehend how different these concepts are from one another. Let's examine just a few of the pairs of words from the lists below so you will get the idea of the differences. The mechanical realm consists of laws, whereas the biological realm consists of opinions and guesses. We always know what makes a clock tick; our laws of physics and mathematics tell us. We are not ever sure what makes people tick; we are left to our opinions and guesses for an explanation. In the mechanical realm, things are predictable; in the biological realm, there is relativity and probability. People are not predictable. Mechanisms are built, but organisms are grown, and so forth.

Mechanical Realm	**Biological Realm**
Mechanisms	Organisms
Made up of machinery	Made up of people
Use laws to explain action	Use opinions or guesses to explain action
Machines are consistent	People change
Machines react to stimuli	People react to their meaning of the stimuli
Machines are externally motivated	People are internally motivated
Machines are built	People are grown
Machines have a price	People have value

To illustrate this point further, let's examine the following pair of differences from the list:

Machines react to stimuli.

People react to their meaning of the stimuli.

Consider the following experiment. Imagine there are two strings suspended from the ceiling. At the end of each string is a steel ball bearing. The two steel balls are at rest and are touching. The weight of each ball is known. If we pull one of the steel balls away to a measured distance from the other steel ball and release it, what happens? Will it collide with the other ball? Is there a mathematical formula to predict how the balls react after the collision? You bet there is. And no matter where this experiment is performed or who does it, the formula predicts the exact outcome every time.

Now a question: What is transferred from one ball to the other when they collide? The answer is force and energy.

Now let us do another experiment. Imagine that there is a 140-pound Rottweiler dog lying on the floor in front of you. You weigh your foot so that you know its mass and you pull it a measured distance from the dog's side. You then kick the dog. Is there a mathematical formula that you can plug the data into that will predict exactly the dog's reaction to the kick? No. There is not such a formula. Why not?

The answer is a simple one. The dog has a brain and a mind. When you kick the dog, you transmit force and energy just as when the steel balls collide. However, you also transmit something else—information. The kick is perceived by the dog's brain, and his mind gives the kick a meaning. We cannot predict the dog's reaction, because we cannot control the meaning he gives to the kick. If the kick means affection, the dog reacts very differently than if it means that he is under attack from a hostile aggressor. For the dog, there is no direct connection between the stimulus (kick) and his response. The dog's brain perceives the kick and his mind gives it a meaning. It is his meaning of the kick that he reacts to.

Humans react to their meaning of stimuli, not to the stimuli itself. Certainly humans are more complicated than any other living organism and they have many more ways of interpreting a kick. If you kick a dog, you might get bitten; but if you kick an employee, you will likely receive a great deal more than that. Leaders must understand this if they are to truly comprehend the behavior of their followers. A leader cannot cause or predict behavior simply by manipulating the stimuli. For this, we should be thankful; otherwise, we would be no more than robots simply reacting like a piece of machinery.

DO NOT CONFUSE THE TWO REALMS

Any supervisor who thinks he can run his department like clockwork, or who tells others that he can motivate his employees, is naive and lacks understanding of the nature of the biological realm. He is also communicating that he essentially draws no distinction between people and all other assets that he manages.

Frederick Herzberg, a human behavior theorist, spoke of the inherent fallacy of the belief that one person can, in fact, **motivate** another person.[1] A supervisor who adopts this view may likely be able to produce concrete evidence of how he or she managed to motivate an employee. That evidence, however, is likely to be measures he or she has taken either to punish or reward the employee. Indeed, the employee will change his or her position once the punishment is threatened or the reward is promised. He or she will likely comply with the supervisor's request in order to eliminate or minimize the threat or to receive the benefit. All the supervisor has really accomplished is to get the employee to **move**. Herzberg describes this as the *KITA* theory of motivation, in which you "motivate" employees by giving them a Kick in the A--. Chicago gangster Al Capone apparently subscribed to this motivation strategy when he said, "You can go a long way with a smile. You can go a lot farther with a smile and a gun."[2]

Gangsters and KITA managers do nothing to help individuals be truly motivated. The more effective approach to motivation, Herzberg asserts, is to recognize that the most a manager can do is create the appropriate conditions in an employee's environment that help the employee find the **instrinsic** motivation he or she needs to perform, just like a gardener maintains gardens and grounds to create opimum conditions for an orange to grow. Stephen Covey, author of *The 8th Habit: From Effectiveness to Greatness*, draws the distinction this way: "You can't lead inventories and cash flow and costs. You have to manage them. Why? Because things don't have power and freedom to choose. Only people do. So you *lead* (empower) people. You *manage and control* things."[3]

PERFORMANCE **CHECKLIST**

1. When the opportunity comes to move into a supervisory role, the more you prepare yourself and can demonstrate that you are ready to take on increased responsibility, the more likely you are to be considered and the more smooth your transition will be. The time to prepare is now.

2. It is one thing to learn theory and prepare for management, but it is quite another to put that knowledge into practice. No matter how much formal preparation you receive in advance, your first few weeks are critical. Seek to begin on the right foot.

3. The notion of supervisor as *boss* has changed dramatically in today's business culture to one where the supervisor is more of a *team leader* or *team facilitator*. Your success as a supervisor comes from working interdependently with team members and engendering employee trust and commitment rather than relying on your authority, power, or status to force compliance and cooperation.

4. There are a number of steps a new supervisor can take to survive his or her first few weeks in the role, including

   a. Use your new power in a sensitive manner
   b. Be patient with yourself
   c. Decide to be a professional
   d. Stay in close contact with all employees
   e. Make changes gradually
   f. Watch the up side—protect the down side
   g. Save some planning time
   h. Redefine your workplace friendships
   i. Adopt new standards of integrity
   j. Let your employees help you
   k. Adopt a learning attitude
   l. Balance home and career

5. In your new role as a supervisor, your initial goals in the first few weeks should be to maintain productivity, build relationships with employees and peers, think like management, ask questions and learn, and stay positive.

6. It is important to understand the difference between the mechanical and biological realms and to understand that people, unlike all other assets you manage, are in the biological realm and require the proper environment and conditions to grow and develop. They cannot be managed like clockwork and other mechanical objects.

TEST YOURSELF

For each statement below, check true or false.

True   False

____ ____ 1. A new supervisor should never seek advice from a subordinate.

____ ____ 2. Previous co-workers seldom, if ever, try to manipulate a new supervisor who was once their co-worker.

____ ____ 3. A professional supervisor should be a buffer between management and employees.

____ ____ 4. It is more important for employees to balance their home and career activities than it is for supervisors.

____ ____ 5. It is a mistake for the new supervisor to try to discover the lay of the land from the person she or he is replacing.

____ ____ 6. It is the responsibility of the employee to initiate contact with the new supervisor.

____ ____ 7. Once you become a supervisor, you should postpone any outside learning and concentrate on your new position.

____ ____ 8. Involving your employees in planning and implementing proposed changes makes them more motivated to adapt to (buy into) them.

____ ____ 9. Criticizing management in front of your employees is a sign to your employees that you are on their side.

____ ____ 10. Your home environment can be a good place to practice your newly acquired leadership techniques.

Turn to the back of the book to check your answers.

Total Correct____

DISCUSSION **QUESTIONS**

1. In moving from the position of a worker to that of a supervisor, what basic behavioral changes should you anticipate?

2. In making the transition to supervisor in the same department, how would you go about building a supervisor–employee relationship with an employee you were close friends with before the switch?

3. If you were the director of human resources, how would you communicate with and try to change the attitude of a new supervisor who had become overly impressed with the power of his or her new position?

4. What are some things that you could do as a supervisor to create and maintain an environment where your employees are motivated to meet the goals of their employer?

5. What are some other differences between the mechanical realm and the biological realm that were not mentioned in the chapter?

6. How can a supervisor balance home life and work life so that one does not jeopardize the other?

CASE: **STRATEGY**

OBJECTIVE

To evaluate alternatives and choose the best approach to use in taking over a new department.

PROBLEM

Renee is being considered for the position as manager for a new department. She has an interview with Bill

tomorrow. In preparation for this interview, she wants your advice on how she should answer questions Bill might ask regarding how she would manage the department, particularly in the first few weeks. She is thinking about one of two basic strategies:

1. Move in openly and freely in a warm and friendly manner. Get acquainted with each employee

quickly. Eliminate any hint of a threatening climate. After one week, slowly withdraw and let the employees know you are the boss by establishing a friendly but firm discipline line.

2. Move in quietly and maintain a discreet distance from each employee. Make little effort to build personal relationships. Give them time to watch your leadership style. Let them discover who is the boss the easy way. After using this approach for a week, relax a little and slowly attempt to establish the warm, friendly relationships and discipline discussed in strategy 1.

Remember, the problem deals only with which approach Renee should take. Support the strategy that puts her in the best position were she to become the new manager.

PLAYERS

If the role-play is used in the classroom: Use only the four management roles (Bill, Ricardo, Yolanda, and Gerald). All the roles are described in the back of the book. Students may draw roles as they enter the classroom, then form a panel in front of the class. Each of the four players should argue the position that best represents the role as described in the back of the book.

PROCEDURE

Have a lively twenty-five-minute discussion of the problem after all players have become involved in their roles. Each player must strongly defend and support one strategy or the other during this period. Every player should have an equal opportunity to defend her or his choice. At the end of the discussion, all four players vote by secret ballot for either strategy 1 or 2, but they need not vote for the one they defended. Votes are then collected and tallied to determine which strategy has the most appeal.

Alternative procedure: Have all students discuss their preferences regarding the two strategies, or alternative strategies, irrespective of specific roles described in the back of the book. Vote among all students to determine which is preferred. If you would prefer that students individually consider their preferred strategy prior to engaging in discussion, have them first complete the "Take-Over Exercise" that follows this case.

CASE DISCUSSION AND QUESTIONS

Discuss a possible blend of the two strategies to fit the leadership style of the supervisor involved (in this case, Renee). How might she blend these strategies to be most effective during her first few weeks as a supervisor? What are the impacts (positive or negative) for adopting one strategy over another, or blending the two strategies, or adopting any other strategy identified through discussion?

TAKE-OVER EXERCISE

Read the Case: Strategy twice, then assume you are giving Renee advice on how to take over the department during the first two weeks. To do this, please write out the advantages and disadvantages of each strategy in the spaces provided next. Keep in mind that your goal is to help Renee establish her role as a manager/leader and reach the highest possible productivity level in the shortest period of time.

STRATEGY 1: (Move in openly and in a most friendly manner.)

Advantages:	**Disadvantages:**
_____	_____
_____	_____
_____	_____
_____	_____
_____	_____
_____	_____

STRATEGY 2: (Move in quietly and stay at a distance.)

Advantages:	**Disadvantages:**
_____	_____
_____	_____
_____	_____
_____	_____
_____	_____

I would recommend that Renee use strategy:___
I would suggest the following compromise:___
Turn to the back of this book to compare your views with the authors.

PERSONAL GROWTH EXERCISE

Examine the role of supervisor in your organization. Identify questions you may have about the position and formulate a plan of action that you can implement to get them answered. You may wish to ask your supervisor or a representative from Human Resources.

TO LEARN MORE

To learn more about surviving the first weeks and months in your role as a new manager, consult the following reference:

Watkins, Michael. *The First 90 days: Critical Success Strategies for New Leaders at all Levels.* Boston: Harvard Business School Press, 2003.

To learn more about the myths and realities of being a manager, consult the following references:

Hill, Linda A. *Becoming a Manager: How New Managers Master the Challenges of Leadership*, 2nd ed. Boston: Harvard Business School Press, 2003.

Hill, Linda A. "Becoming the Boss," *Harvard Business Review*, vol. 85, no. 1 (January 2007), 49–56.

To learn more about Frederick Herzberg's theories, consult the following references:

Herzberg, Frederick. *Work and the Nature of Man.* New York: World Publishing Co., 1966.

Herzberg, Frederick, B. Mausner, and Barbara Snyderman. *The Motivation to Work*, 2nd ed. New York: John Wiley & Sons, 1959.

NOTES

1. Herzberg, Frederick. 1987. "One more time: How do you motivate employees?" *Harvard Business Review Classic* (September–October); 5–16 (reprint, *Harvard Business Review* 46(1): 53–62).

2. The Quotations Page, http://www.quotationspage.com/quotes/Al_Capone (accessed January 26, 2008).

3. Covey, Stephen R. 2004. *The 8th Habit: From Effectiveness to Greatness.* New York: Free Press, p. 101.

Improving Productivity
Leading Teams
Communicating Effectively
Managing Conflict
Improving Performance
Managing Time
Benefiting from Change

chapter **three**

THE SUPERVISOR'S ROLE AND RESPONSIBILITY IN THE MODERN ORGANIZATION

"Model the behavior you desire from others."

Cliff Goodwin

PERFORMANCE COMPETENCIES

After you have finished reading this chapter, you should be able to:

- Describe five benefits that supervisors receive from their position in management

- Describe five to seven ways to put more leadership into your management style

- List and describe three sources of power

- Describe three ways to increase motivation through mutual rewards

- List and describe two ways a supervisor can help employees find value in their job

For years the role of the working or front-line supervisor has been considered by many organizations to be little more than a stepping-stone into management. Business and management schools devoted their attention primarily to teaching principles and theories applicable to upper management. Many professors figured their graduates would hold down beginning supervisory roles for a short period and then move into something more challenging. How things have changed!

Top Management

Middle Management

Supervisors

Employees

Typical Organizational
Chart

Today's organizations are complex. Some of the complexity is due in part to the following:

- A more culturally diverse workforce than ever before.
- Molding a productive team out of a mix of full-timers, part-timers, "temps," and contract workers.
- Implementation of quality and productivity programs such as: ISO certification and six sigma, JIT and lean manufacturing, and organizing work using self-directed teams.
- Enforcing the ever-growing number of employment laws pertaining to: hiring and dismissal, anti-discrimination, sexual harassment, disability accommodation, workplace violence, FLMA, OSHA, HIPPA, worker's compensation, overtime, and ergonomics.
- Globalization and international competition, downsizing, outsourcing, and flattening the organizational structure by removing levels of management.

THE GOOD NEWS FOR SUPERVISORS

To meet all the challenges inherent in the complexity of modern organizations, the role of the front-line supervisor has changed dramatically. This is great news for someone aspiring to become a front-line supervisor because, while challenging, these changes present tremendous career and growth opportunities.

1. *The stature of the front-line supervisor has been elevated.* Instead of being a bit player at the bottom rung of the management ladder, the supervisor has become a key position. The obvious reason is because many middle- and upper-level management positions have been eliminated. Organizations are "flattening" their organizational hierarchy. There are fewer middle- and upper-level managers in flat organizations. The flat organizational structure means that more authority, power, and responsibility are being delegated to lower-level managerial positions. The talent and skill of the supervisor in a flat organization is a major factor to its success.

2. *Empowerment of the supervisor's job is ongoing.* Some of the "power" previously held by those whose jobs have been eliminated will be delegated to the supervisors they used to supervise. This shift means that the line supervisor or "team leader" of the past can take a more positive stance. She or he can submit new suggestions with more freedom and more influence. In short, the line supervisor will play a bigger role in the total management team. Upper management (those left) will have to listen more and react to what they hear.

3. *Supervisors have more autonomy.* With fewer directives to follow, fewer inspections from those above, and fewer people to please, supervisors have the power and responsibility to run their departments or "teams" more like the owner of a small business might do. Supervisors will be encouraged to operate with more authority while expecting to be held accountable.

4. *Supervisors receive more advanced training.* As upper management shifts additional responsibilities to their front-line supervisors, they will provide

more training to help them succeed. In addition, more supervisors will appoint assistants and prepare them for temporary "takeover" roles when they are absent. In other words, front-line supervisors will move closer to those upper-management leaders who remain with the firm and whose roles, in turn, will be expanded.

5. *Supervisors derive tremendous personal benefits from their role in today's business culture.*   For example:
    - Effective supervisors will be easier to spot and will receive "first call" on promotional possibilities.
    - Women who excel as front-line supervisors will discover that the so-called glass ceiling is less likely to affect them.
    - The challenges of front-line supervision provide a great training ground and preparation for upper-management positions.
    - Supervision offers the opportunity to engage in meaningful and challenging work that will enhance one's self-respect and the respect from others.
    - Supervisors will receive more immediate positive reinforcement of their contribution to organizational success as a result of leading their employees through collaborative and team-based approaches than was possible through former top-down management methods.
    - Supervisors will have greater opportunities to engage in continuous learning, which is a top motivator.

DEVELOP YOUR SUPERVISORY SKILLS

All these changes mean that employees or team members who aspire to become supervisors will be expected to demonstrate their acceptability with more force and enthusiasm. Not only will their personal performance and contribution to the higher performance of others be evaluated, but management will evaluate how well prepared they are to assume the role of the supervisor. Obviously, being accepted as a new supervisor will be more of an achievement in the future than it has been in the past.

If, at this point, your long-term career goal is to get into upper management and you wish to qualify as a supervisor as soon as possible to speed things up, here are three necessary steps to consider:

Step 1. Put practical experience first. The job of the supervisor in most organizations is 90 percent application. It is getting the job done. Theory is great, but it is even greater when practical techniques are learned and practiced first. The focus on experience does not mean that strategy theories are to be ignored. The more theoretical background one has, the better; but in starting a career, your first goal should be to survive as a supervisor, your second goal should be to become a superior supervisor, and your third goal should be to make the move into upper management.

Marty desires to eventually graduate from a four-year university, but being a realist, she knows she must earn her own way step by step. Her first step is to earn an associate or two-year degree from a local community college. Her next step is to become a supervisor to obtain some practical experience in management. After gaining experience she expects to graduate from an accredited university with a bachelor of arts or bachelor of science degree. Marty figures that the theory and advanced courses in statistics, data processing, and so forth, will have more meaning to her after she has had some supervisory experience. It will speed up her transition and put her in a position to occupy a higher management role.

Step 2. Learn the techniques of supervision by becoming an assistant supervisor or group leader when the opportunity arises. You can learn a lot about being a supervisor from working as an employee. You can also learn the skills of supervision and leadership by completing a course in supervision. The best option is a combination of both. There is no better substitute for being an understudy to an outstanding supervisor for a period of time. It is generally better to learn to walk before you run. Many colleges have internships or cooperative education opportunities in which you can gain experience and earn college credits at the same time.

Drake recently graduated from a university as a business management major. He anticipates it may take him the better part of a year, perhaps more, to become eligible for a job as a supervisor. He is more than willing to build his experience, but he wants to qualify as a supervisor by first being an assistant. Drake wants the experience of working closely with a model supervisor who can give him the kind of help he can never get from a textbook. He feels he must become a star supervisor if he is to move into upper management within a two- or three-year period. The right mentor could be the ticket he is seeking.

Step 3. Place emphasis on managing your personal life better now so that you can manage a department or team better at a later date. At first this step may not seem appropriate. What does the way you manage your personal life—going to college, working part-time, working out regularly, spending time with family, and so on—have to do with becoming a superior supervisor? The answer is plenty. These skills will assist you in reaching the lifestyle you desire as well as help you become an effective supervisor and manager.

LEADERSHIP AND SUPERVISION

Leadership is not a gift awarded to some and denied to others. No magic is involved, and no special personality or unusual charisma is required. Most individuals who truly wish to become leaders can develop leadership ability. Leadership is stepping out in front of others with confidence, taking charge, and earning the support of followers.

A perceptive observer can sense the presence of strong leadership. The group under observation is pulling together in an organized, efficient manner. Members show enthusiasm and a sense of direction. Tension is absent because everybody expects to benefit from the group's activity. Everybody supports the leader because of respect that the leader has earned. A strong leader is as important in a traditional department as in a team arrangement, although the leadership styles are different.

For most workers the leadership-building process starts when they become supervisors. Some may get a head start through experience as club officers, team captains, chairpersons, and officers in trade or volunteer organizations, but supervisory jobs are the primary leadership builders.

Developing and maintaining effectiveness as a supervisor is foundational to becoming a leader. It is impossible to be a good leader without being a good supervisor or manager. Those who become leaders without first becoming supervisors must ultimately learn management skills such as setting priorities, learning to delegate, and applying other principles and techniques covered in this book. They must do these things to free themselves to lead. Many supervisors become so bogged down with administrative details that they do not have time to put more leadership into their management styles, denying themselves the opportunity to move up the ladder to higher management/leadership positions.

The better you are as a supervisor, the more freedom you will have to lead. Although most people are in middle- or upper-management positions before they have had the opportunity to stretch their leadership "wings," it can all start at the supervisory level. It is the combination of management and leadership that usually creates upward mobility.

Leadership is often the missing ingredient to greater productivity. Leaders who meet the needs of their followers inspire greater productivity than managers who do not.

Your leadership style should reflect your personality. Although you can learn about leadership from others by using them as models, you must nevertheless create your own style, a style that reflects your personality, supervisory approach, and the kind of leader you want to be. You can learn a lot about leadership by observing your superiors, but you should feel free to adapt or reject their methods in forging your own individual style.

In building your own leadership style, it is important that you identify your strong personal characteristics and strengthen them. Your style is an extension of these characteristics. When you emphasize a unique trait, such as a strong, powerful voice, you are building a style that causes you to stand out from others. It is vital, however, that you channel your special characteristics into certain areas that reflect strong leadership.

BECOME AN EFFECTIVE COMMUNICATOR

The first step in putting more leadership into your supervision is to become a more dynamic communicator. Employees will follow leaders who speak with authority. They want them to sound like leaders.

Dixie was an outstanding supervisor, but she was so soft-spoken in her approach to group meetings and counseling that those in her department became impatient. Some even went so far as to say she was too nice. Dixie's superior and mentor, a woman with a strong, commanding voice, suggested that Dixie take a course in public speaking. Dixie rejected the idea but took the suggestion to mean that she should demonstrate more leadership through her voice. She started to exercise more control through her voice in both private counseling and group sessions. Within three months her superior complimented her on the change and asked what grade she had received in her public speaking course. "I didn't take one," Dixie replied. "I used you as a model and made the changes myself."

Of course, speaking with confidence is only one part of your communications system. A good communications system is a planned program of daily two-way communications to keep those who work for you informed. An effective communications system can include all or part of the following: daily personal contact with workers on the site, a bulletin board where both supervisor and employee can leave messages that will be picked up daily, regular group staff meetings, informal communications during break periods, and use of in-house communications media (newsletters), telephone calls, distribution of personal notes, e-mail, and voluntary or designed counseling sessions. Each leader must design a two-way system that works on a daily basis. A breakdown in the communications system is as serious as a breakdown of production equipment.

Why is such a system so important? It is essential to keep everyone informed and prevent misunderstandings. Not knowing what is going on destroys morale. When workers are involved in decisions, or at least informed, they can cope with changes. Being left out in the cold develops hostility that can even lead to mutiny in extreme cases. Employees need to know how they are doing as individuals and how their contribution relates to departmental goals. Knowing their status provides job security and reassurance, which many need daily. When employees know where they stand, they relax and produce more. Within the security of the group, they feel they belong. A good communications system keeps workers from feeling neglected, misinterpreting, or becoming suspicious. It keeps them involved.

Leaders need the ideas that can come only from their followers. They must listen to suggestions and then give credit to those who make them. A good leader discovers problems and solves them before they become disruptive. The only way to make such discoveries is through a sound two-way communications system that brings problems to the attention of the leader. Weak and ineffective leaders usually discover problems too late. A leader with a strong and commanding voice who does not have a two-way communications system eventually loses the respect of followers. A leader with an authoritative voice and a well-maintained communications system has the winning combination.

As managers move into leadership roles, they go through a transition similar to a baseball player's experience in shifting from the minor to the major leagues. In no area is this change more dramatic than in communications. Recognized leaders give high praise to Dale Carnegie and similar courses and public-speaking teachers for preparing them to lead. In recognition of the need for special training in this area, some professors are now suggesting that business administration majors earn a minor in communication arts. Demonstration of good communication skills remains essential for success in today's competitive job market.

INCREASE MOTIVATION THROUGH MUTUAL REWARDS

The best way to convert employees into motivated followers is to put into practice the Mutual Reward Theory (MRT). The supervisor (leader) and employee (follower) can create and maintain a mutually rewarding environment. For example, the supervisor can provide an enjoyable and consistent work environment; an opportunity to learn; an ability to participate in matters that affect their work routines; and freedom to voice their concerns without being stifled. The employee can provide productivity, dependability, and a high level of motivation to meet the goals of their leader. A natural reward exchange takes place between supervisors and followers, and rewards should be mutually satisfying.

It stands to reason that a leader cannot be a leader without having employees who are willing to follow him or her. But what separates one manager who is able to instill the desire to follow from another manager who is not? How can a manager become a leader by instilling this willingness to follow? Three basic factors are involved in this transition:

1. Employees cannot be forced or cajoled into becoming followers. It is a purely voluntary action on their part. If they want to move in the direction the leader has chosen, they follow. The reason they will follow is that it is to their advantage to do so.

2. The vision projected by the leader is a primary converter. The goal or mission presented must offer the promise of transforming the nature of the work and raising expectations to a high level, so that following is a natural and enjoyable thing to do.

3. The character and personality of the leader play a significant role in the conversion. Sometimes charisma is present; sometimes it is not. There must, however, be a high degree of confidence, trust, integrity, and a strong belief that life will become better by following.

All leaders go about converting employees to followers in their own way. The supervisor who provides unusual opportunities for self-improvement, for example, may gain an increase in productivity in return. Mutual rewards strengthen the relationship and enhance the image of the leader. Both parties come out ahead, and they know it.

Leadership, in a sense, is an impression in the mind of the follower. If the needs of the worker are satisfied, the supervisor appears to be a good leader; if the needs are not satisfied, then the worker feels thwarted and neglected and has a poor image of the supervisor. And when workers produce at high levels because their needs are amply satisfied, they convert their supervisors into leaders in the view of upper management. They make their supervisors leaders.

When Ralph was first introduced to MRT, he dismissed it as nothing more than the old truism, "You scratch my back and I'll scratch yours." But later, after a discussion with a superior he respected, he decided to try it. As a supervisor, he discovered that he could furnish many rewards he had previously neglected. When he sat down with an employee and openly discussed the reward exchange that was possible between them, a better relationship and higher productivity resulted. In six months Ralph had progressed from a good supervisor and average leader to a better supervisor and a good leader. Through the application of MRT, he had put more leadership into his management style.

RECOGNIZE YOUR SOURCES OF POWER

Leaders have three basic sources of power to draw on. They are:

1. *Position power.*   The power that comes from your managerial position as a supervisor. Anyone in your job as a manager has the same power. It gives you authority to require certain behavior from your workers. You must be careful, however, not to overuse this source.

2. *Knowledge power.*   The power that comes from having technical knowledge, expertise, and experience pertaining to the tasks that the employees you manage are responsible for doing.

3. *Character or personality power.*   The power that comes when you demonstrate a strong sense of self-esteem, self-confidence, and honesty. Some might refer to this as *personality power* because of the outward manifestations of inner qualities to which followers are attracted. Others might refer to this as *character power* because it is only through these inner qualities, such as integrity, honesty, ethical frameworks, fairness, and so on, that produce the personality traits to which followers are attracted. Either way, the source of power in this instance relates to intrinsic qualities of the leader rather than more external qualities such as knowledge and position power.

You should draw carefully from the power bank composed of your position, knowledge, and personality, but you should not hesitate to draw from it when necessary. Without it, a department cannot reach productivity goals. When such goals are not reached, everyone suffers. Utilizing your power sources in a sensitive and balanced manner may be the best way to put more leadership into your style.

Janice knew she had replaced an authoritarian manager. After careful consideration, she decided she could gain greater productivity from the nine workers in her department if she relied primarily on her knowledge power and soft-peddled her position and character/personality power. Janice said to herself, "If I can teach them more about the automated equipment and increase their competencies, they will sense my knowledge power and little else will be necessary." Things progressed in a satisfactory manner for some time, but gradually her employees began to slow down and take advantage of her. Janice had made the classic mistake of depending on one source of power. She quickly fell back on her position power by demonstrating her strength as a firm, no-nonsense supervisor. In addition, Janice became a stronger personality—using her special characteristics (warm voice, persuasive manner, etc.) to project more leadership. It took only a few weeks to return to higher productivity and a more cohesive department.

MAKE DECISIVE DECISIONS

In all leader–follower situations, good decision making surfaces as a characteristic that followers value highly. Leaders say the same thing in many ways:

> "Poor decision making is the downfall of most leaders."

> "Decision making is a symbol of leadership."

> "It's not just making good decisions, it's making them with authority and decisiveness."

Do not be afraid to make a decision—that's what leaders do. Although you will eventually be judged by the quality of your decisions and your long-term record, the way you announce your decision is important. A good decision forcefully announced communicates the presence of leadership. In fact, a poor decision forcefully announced communicates the presence of leadership. A poor decision timidly announced communicates the absence of leadership. Even an excellent decision announced in a wishy-washy manner turns out to be weak if it is not accepted and put into operation by followers.

From the viewpoint of followers, leadership is decisiveness. A strong leader carefully analyzes the problem and then chooses one direction or another with confidence. Supervisors who straddle the fence and sweep problems under the carpet do not communicate strong leadership.

Kenneth had spent all afternoon evaluating the new advertising campaign. He had seen all the layouts and considered their probable impact on sales and on the corporate image. He was not satisfied with the program, but he had no time to develop a better proposal. He decided to support the advertising staff, accept their plan, and do everything in his power to make it work. He called in the staff and complimented them on their proposal. Then he wrote a short and enthusiastic article about the campaign for the in-house bulletin. In every possible way, he communicated the idea that the right decision had been made. As it turned out, the advertising program was moderately successful, primarily because of the enthusiasm behind it. Equally important to Kenneth, he had protected his leadership image. In fact, he was never criticized because the program's success was only moderate. His staff and other followers continued to support his leadership.

Leaders who expect to bat a thousand in making sound decisions will, of course, fall short of their expectations. But those who are afraid to make any decisions are doomed to failure. Although you can't expect to win them all, you can win often enough to keep your workers' respect. And a decision made with confidence has a better chance of success because your employees will try to make it work. But when you are indecisive, you are already behind in the game.

Workers often interpret your decisions from a personal point of view. "Does the decision give me more or less job security? Will it enhance my career progress or slow it down?" Employees like decisions that are good for themselves as well as for the organization. The skillful leader makes sure that employees see how they benefit from whatever is best for the organization. Involving your followers in decision making increases their motivation.

Decisions that involve too many compromises do little for the supervisor's leadership image. Those decisions that are based on facts and made with gusto are usually well received. A good decision maker inspires respect. Employees feel they are in good hands, and the department is making progress and headed in the right direction.

LIVE AND MODEL THE COMPANY MISSION

Leaders must furnish direction. They must lead their people in doing work that produces products or provides services that have meaning and significance.

Peter Drucker, America's foremost management consultant, recently deceased, discusses the importance of a single organizational goal for both managers and employees in his book *Management: Tasks, Responsibilities, Practices.*[1] In *Execution: The Discipline of Getting Things Done,* Larry Bossidy and Ram Charan emphasize that effective leaders set a few very clear goals (three or four) because fewer priorities will produce better results from the resources available.[2] In contrast, leaders who are unable to define the few most important goals and identify and push to accomplish too many goals will realize more limited results because of the struggle workers will have in attempting to meet multiple and often conflicting priorities all at once. When one or only a few goals exist and are clearly articulated, they can and should be converted into a mission. A mission has two purposes: It gives the whole organization (managers and employees alike) a sense of unity and purpose, and it keeps everyone moving with enthusiasm in a clear direction to accomplish it.

The leadership in any company can help its employees at any level, regardless of the work they do, find purpose and value through establishing, communicating, and modeling a mission that elevates the work they do beyond the mere provision of services or production of goods. The mission statement is the beginning. Consider the following example of a Christmas tree manufacturer.

Holiday Delight Christmas Tree Company had been in business for more than fifty years. During much of this time, it had grown as a company and had acquired a huge share of the manufactured Christmas tree market. However, in the past few years, the public's taste in manufactured trees had changed in favor of real trees. This was due in part to perceptions about the ecological effect of manufactured trees, especially when it came time to dispose of them. With these perceptions came a growing discontent and loss of spirit among the workforce. Holiday Delight leaders needed to respond.

Through a process of conversations and meetings that included staff at all levels, the company came up with the following mission statement:

> "Our business is saving twenty trees for every beautiful tree we manufacture in an environmentally responsible way."

The company derived this mission based on the following information about its business:

1. *Despite recent trends, there was still a huge market of families that did not want the mess and inconvenience of buying, cutting, hauling, maintaining, and disposing of a live tree every year.*

2. *Its trees are spectacularly beautiful and emulate real trees, delighting their customers. Further, they were durable and guaranteed to last at least twenty years, if not longer, thereby saving at least twenty live trees from cutting in the course of its "lifetime."*

3. *The company has become more environmentally responsible over time in the production of its trees. It uses recycled materials as much as possible, and it provides instructions in its packaging regarding the disposal of its trees in an environmentally friendly way.*

With this mission, the company is not just manufacturing fake trees; it is also manufacturing quality trees in environmentally responsible ways while saving real trees from being cut down. This is a loftier mission than just making fake trees and one that its employees can respect.

When employees understand the mission and know that their management, supervisors, and peers believe in it and defer to it when making decisions, it becomes an identifying characteristic of its corporate culture. Top management ultimately has the responsibility for writing the mission of the company they lead. Effective leaders realize, however, that any mission statements should be formulated with considerable input from all who play a part in living the mission. This means from all employees at all levels within the organization.

Supervisors play a key role in making the mission a reality. They must know the mission, buy into it, and explain and communicate it to their direct reports. They must act congruently with the mission statement and not be at odds with its intended purposes. They need to explain to each employee how his or her contribution is important to the accomplishment of the mission. Unless the mission statement is adopted at all levels of the company and understood by all, it becomes a useless document.

Supervisors at Holiday Delight Christmas Tree Company demonstrated to their employees the magnitude of their value to the world by providing data on the number of live trees the company actually saved per year. They also helped employees gain pride by providing information on how well the company is doing in relation to its competitors, including the live tree market. They went further still and communicated through employee communications, annual reports, and advertising how their efforts contribute to protecting the environment, and also donated a portion of profits to organizations dedicated to forest preservation initiatives. Employees soon regained confidence in their company and its value, and felt proud to say that they work for the number one company in their industry.

Often an organization's mission is implemented from the bottom up and the supervisor becomes its most important and influential cheerleader. Effective teamwork is possible only when all share in the common mission of their company. The supervisor must drive this process.

Managers and supervisors who give only lip service to their company's mission underestimate the importance of having a unifying vision or mission. The mission should provide a higher purpose for the work the employees do. People are motivated to work for an organization that has a lofty mission, one they are proud to tell their family and friends about. It is also the reason that work is, for many, more than just a paycheck.

HELP EMPLOYEES FIND VALUE IN THEIR WORK

Respected leaders acknowledge that people do not live or work for bread alone. They realize that employees want something beyond dollars, benefits, security, promotions, recognition, and the promise of retirement. They want to be a part of

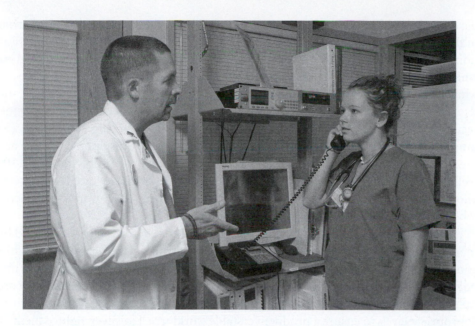

something important, to be a part of something that is greater than and beyond their own self-interests. Workers become followers when they become part of an effort that has significance. They feel differently when they are a part of a movement, wave, or team. It is not just little personal victories that most employees seek; rather, they want to dedicate themselves to something greater than themselves. People who find ways to do this are said to be *self-actualizing.*

Supervisors play a lead role in helping their employees find value in their work. This may be easier to do for some careers and for some companies than for others. For example, a medical doctor is generally held in higher esteem in our society than a production worker in a Christmas tree manufacturing plant.

What we do for a living is very important to us. If you don't agree, ask yourself, "How long does it take two people who meet for the first time to begin talking about what each does for a living?" For most people it comes up quickly, especially when they are proud of their careers and proud of the company for whom they work. It is incumbent on the supervisor to help employees make connections between the day-to-day activities of their jobs to what those activities contribute to higher company and society goals. This is equally true for the doctor and the production worker.

Employees desire to have their work valued by society in general and by their management in particular. Valuing employees and the work they do is a requirement of managers and supervisors. It is a prerequisite ingredient to motivation. It is the rich soil in the well-kept garden.

MEET EMPLOYEES' LEGITIMATE NEEDS

Finding value in their work is one of an employee's highest needs. An employee has many needs and the more a supervisor can address them, the more he or she will do to gain the employee's commitment.

Where supervisors often struggle is understanding what an employee's legitimate needs are and what needs are most critical to engender this commitment. In particular, they tend to overlook their needs for intrinsic rewards (e.g., satisfaction in the job itself) in favor of seeking to satisfy more extrinsic needs (e.g., compensation). Comprehensive surveys have been performed which have asked over time what employees feel they need in their work and then compared their responses to what their employers believe their employees want. In one well-known survey, the ten needs were listed by employers in rank order as follows: (1) good wages; (2) job security; (3) promotion/growth opportunities; (4) good working conditions; (5) interesting work; (6) personal loyalty to workers; (7) tactful discipline; (8) full appreciation for work done; (9) sympathetic help on personal problems; and (10) feeling "in" on things. In contrast, employees ranked interesting work, full appreciation of work done, and feeling "in" on things as the three most important needs. Job security and good wages were ranked fourth and fifth.[3]

These findings are consistent with the hygiene/motivator theory developed by management theorist Frederick Herzberg.[4] Herzberg theorized that matters like good wages, good working conditions, and proper and fair supervision, while important, did nothing to increase employee motivation and commitment. They are called *hygiene factors* because an employer must always seek to maintain them at appropriate levels to ensure a productive, stable workforce. However, reduce them or take them away, these factors will serve to demotivate employees. *Motivators* are factors like those listed among the top three of the survey by employees, as well as factors like growth opportunities and increased responsibility, which are more instrinsic to the employee and the value and satisfaction he or she derives from the work itself. Create conditions where these values can be satisfied, and employee motivation and commitment will increase.

It is important to note that all ten of the needs listed in the survey matter to employees. Nothing in this list is unimportant. No one would dare say that good wages and job security are unimportant. They clearly are. Given the variance in understanding between what employers and employees think about these matters, however, managers and supervisors are on notice to take special care in meeting needs that are more likely to motivate employees and engender true commitment. Without minimizing the need to provide fair compensation and to meet other extrinsic needs, effective supervisors resist "throwing money at the problem" to engender employee commitment and focus instead on what they can do to meet employees' instrinsic needs.

CREATE A POSITIVE FORCE

By drawing on all power sources, especially personality or character power, a leader creates and maintains a positive force that pulls followers in one direction with enthusiasm and dedication. Nothing is ever dull or routine in the presence of a leader with spirit and a sense of purpose. The workplace becomes infused with energy and enthusiasm. The place is "jumping"! This physical, psychological, and spiritual *force* constitutes the heart of followership.

Like any power system (generator, battery storing an electrical charge, etc.), the supervisor must be that central force that keeps the communication network alive, provides the vehicles to deliver rewards, creates good decisions, meets employees' legitimate needs and helps them find value in their work, and, drawing heavily from his or her power sources, leads the organization to high productivity and success in the direction of an established mission.

When Bernie took over as supervisor, apathy prevailed. The staff was lethargic and difficult to motivate. Within six weeks, the opposite was true. Employees were full of energy and anxious to contribute. How did Bernie turn things around? He held a meeting with his employees and explained the company's mission to them. He explained how important their work was to the company and how the company's products really benefited the community. He gave statistics on how well the company was doing and how well respected it was within its industry. He provided each employee with a sense of purpose by explaining to each one how her or his work directly impacted the company mission. Collectively, they began to feel real pride for the company and for each other. No one felt unimportant or unappreciated. His direct reports responded as valued employees often respond: they gave their all to their work. They gave their creativity and talents to their work.

By carrying out the responsibilities of a supervisor as outlined in this book, you will automatically develop a certain amount of leadership. But don't stop there. Once you survive and then begin to thrive as a successful supervisor, you may accept the challenge of becoming a manager/leader. You may choose to rise to the highest level of leadership and become a CEO. Keep in mind that your future as a manager or leader is based on the success you achieve as a beginning supervisor.

PERFORMANCE **CHECKLIST**

1. Today's organizations are complex. The good news for supervisors is that this presents tremendous career and growth opportunities. They are more empowered, have greater autonomy, and have opportunities to receive more training opportunities than ever before. They also derive tremendous personal benefits from being front-line supervisors, such as having a great training ground to prepare for upper-management positions; less concerns about the glass ceiling for women supervisors; and opportunities for meaningful, challenging work and to engage in continuous learning.

2. Someone wanting to be a supervisor can develop quick supervisory skills by putting practical experience first, learning from other supervisors by serving first in an assistant, intern, or apprentice-type supervisory role, and managing his or her personal life in a way that helps further develop leadership skills.

3. Some supervisors become so busy with day-to-day activities and the business of supervision that they don't take time to put more leadership into their management styles. Specific ways to do this are:
   a. Become an effective communicator by learning to communicate confidently and building effective two-way communication systems with your team members.
   b. Motivate employees through mutual rewards, which involves working with employees to achieve a fair exchange of recognition and rewards for employees for their efforts and commitment to their work and the organization.
   c. Recognize and appropriately utilize your sources of power, including your position, knowledge, and character or personality sources of power.
   d. Live and model the company mission so that employees see the connection between their day-to-day work activities and the contribution their efforts make to company goals and larger societal goals.
   e. Help employees find value in their work, regardless of what they do or what status and value society would otherwise give their efforts.
   f. Help meet your employees' legitimate needs, understanding the difference between intrinsic and extrinsic needs and how to address each.

TEST **YOURSELF**

For each of the following statements, check true or false.

True   False

1. The many new responsibilities that will be assumed by the supervisor of today need **not** apply to team leaders.
2. In the future, most college business majors will be able to skip front-line supervisory roles and enter at a higher level.
3. Even though they will receive less support from their superiors, future supervisors will play more important roles.
4. Team leaders and supervisors will make fewer but more important decisions in years to come.
5. Women who excel as supervisors will find upper-management roles more accessible.
6. The power previously held by middle-management people (some whose positions have been eliminated) will be absorbed only by higher-management people.
7. Supervisors and team leaders will have more superiors to please.
8. You can't learn much about becoming a skillful supervisor while you are working as an employee.
9. College internships or co-op education opportunities can help you gain experience and earn college credit at the same time.
10. Paying employees more money does not truly motivate them to perform better.

Turn to the back of the book to check your answers.
Total Correct ____

DISCUSSION **QUESTIONS**

1. What changes have occurred to make the job of supervision more complicated in today's organization?
2. What are three levels of skills that supervisors must develop?
3. How could you gain experience and knowledge about being a supervisor before becoming one?
4. Do you agree with the statement that it is impossible to be a good leader without being a good supervisor or manager? Explain fully.
5. What are some of the benefits supervisors get from their jobs?
6. What leadership skills do you think are necessary to be an effective supervisor?
7. What role does a mission statement play in enhancing motivation?

CASE: WHAT DO **EMPLOYEES WANT?**

OBJECTIVE
To determine what employees want most from their jobs.

PROBLEM
Bill wants Ricardo to incorporate effective leadership in his supervision of employees in order to enhance their satisfaction and dedication to the goals of the company and thus achieve greater productivity.

PROCEDURE
All non-management players (five roles) select from the following employee list what they believe are the **five most important employee needs** that Ricardo should provide in order to accomplish Bill's request. In a separate group, all management players (four roles) choose from the management list the five rewards they feel would do the most to increase productivity. Those in the class or seminar not assigned roles should make their own selections, either individually or as a group.

After twenty minutes, a member of the employee group and a member of the management group will write their selections on the board. Each group (in turn) will explain their five choices out of these long lists. Thoroughly discuss any differences that emerge between the two groups' lists. In what ways do management and employees differ regarding employee needs and why? In what ways do they agree?

CASE DISCUSSION

Discuss how Ricardo could meet these needs in his department.

EMPLOYEE NEEDS

- Opportunity for self-improvement on the job
- Freedom from close supervision
- Ample time for socializing
- Freedom to take breaks without following a schedule
- Opportunity to express oneself in group situations
- Chance to have some enjoyment on the job
- Opportunity to rotate among different tasks
- Credit for accomplishments
- Involvement in the decision-making process
- Knowing what is going on
- Opportunity to use limited work time for personal business
- Chance to learn the supervisor's job
- Opportunity to talk about personal problems
- Chance to extend coffee and lunch breaks without asking permission
- Opportunity to use the telephone for (local) personal calls

- Assurance that the job is secure
- Having a supervisor who is accessible
- Knowing about changes in advance
- Selecting one's own vacation schedule
- Learning new things from one's supervisor
- Other:

MANAGEMENT NEEDS

- Quality work
- High productivity
- Acceptable attendance record
- Creativity
- Cooperative attitude toward co-workers
- Cooperative attitude toward management
- Desire to learn
- Self-motivation
- Willingness to accept new assignments
- Willingness to pitch in during emergencies and, if necessary, work overtime
- Willingness to teach co-workers
- Tolerance of problem co-workers
- Minimum of socializing on the job
- Control over misuse of the telephone for personal reasons
- Awareness of safety regulations
- A consistently positive attitude
- Other:

PERSONAL GROWTH **EXERCISE**

Study your company's organizational chart. Locate the various managerial levels, like the position of supervisor or of front-line management. Discuss the organizational characteristics that come from this organizational structure and what it may mean for your development as a leader in order to be successful in your current role and to be considered for future roles in management. What specifically do you need to do in your organization to put more leadership into your management style?

NOTES

1. Peter F. Drucker, *Management: Tasks, Responsibilities, Practices.* New York: Harper & Row Publishers, 1973.

2. Larry Bossidy and Ram Charan, *Execution: The Discipline of Getting Things Done.* New York: Random House, 2002.

3. Kenneth Kovach, "Employee Motivation: Addressing a Crucial Factor in Your Organization's Performance," *Human Resource Development*, Ann Arbor, MI: University of Michigan Press, 1999; Kenneth Kovach, "What Motivates Employees? Workers and Supervisors Give Different Answers," *Business Horizons* 30 (1987), 58–65; James R. Lindner, "Understanding Employee Motivation," *Journal of Extension* 36, no. 3 (June 1998), http:// www.joe.org/joe/1998june/rb3.html (accessed December 13, 2007).

4. Frederick Herzberg, B. Mausner, and Barbara Snyderman, *The Motivation to Work*, 2nd ed., New York: John Wiley & Sons, 1959; and Frederick Herzberg, *Work and the Nature of Man*, New York: Thomas Y. Crowell Co., 1966.

HUMAN RELATIONS AND COMMUNICATIONS: THE KEY TO SUCCESSFUL SUPERVISION

"The only things that evolve by themselves in an organization are disorder, friction, and malperformance."

PETER DRUCKER

chapter **four**

ACHIEVING PRODUCTIVITY THROUGH PEOPLE

"Never be doing nothing."

Sir Walter Scott

Improving Productivity
Leading Teams
Communicating Effectively
Managing Conflict
Improving Performance
Managing Time
Benefiting from Change

As you move successfully from the role of worker to that of supervisor, an amazing transformation will take place in the way you look at things. You will suddenly find yourself more interested in John than in the machine he operates; more concerned with Helen than with the records she keeps; and more involved with Hank as an individual than with the work he turns out.

Your attention will shift from things to people, from the job itself to the person who performs the job. In short, you will need to become people oriented.

Terms such as *human relations*, *human behavior*, *motivation*, *attitude*, *sensitivity*, and *leadership style* will take on new meaning. Human understanding will earn the same priority in your scheme of things as job know-how. Helping Roberta increase her productivity will be as important as getting one of your reports out on time. Improving Dick's attitude will command your attention along with production figures, deadlines, and work schedules. You must make the shift from a job-centered employee to a people-centered supervisor.

Why is this transition necessary? Why must the new supervisor become so people oriented? Why must she or he learn to focus attention more on people than on the job itself? The answer lies in a simple, basic truth: A supervisor achieves productivity through people. Your success will be determined by the outputs of those you supervise.

PERFORMANCE COMPETENCIES

After you have finished reading this chapter, you should be able to:

- List three fundamental reasons why a supervisor must work through people to gain productivity

- Calculate productivity using the productivity formula

- Identify barriers and solutions to achieving increased productivity

- Describe Maslow's Hierarchy of Needs theory

- List and describe five ways to create and maintain a motivating environment

YOU CAN NO LONGER DO IT YOURSELF

The moment you become a supervisor, the production work you do yourself becomes secondary to the relationships you build with the people who do most of the actual work. Even though you may be able to do the job better or faster than those who work for you, and even though you would enjoy doing it yourself, you must turn it over to your employees. You must achieve productivity by learning how to direct, train, create, and maintain a motivating environment. You can seldom afford the luxury of doing it yourself. In other words, in terms of production work in the department, you will contribute more by doing less. Here is how the process works.

1. If you remain an employee, you are primarily responsible for your own job performance and productivity. Your productivity is measured and compared with that of others, and is the focus of your concern. As a supervisor, you are responsible for the productivity of everyone in your department. Consequently, management will be interested in measuring departmental productivity and not what you produce yourself.

2. Obviously, you cannot increase productivity substantially through your own production. You cannot supervise effectively and produce at a high level at the same time—you are only one person, not two or three. Even if you arrive at work two hours early and leave two hours late every day to do production work, the increase in total productivity would not be substantial, and, of course, you could not continue at such a pace for long.

3. Therefore, as a supervisor, you can maintain or increase productivity substantially only through others. You cannot do it by yourself. If you do not accept this fact, you will never be happy as a manager.

When you become a supervisor, you must learn to let the personal satisfaction of working with people replace the satisfaction you previously enjoyed in working with things. Your future is in the hands of those you supervise, so you must take pride in creating the kinds of relationships that will motivate people to achieve the productivity you desire. First, create the relationships; then work through them to achieve your productivity goals.

Create and maintain an atmosphere of respect and trust. By listening and following through on your employees' suggestions, going to bat for them with your superiors, recognizing their individuality, and, above all, demonstrating two-way communication, you will build trusting relationships.

KINDS OF PRODUCTIVITY

Because your future as a supervisor is so dependent on what you achieve through the productivity of the people you lead, let's examine the facts and theory involved. First, a sound understanding of productivity is important. *Productivity* is a word dear to the hearts of all managers. And well it should be. Productivity in its broadest meaning is the major purpose of all American business and government organizations and forms the foundation of our profit system. It permits us to compete favorably with other countries and is responsible for all the materials and services we enjoy. Only through the productivity of individuals (and machines operated by individuals) do we achieve our gross national product (GNP), the sum total of all tangible goods and services produced in this country during a given period of time. As a supervisor, however, you are concerned with only two kinds of productivity: individual productivity and departmental productivity.

Individual Productivity

As the term implies, *individual productivity* is the performance or contribution of one person over a specified period of time. It may mean the amount of materials produced, the ideas contributed, the sales achieved, or the quantity or quality of clerical services rendered. Every job has its own special kind of productivity or contribution. Most jobs, however, will fit into one of the following classifications:

- *Tangible productivity.* The factory worker who operates a machine on an assembly line contributes to the manufacture of the item in a form that can be seen and measured by management, so standards or norms can easily be established. For example, if the average employee produces sixty units per hour, and employee A produces seventy units, then it is easy to measure how far above the standard A's productivity is. In addition to factory work, tangible productivity applies to repairing or altering tangible products.

- *Sales productivity.* A salesperson in a retail store knows how her or his performance compares with that of others because management keeps a record of each person's dollar sales per hour. An individual's productivity can also be compared with a norm. For example, if sales amounting to $90 per hour is the standard for salespeople of a given classification, and one salesperson's sales amount to $100 per hour, her position above the norm is easily measured. However, retail salespeople should not be measured entirely on the basis of dollar sales. Because they must also contribute to stock work, housekeeping, and other departmental nonselling functions, their productivity base is larger than selling alone.

- *Service productivity.* Many employees who do not produce tangible goods or generate dollar sales perform vital services that contribute a different form of productivity. Most of these services come under the classification of *customer relations.* For example, telephone operators do not produce anything you can see, nor do they normally sell to customers, yet the services they perform are basic to the company they represent. The same is true of the services provided by police officers, bank tellers, nurses, supermarket checkers, waiters and waitresses, postal employees, and many others. Although these intangible forms of productivity are sometimes difficult to measure and compare scientifically with norms, they are important to supervisors and the organizations they represent.

The productivity of all individuals is measured to some extent. If an objective measurement is impossible, a subjective measurement is attempted, perhaps comparing one individual with another. The measurement of individuals is vital to good personnel administration and management and must be accepted as part of employment (see Chapter 14). The important thing, of course, is to measure the productivity and performance, and not the personality of the individual.

Departmental Productivity

Departmental productivity is the sum total of all productivity (by machines and people) that comes from a department or section within an organization. Like individual productivity it can also be tangible, sales, service, or a combination of these and other forms. Just as one individual is compared with another, so are departments. It is easier, however, to measure the productivity of a department scientifically because it can usually be reduced to figures and accounting data from which management can make its analysis. The important thing to realize is that department productivity becomes your responsibility the moment you become a supervisor. You must live with the figures, reports, and comparisons on a day-to-day basis. If productivity goes up, you are rewarded; if it goes down, you must come up with some explanations. Your reputation in the company will be tied to the productivity record of your department regardless of how much you contribute individually.

Management is defined as planning, organizing, directing, coordinating, and controlling activities to achieve productivity goals. From a human relations point of view, this process boils down to specific things you do to get work done through and with other people. No manager or supervisor can do it all alone, and frequently the more tasks he or she does personally, the lower the total departmental productivity that is achieved. Working supervisors, those who are expected to produce pieces or render services, often have lower departmental productivity than nonworking supervisors.

Shipping Department Example. Despite the fact that Woody felt he already had more than he could handle, he was given new duties in addition to running the shipping department at the paint factory where he had been a supervisor for five years. How could he pitch in during high-activity periods to maintain shipping schedules if he had to supervise workers in another section? He decided to lay the cards on the table with his six-person shipping department staff. His basic comment was, "I've been able in the past to help out during peak periods, but I can no longer do it. In the future it will be up to you to maintain schedules without my

personal productivity unless there is an emergency. How you do thi̶̶̶̶̶
you can come up with some time-saving procedures, I will go along w̶̶̶̶̶

Six weeks later, after the crew had made a number of helpful suggesti̶̶̶̶
ping schedules were achieved without personal help from Woody, and whe̶̶̶
member of the staff resigned, a replacement was not necessary. Woody learned t̶̶̶
his crew had not been working up to their potential because they could rely on him̶
to step in and produce during busy periods.

Banking Example.

Alice, an operations officer for a savings and loan facility, devoted so much time to training a few people to operate computers that other employees felt neglected. She finally turned computer training over to another. Result? Because she was able to improve relationships, efficiency increased to the point where the facility was able to maintain a high level of service with one less employee.

Health Care Example.

Frieda, a registered nurse in a long-term health care operation, decided to delegate a series of duties to her three ward nurses so that she could devote more time to building relationships with the twenty nurses aides under her supervision. Result? The quality of care increased and costs went down.

Please study the following chart for a moment. Notice that each employee has an individual productivity gap. This gap represents the difference between what each employee is currently producing and what could be produced under ideal conditions. Notice, also, a departmental productivity gap between what the department is currently producing and what could be produced.

The goal of the supervisor is to close the departmental productivity gap. Because supervisors have a limited supply of time and energy, their time and energy should be spent helping employees close individual productivity gaps. This goal is accomplished primarily by building better human relationships with employees and creating an environment where they will be motivated to reach their own potentials. The remainder of this book will be devoted to helping you learn how to accomplish this goal.

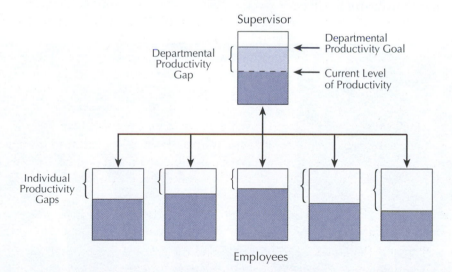

The new supervisor soon learns that a difference almost always exists between an employee's daily performance and his or her capacity to perform. Whether large or small, a productivity gap of some size is natural and should be expected in all employees. Such gaps are, of course, difficult to measure accurately for two reasons: (1) the true potential capacity of an individual cannot really be determined because it is made up of elusive factors such as mental ability, inner drive, perception, attitude,

…is up to you. If
…th them."
…ons, ship-
…n one
…hat

…nal stability; and (2) job productivity is difficult to meas-
… of a worker is fluid, moving up and down on an hourly,
…ne time an employee can have a wide gap (anybody can
…her times it can be narrow. In other words, productivity
…down, depending on many internal and environmental
…control some, but not all, of these factors.
…upervisors should be sensitive to changes in productiv-
…. When an employee shows progress in closing the gap
… productivity and the potential capacity, the supervisor
… happens, she or he becomes disturbed. The smaller the
…oductivity, and nothing is more important to the super-
…hall wonder the supervisor wants to know every tech-
…ch gaps.
…ing, I get the picture. I see why I must step in and help
…ith their capabilities. But how do I learn to motivate my
…y to their capacities? How can I increase productivity in
…ore equipment or more employees?

Calculating Productivity

Simply put, *productivity* equals *output divided by input*. It is written as the following formula:

$$P\,(\textit{productivity}) \;=\; \frac{O\,(\textit{output})}{I\,(\textit{input})}$$

By manipulating output or input, we affect productivity. High productivity usually means that the organization is efficient. The more efficient the operation, the more successful it will be.

Output is anything your company produces. *Inputs* are the things it takes to produce output. For example, let us say that 1 person in a delicatessen produces 100 of the deli's signature sandwiches in 2 hours. Productivity for making those sandwiches is calculated by plugging this data into the productivity formula:

$$\text{Sandwich productivity} = \frac{\text{Output (100 sandwiches)}}{\text{Input (2 hours)}}$$

Dividing 100 by 2 hours provides the productivity for making the sandwiches. In this case, this individual's productivity in making these sandwiches is

50 sandwiches per hour of work

The rate of productivity affects the unit cost for producing the sandwiches. If our sandwich maker collects $8.00 per hour worked and it takes him 1 hour to make 50 sandwiches, the cost per sandwich is calculated by dividing $8.00 by 50 sandwiches. The result gives us the amount of money it costs (in labor) to make 1 sandwich:

$$\frac{\$8.00 \text{ (labor cost)}}{50 \text{ sandwiches}} = \$.16 \text{ or 16 cents}$$

It takes 16 cents worth of labor cost to produce each sandwich. Of course, to calculate the total cost of the sandwich, we need to add in the cost of the ingredients as well.

Knowing the level of productivity can help the organization establish the correct price to charge its customers for its goods or services.

Add Value by Increasing Productivity

There are many ways to increase productivity. Reducing mistakes, errors, and waste of any kind; training employees; and investing in modern and efficient equipment are a few common ways to increase productivity. In some form or another, all organizations measure their productivity. Productivity levels can be calculated on a single operation or task. It can also be calculated on the organization as a whole. The organization's level of productivity provides evidence on its overall efficiency and financial health. Supervisors who raise productivity without sacrificing the expected level of quality add value to their organization. Adding value is a sure way to success.

INCREASING PRODUCTIVITY BY RESOLVING PERFORMANCE BARRIERS

The previous discussion illustrates the importance of understanding and analyzing performance gaps that are causing individuals or departments to not achieve the full level of productivity that is possible. Put another way, it is important to analyze the difference between an individual or department's current level of performance and expected level of performance and to then fill, or close, the performance gap.

The previous discussion also provides examples of the ways in which this gap can be measured, depending on the type of industry and the product involved. As noted, this product is not always tangible but may be more in the form of services that the industry provides. Determining this measure is not always easy. Nonetheless, you must have a clear picture of the expected level of performance for any particular position or team or departmental function so that you have a clear picture against which to judge current performance levels. Typically, for any position, you should be able to collect appropriate data through sources such as direct observation of performers in similar positions as the individual being analyzed; industry standards indicating the level of performance that should be expected for the position in question; concrete statistics showing the expected average level of performance for multiple performers in the position over time; and records, evaluations, and other data of performance for the specific individual being analyzed before a decline in performance was observed.

Once you have obtained this measure, you then know the extent of the gap you must fill. You must then come to an understanding of what is causing the gap in the first place. These causes are referred to as *performance barriers*. Once these barriers are identified and appropriate solutions have also been identified and implemented, we should see the gap close so that the individual or the department returns to the expected level of performance. This analytical process may be illustrated as follows:

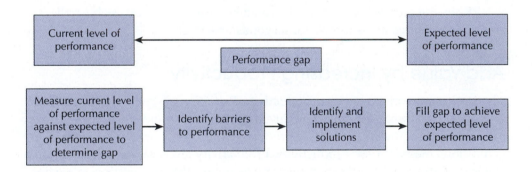

But what are these barriers and how do you address them? As the supervisor, you must work closely with the individual or team to identify these specific barriers. There are essentially two kinds of barriers that impact individual or team performance: external and internal. Typically, as much as 80 percent of all such performance barriers are the result of external factors beyond the individual's or team's control. If you want to fill these gaps, you and the organization overall must seek to identify and implement solutions to these barriers in order to improve performance. Only 20 percent of all potential performance barriers relate to matters within the individual or team's direct control. While it is ultimately up to the individual or team members to address and overcome these barriers, there are solutions that you can assist in implementing that will provide the appropriate conditions to allow the individual or team members to improve performance.[1] A description of these potential barriers and possible solutions follows.[2]

Potential Barriers	Possible Solutions

External—intangible (pertaining to the environment)

Organizational Systems and Processes
- The process of how tasks are completed, in what order, and who is responsible
- Work flow issues, including the sequencing of tasks and allocation of work among individuals and teams
- Organizational practices and policies, including who is responsible for decision making and who has access to decision makers (and who doesn't)

- Ensure employees have access to anyone in the organization on who they must rely to get work done, including managers in other departments
- Realign responsibilities among employees and across teams and departments
- Form process improvement teams to identify and resolve bottlenecks
- Examine job descriptions and duties to address task-alignment and job-design problems

Incentives
- The messages employees receive about their importance and the importance of their work toward contributing to team and organizational goals
- The associated behaviors employees exhibit in response to these messages (positive or negative)
- The mechanisms by which these messages are conveyed (or not), such as feedback, coaching, compensation, rewards and recognition, etc.

- Schedule informal feedback meetings for coaching purposes
- Begin a recognition program utilizing "low-cost" and "no-cost" methods for recognizing, rewarding, and appreciating staff
- Introduce job-enriching tasks
- Assess compensation structures to ensure they are equitable

External—tangible (pertaining to resources needed to perform)

Cognitive Support
- Guides, job aids, and documentation that show employees how to do their jobs
- The effect their use or non-use has in facilitating the work to be completed efficiently and effectively
- The clarity in which these guides demonstrate how tasks should be completed, or fail to do so

- Work with employees to develop simple instuctions and diagrams and standard operation procedures
- Develop intranet and other electronic media to share operating procedures and make them accessible at all times

Tools
- The "hardware" needed to perform job responsibilities
- Includes work tools (for manufacturing jobs), computers and related software, calculators, automobiles, office equipment and supplies, telecommunication devices, etc.
- The impact that the availability, absence, usability, and repair of such tools have on performance

- Identify areas where technology or the enhancement of existing technologies will help staff work more efficiently and effectively, and make modifications accordingly
- Update computers, programming, and software as needed
- Purchase new media, tools, and equipment or ensure existing tools are in good repair

Physical Environment
- The physical space in which task completion takes place
- Includes noise, light, temperature, physical layout, air quality, ergonomics, work atmosphere, etc.
- The impact these issues have on facilitating or hindering work

- Perform ergonomic, air quality, and other OSHA-type assessments and make improvements
- Accommodate specific concerns regarding lighting, noise, temperature, etc.
- Assess the work climate and general work atmosphere and make adjustments
- Examine OSHA and occupational injury records and make corrections where injury patterns are identified

(*continued*)

Potential Barriers	Possible Solutions
Internal (pertaining to the individual performer)	
Skills/Knowledge	
• The entent to which employees possess the requisite technical knowledge and interpersonal skills to complete job responsibilities	• Provide weekly/monthly "release time" to attend workshops and complete on-line training modules
• The extent to which employees receive continual training to keep skills and knowledge current	• Provide timely performance feedback and coaching
• The employee's personal motivation (or lack thereof) to contiually develop skills	• Create opportunities for team members to meet and train one another on new skills
	• Make pursuit of job-related training an expectation of the job that will be evaluated
Inherent Ability	
• The traits and characteristics held by individuals that are relatively stable and enduring over time, e.g., introversion/extroversion, conscientiousness, openness to new experiences, agreeableness, emotional stability, etc.	• Complete "interest inventories" to identify traits and characteristics and realign work assignments among team members accordingly
• The match or mismatch of these traits and characteristics and the position in question, and the impact these issues have on performance	• To the extent possible, focus on strengths and compensate for weaknesses through appropriate trade-offs between team members and their duties
	• Incorporate cross-training among positions to increase variety

When you analyze these barriers and identify and implement solutions, do so carefully, paying special notice to the 80/20 rule described previously. One mistake supervisors can make is to seek to "fix" employee performance problems by directing their focus almost exclusively on the individuals themselves under the assumption the performance problems are inherently internal to the performer. When we fail to properly analyze performance problems and correct external barriers, we not only fail to fill the performance gap, but we also frustrate employees and, in the worst case, create tremendous resentment and distrust through the pressures we place on them to improve performance.

Of course, 20 percent of all performance barriers are internal. The discussion that follows concerning motivation provides additional insight on how to address these issues.

MOTIVATION AND PRODUCTIVITY

Many things can happen, either on or off the job, to cause an excellent employee to drop suddenly in personal productivity. In dramatic situations of this nature (when the cause might be highly personal), the supervisor may wish to give the employee a few days to bounce back without interference. But if too much time passes with no improvement, the supervisor should try to discover the cause and take immediate steps to bring productivity back to the previous level. Hoping that time will take care of the problem can be wishful thinking. Take the case of Bernie, for example.

For the past week, Bernie had been producing far beneath his potential as a home-appliance repairman. Most of his co-workers averaged thirty-two house calls the previous week (average labor billings $2,400), while Bernie averaged only twenty-one calls (average billings $1,600). Why? Were Bernie's calls more difficult and time-consuming?

Was he less capable, so that it took longer? Were some unknown personal reasons behind the gap between what he was doing and what he could do?

Bernie's supervisor took time to look at his previous record and discovered that Bernie had been above average in productivity until the previous Friday, when his productivity gap dropped suddenly to about 50 percent of his normal level. Bernie's supervisor tried to remember any specific circumstance that day that might have been the cause. Then it hit him. That was the day the new truck arrived and was assigned to Frank. Was Bernie upset about it? Through a quick counseling session with Bernie, the supervisor verified his hunch. Bernie, thinking he had seniority over Frank, had expected to be assigned the new truck and was understandably upset when he didn't get it—so upset, in fact, that he seriously thought about resigning. In a long heart-to-heart talk, the supervisor was able to convince Bernie that his assumption had been wrong and that Frank was entitled to the new truck. The next day, Bernie's productivity started going back up. The supervisor had done a successful emergency repair job. Rather than wait around, he moved in and corrected the situation before Bernie's productivity drop seriously hurt the department or before Bernie resigned.

Communication failures, misunderstandings, and damaged egos can occur in any department, so the supervisor must constantly be on the alert for sudden drops in individual productivity. You cannot always afford to wait to discover whether the problem is job-related.

Not all drops in productivity are sudden and dramatic. Sometimes a slow deterioration does not show up for weeks or months. In such instances the supervisor may not be able to find a tangible cause for the widening gap, making corrective action much more difficult. For example, what about the person who has become disenchanted with the job and the company? What do you do when an employee has temporarily lost sight of a previous goal or has a change in attitude that defies understanding? To illustrate the problem, let's look at the case of Gilbert.

In less than two years with the organization, Gilbert had reached a position of high responsibility in his department. During the past three months, however, he had shown a noticeable productivity gap. Gilbert's slow loss of drive was reflected in reduced efficiency and generally weaker performance. Gilbert's supervisor decided to try some motivational counseling. She called Gilbert into her office and began as follows.

"Good morning, Gilbert. Thanks for accepting my invitation to drop by. It's been a few months since you and I had a good chat. Tell me, how are things going for you?"

"Well, pretty good, I guess. I still like the job and the company. I haven't heard any complaints."

"Yes, I still feel you have excellent long-range potential with us. By the way, have you ever thought about where you might like to be in our organization in five years? Do you have a personal goal? Are you, for example, preparing for a job similar to mine?"

"Well, at first when I was really gung-ho, I decided to become a supervisor within three years, but I guess my goals are less crystallized now. Reality is quite different from optimistic first plans, I guess."

The conversation that followed between Gilbert and his supervisor lasted forty minutes. During that time, they had a free exchange of ideas on many subjects, but most of the talk centered on Gilbert's future. At the end, Gilbert admitted that he had lost his focus on a goal, and it had been affecting his work. He expressed his pleasure in getting the problem out in the open. It was forty minutes well spent because Gilbert's productivity started going back up within the next few days. In fact, soon it was higher than it had been previously. Before the year was out, Gilbert was promoted to supervisor of another department. Talking things over had apparently restored Gilbert's goal and renewed his personal confidence in his ability to achieve it.

You can sometimes improve motivation by giving employees special assignments, rotating jobs when feasible, or providing special learning opportunities. Everything you do as a supervisor will have an impact on the motivation of those who work for you. In turn, the degree of their motivation will determine the productivity level of your department.

MOTIVATION THEORIES

Management books are full of motivational theories. Some, properly interpreted, can be useful to the beginning supervisor. Here are two examples.

Hawthorne Experiments

From 1927 to 1932, the Western Electric Company conducted what are now known as the Hawthorne experiments. These experiments showed that no matter what improvements were made (rest periods, free hot lunches, etc.), the productivity of the group increased. Why? The employees were made to feel important; making any improvement gave them more status and respect. Until these experiments were made, management had accepted as self-evident that the way to improve the rate of production was to improve machinery, provide better lighting, and make similar physical changes. The Hawthorne experiments proved that the emotional climate of the worker is just as important and has positive effects on employee attitudes, which in turn affect productivity positively.

Many psychologists claim that employees' inner needs must be satisfied before they can reach their personal potentials. They divide needs into primary and secondary. A *primary need* is physiological, such as hunger; a *secondary need* is one that satisfies the mind, ego, or spirit.

Maslow's Hierarchy of Needs

One of the best-known need-priority lists was established by Abraham Maslow. [3] He theorized that all humans have five needs that can be prioritized in a hierarchy or pyramid, as follows:

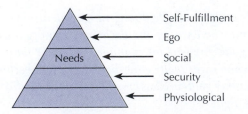

This theory has some intuitive appeal. It helps supervisors understand their employees' reaction to changes in the organization that affect them and to decisions made by their company's leaders.

The crux of this theory is that workers are motivated to meet the lower-level needs before they are motivated to meet the needs above them. For example, an organization that is getting ready to lay-off half its work force will not be able to motivate its employees by sponsoring a softball team. A lay-off threatens employees' survival and security needs, which are satisfied by their paycheck. Employees will be more motivated to regain their level of satisfaction at the security level than attempt to meet the higher level social need. In other words, you must satisfy your need for food and security before social needs become motivating. Likewise, employees will satisfy social and ego needs before self-fulfillment is possible.

Today, employers do an adequate job of helping satisfy the first three levels of needs: physiological, security, and social needs. This is partly due to state and federal regulations and laws. We have OSHA to ensure our safety, employment laws that protect us from capricious and arbitrary firings and layoffs, and plenty of opportunities to socialize on and off the company property. As a supervisor, concentrate on helping your employees satisfy their ego and self-actualization needs. This is not difficult to do, and often costs very little. For instance, when you ask your employees for advice on how to make a change that affects them, you send the message to them that their ideas (and they as people) are important to you and the company. This helps satisfy their esteem need because it makes them feel valued.

Organizations attempt to meet each level of needs by providing, among other things, the following:

> Physiological or survival needs—safe working conditions, adequate pay, health benefits

> Security—job stability and security, savings account, retirement plans

> Social—opportunity to work with others, team projects, break areas, company sponsored softball team, company picnics

> Ego—awards, pats on the back, seeking employee input, participative management, advancement opportunities

> Self-actualization—tuition reimbursement, career and professional development opportunities, work/life balance, participation in corporate-sponsored community service days

SUPERVISOR–EMPLOYEE RELATIONSHIPS AND PRODUCTIVITY

A supervisor is responsible for creating and maintaining a motivating environment—an environment in which all employees are motivated to do their highest quality and most productive work. The following five tips will help you do this.

1. *Building good relations with employees is more important than being able to do their jobs skillfully yourself.*   The technical skills you have are important because you must know how to do something before you can teach and supervise others; however, your emphasis as a supervisor will be on transmitting your skills through sound relationships rather than being capable of doing all the tasks yourself.

2. *Spending time to restore or improve your relationship with an employee whose productivity has slipped is the most important thing you can do with your*

time.   As a supervisor, you will have multiple responsibilities. In all likelihood, you will have more things to do than time to do them, so it will be necessary to sift out and assign suitable priorities to your responsibilities. Top priority should always go to keeping the productivity of others as high as possible. When the productivity of one employee slips, you must be aware of it immediately and begin trying to do something about it within a reasonable period of time. Identifying and providing solutions to performance barriers are key methods for doing this.

3. *Management expects you to achieve high productivity from new employees in a hurry.*   Today, a faster payoff is expected from new employees than was true in the past for several reasons:
   a. Employees have a shorter span of employment today, moving from one job to another more quickly. So, if the mobile employee is going to make a productivity contribution, he or she should do so without wasting any time.
   b. The pace in most organizations is faster today. Orientation periods have been speeded up, and training time (both on the job and in formal classrooms) is more limited.
   c. Training today is more expensive.
   What do these factors mean to you as a supervisor? It means you must build relations with new employees as early as possible and train them quickly so that they reach a good productivity level in a shorter span of time.

4. *Your future promotions will be based on the productivity of the people who work for you now.*   Many factors are considered when management promotes a front-line supervisor to a more responsible middle-management position, but nothing influences a favorable decision more than a supervisor's human relations skill to motivate sustained productivity from people. To ignore, underestimate, or downgrade this principle in any way will surely damage your career.

5. *When you think of higher productivity, you must think of quality.* Corporations have discovered that higher productivity and higher quality are necessary to compete domestically and internationally. Stockholders and executives know they are dependent upon front-line supervisors to achieve these goals.

Supervisors occupy a unique and sometimes contradictory role. Although they must possess the knowledge and skills to do specific jobs they ask their employees to do, they must refrain from doing these jobs so that they can manage. They must be content to teach others how to reach their potential. They must reach their own goals through the efforts of others. It takes a special perspective and sensitivity to achieve success in this role.

PERFORMANCE **CHECKLIST**

1. The moment you become a supervisor, you must achieve productivity by learning how to direct, train, create, and maintain a motivating environment. You can seldom afford the luxury of doing it yourself. In other words, in terms of production work in the department, you will contribute more by doing less.

2. As a supervisor, you must work to increase and maintain the individual productivity of each employee you manage as well as overall departmental

productivity. *Individual productivity* is the performance or contribution of one person over a specified period of time. *Departmental productivity* is the total of all productivity (by machines and people) that comes from a department or section within an organization.

3. *Productivity* equals *output divided by input.* *Output* is anything a company produces. *Input* is anything it takes to produce output. By manipulating output or input, we affect productivity. High productivity usually means that the organization is efficient. The more efficient the operation, the more successful it will be.

4. To improve productivity, you must first analyze the difference between an individual or department's current level of performance and the expected level of performance. Once you have obtained this measure, you then know the extent of the performance gap you must fill. You must then come to an understanding of what is causing the gap, referred to as *performance barriers.* Once these barriers are identified and appropriate solutions have also been identified and implemented, the gap closes and productivity increases.

5. In general, only 20 percent of the barriers to effective performance are the result of causes internal to the employee. Common internal performance barriers are the lack of inherent ability and lack of appropriate skills or knowledge to perform specific tasks. On the other hand, as much of 80 percent of performance barriers is the result of causes external to the employee and beyond his or her control. Some of these external barriers pertain to the work environment such as incentives and organizational systems and processes. Other external barriers pertain to the resources employees need to perform such as cognitive support, tools, and the physical environment. Supervisors must be careful to address external barriers and not put all the burden on employees for performance problems.

6. When there are performance issues involving individual performance, Maslow's hierarchy of needs theory serves as a good model to identify and implement appropriate measures to motivate employees. In particular, employers must consider specific ways they can address each of the five needs identified in Maslow's model: physiological, security, social, ego, and self-actualization.

TEST YOURSELF

For each of the following statements, check true or false.

True   False

1. The Hawthorne experiments demonstrated that *any* change in the treatment or environment of the worker causes an increase in productivity.

2. Employees promote their own supervisors through their personal productivity.

3. Individual productivity is easier to measure than departmental productivity.

4. *Managing* is defined as planning, organizing, directing, coordinating, and controlling activities to achieve productivity goals.

5. Maslow's list of needs indicates that physiological needs cannot be met until self-realization needs are met.

6. Upper management measures only the personal productivity of a supervisor.

7. In general, focusing most of your attention on an employee's performance deficits rather than other factors impacting his or her performance will more quickly lead to improvement.

8. A *performance gap* is the difference between current performance and expected performance for someone in the employee's position.

9. *Output* is what a company produces. *Inputs* are the things it takes to produce output.

10. An example of an internal barrier affecting an employee's performance is the absence of effective job aids and documentation explaining how to accomplish tasks.

Turn to the back of the book to check your answers.

Total Correct_____

DISCUSSION **QUESTIONS**

1. Why might it be extremely difficult—perhaps impossible—for a worker who has been in a highly skilled job for ten years to become a successful supervisor?

2. When, if ever, would a supervisor be justified in saying, "It's easier to do it myself"?

3. Does it take as much patience and understanding to be a good supervisor as it does to be a good teacher, coach, or minister? Explain your answer.

4. Do you agree that 80 percent of performance problems are typically due to external factors beyond employees' control? What has been your observation where you have worked as an employee and/or supervisor? How would your acceptance or rejection of this 80/20 principle impact the way you manage employees in the future?

5. What things might supervisors do in order to create an atmosphere in which their workers can meet their social, ego, and self-fulfillment needs?

CASE 1: **APPROACH**

Yesterday, Marty was promoted to the role of supervisor in a department where customer relations has top priority. In fact, Bill told him he received the promotion because of his outstanding skills with people and his contagiously positive attitude.

Marty is pleased with the opportunity and hopes that it will be the first step on a path that will bring him additional promotions. He decides on the following approach.

First, he thinks he can eliminate all training in how to handle customers by being an ideal model. He feels strongly that to work well with people, an individual must be natural, and he does not want to impose his own customer relations techniques on the personalities of others. He feels that if he sets the pace and becomes a good example, employees will accept the challenge and develop their own style. They will not need specific suggestions from him. He intends to come to work early and stay late to do supervisory paperwork so that he can spend more time out front with customers.

Second, because satisfied employees are the key to success, he wants to be a "good guy" instead of a disciplinarian. He feels a permissive, relaxed working environment is essential if employees are to be natural and effective with customers. He feels that if he is more accessible to his employees, they will come to him with their problems, and he can develop stronger personal relationships.

Do you see any pitfalls in Marty's approach? What suggestions might you make? Turn to the back of this book to compare your thoughts with those of the authors.

CASE 2: PERFORMANCE **BARRIERS AND SOLUTIONS**

Review the role profiles for the members of Ricardo's team, including Karl, Giselle, Marty, Renee, and Julie. For each, using the performance gap analysis and barriers/solution discussion provided in this chapter, identify the potential barriers keeping each employee from performing to their full potential and possible solutions to improve their performance. Conduct the same analysis for the team as a whole. What barriers and solutions would you suggest? Would you say performance relates more to internal or external factors? Why or why not? If you feel you have insufficient information to assess team or individual performance problems, what more would you need to know or do to determine the barriers and identify and implement solutions?

PRODUCTIVITY **EXERCISE**

This exercise will help you identify the kinds of motivational factors that may help your employees close their productivity gaps. Read the ten factors listed below, then rank the one you feel would be the most effective motivator at the top of the pyramid and so on down the line. Once you have completed the pyramid, ask one of your employees (or a fellow student or friend) to complete the same exercise. To gain new insight, match and discuss your answers.

- More recognition
- Involvement in decision making

- Opportunity to be heard
- Opportunity to learn
- Sharing problems and challenges
- Freedom from close supervision
- Being trusted and respected as an individual

- Getting time off to handle personal problems
- Enjoying some fun on the job
- Opportunity to discuss personal plans and goals

Turn to the back of this book to compare your view with that of the authors.

PERSONAL GROWTH **EXERCISE**

Calculate your department's productivity in one area and think of several ways to increase it. To do this, analyze the performance gap and the performance barriers and identify possible solutions to eliminate the gap.

TO LEARN **MORE**

To read more about Abraham Maslow's theories, refer to the following texts:

Maslow, Abraham H. *Motivation and Personality*. New York: Harper & Row, 1954.

Maslow, Abraham H. *New Knowledge in Human Values*. New York: Harper & Row, 1959.

Maslow, Abraham H. *Toward a Psychology of Being*. Princeton, NJ: D. Van Norstrand Co., 1962.

Maslow, Abraham H. *Maslow on Management*. Hoboken, NJ: John Wiley & Sons, 1998. (Originally published as *Eupsychian Management*. Homeward, NJ: Richard D. Irwin, Inc. and Dorsey Press, 1965).

NOTES

1. Wile, David, "Why Doers Do," *P & I Journal* 35, no. 2 (February 1996), 30–35.
2. Adapted from Ibid.
3. Abraham H. Maslow, "A Theory of Human Motivation," *Psychological Review* 50 (1943), 370–96.

chapter **five**

THE SUPERVISOR–EMPLOYEE RELATIONSHIP

"In order for me to look good, everybody around me has to look good."
Doris Drury

PERFORMANCE COMPETENCIES

After you have finished reading this chapter, you should be able to:

- Identify the psychological ingredients or factors in a typical supervisor–employee relationship

- Describe five ways to build a stronger relationship with your supervisor

- Explain three characteristics found in most relationships

- List the five foundations for good human relations and how to put them into practice

"*S*orry to put this additional responsibility on you at this time, but you know how it is . . ."
"*Here's a new report we have to get back to headquarters by Friday, even if it means letting something else slide.*"
"*J.B. has called another special meeting for tomorrow afternoon . . .*"

The new supervisor soon learns that a constant stream of additional and unexpected time-consuming duties filters down from above. Most supervisors occasionally feel that they need more arms and legs and a twenty-four-hour workday to give full attention to their growing list of responsibilities. But no matter how many or how urgent your multiple responsibilities may be, one must take priority over all others: your responsibility to build and maintain a productive relationship with each employee under your immediate supervision. No other single responsibility demands the same degree of attention.

Why? As we discovered in Chapter 4, building a good relationship with an employee is the best way to close the employee's productivity gap. It also promotes your own personal effectiveness and productivity as a manager because when you take the time to develop these relationships and guide employees in their work you are better able to produce more quality work through their efforts with less need for you to perform these tasks so that you can focus on broader managerial goals. Only through good relationships combined with strong, sensitive leadership can a cohesive department be built. The quality of relationships constitutes the fabric of the department. If relationships fall apart, the whole operation is weakened. If you do not learn to build and maintain these relationships skillfully, your days as a supervisor will be full of turmoil, and you will not reach your potential as a manager. Building interpersonal relationships is the key to success as a team leader.

What is the all-important relationship that exists between the supervisor and each employee? What is its function? How can a productive relationship be built?

THE RELATIONSHIP CHANNEL

Perhaps a supervisor–employee relationship is best perceived and understood as a line that exists between the two, a kind of psychological channel through which all communications, reactions, and feelings must flow back and forth.[1]

Through this relationship channel, each party views, interprets, and reacts to the other. The openness—the amount of freedom or naturalness—of this line contributes to the quality or tone of the relationship, which, in turn, is the essence of the working arrangement. Here are three characteristics found in most relationships, which apply to the relationship itself and do not describe the individuals themselves.

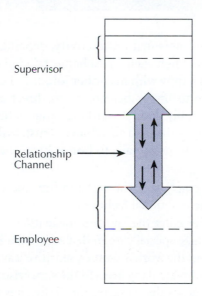

1. *Two-way communication.*   This is the lifeblood of the relationship line. You keep a relationship alive and healthy through an input of words and nonverbal signals from both ends. Just as all parts of the human body must receive a constant supply of fresh blood to survive, a relationship is kept alive with an exchange of ideas, given strength by words, and kept in good repair through talking. Parties at both ends of the line must contribute. An open dialogue keeps the relationship healthy. In management parlance, the operative word is *feedback* and both parties in the supervisor–employee relationship need it—continuously, even desperately at times. To repeat: *feedback is two-way*, including employee to supervisor, and not just supervisor to employee as is commonly assumed.

2. *Mutual Reward Theory (MRT).*   MRT states that the relationship between supervisor and employee is enhanced when a good reward exchange occurs between them. For example, the supervisor may provide the employee with the freedom to work with minimum supervision, personal recognition, and involvement in decision making. In return, the employee

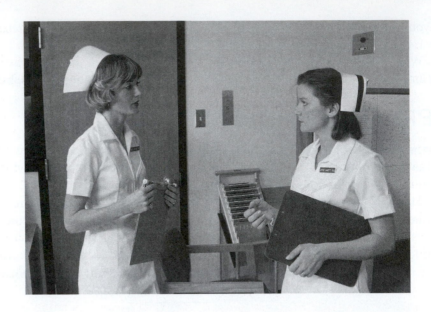

may provide high personal productivity, dependability, and cooperation with co-workers. When such an exchange takes place, both parties benefit. The employee is happy with his or her job, and the supervisor's reputation is enhanced due to his or her ability to direct and support employees. Without a reasonably good reward exchange, a healthy, productive, long-term relationship is difficult to achieve. Trust is also violated when either person in the relationship fails to honor his or her part of the agreement in the exchange.

3. *The presence of emotion.*   The relationship line can become emotionally charged. Extreme emotional feelings of either the employee or the supervisor can sometimes enter the line and make it difficult to handle. Therefore, you must often take special care in dealing with a highly charged situation. You must go about the work in a quiet, sensitive way. Sparks generated by uncontrolled emotions are dangerous to the supervisor–employee relationship. Although both parties share this responsibility, it is the supervisor who must keep the line under control, managing to control his or her own emotions and responding appropriately when employees' emotions run high.

You, as the supervisor, are primarily responsible for the condition of any given employee relationship. You must take the initiative to keep it healthy. If it fails, you cannot blame the employee. You need the cooperation of the employee and must assume the responsibility for getting it.

What happens when, despite your best efforts, the employee doesn't meet his or her end of the agreement to build a workable relationship? You may have a problem employee. When faced with this situation, you have at least three possible solutions: (1) Involve the employee by asking for suggestions on how to improve the relationship. Perhaps some aspects of the relationship concern the employee, and you can manage differently if you better understood these concerns. Perhaps there are differences in learning or communication styles or in your personalities that you can address. If nothing comes of this approach, you may have to (2) initiate action to transfer the individual to another supervisor who has a different leadership style and personality, which might be more successful than yours. This action should be taken in all cases where the employee has made a sincere effort to be productive. If neither of the two previous suggestions solves the problem, you may have to (3) consider ending the employment relationship. This option should be utilized only when it becomes clear that the employee is unable or unwilling to hold up his or her part of the agreement with you or another supervisor to which he or she was transferred. This option may be the most difficult thing you are called on to do as a supervisor, but sometimes it is inevitable. More often than not, such action is best for both the employee and the organization. If you choose to take this action, be sure that all company procedures and policies are honored. In most cases, this means checking with the human resources department to make sure that the rights of the employee have been protected and that no laws have been violated.

A variety of supervisory jobs are available. Some supervisors direct large numbers of employees, others only a few. Some work with highly technical equipment, others with customer services. But no matter what the supervisor's scope or the complexity of the job, a supervisor faces no greater challenge than building and maintaining healthy relationships with those who look to her or him for leadership. To accept the challenge fully means to plunge deeply into human relations. It means taking a deep, clear look at your own behavior, for one thing is certain: You get back the kind of behavior you send out.

BUILDING SOUND RELATIONSHIPS

Now that you see why you must build and maintain good employee relationships, how will you do it? Listed here are some suggestions.

1. *See the relationship first and the employee second.*   The previous discussion invited you to view the employee through a relationship channel in order to become more objective and professional in dealing with employees. By concentrating more on the relationship, you will become less involved in the personality of the individual and will probably be less motivated by any unconscious prejudices that you may have. You will also be more scientific in your approach to problems, more aware of your own responsibilities, and more successful in achieving the productivity you seek. This approach also provides insulation against unwise personal investments.

    When Sylvia first took over the department, she dealt only in personalities, attempting to understand and deal with the individual traits of her staff. Resentment developed because her employees thought she was prying into their private lives. Later, Sylvia backed away and started to view each worker through the relationship channel for which she had primary responsibility to keep open and healthy. Not only did this more professional approach result in more respect from her staff, but Sylvia felt better about herself because she knew she was more objective and fair.

2. *Don't play games with relationships.*   A relationship is not a toy or game with which the supervisor is free to experiment. Relationships should be honored and treated with deep respect and sensitive consideration. If you hurt the relationship between you and your employee, you may lower productivity. The employee may at times seem too far away to be hurt by your actions, but she or he will certainly be aware of your attitude.

3. *Keep all relationships on a business basis.* In most cases, it is best to keep your business and personal lives balanced. You may find it hard to have both a working and a personal relationship with the same person (regardless of gender) without losing your objectivity and hurting both your careers. For some people in some situations, a working and a social relationship can be combined. However, if either you or those you supervise cannot handle this kind of closeness without a distortion of the on-the-job relationship, do not try to blend the two.

4. *Don't build one relationship at the expense of another.* The goal of the supervisor should be to build and keep relationships with all employees equally. Like the parent of several children, the supervisor should show no favoritism, despite the fact that one employee may need more help than another. In building one relationship, it is easy to neglect others, resulting in increasingly negative reactions from the other employees. It is similar to the problem faced by the stagecoach driver who attempts to get each of six horses to pull an equal share of the weight at the fastest possible speed over the long haul. It is difficult to hold the reins with just the right touch. To avoid imbalances, the supervisor must occasionally review the state of relationships with all employees in the department. If one relationship has been built at the expense of another, immediate repair work should be the first priority.

   The following checklist can assist you in equalizing communications and rotating assignments.

SUPERVISOR'S CHECKLIST

☐ Talk to employees with the same frequency.

☐ Pay as much attention to employees whose interests are different from yours as those with whom you have more in common.

☐ Find *something* to appreciate about each employee.

☐ Rotate less desirable tasks.

☐ When assigning new tasks, follow criteria clearly defined and known to your employees.

☐ When assigning new tasks, keep in mind opportunities for cross training and skill building.

☐ Communicate your expectations of what is a fair workload for all employees.

---

5. *Build your relationship with a new employee quickly and carefully.* When a new employee comes into your department, you have a good opportunity to build a healthy, lasting relationship from scratch. Take time for this task. Do what is necessary to make new employees feel at home, give them the confidence needed to be productive, and help them build sound working relations with the other employees. Orient new employees to their new surroundings, taking time to introduce them to their co-workers. If you move in quickly and build the right kind of relationship with new employees, especially those

from different cultures, they will respond with quick productivity, and the relationship itself will last through the many demands made on it later.

6. *Relationships require daily maintenance.*   Just like certain pieces of complex machinery, relationships need daily maintenance. They need to be constantly lubricated with recognition, oiled with attention, and polished with kindness. A good relationship must be protected, nurtured, and closely observed lest it fail because of neglect. Experience shows that the productivity payoff is more than worth the attention.

7. *Repair damage quickly.*   No matter how skillful you become in building relationships, a break now and then is likely to occur. When such disturbances surface, you should quickly make whatever repairs are necessary. Sometimes it means readjusting workloads, schedules, or procedures, or perhaps it requires an apology from you. Whatever it takes, you must move quickly. If the break is beyond repair or requires an outsider, take the problem to your supervisor or human resources director.

In addition to building and maintaining good relationships with employees, you must not neglect relationships with fellow supervisors.

FIVE IRREPLACEABLE FOUNDATIONS

Supervisors can employ many relationship-building techniques, depending on their styles and environments, such as the following:

- *Good listening skills.*   Only through listening can supervisors discover the special rewards their employees seek as part of the bargain under the Mutual Reward Theory (MRT), or identify problems and their solutions before they grow into major conflicts.

- *Flexibility.*   Supervisors should remain flexible enough to accommodate harmless personal requests (like leaving early to take care of important personal business) when productivity is maintained and problems with other employees can be avoided.

- *Consistency in style.*   Employees do not respond well to supervisors who are unpredictable in their behavior or in their expectations of others.

- *Being a good one-on-one counselor.*   Without playing psychologist, providing timely support and understanding sends a message that you care and want your employees to succeed.

The list goes on, but nothing—absolutely nothing—is more important than application of the five foundations. These can literally make or break you as a supervisor.

1. Give Clear and Complete Instructions

As a supervisor, you have a certain amount of *knowledge power*. You know more about how to perform certain tasks than most of your employees. How effectively you transmit this knowledge is the key to your relationships. When instructions are clearly and completely given, the employee knows exactly what to do and feels good about it; however, when instructions are hazy and incomplete, the employee loses confidence in the supervisor, and their relationship deteriorates. To feel secure, the employee must know what is expected and possess the skills to do his or her job.

As a supervisor, take time in giving instructions. When possible, use visual illustrations. Follow the basic teaching techniques of keeping things simple and logical and providing examples. When you give instructions, make sure they are clear and complete by asking for feedback. Then, follow up by checking the following day to see whether the instructions were put into practice correctly. Provide further clarification as needed.

With many important problems facing him, Jake nevertheless took time to demonstrate patiently to Mary, an insecure new employee, how to operate a complicated and dangerous machine. Jake gave Mary more than two hours of his time, including two follow-ups, so that all errors were eliminated. On her second day at work, Mary felt completely competent and her productivity was almost up to average. This training happened more than a year ago, and Mary has yet to have an accident. Furthermore, Jake has had a strong, sound relationship with Mary from the very start.

2. Communicate: Let People Know How They Are Doing

To keep supervisor–employee relationships in good repair, take time to let employees know how they are getting along. Most employees (especially new ones) want to know how to do their jobs better and will welcome help if it is provided in the right way. They also want to know when things are going well and when you are pleased with their performance. Don't let them feel that they are working in a vacuum and that you do not care. Tell them.

Employees respond quickly to any stimuli created by you, and can also sense the reaction of fellow employees. But the thing that hurts them most is neglect. They want to feel that they are an important part of the department, and they know that their future depends on your training and support. An excellent way to keep the relationship in good working order is to provide both training and support. Being open to the needs of your employees will help create effective two-way communication.

Mrs. Browne is a highly capable night supervisor of nurses in an Atlanta hospital. She does not, however, believe in letting people know how they are doing. She almost never tells a nurse when she or he does well, but she comes down heavily when a violation occurs. As a result, she has more personnel problems than any supervisor on the staff. Nurses are constantly asking to be transferred to other wards. Mrs. Browne has been passed over for a promotion for three years in succession.

3. Give Credit When Due

Employees need positive reinforcement now and then if they are to keep their personal productivity at a high level. They need the compliment you intend to give before you get too busy with something else; they need recognition. Look for extraordinary quality performance from those who work for you. Sometimes it is best to give credit in front of the entire department. More often, however, it is best given privately. Praise should be given freely, sincerely, and most important, when it is due. To achieve this goal, you must constantly have your "radar" turned on to observe behavior that is deserving of credit. Supervisors who fail to give credit when it is due, or who are stingy about it, often have standards that are far above levels the employee is capable of reaching and are afraid that giving credit would be misinterpreted as undeserved flattery. This attitude leaves the employee feeling small and insignificant, and usually results in lower productivity. It is necessary to be sincere in giving credit, and it is wise to be generous with giving it.

Karen handles certificates of deposit for her bank, which means she frequently deals with senior citizens who have accumulated enough money to purchase them in amounts of $10,000 or more. Many of these people become extremely nervous when making decisions. A few are overly talkative and difficult to send on their way. Others have hearing impediments. Last week at a staff meeting, Karen's supervisor complimented the entire staff on the improvements they had made in dealing with these customers and singled out Karen for special mention. The following day, Karen told her supervisor that she had been thinking of leaving because she did not feel appreciated. She thanked the supervisor.

4. Involve People in Decisions

Certain problems may arise that only the supervisor can solve. The wise supervisor knows, however, that many problems can be solved with employee participation. When you involve employees in departmental problems that concern them, you accomplish at least three goals:

1. You give them a chance to learn about the operations of the department, thus preparing them for future promotions.
2. You build their confidence by providing decision-making opportunities, and as a result, their productivity increases.
3. You improve the departmental climate by bringing people closer together, thereby reducing friction and misunderstandings.

Often the benefits of letting employees come up with solutions can prove more helpful than the solutions themselves. When employees help make decisions, they grow and you gain. Involvement makes people feel important, challenged, and stimulated. It can release talent and increase productivity as nothing else can.

Make it a practice to turn over appropriate problems to the people who work for you. Let them struggle with solutions even though you could easily find the answer alone. Once they have an answer, accept it gracefully, giving their solution your full support. Employees often give greater support to their decisions than to those handed down by the supervisor. Do not, however, come up with your own answer and just wait for someone to match it, intending to do what you planned all along. Tricking employees into thinking that they are helping you find a solution to a problem that you have already picked is manipulative. Employees find out quickly that you cannot be trusted.

Marla, the owner of a successful boutique in an enclosed shopping center, had been paying a freelance window trimmer to change the front display twice each month. Her three full-time salespeople were so critical of the displays that she asked them to decide whether to keep the professional or to rotate the job among themselves. They said they would like to do it themselves. After two months, Marla had to agree that not only were the displays better, but all three salespeople were better motivated.

5. Maintain an Open Door

The supervisor who is easy to approach builds better relationships than the aloof supervisor who is hard to see and difficult to talk with. Encourage your employees to come to you freely with suggestions, with complaints, or for counsel. To allow this communication to happen, you must avoid building physical or psychological barriers between yourself and each employee. Rather, try to establish and practice an open-door policy through which free, open, and healthy communication practices can be built. Fear or distrust can prevent good communication and hurt relationships. Merely keeping the door to your office open and telling employees to drop by is not enough. You must work to create a nonthreatening, welcome atmosphere that will cause employees to come to you. Seeking them out by walking around and visiting them is an effective strategy for opening doors.

Tricia was the supervisor of an office staff of twelve. Unfortunately, her office was enclosed in glass and visible to all employees. They could not hear her conferences, but they could observe them. As a result, despite her best efforts, no one wanted to be made conspicuous while talking over problems in the supervisor's office. Her solution was to schedule and conduct short discussions once a month with each employee at a special location in the employee cafeteria. These meetings took time she could ill afford, but it greatly strengthened relationships, and productivity increased.

USING THE FIVE FOUNDATIONS

These five irreplaceable foundations, then, serve the supervisor in building and keeping healthy, productive relationships with employees. Obviously, it doesn't take a mental giant to understand them, nor does it take a supervisor with twenty years of experience to put them into practice. Why, then, are they so frequently taken for granted and so seldom used? Following are three possible reasons:

1. Some ambitious supervisors spend their time seeking more sophisticated replacements instead of realizing that these five foundations will serve them well.

2. Some supervisors give these foundations lip service by claiming to use them when, in fact, they do not. They say one thing and do another, but the people they supervise know the truth.
3. Some supervisors accept the foundations at face value and honestly try to use them, but fail because they do not use them consistently day after day.

How can you tend to these five foundations and use them naturally in your daily contact with employees? First, you must make a personal commitment to the five foundations, convincing yourself of their value. You must believe they are sound human relations principles. Second, you must incorporate them into your way of working with your employees, integrating them into your daily routine. You must practice what you believe. The more you practice these five foundations, the better you become at using them.

DEALING WITH A DEMANDING SUPERIOR

And you thought, as a new supervisor, that developing effective relationships with the employees you manage would be challenging! Indeed, your most difficult supervisor–employee relationship challenge may be the one you have with your boss. It is one thing to deal with a superior as a regular employee; it is another ballgame when you as a manager must build and maintain a strong, open relationship with another person in management. Upper-management people can often be more demanding (with vastly different behavioral patterns) than those at the beginning supervisory level. This distinction does not mean you should be intimidated by a powerful person. Three suggestions might assist you in this respect.

- Your new supervisor is more of an equal because you are both members of the management team.
- You can initiate communications more easily because the traditional employee–boss barrier has been eliminated.
- You can often be more assertive (express greater leadership) because you represent the welfare and productivity of your own team.

Your responsibility to your employees in no way means that you have less of a responsibility to build a stronger relationship with your supervisor. Just the opposite! In building these relationships, the following tips may be helpful:

1. Keep in mind that the more you act like a manager, the more you will be treated like one by other managers.
2. Be concerned with the relationship between you and your boss, and not with her or his personality. If you concentrate on the relationship, you can (with experience) get along with almost any personality your supervisor may possess, including those with unusual quirks, mannerisms, and styles of leadership.
3. Demonstrate productivity and quality performance first and good human relations second. You want your department to excel, but you do not want disruptive employees to go over your head by jumping the chain of command.
4. Don't be a problem supervisor. As a supervisor, you do not want problem employees in your department; by the same token, your superior does not want problem supervisors. He or she may be less apt to intervene and counsel

you on your behavior than you would one of your own employees because it is expected that you have outgrown the need.

5. The more effectively you handle your own departmental problems, the more you will be appreciated.

Hopefully, your new superior will become a mentor and show you the "ropes" of upper management. Your challenge is to give her or him a reason to help you learn and succeed.

PERFORMANCE **CHECKLIST**

1. The three characteristics of effective supervisor–employee relationships are two-way communication, the proper exchange of rewards between the parties, and the presence and ability to manage emotion.

2. When, despite your best efforts, an employee fails to hold up his or her end of the exchange in the Mutual Rewards Theory, you have three alternatives: (1) Seek input from the employee on concerns that may affect your relationship that you can address and hopefully correct; (2) Transfer the employee to work with another supervisor, where a more effective relationship may be possible; (3) End the employment relationship. The third alternative should be utilized only when the employee is unwilling or unable to build a good relationship with you.

3. To build a strong relationship with an employee, separate the relationship from the personalities involved, keep the relationship on a business basis, don't play games with the relationship, don't build one relationship at the expense of another, maintain the relationship on a daily basis, and repair damage quickly.

4. The most effective relationship-building methods are encompassed in the Five Irreplaceable Foundations, which are: (1) Give clear and complete instructions; (2) Let people know how they are doing (communicate); (3) Give credit when due; (4) Involve people in decisions; and (5) Maintain an open door. You must make a personal commitment to these five foundations, convincing yourself of their value, and practice applying them in your relationships with employees on a consistent, daily basis.

5. Your most challenging supervisor–employee relationship may not be with the employees you manage, but with your boss. Use similar techniques as described in this chapter, but also remember that your boss' concerns will lessen when you demonstrate your productivity and commitment to quality, that you are not a problem supervisor to which your boss must always attend, and that you are capable of managing your departmental issues without need to continually seek his or her direction.

TEST **YOURSELF**

For each of the following statements, check true or false.

True   False

____   ____   1. A beginning supervisor would be wise to master the five foundations quickly and supplement them with other management skills later.

____   ____   2. Generally speaking, you get back the kind of behavior you send out.

____   ____   3. Breakdowns in working relationships should be given time to mend themselves.

____   ____   4. Many relationships require daily maintenance.

____   ____   5. One employee relationship should never be strengthened at the expense of another.

____   ____   6. See the employee first, the relationship second.

____   ____   7. Those who accept the five foundations as irreplaceable automatically integrate them into their behavioral patterns.

____ ____ 8. The easiest and most productive time to build a relationship is when an employee first joins a department.

____ ____ 9. Supervisors should never take significant action regarding an employee before they are certain the action is in compliance with organizational policies and procedures and does not violate individual rights.

____ ____ 10. A failed working relationship between a supervisor and employee can become successful by asking the employee for suggestions on how to improve the relationship.

Turn to the back of the book to check your answers.

Total Correct____

DISCUSSION **QUESTIONS**

1. How important is the Mutual Rewards Theory (MRT) in maintaining good relationships between supervisors and employees? Use your personal experiences as both a supervisor (if any) and an employee to support your answer.

2. In a work context, why is it important to separate the people from the personalities involved when managing interpersonal relationships, either your own or between two or more employees you manage? What are the advantages in doing this?

3. Why do the authors claim that the five foundations are irreplaceable? Do you agree? If not, what would be your "top five" irreplaceable foundations? Why? (Note: Having a personal list that exceeds five is acceptable.)

4. Which of the five foundations would you give top priority? Which one would you give the lowest? Why?

5. List some reactions you would have if your supervisor practiced these five foundations with you.

6. How much time should the new supervisor devote to building relationships with their supervisors and peers? What precautions, if any, should be taken?

CASE 1: **INTERVENTION**

OBJECTIVE

To discover the dangers of intervening when an employee's attitude becomes highly negative.

PROBLEM

Marty showed up this morning with a dramatic change in his attitude. Normally positive and pleasant, he is sullen and uncooperative today. Already indications are that his attitude may hurt the productivity of others. Bill is certain that this problem is personal and not connected with the job. Bill feels he has three possible alternatives for dealing with the situation, and he would like your advice. Which should he choose?

1. Immediate intervention through a private talk. Nip the problem in the bud by moving in before group productivity suffers.

2. Give Marty two or three days to solve his problem before intervening. Even if productivity suffers, he has a right to solve his own problems. He has been an excellent employee. Why take the risk of offending and possibly losing him?

3. No intervention. Marty will eventually solve his own problem, and Bill should do nothing in the meantime. Managers have no right to invade the privacy of employees, no matter what happens to productivity.

PROCEDURE

Each student selects his or her intervention choice among the three alternatives provided and writes at least three reasons for this choice. Also, consider any side factors that should be taken into consideration when the intervention takes place. Assume that the problem Marty faces is personal and not connected with his job. Then, engage in the discussion and be prepared to defend your answers vigorously.

CASE DISCUSSION AND QUESTIONS

Follow-up discussion should center on the way Bill might intervene without offending Marty. A key consideration is how Marty might feel about the intervention selected. What kind of intervention would he have accepted? When would he be most receptive to intervention? Why and how would each possible intervention work or not work under the circumstances? Are there any other interventions beside the three identified that you would suggest?

CASE 2: **REQUEST**

Bill walked into his office yesterday morning and found a special letter in his in-basket. It reads as follows:

Dear Bill:

Yesterday I received a big shock. My boss, Gerald, told me he was preparing the necessary papers for my dismissal. I was so upset that I hardly remember what else he said.

When I finally got around to asking him why, he told me that I was habitually late for work in the morning, that I had been warned a number of times, and that he would not tolerate any further lateness. I hate to go over his head to you, but I am desperate. It is true that I'm late about fifteen minutes two days a week, but let me give you some background.

I was hired three years ago, after my husband died. I am forty and am the sole support of my three children, the oldest of whom is fourteen. My reason for being late is that I must get my three children off to school. It's not easy. This whole thing never bothered Yolanda when I was in her department. In fact, she often complimented me and simply asked me to do the best I could about my lateness.

The company has been good to me, and in appreciation I am really dedicated to this job. I work faster and more accurately and waste less time than anyone else in the department, despite the fact that I never receive credit and am not told how I am doing. I'd like to talk with Gerald about my personal situation so that he might understand my concerns and how I want to work things out, but I don't feel he is that approachable. He is so focused on just getting the job done. I often work through coffee breaks and even part of my lunch hour to make up any time I owe the firm because of occasional lateness. I don't think he recognizes that fact.

Would you please review the situation for me?

Sincerely,

Jane Pitts

Assuming you are Bill, how would you deal with this problem? It appears that Gerald may not be practicing the five irreplaceable foundations, or do you have the full story? Should he be reminded? Should you intervene on behalf of Jane Pitts? Outline the steps you would take.

(Turn to the back of the book to compare your thoughts with those of the authors.)

COMMUNICATION **EXERCISE**

Assume that management has selected you to talk to your peers about the five irreplaceable foundations. You decide that the best approach is to present appropriate examples from your own work environment (production, service, retailing, banking, and so on). In preparing for your talk, you decide to improve on the textbook by writing out your own personal definition of each foundation and to illustrate it with the best specific application you can think of. (See the author's comments in the back of the book.)

My personal definition of giving clear and complete instructions is:

My example is:

My definition of letting people know how they are doing is:

My example is:

My definition of giving credit when due is:

My example is:

My definition of involving people in decisions is:

My example is:

I intend to communicate what is meant by an open-door policy as follows:

My example is:

PERSONAL GROWTH **EXERCISE**

Identify three things that your supervisor does that lead you to believe that you are an important contributor to the goals of your organization. How would you model these behaviors as a new supervisor?

TO LEARN **MORE**

To learn more about building relationships with employees and providing feedback and appropriate rewards and recognition, refer to the following references:

Covey, Stephen R. *The 7 Habits of Highly Effective People.* New York: Simon and Schuster, 1990.

Hiam, Alexander. *Motivating and Rewarding Employees: New and Better Ways to Inspire Your People.* Holbrook, MA: Adams Media Corporation, 1999.

Kaye, Beverly, and Sharon Jordan-Evans. *Love 'Em or Loose 'Em: Getting Good People to Stay.* San Francisco: Berrett-Koehler Publishers, 1999.

Kouzes, James M. and Barry Z. Posner. *Encouraging the Heart: A Leader's Guide to Rewarding and Recognizing Others.* San Francisco: Jossey-Bass, Inc., 1999.

Maurer, Rick. *Feedback Toolkit: 16 Tools for Better Communication in the Workplace.* Portland, OR: Productivity Press, 1994.

Nelson, Bob. *1001 Ways to Reward Employees.* New York: Workman Publishing, 1994.

Nelson, Bob. *1001 Ways to Energize Employees.* New York: Workman Publishing, 1997.

NOTE

1. Elwood N. Chapman. *Your Attitude Is Showing,* 9th ed. Upper Saddle River, NJ: Prentice Hall, Inc. 1996, p. 46.

chapter **six**

CREATING A PRODUCTIVE WORKING CLIMATE

"People who produce good results feel good about themselves."
Kenneth Blanchard

PERFORMANCE COMPETENCIES

After you have finished reading this chapter, you should be able to:

- List the steps you would follow to create and maintain a productive working climate

- Choose and maintain an appropriate discipline line that will promote a productive working climate

- Describe three ways in which management of your company offers its employees purposeful and meaningful work

- Describe three ways in which your management encourages continuous learning

- Describe three ways in which your management provides timely, accurate, and specific feedback on performance

As a supervisor, your attitude is always showing. All the employees in your department have a special kind of radar that permits them to read and evaluate your disposition each day. It gives them a chance to size up and adjust to your present temperament or mood. If you drag into the office with a grouchy, negative attitude, your employees will get the signal and back away from you, going about their jobs with little enthusiasm and avoiding contact with you. If, however, you walk in with a positive attitude, the opposite can happen. They may pick up your mood, show more enthusiasm, and look for chances to communicate with you.

When you are positive, it is easier for those who work for you to be positive; when you show a sense of humor, it is easier for those who work for you to laugh; when you show confidence, it is easier for others to have a productive day. Your behavior and attitude affect the departmental pace, mood, climate, and culture.

DEVELOPING THE RIGHT CLIMATE BY EXAMPLE

The example you set contributes more than anything else to the working climate in your department. The speed at which you work sets a tempo for others. The friendliness you show toward customers or fellow employees sets a norm for others. The energy and enthusiasm you put into your work are transmitted to those who work for you. Most of your employees expect you to set standards through your personal behavior. They observe your every move: how you answer the telephone, the speed at which you work, and the way you communicate. In other words, as a supervisor, you are always in the spotlight. You are the model.

One of your employees can afford a bad day, but you cannot. It is the price you pay for your leadership role. You are the supervisor, and as such, you must consistently set the best possible example. Consider some common situations where you have the opportunity to step up and set the example for those you lead.

Handling Emergencies

The way you handle emergencies shows your real character more than circumstances do. If you lose your cool under stress, the security of those who work for you will be seriously undermined. Take Marcia, for example.

Marcia was recently hired to manage a government office located on a busy street in a rough section of a major city. She had more than ten men and twenty women working for her, and she knew that she was being tested in many ways. She had not yet been accepted by the staff. One day, an automobile crashed through the front window, caught fire, and created general chaos. Marcia handled the situation calmly, efficiently, and without losing her head. From that moment on, she was fully accepted as part of the staff.

Marcia's behavior under stress demonstrated her leadership and gave the staff the security it needed. As a result, the working climate became more relaxed and productivity increased. You should never fake an emergency to enhance your image with your staff, but if one comes along, do not panic; follow procedures and involve others in decisions.

Reacting to Employee Mistakes

Nothing is more deflating to the ego or more embarrassing than to make a stupid mistake in front of others. Yet we all occasionally do it. The way you react to such mistakes by your staff members will greatly affect the climate you are attempting to build. Take Morton, for example.

Morton was the bank manager of a small branch office. He had been in charge only two days when Hazel, carrying a large, heavy tray of coins, slipped on the newly polished floor and spilled everything. After helping Hazel to her feet, Morton calmly got down on his knees and helped retrieve the many coins. He showed no anger, no disgust, no impatience; in fact, he asked one of the other women to take Hazel to the employees' break room while he counted and verified her cash drawer. As a result, everybody relaxed and Morton was well on his way to establishing a healthy, productive working climate.

Employees are sensitive to the way a fellow employee is treated, and when Morton built a good relationship with Hazel, he enhanced his relationships with the rest of his staff.

Absorbing Pressures

The way you handle pressures from above affects the working climate. Every supervisor is occasionally on the receiving end of certain demands from people in higher positions. When such a demand is made, you have two choices: You can pass the pressure on by calling a staff meeting and chewing everybody out, or you can absorb as much of the pressure as possible without passing it on. Here's the way Steve, a section manager in a large factory, reacted.

It was Steve's first job as a supervisor, and in his anxiety to accomplish many things in the first two weeks, he had neglected to have his staff do the necessary cleaning up. As a result, the section was dirty and messy. Predictably, a high-level manager made a routine inspection late one afternoon and reprimanded Steve privately—and emphatically—for the condition of his area. Although he was emotionally upset and was tempted to chew out his staff (after all, it was their fault), he absorbed the pressure and said nothing that day. The following morning, Steve discovered his staff was busy cleaning things up. Apparently, someone had heard the reprimand Steve had received and passed the word along. Steve never had to say a word to his staff. They respected his willingness to take a beating on their behalf without passing it on. From then on, Steve had little trouble keeping a clean and tidy department.

Communicating Changes

The way you react to changes and communicate them to your staff is critical to a productive working climate. Changes constitute a challenge to the supervisor. In fact, organizational changes are the source of most pressures felt by management and non-management alike. The better you are at adjusting to change, the easier it will be for your employees to accept changes, and the more productive your working climate will be. Even more important is the manner in which you communicate forthcoming changes to your employees.

Doreen received word Friday evening after all of her employees had left for the weekend that her department would be transferred to an older, less-desirable building. She took time on Saturday to inspect the new location and work out a tentative floor plan. She announced the change in a positive way Monday morning and asked employees for input on her plan. Before the day was over, everyone had made a good adjustment, and some employees were even looking forward to the additional freedom that would result from being more isolated.

MAINTAINING THE APPROPRIATE LEVEL OF DISCIPLINE

The employees you lead will be very attuned to the example you set with respect to the degree of authority, firmness, and control you exert as you manage them as compared to the degree of freedom, autonomy and control you place in their hands. How much freedom do you give them? At what point do you draw the line and rein them in? In other words, what is your **discipline line** or, if you prefer, authority line? The discipline line defines what employees are permitted to do without violating procedures, policy, and working standards.

A Low, Permissive Discipline Line

A low, or permissive, discipline line permits maximum freedom because it calls for a minimum of control or supervision. For the most part, employees in this

environment need to be self-disciplined rather than have discipline imposed on them. A permissive line works best when employees are well trained, knowledgeable, and experienced in doing their jobs. The more trust a supervisor has for his or her employees to conduct themselves in a mature manner, the less the need for imposed discipline.

A High, Tight Discipline Line

A high, or tight, discipline line limits employee freedom. In some cases, these restrictions are necessary. Tight discipline is appropriate, for example, when the work is highly regulated by safety rules and regulations that are imposed by forces outside the organization. For example, a tight line would be appropriate in an atomic energy plant, where safety is a paramount concern. In a department that has high turnover rates and whose employees lack training and experience, a tight discipline line is usually needed. The age and maturity of employees must also be considered. Teenagers working in a fast-food restaurant may need to be more closely controlled and supervised.

Generally, well-trained mature employees that can be trusted to do their jobs are irritated by a tight discipline line. Often these employees conclude that their supervisor does not trust them.

During her first few months as a supervisor, Billie permitted her discipline line to be low and permissive. In her previous job, she had some great employees who needed little or no supervision. She preferred a low line of discipline. In her new department, her employees were not well trained in their jobs and several were new due to higher than average turnover. She did not closely supervise her employees because she felt that she could trust them to follow the rules and procedures clearly outlined in their employee handbook. For the most part they did. But as time passed, there were too many mistakes occurring. Productivity began to go down, and horseplay got out of hand. Just the other day an employee just missed being injured when he did not follow the proper procedure for cleaning a piece of equipment. Several employees were abusing their break and lunch times. She decided that her line was too low and she needed to tighten it up.

Balancing Compassion and Control

The inexperienced newcomer to supervision may think that it is impossible to demonstrate compassion and maintain a tight discipline line at the same time. Not so. Compassion for others can be communicated in any working climate. In fact, if handled in a sensitive manner, employees may accept a stronger, higher discipline line from a more compassionate supervisor. Some less-permissive supervisors consistently demonstrate that they care deeply for their staff members. Discipline in this context must not be confused with punishment. The discipline discussed here does not refer to the progressive measures employers take to enforce employee compliance and cooperation when employees behave badly or are not performing to expectations. Rather, the form of discipline discussed here is analogous to the ship captain who ensures discipline is maintained so that operations run smoothly and the crew and its cargo safely reach port. Hence, the expression, "He runs a tight ship." In such environments, compassion and tight controls on employees are not incompatible and may be, in fact, what employees need to feel supported.

Creating the Right Discipline Line for the Working Climate

Once you find the right discipline line for the work situation, maintaining it will require daily attention. To illustrate, let's look at three hypothetical situations in the same work environment.

Rick is currently running a rather tight department. His discipline line leaves little room for socializing and a narrow margin for error. The atmosphere is one of strict compliance. An experienced outsider observing the situation senses that the department might be slightly overcontrolled, overmanaged, and overstructured. The productivity and quality levels are average.

Ron operates a loose department. He sometimes gives his employees more freedom than they know how to handle. The work gets done, but because of excessive horseplay, occasional errors crop up that must be corrected. Ron feels that employees resent close supervision, so he stays clear except when he feels it necessary to become more involved. The atmosphere is one of noisy relaxation. A trained observer senses an absence of direction. The productivity and quality levels are slightly below average.

Susan is following a middle-of-the-road philosophy. The discipline line is there, but it is not overpowering and restrictive. She tries not to be too permissive, but consciously avoids overcontrol. As a result, she does a balancing act between the two. She strives to create a democratic climate in which employees have a degree of freedom but still welcome her leadership, if and when necessary. To the perceptive outsider, the atmosphere is businesslike, with more than average communication between employees. The productivity and quality levels are above average.

You will recognize that these examples represent the three classic climates: autocratic, permissive, and democratic. You can find, of course, many variations of each. Although it is estimated that the great majority of working climates fall into the democratic classification, in some situations either an autocratic or permissive climate is more productive. In work environments like the ones depicted here, however, clearly they are not.

How can you tell when you have created the ideal discipline line for the working climate? In answering this question, consider the following three points:

1. You must create the departmental working climate that works best for you and those you manage. This will come through trial and error based on a balance between work demands and what employees respond to best when working to meet these demands.

2. Your barometer for determining whether you have chosen the right discipline line is when you have achieved a working climate that generates the highest-quality productivity (measured by sales, production units, quality control reports, or service standards) and relationships between employees and their supervisor. In contrast, the characteristics of a poor climate are complaints, human relations problems, absenteeism, employee rip-offs, hostility, errors, and a general lack of enthusiasm. Like a custodian controlling the temperature in a room, the supervisor should occasionally take readings and make adjustments.

3. Climates change according to the needs of the department and its employees. The major reasons for the deterioration of formerly productive departments are neglect, failure to alleviate controllable pressures, and the inappropriate setting of the discipline line. For example, a supervisor with a low, loose discipline line will have more problem employees when those employees lack self-discipline or lack work-related training. Many are unable to discipline themselves. You are never done adjusting your discipline line. As work demands increase or diminish and as your employees' level of maturity and experience changes, you must adjust your discipline accordingly.

MONITORING YOUR DISCIPLINE LINE

You cannot maintain a good working climate without giving it some personal attention. You must work at it daily by contributing new ideas and lively comments, injecting a little humor to keep employees reacting in positive ways, inserting some deserved compliments to help motivate people, and, above all, communicating. Obviously, you must do a great deal of testing and experimenting before coming up with a satisfactory climate. Do not expect immediate results. Even after you have achieved a good climate, it is not easily maintained. Constant work is required. However, the supervisor who eventually does create and maintain an effective working climate can thereby establish good productivity records and enhance his or her personal progress. Here are some suggestions to keep in mind as you work toward this goal.

High or Low, Make It a Firm Line

Err on the side of strong leadership. A strong leader is one who provides the correct balance of control and freedom in her or his area of responsibility. Most employees prefer consistent leadership behavior, whether strong or weak. Being able to predict a supervisor's reaction has a stabilizing effect on employees. Most employees cannot function well in an atmosphere devoid of leadership and direction. They want decisive leadership and work best in a predictable, controlled environment. The fewer rules the better in most situations, but the rules must be clear and they must set a firm, clear line that all perceive accurately.

Joyce moved in as the new store manager quietly and in a warm and friendly manner, but she set a much firmer discipline line than her predecessor. Productivity (measured in sales) was up 20 percent the first month. Later, some of her employees told her what it was like to work under the previous manager: "I didn't feel like I was headed anywhere." "There was little satisfaction in doing good work." "Time goes much faster under your supervision." "If there is anything that frustrates me, it's a manager who doesn't lead."

Consistency Is the Key

Find the ideal climate for your department and then maintain it. Be consistent in the way you treat your employees and predictable in the way you handle your duties as a supervisor. Daily inconsistency keeps everyone on edge and holds productivity down.

Raymond, an operations manager for a branch bank, set his discipline line on a daily basis. When he was in a light mood, he was extremely friendly and tolerant (lowering the line); when he was in a serious mood, he was stern and demanding (raising the line). In less than two months he had lost two employees, and two others had requested transfers. When asked why, one replied, "He expects us to adjust to his mood every day, and we never know just what to expect. He's inconsistent and unpredictable. It's worse than dealing with your own children." Another employee said, "Once you get used to the rules, he changes them in a capricious manner that leaves me disturbed and angry. I would prefer a less capable but more consistent manager."

Seek Feedback from Employees

One way to get feedback from your staff is to mingle a little with your employees during breaks. If the timing seems right, ask how things are going and then listen to the responses you receive. Be open to their feedback. If you are trusted, you may hear complaints or compliments. If you receive few complaints, you probably have the kind of climate you want; if you receive many complaints, things must be out of balance, and you should adjust your discipline line. It is easier to make small adjustments to a working climate than to make major repairs. If you listen to employee complaints and value their input, you may receive information that leads to greater productivity.

Fine-Tune Your Discipline Line

Adjust your discipline line frequently and gently. Maintaining the right discipline line or climate takes sensitive maneuvering. The supervisor who overreacts one way or the other often must start from scratch. Here is a classic example.

About three months ago, things were going well in Chuck's department. Production was high. Morale was great. Apparently, Chuck had come up with the perfect climate, so he relaxed and became more permissive. He felt he could trust his staff. Two weeks later,

things began to go wrong. Productivity dropped and mistakes increased. Chuck, over-reacting, moved in and tightened the discipline line harshly and emotionally, resulting in even lower productivity. Employees didn't want to work hard for someone who gave them freedom one day and took it away the next. Chuck needed to learn that sudden, drastic adjustments to his discipline line can easily boomerang. The best policy is to take frequent soundings and make minor adjustments.

Maintain a Lively Climate

Lighten the climate with a sense of humor. It is easy for the supervisor, weighed down with many responsibilities, to become too serious about the job. When it happens, a cloud of gloom may settle over the department. The sensitive supervisor, seeing this situation beginning to develop, will break it up with a little fun or appropriate humor, and lighten up the mood. Take Odessa's situation as an example.

Odessa operated a highly successful fast-food franchise. Most of her employees were part-time high school and college students. Knowing that she could pay only minimum wages but needing dependability and high performance, she did everything possible to make the work fun and status-building among the employees' peers, who were frequently customers. After the store was closed, her employees would play their favorite music over the P.A. system. Her employees would dance and sing along—so did Odessa. Odessa's motivation for her actions? She says, "It is nothing more than a human relations safety valve that permits everyone to let their hair down harmlessly for a short period. It releases the pressure and helps me keep the working climate I need to be successful."

Keep Employees Challenged

Employees, generally speaking, have more positive attitudes when they are busy. Idle workers usually become bored and eventually negative. By keeping employees busy through advanced planning and delegating, the supervisor will create a more positive working climate and reach higher levels of productivity. The most difficult job in the world is one in which an employee has too little to do. The effective supervisor will see that no such jobs exist under his or her direction.

Communicate Daily

The most disastrous thing you can do as a supervisor is break off communications with your people. This breakdown usually happens when managers get so busy with reports, planning, research, and other activities that they stay hidden in their offices too long. Loss of communication—for any reason—will destroy morale and productivity faster than anything else. It is only through daily communication that you can measure the atmosphere and decide if you need to adjust your discipline line. Because of this concern, some supervisors force themselves to get away from their other responsibilities once each day for the purpose of casual communications with their employees. It is a sound practice.

Manage Workplace Technology Issues

Probably the single most important contributor to increased productivity in your company has been the personal computer and related information technologies. It is hard for many supervisors to imagine how they could ever complete their tasks without their computer: production machines are run by them, and important reports and records are created with them and filed in them. To be successful, the supervisor must be proficient in using the computer. If you are not, it is a good idea to seek out computer training classes. Continuing and professional education opportunities are readily available through local colleges as well as local libraries or high schools that offer adult evening classes.

One problem that has arisen with the computer in the workplace is use of the computer for personal business while at work. Employees sometimes use their computer to surf the Internet for their own purposes. Some use e-mail to send personal messages to friends and family. Employers everywhere are struggling with the question of how to control non-business computer usage. A survey by Vault.com on Internet use revealed that 87 percent of employees surveyed surfed non-work-related websites while at work, and 53 percent of these employees did so every day. Many companies now use some type of tracking software that lets them monitor Internet use at work. Even so, 56 percent of the employees in this same survey do not worry about their personal e-mail and Internet use being monitored. Further, only 35 percent believe such activity decreases productivity.[1]

On-the-job Internet and other uses of company IT systems and devices (e-mail, cell phones, hand-held devices, etc.) raise tough questions concerning managing the appropriate discipline line to foster a good working climate. Overuse can be reduced by making it clear that Internet use will be monitored for signs of abuse. Some experts urge employers to establish Internet-use policies that permit moderate use, particularly during non-work hours. As a supervisor, you must know your company's policies on these issues and enforce them on abusers by following established disciplinary procedures. If your company does not have policies governing the use of company IT systems and devices, including the Internet and e-mail, employees may take advantage of this situation, and as a result, their productivity may decrease.

If the decrease in productivity is unacceptable, the supervisor may be forced to take disciplinary action against the employee. An employee cannot, however, be held accountable for disobeying a rule that does not exist. In such cases, policies governing lack of productivity or abuse of personal time become the supervisor's only recourse for taking disciplinary action.

AN IDEAL CLIMATE ENCOURAGES SELF-MOTIVATION

The ideal working climate is one that creates self-motivation in workers. As discussed in previous chapters, it is generally recognized today that in most work environments traditional motivational techniques do not work well. Supervisors get little response from most workers through pep talks, contests, pay increases, and traditional forms of counseling. In a large number of cases, a worker is either self-motivated or not motivated at all. Maintaining the proper environment may enhance the possibility that the orange seed will be motivated to grow, but does not guarantee the orange seed will grow into a tree and bear fruit. Like the hypothetical orange discussed in Chapter 2, our employees are living organisms, not machines, and their motivation is internal to them. Like the orange, the person chooses to move. No amount of coaxing will motivate growth. He or she can't be forced.

The contemporary supervisor is challenged to create an environment where, without prodding, workers will want to achieve. In short, employees "catch" motivation from the surrounding climate, a climate created primarily by the way the supervisor supervises. When an atmosphere of confidence and involvement is created, the worker feels good about his or her role and wants to reach out to achieve. Creating and holding on to such a climate is one of the most difficult challenges both new and experienced supervisors face. Research has shown that an environment conducive to internal motivation exhibits the following three characteristics:

1. Purposeful and meaningful work
2. Continuous learning
3. Accurate, timely, and specific feedback on performance

Let's look closely at each of these characteristics.

Purposeful and Meaningful Work

Supervisors must communicate to their employees that they consider them to be valuable to the company. Telling them is necessary but not sufficient. Here are some things the supervisor can do to create purposeful and meaningful work for their employees.

1. Involve them in planning changes. Many times employees are informed or included in the change process only at the implementation stage. When possible, include your employees in change from the beginning; involve them in the planning stage of a change.
2. Meet with employees as a group on a regular basis. During the meeting, dedicate a portion of time to seek their input and opinions on issues important to the department, not only when planning change but in solving

problems and making decisions as well. Their input is especially important when the solution of a problem changes any aspect of an employee's work routine.

3. Show them how their contribution affects the department's or the company's welfare. In some cases, the supervisor may be able to show how the company's products or services enhance the lives of its customers and society in general.

Sometimes employees are told that if they do not like what is happening they can quit. Do not send such a message unless you are prepared to deal with a negative reaction. Doing or saying things that devalue employee contributions quickly and thoroughly undermines the feeling of having purposeful and meaningful work.

Continuous Learning

A job that continually challenges the employee to learn is crucial to motivation. If a job is mastered easily, it may become boring or monotonous to the one doing it. Motivating environments contain elements that require the employee to build new skills in order to complete the job. Here are some things the supervisor can do to provide learning opportunities.

1. *Engage in continuous improvement.* Encourage your employee to seek new techniques, new technology, or improvements to the existing work. Provide opportunity for employees to learn more about their job, company, or industry. Many companies provide in-service training on a variety of topics such as new computer software, financial planning, or supervision. The supervisor can set the example by personally engaging in training opportunities.

2. *Provide opportunity for education beyond the job.* Some companies provide tuition reimbursement for employees enrolled in college. Encourage the use of this opportunity, and adjust work schedules to accommodate school schedules when possible. Supervisors who simply change a set work schedule that makes it impossible for an employee to complete a class begun under an old schedule undermines trust.

Employees can really get hooked on training and development at work. Well-trained employees who seek to keep their skills current are motivated employees.

Accurate, Timely, and Specific Feedback on Performance

Employees want to know how well they are performing. Feedback is the cornerstone of both growth and productivity. While many companies impose feedback mechanisms between supervisors and employees through formal performance evaluation processes, the quarterly, semi-annual, or annual meetings established through these processes are inadequate measures for providing feedback if they are the sole mechanisms supervisors use to provide meaningful feedback. Rather, supervisors must strive to provide feedback on a daily or weekly basis as needed to support employees' success.

Some key points to consider when providing feedback are as follows:

1. Be upfront about why you are meeting, and the precise performance issue you wish to discuss. Whether the feedback is positive or negative, don't vacillate regarding your purpose in discussing the performance issue.

2. Provide feedback as soon as you observe the behaviors you wish to discuss. This not only makes the employee's recall of the behavior or event more likely, it also ensures that the employee has the opportunity to correct performance rather than continue on the false impression that his or her performance is acceptable. If the feedback is positive, its timeliness provides quick reinforcement to continue on the performance track she is on.

3. Describe the specific behaviors, results, or outcomes you observed. Rather than being accusatory ("Your work was sloppy") or vague ("Nice job"), state the precise facts on which you would like to offer praise or correction.

4. Inform the employee regarding the impact of his or her performance, such as how it contributed to team or organizational goals or how it hindered them. Be clear how poor conduct offended a co-worker or customer, or how a customer was complimentary and would return again because of the employee's exemplary service.

5. Provide opportunity for the employee to respond to your feedback and offer suggestions for improving performance. As the supervisor, acknowledge this is a two-way conversation and that you are not only open to his or her input to improve performance, but that you would welcome feedback on how you can improve your performance as his or her manager.

6. Offer encouragement that you have full confidence in the employee's ability to bring his performance up to expected levels or to reinforce good performance by stating you look forward to seeing more of the same.

In providing feedback, supervisors must look for opportunities on a daily and weekly basis not simply to correct performance deficits when they arise but to praise good performance when it is observed. Feedback is not simply a tool for correction or reprimand, but is doubly useful to reinforce good work. This is where true motivation resides in your employees. And as Ken Blanchard has written, truly meaningful, consistent feedback need not be drawn out or belabored, but can be effectively delivered in a minute and lead to immediate change.[2]

PERFORMANCE **CHECKLIST**

1. Creating a productive working climate begins with you as the supervisor by the example you set and how you handle matters such as responding to emergencies, reacting to employee mistakes, absorbing pressures, and communicating changes.

2. Creating a working climate that is most productive depends also on setting the appropriate discipline line. A lower, permissive line is appropriate for most situations, particularly where employees are mature and where trust is high. A higher, tighter discipline line may be more appropriate, however, for industries that are more heavily regulated or

where safety is a paramount concern, and also where the level of maturity and experience of the employees is less.

3. Regardless of the discipline line that you set, you must continually adjust it to meet the changing work demands and level of maturity and experience of the employees you manage. The barometer to determine whether the appropriate discipline line has been established is when a working climate exists that maximizes productivity (measured by sales, production units, quality control reports, service standards, and similar

measures) and fosters positive working relationships between the supervisor and employees.

4. A supervisor must always give personal attention to maintaining the appropriate discipline line to foster the best working climate. To do this, she or he should maintain a firm, consistent line (whether high or low); seek feedback from employees daily; fine-tune the discipline line as needs and demands require; maintain a lively, engaging work climate; keep employees challenged; and communicate daily.

5. An ideal climate encourages self-motivation. Supervisors must create environments where, without probing, employees want to achieve. To foster a working environment that encourages self-motivation, supervisors must provide purposeful and meaningful work; opportunities for continuous learning, and accurate, timely, and specific feedback on performance.

TEST YOURSELF

For each of the following statements, check true or false.

True   False

___   ___   1. The higher the discipline line, the greater the freedom provided to employees.

___   ___   2. The kind of work done in a department has little to do with the level of the discipline line.

___   ___   3. The more free time employees have on the job, the more positive they are.

___   ___   4. Once the ideal discipline line has been achieved, it does not require adjustment.

___   ___   5. Compassion and exercising authority are incompatible.

___   ___   6. The ideal working climate is the one that does the most to trigger the self-motivation of employees.

___   ___   7. The supervisor's behavior and attitude affects department pace, mood, climate, and culture.

___   ___   8. Department climate rarely changes year to year.

___   ___   9. A strong leader is one who provides the correct balance of control and freedom in his or her area of responsibility.

___   ___   10. Listening to employees' feedback and valuing their input leads to increased productivity.

Turn to the back of the book to check your answers.

Total Correct____

DISCUSSION QUESTIONS

1. a. Describe three ways in which management of your company offers its employees purposeful and meaningful work.
    b. Describe three ways in which your management encourages continuous learning.
    c. Describe three ways in which your management provides timely, accurate, and specific feedback on performance.

2. Give an example of a supervisor whose discipline line is either too firm or too lax, resulting in low productivity. How should the supervisor modify his or her discipline line to get better results?

3. Do you agree that compassion and strong discipline are compatible? Defend your position.

CASE: CLIMATE

OBJECTIVE

To gain insight into causes of poor employee morale and to learn ways to restore a productive climate in a demoralized department.

PROBLEM

Ricardo has just returned from a disturbing private conference with Bill. He was told that his department productivity had dropped more than 20 percent in the past sixty days. Bill didn't pull any punches. Ricardo must get employee morale and productivity back up. Ricardo is upset, and feels that he has been considerate with his employees, who are now letting him down. He knows that things have been going badly in the department. Productivity is down; morale is low; griping is high; mistakes have been too frequent. What should he do? After considerable soul-searching, Ricardo comes up with ten steps he might take to restore a healthy working climate in the department. Ricardo wants advice to help him determine which steps would help and which might do more harm than good. (Readers not involved in group role-playing are invited to go directly to the list.)

RICARDO'S LIST OF PROPOSED ACTIONS

1. Call a fifteen-minute department meeting. Release the productivity figures and make it clear that you expect immediate improvement.

2. Instead of a group meeting, take time to counsel each of the five employees on the matter privately. If an employee's productivity is down, be frank about it; if it is mediocre, discuss what can be done to improve it; if productivity is good, be complimentary.

3. Say nothing, but start tightening the department's discipline line through your actions. Set a more disciplined climate without talking about it.

4. Start immediately to correct all violations or unacceptable behavior you spot through private conferences in your office. Be pleasant but firm. Supervisors must use language that tells employees what specific behavior is acceptable and unacceptable. Generalities do not change behavior. When making an assessment of another's behavior, back it up with specific examples.

5. Withdraw and act hurt until the employees feel sorry for you and, as a result, come around.

6. Start involving your employees in selected departmental problems that you previously handled yourself.

7. Have an off-the-job party at your home for all five employees.

8. Give each employee a written report of the productivity drop and ask for written feedback on what might be done to get back to previous productivity levels.

9. Go to Bill with this list and ask him for suggestions.

10. Spend more time with employees, listening to their complaints, working beside them, having coffee with them during breaks, and generally circulating to improve communications.

PROCEDURE

Break the class up into teams, each with four to six members. Each team then selects a spokesperson to summarize the team discussion. Have each team spend twenty minutes doing the following: (1) Eliminate those steps that might do more harm than good. (2) List the remaining steps and number them in order of preference. (3) If possible, come up with an action that the group prefers over any of those listed.

Once finished, each group should put its list on the blackboard. Take ten minutes to discuss differences. Everyone then votes for the list they feel will be most effective in getting productivity back up to the previous level.

CASE DISCUSSION

Discussion should center on (1) differences among the answers of the teams, (2) whether any formula would actually restore high productivity, and (3) what caused the department to become demoralized.

RESTORING MORALE **EXERCISE**

Read the case again. After you have finished, eliminate all actions on Ricardo's list that you feel would do more harm than good. Next, weave those that remain into a personal "action package" that you think would turn the department around. In your own words, write out this strategy in the spaces provided.

PLEASE ANSWER THE FOLLOWING QUESTIONS

The single word that I feel best explains the cause of the deterioration of Ricardo's department is:

Why do you feel that your "action package" will turn the department around?

How long do you think it would take?

To compare your steps and views with those of the authors, turn to the back of the book.

PERSONAL GROWTH **EXERCISE**

Identify three ways your company measures the productivity of your department. Ask your employees how these areas can be improved. If you use their ideas, be sure to give them the credit!

NOTES

1. Vault.com. "2005 Internet Use in the Workplace Survey Result." http://www.vault.com/surveys/internetusesurvey/home.jsp (accessed January 17, 2008).

2. Ken Blanchard, *One Minute Manager*. New York: The Berkley Publishing Company, 1981.

chapter **seven**

QUALITY CONTROL AND CONTINUOUS IMPROVEMENT

"Quality is everyone's responsibility."

W. Edwards Deming

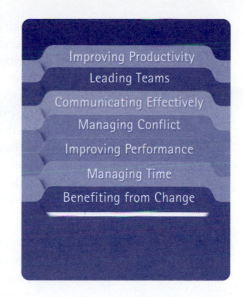

Improving Productivity
Leading Teams
Communicating Effectively
Managing Conflict
Improving Performance
Managing Time
Benefiting from Change

Any supervisor working in a profitable company today will tell you how important quality is to its bottom line. It is a simple fact that without a high level of quality, the company's days are numbered. Manufacturing plants and service organizations, large or small, throughout the country and world have embraced a quality-minded philosophy.

Competitive, world-class organizations are committed to producing high-quality products and providing high-quality services. Top management recognizes the critical need for the merger of a sound quality philosophy with the production of goods and services. Globalization, foreign competition, and rising prices of raw materials due to diminishing natural resources combine to make quality one of the foremost goals in modern industry. The level of quality directly impacts the amount of waste and rework a company experiences. Waste and rework increase costs and thus consume profits. Eliminating waste also has a positive effect on our environment. It takes less energy and material when quality rises. Quality is every employee's responsibility.

A BRIEF OVERVIEW OF QUALITY

The push for higher quality has revolutionized the way business is conducted. Theories and philosophies have been developed and disseminated throughout the world. Three of the best-known and widely published quality gurus are W. Edwards Deming, who outlined his now-famous Fourteen Points to achieving quality[1]; Philip Crosby and his Quality Management Grid[2]; and Joseph Juran, who proposed a universal way of conceptualizing quality control and quality improvement, which he called the Quality Trilogy.[3] The tremendous impact of these

PERFORMANCE COMPETENCIES

After you have finished reading this chapter, you should be able to:

- Explain management's responsibilities in leading a quality system

- Describe how quality affects productivity, as well as employee and customer satisfaction

- Explain three reasons why supervisors are often in the best position to champion training programs

- Explain confirming signs and negating signs and describe the exchange rate between the two

- Explain and facilitate simple process improvement efforts for your team

American pioneers in quality control is incalculable. Collectively, their philosophies have literally changed the fundamental values of industries throughout the world. These philosophies share the belief that improvement is a never-ending process, and that training in quality control should be open to employees at all levels.

This revolution in quality in the United States has its roots in efforts to standardize production methods for the military during World War II, and continued in response to the emphasis on quality and resultant competition from Japan, particularly in the automotive and electronics industries in the 1970s. In addition to Deming, Juran, and Crosby and their contributions, a number of quality methodologies, programs, and standards for measuring quality have developed and are used, to varying degrees, in industry to present. These include:

Total Quality Management (TQM).   TQM is a people-focused management system that focuses on increasing customer satisfaction while continually reducing costs. Although it uses scientific methods for assessing quality and associated costs and constraints and implementing improvement, it takes a total systems approach in which all functions, processes, and departments across the organization, and all employees at all levels, are integral to ensuring success in the manufacture of products or delivery of services. TQM stresses learning and adaptation to continual change as essential to achieving this success.

Six Sigma.   The term *Six Sigma* was coined by Motorola as its methodology for improving business processes by minimizing defects and refers to the statistical measurement indicating there are only 3.4 defects out of every 1 million opportunities to produce a defect, or virtually zero. It is an organizational approach where companies make decisions based on data, seek roots of problems, define defects based on customer requirements, and track leading indicators of problems to prevent them from happening.

Lean Production.   *Lean production* refers to the continuous flow of products or services to the customer at the moment it is needed and to the customer's specifications. It focuses on increasing productivity and quality while reducing inventory and shortening lead time from floor to customer. Its principles include workplace safety, order, and cleanliness; just-in-time production; built-in Six Sigma quality; empowered teams; visual management to track performance and provide immediate feedback on a daily or even hourly basis; and continual pursuit of perfection.[4]

International Standards Organization Quality Management Standards.   The International Standards Organization (ISO) has developed a series of quality management standards that support the quality philosophy. Specifically, it has developed a set of five such standards, ISO 9000–9004. The American National Standards Institute (ANSI) and the American Society for Quality Control (ASQC) developed the ANSI/ASQC Q9000–Q9004. In addition, specific standards also exist for automotive, aerospace, and telecommunications industries and for environment management. These standards have been revised over the years, and organizations must continually address these revisions. Organizations competing in the global market must achieve the quality levels dictated by these standards.

In addition to these and other programs and methodologies, a number of prestigious national and international quality awards are available to which companies apply and compete to be recognized for their commitment to world-class quality. These awards include the Malcolm Baldridge National Quality Award, the European Quality Award, and the Deming Prize, Japan's highest quality award. The standards for receipt of these awards are high and the review process is rigorous. For example, to receive the Malcolm Baldridge National Quality Award, recipients must have demonstrated performance excellence in seven categories: leadership; strategic planning; customer and market focus; measurement, analysis, and knowledge management; workforce focus; process management; and results. Malcolm Baldridge National Quality Awards are awarded to organizations involved in manufacturing, small business, service, education, and healthcare.[5]

The quality movement in the United States is pervasive and extends beyond manufacturing industries and includes areas like service, healthcare, education, and government. For professionals involved in these and other industries, the most prominent professional organization to which they can belong is the American Society for Quality (ASQ) (formerly the American Society for Quality Control). ASQ provides its members with the latest information on quality standards, processes, and procedures. It also offers a curriculum of courses that lead to a certification in quality control. Supervisors should seriously consider joining this organization. Supervisors who earn a certificate in quality control greatly increase their value to their employers. This translates into increased income, advancement, and career satisfaction.

MANAGEMENT COMMITMENT TO THE QUALITY PROCESS

The various philosophies, programs, methodologies, and awards discussed promote a common goal of developing an integrated total quality system by engaging in continuous improvement. They also share the belief that managers and supervisors play an enormously critical role in achieving and maintaining high standards of quality.

To illustrate this point, all fourteen points in Deming's philosophy pertain to the managers. According to Deming, workers, management, vendors, and investors are on the same team. It is management who creates the culture of worker "ownership" of the improvement process. Management creates the culture that enables workers to feel comfortable enough to recommend changes. Management develops the strategic plan for implementing the quality initiative. Through their plan, resources necessary to fund the process of change are allocated. Additional investments in tools, machinery, equipment, and materials might have to be made. Quality parts cannot be produced on worn-out or obsolete equipment. Training is integral to individual performance. Employees must know exactly what to do. Training is ongoing. It starts when employees are hired and continues throughout their time with the company. There are sizable indirect costs associated with training that the organization must absorb. For example, training will impact the quantity of production. It may suffer as workers leave their workstations to receive classroom training or when they meet regularly with their process improvement team. Significant improvements come from well-trained employees.

It is vital that management personnel face up to their responsibility. They must plan for the added costs that improvements will bring. It is equally important that managers model the proper attitude. Enthusiasm is contagious and management must demonstrate their commitment beyond funding. They must demonstrate enthusiasm for the process. The continuous improvement process inevitably brings many changes and management's reaction to change will be watched and monitored by the workers. Workers' attitudes and willingness to embrace the process will be influenced chiefly by the example management sets.

NEGATING AND CONFIRMING SIGNS OF MANAGEMENT COMMITMENT

While management may implement quality management programs, it is not always committed to them. Management shows signs of its commitment through its slogans, its talk throughout the organization about quality principles, the training it provides supervisors and employees, its continuous improvement teams (CITs), and other efforts. Yet, in some organizations, managers may say they value quality, but their behavior says something quite different. When management behaves incongruently in this fashion, employees will believe the behaviors and not the slogans and words. Managers who say one thing and do another are bound to fail.

Let us consider a story that illustrates clearly what can happen when managers try to fool their employees into thinking they value something when they really don't.

Twelve production (non-management) employees from the same manufacturing plant voluntarily gathered together in a nearby college classroom one Saturday morning at the urging of Leonard, one of their peers. He was taking a supervision class at the college and informed them about a series of public lectures given by a well-known professor at the college regarding various topics. The subject for this session was about how managers communicate their values to employees. After introductions, the professor began a conversation by asking the participants to tell him what they thought their managers valued. He recorded their responses on the white board under the heading:

Things our management values

Themselves

Profits

Customers

Product quality

Production quantity

The company's image and reputation

The professor looked at the list and circled **Product quality.** *He said that he was conducting research on quality and would like to ask them some questions about that item. His first question asked them how they knew their management valued product quality. They thought for a moment and gave him their responses, which he put on the board under the following heading:*

Confirming signs

Slogans and banners about quality hanging all around the plant

Conducting line inspections and having a quality control department

Holding products to tight tolerances and specifications

Not shipping a bad part

Frequent meetings of quality improvement teams

He looked at the list for a moment and then asked them to tell him things that their management did **not value.** *After a brief silence one of them shouted out,* **"Product quality."** *Almost instantly, the others agreed. The professor wrote their response under the heading:*

What our management does NOT VALUE

Product quality

The professor stepped back with a puzzled look on his face. He then pointed out to them that they had just contradicted themselves. Previously they said their managers valued quality, and now they said they don't. Several justified their response by explaining that their managers only say they value product quality, when in fact they really don't. They all seemed to agree that this was the case. The professor asked them how they knew that managers really did not value quality. He wrote their response on the board under the heading:

Negating signs

Management won't ship bad parts when there are only a few, but
if there are a thousand bad parts, they will ship them all in order
to meet their production quotas.

The professor then asked that they look at the **Confirming Signs** *list and at the* **Negating Signs** *list. After a moment, he asked them the following question: "How many negating signs does it take to wipe out all the confirming signs?" In unison, and much to their surprise, they said aloud,*

"ONE!"

The professor was astounded by their remark. He summarized what he had just witnessed. All those confirming signs that management communicated to them were wiped out or

negated by a single action—management's decision to ship a thousand bad parts. They all agreed that the professor was correct. He pointed out to them that this is a very high exchange rate. In effect, one negating sign wiped out numerous, if not all, confirming signs. The professor then led them in a conversation that focused on the dangers of communicating negating signs. The employees discussed how they pay attention to the words and deeds of their leaders. Employees expect their leaders to behave in a congruent manner and, when they don't, employees withhold respect and trust. They said they feel that management is lying to them and wonder what other lies their management is telling. They were confused by this duplicity and thought it quite unethical, immature, and totally unnecessary. They could not come up with any reasonable justification for their management's behavior.

The exchange rate may not always be as high as it is in this example, but managers must be very mindful of the fact that employees pay attention to their behavior and will draw conclusions about the things valued by managers. Acting incongruently will bring negative consequences and the organization will suffer. Try to minimize communicating any negating signs. Supervisors should always strive to have their deeds match their words.

MANAGEMENT'S RESPONSIBILITIES

Quality is not just the responsibility of one person or one department in the organization as it once was. Today, everyone from the CEO to the production worker or service provider is directly responsible for quality. Supervisors play a key role in the success of any quality initiative. They serve the vital communications link between management and the employee. They must understand both the challenges of the workers and expectations of top management. The quality philosophy is set into motion by the workers under the leadership and guidance of their supervisor. Often, supervisors must coordinate and schedule regular in-service training sessions for their direct reports. It is imperative for supervisors to demonstrate a positive attitude toward training by encouraging all employees to take part. Training to gain skills in quality control must be a top priority for the supervisor. Their attitude and commitment to quality serves as the role model for all employees.

Employees are the fundamental asset of any company. They should be knowledgeable of all expectations placed on them. They must know exactly what is expected of them when it comes to quality. A clear idea of these expectations will create an environment where workers will take pride in their work, feel more secure, have high morale, and produce high levels of productivity. Very few employees desire to go to work and produce substandard products or provide substandard services. Having pride in one's work is highly motivating. Workers must be trained in all aspects of quality improvement. Supervisors are often in the best position to champion training programs offered in and out of the company. They might be expected to train their employees. Supervisors directly help management create a climate for innovation and continuous improvement.

TOOLS FOR MEASURING QUALITY

Producing a quality product or providing a quality service that customers are willing to buy is not a new concept. However, using systematic record keeping and tracking quantitative data involving statistical principles are modern concepts.

Today's supervisor must be able to collect data and understand principles of data analysis. Supervisors need to be trained in statistical methods used in analyzing performance data. Supervisors are required to use many tools for measuring quality. Some of the more typical tools are check sheets to record patterns or trends for a product or service, Pareto diagrams for prioritizing problems based on their importance, flowcharts that show pictorially the sequence of events in a process, cause-and-effect diagrams that examine all possible causes for a quality defect, histograms that chart the frequency or number of occurrences of a particular aspect of a product or a process, control charts that monitor production as it occurs, and scatter diagrams that graph pairs of numeric data on two axes with one variable on each axis to determine the correlation between the variables. Extensive descriptions of these and other tools, their purpose and instructions for use are available on-line on the American Society for Quality's website.[6] The objective of this chapter is not to teach you how to use these tools, but to emphasize their importance and to encourage supervisors to learn how to use these tools as soon as possible. They are fundamental quality control tools. Any supervisor who wishes to grow and prosper in today's organizations must comprehend how to use these concepts and integrate them into their daily work routine. Sign up for any type of quality training your company provides or any similar course your local college offers. They may offer a series of courses leading to a certificate in quality control.

IMPLEMENTING CONTINUOUS IMPROVEMENT IN YOUR TEAM

Although many quality improvement issues involve complex systems that impact numerous processes, functions, and departments within an organization, managers must also implement quality improvements at a much smaller scale within their work units. There are numerous issues involving work flow, customer service, communication, data management, and other matters that are solely within your team's purview that can make a big difference in enhancing the functioning of your team.

One tool you can use to implement continuous improvement in your team is the *plan-do-check-act model,* also called the *Deming Cycle* or the *Shewhart Cycle.* This model is described as[7]:

Plan: Identify an opportunity and plan for change.

Do: Implement the change on a small scale.

Check: Use data to analyze the results of the change and determine whether it made a difference.

Act: If the change was successful, implement it on a wider scale and continuously assess the results. If unsuccessful, begin the cycle again.

To engage in a continuous improvement effort with your team, consider these basic steps:

1. Assemble the team to identify a specific process issue requiring improvement.
2. Engage in processes to identify root causes of the problem. Many of the tools listed in this chapter may assist you to do this.

3. Chart the current process used. Typically, some form of flowcharting will assist you to do this. The most commonly used symbols in flowcharting are as follows:

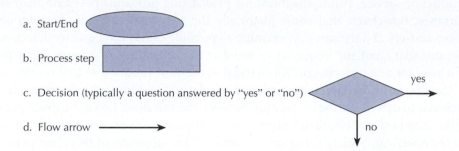

a. Start/End

b. Process step

c. Decision (typically a question answered by "yes" or "no")   yes

d. Flow arrow ⟶   no

To illustrate the basic flowchart process, the diagram that follows provides a rather exaggerated process that a short-order cook at a delicatessen might go through to prepare an order for a corn beef sandwich on rye with potato chips to go. Though flowcharting systems in your work are undoubtedly more complex than this, this example illustrates the many seemingly simple steps that must be accounted for when flowcharting. You must be careful to chart each step in order to identify whether each step is necessary or if some steps are redundant or otherwise unnecessary.

4. Chart the ideal process that the team envisions will improve the process. Typically, when compared to the current process, this will reveal the opportunity to eliminate steps that are redundant, time-consuming, or inefficient in other ways.

5. Agree on the ideal model and identify the barriers and bottlenecks that may prevent its implementation and discuss how to address them. Are there arbitrary policies, practices, and procedures that need to be corrected? Are there others outside the team who have some control or ownership over the current process with whom the team must negotiate? Are there impacts upstream or downstream that must also be addressed in order to realize this new model?

6. Determine who will address the barriers and bottlenecks identified, the timeline and deadlines for addressing them, and then proceed to address them.

7. Implement the change. Determine how you will measure the effectiveness of the change and evaluate the new process accordingly.

8. Check progress at the agreed-upon time. Make modifications as necessary. If change proves ineffective, return to the initial steps to identify causes and create a new ideal process. Note: If significant change is still needed beyond minor modifications, chances are that sufficient time was not spent to identify causes. For example, it is possible that the process itself is sufficient, but factors like personality clashes, lack of sufficient resources, or a lack of commitment among team members or others outside the team needed to implement the process are the true culprits of the inefficiencies.

Hypothetical Flowchart for Filling a Delicatessen Order

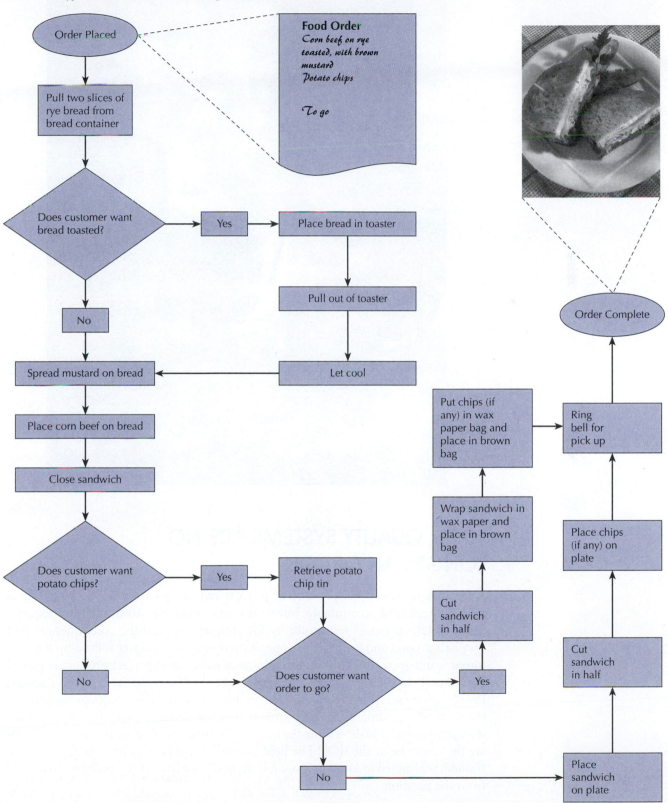

TOTAL QUALITY SYSTEMS ARE NO LONGER AN OPTION

A continuous quality improvement process requires accountability. Not only is management held accountable, but so is every employee. Accountability requires that you take personal responsibility for your actions and the consequences that they bring, good and bad. Frequent performance reviews, closer follow-up if a customer is unhappy, and almost zero tolerance when an imperfect product is placed prematurely in the hands of a customer or client are ways to foster accountability. People, processes, procedures, machinery, materials, and the vendors who provide them are all accountable for their quality. Causes for lapses in quality must be investigated in order to determine the causes. If it turns out that an employee's actions are the cause, he or she should be held accountable. The employee may need to be trained, reassigned to another job, or, if these do not correct the problem, removed from the position.

When Sylvia was hired and trained to do high-precision work in a high-tech factory, she was amazed to discover that she would go through a weekly performance review for the first two months and a monthly review thereafter. The next thing she discovered was that quality standards had permeated the entire organization, and that her co-workers took great pride in the part they played in turning out the best possible product. After surviving her probation period, her supervisor said: "Sylvia, we are pleased to have you aboard. We are also pleased that your productivity is above average without sacrificing quality. I consider you to be a quality employee working for a quality outfit. Although our standards are high and there is always some pressure involved, you will discover that there is a lot of job satisfaction working here, and there are times when we relax and have a lot of fun."

The swing to quality while maintaining high quantity levels is the number one story in the world of business today. This change is primarily responsible for the success America is having in foreign markets. As a new supervisor, it is imperative that you evaluate just where your firm stands as far as quality is concerned. Is your company still in the talking stage? Have they adopted a workable plan? Or have they reached a high level of maturity in their ability to manage quality?

No matter what commitment your employer makes to quality, the commitment you make to yourself is the key to your future career success. If you are committed to getting your employees or team members to put customers first, producing the best product or service possible, and keeping improvements on a steady, consistent basis with frequent accountability, you are on the winning track. You will be playing the supervisory game under the best possible game plan.

PERFORMANCE **CHECKLIST**

1. The quality philosophies developed by quality gurus like W. Edwards Deming, Joseph Juran, and Philip Crosby; as well as programs and methodologies like TQM, Six Sigma, Lean Production, and the ISO 9000 Series; and national and international awards like the Malcolm Baldrige National Quality Award all promote a common goal of developing an integrated total quality system by engaging in continuous improvement. They share the belief that managers and supervisors play an enormously critical role in achieving and maintaining high standards of quality.

2. Management shows signs of its commitment through its slogans, its talk throughout the organization about quality and quality principles, the training it provides supervisors and employees, its continuous improvement teams (CITs), and other efforts. Yet, in some organizations, managers may say they value quality but their behavior says something quite different. When management behaves incongruently in this fashion, employees will believe the behaviors and not the slogans and words. These are known as negating and confirming signs of management's commitment to quality.

It only takes one negating sign to put into question management's true commitment.

3. Supervisors need to be trained in statistical methods used in analyzing performance data. Supervisors are required to use many tools for measuring quality. Some of the more typical tools are check sheets, Pareto diagrams, flow charts, cause-and-effect diagrams, histograms, control charts, and scatter diagrams.

4. Supervisors can implement continuous improvement of processes within their team by utilizing the *plan-do-check-act model*. A practical process for doing this includes these steps: (1) assemble the team and identify the issue needing improvement; (2) identify root causes of the problem; (3) chart the current process using flowcharting; (4) chart the ideal process to identify steps that can be eliminated; (5) identify barriers and bottlenecks to realizing the ideal model; (6) address the barriers and bottlenecks; (7) implement the change; and (8) monitor the implementation, making modifications or returning to identify root causes if implementation is unsuccessful.

TEST YOURSELF

For each of the following statements, check true or false.

True   False

____ ____ 1. Having quantity receive preference over quality is desirable.

____ ____ 2. Quality control is 100 percent a manufacturing function.

____ ____ 3. A major training effort is necessary for a supervisor to improve quality in her or his department.

____ ____ 4. Continuous improvement is a philosophy that never ends; that is, improvements need to be made on a steady, continuous basis.

____ ____ 5. International companies are forcing some United States firms to adopt high-quality standards.

____ ____ 6. The level of your personal commitment to quality will have little to do with your career success.

____ ____ 7. Quality control can be applied not only to enhance your department's productivity, but also your career.

____ ____ 8. An effective quality system focuses on customer needs and quality made products.

____ ____ 9. One tool for continuous improvement is the *plan-check-do-act* model.

____ ____ 10. If, on balance, confirming signs of management commitment to quality are more than negating signs, employees and customers will be assured of the organization's commitment to quality.

Turn to the back of the book to check your answers.
Total Correct ____

DISCUSSION QUESTIONS

1. Why is everyone from the CEO to the production worker or service provider directly responsible for quality?

2. Explain why supervisors are often in the best position to champion training programs on quality offered in and out of the company.

3. What changes do you feel would take place in the work environment of a company that adopts a quality-oriented philosophy?

4. Describe some "confirming signs" that your managers communicate about their commitment to quality, and describe any "negating signs" they communicate.

CASE: PHILOSOPHY

SITUATION

Bill has returned from a two-day seminar at the home office in which the importance of quality was discussed in detail. A company-wide initiative on improving quality is going to be rolled out. All areas of the company will focus on improving quality. The first step is to provide training on quality to all employees and the first training session will cover the fundamental tools of quality control.

Bill was told that all of his employees must have a positive attitude toward the quality initiative in general and toward all training programs specifically. To kick off the initiative, all employees, including supervisors, will attend a twelve contact-hour training program where they will learn how to use the fundamental tools

of quality control in completing their jobs. A quality expert was hired by the company to conduct the training session.

OBJECTIVE

Gain the support of all supervisors and employees for the quality program.

PROBLEM

Attention to quality has not always been consistent at the company. This is especially true in Ricardo's department. Just last week, Bill ordered Ricardo to ship a load of product to one of its largest and oldest customers. The quality of the product was questionable. It did not meet the quality specifications set by the quality control department. Some of Ricardo's employees knew about the shipment and were confused and even a bit angry that the product was shipped. This type of thing happens periodically in all departments. Some employees have made the statement that "Bill cares more about profits than he does about the customer." Several employees have also complained to Ricardo about how poor quality will one day cost them their jobs if this sort of thing doesn't stop.

Bill called a meeting with the supervisors to determine the best way to conduct the training. Since all employees are expected to attend, scheduling will be critical. Bill does not want productivity to go down due to the training.

PLAYERS

Bill and the supervisors: Ricardo, Gerald, and Yolanda.

PROCEDURE

Use a fishbowl arrangement. Have the four players circle their chairs in the middle of the classroom so all other students in the class can see and hear their meeting. Bill and the supervisors will discuss all pertinent factors related to the company's quality program. The discussion should last approximately ten minutes.

CASE DISCUSSION AND QUESTIONS

A facilitated discussion involving the entire class should be conducted. Discuss the issues brought up by the players and discuss new ones as they arise. Focus on some of the challenges facing the quality initiative in Bill's area. How will the supervisors gain the acceptance from their employees for such an initiative? How will they overcome their past practices of shipping bad parts?

IMPLEMENTATION **EXERCISE**

In completing this exercise, assume one of the two follwing conditions regarding the organization in which you work or an organization of which you are familiar: (1) You are a supervisor or team leader who is currently adopting a total quality system; or (2) You are the training director of a firm that is considering the adoption of a quality system.

Further, assume that you have made a survey and there is a sizable "gap" between what your current product quality, customer service, and accountability levels are and what they should be. Based on what you know of this organization, please list non-acceptable levels below.

Product Quality	Customer Service	Accountability
10	10	10
9	9	9
8	8	8
7	7	7
6	6	6
5	5	5
4	4	4
3	3	3
2	2	2
1	1	1

Your goals over the next six months are as follows:

Product Quality	Customer Service	Accountability
10	10	10
9	9	9
8	8	8
7	7	7
6	6	6
5	5	5
4	4	4
3	3	3
2	2	2
1	1	1

What measures would you initiate to meet your goals? Please list three each for Product Quality, Customer Service, and Accountability.

PERSONAL GROWTH **EXERCISE**

If your company is involved in a quality initiative, discuss the advantages and disadvantages of the effort.

NOTES

1. W. Edwards Deming, *Quality, Productivity, and Competitive Position.* Cambridge, MA: Center for Advanced Engineering Study, MIT, 1982.

2. Philip B. Crosby, *Quality Is Free.* New York: McGraw-Hill, 1979.

3. Joseph M. Juran, *Juran on Planning for Quality.* New York: The Free Press, 1988.

4. Bruce A. Henderson and Jorge L. Larco, *Lean Transformation: How to Change Your Business Into a Lean Enterprise.* Richmond, VA: The Oaklea Press, 2000, pp. 45–66.

5. National Institute of Standards and Technology, "Frequently Asked Questions about the Malcolm Baldridge National Quality Award," http://www.nist.gov/public_affairs/factsheet/baldfaqs.htm (accessed January 14, 2008).

6. American Society for Quality, http://www.asq.org.

7. American Society for Quality, "Continuous Improvement," http://www.asq.org/learn-about-quality/continuous-improvement/overview/overview.html (accessed January 14, 2008); Mary Walton, *The Deming Management Method.* New York: Putnam Publishing Group, 1986, pp. 86–88.

chapter **eight**

THE EFFECTIVE WORK TEAM

*"The productivity of a work group seems to depend on how the group
members see their own goals in relation to the goals of the organization."*
Paul Hersey

Improving Productivity
Leading Teams
Communicating Effectively
Managing Conflict
Improving Performance
Managing Time
Benefiting from Change

A major restructuring of organizations is taking place in the
United States. Downsizing, thinning out of middle-management positions, and greater international involvements are in
progress. These and other unsettling changes are necessary to enable
firms to reach higher quality and productivity levels in their efforts to
remain competitive. It is the challenge of our times!

In previous chapters, you studied the fundamentals involved in
creating good relationships as a traditional supervisor. You may not
have been aware that everything you learned is even more applicable
in becoming a team leader. In fact, if you think back, you will realize
that everything you have absorbed, once put into practice, would
make you a successful coach. This capability can be highly significant
to your future because of the following trends:

> A steady movement away from the traditional pyramid depart-
> mental structure to the circle or team arrangement.

> Increased empowerment, which means that team and depart-
> mental personnel are given more autonomy to make decisions,
> take action, and enhance their own roles.

> The changing demographic composition of units, which is be-
> coming more representative of all domestic and international
> cultures and includes four generations working together.

FROM THE PYRAMID TO THE CIRCLE

The traditional department with authority and responsibility held
tightly by the supervisor is giving way to a new, more productive
team approach. Study the comparisons illustrated in the figures
below.

PERFORMANCE COMPETENCIES

After you have finished reading this
chapter, you should be able to:

- Describe six rules to follow to
  become an effective team leader

- Describe five techniques for
  leading culturally diverse teams

- Describe three team roles in
  team meetings and explain how
  they affect teamwork

- Explain the seven normative
  conditions for effective teams

- Define *synergy* as it applies to
  team performance

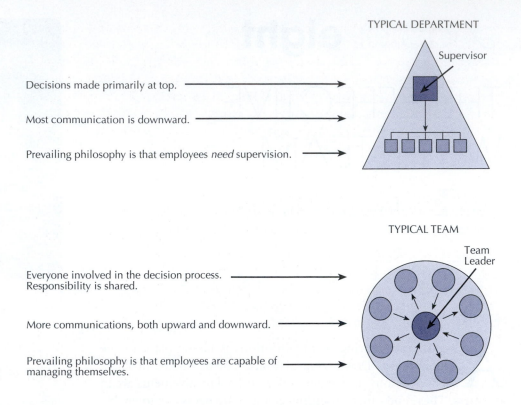

TYPICAL DEPARTMENT

Supervisor

Decisions made primarily at top. $\longrightarrow$

Most communication is downward. $\longrightarrow$

Prevailing philosophy is that employees *need* supervision. $\longrightarrow$

TYPICAL TEAM

Team Leader

Everyone involved in the decision process. $\longrightarrow$
Responsibility is shared.

More communications, both upward and downward. $\longrightarrow$

Prevailing philosophy is that employees are capable of $\longrightarrow$
managing themselves.

TRANSITION DANGERS

In making the transition, it may help traditional supervisors to think of themselves as "boundary managers" instead of direct, forceful bosses. That is, a supervisor acts as a team "facilitator" as well as a leader–supervisor. As a boundary manager, he or she will spend more time coordinating productivity efforts with other departments, obtaining resources the team needs, and negotiating conflicts inside and outside team boundaries.

A *team boundary* is the sphere of responsibility or work area of the team. A boundary manager is needed when a problem transcends the team's boundary. The team hands the problem off to the boundary manager and he or she takes it from there. The sharing of authority once held only by the supervisor can sometimes cause a leader to feel isolated and ineffective. Should this feeling arise, the leader might mistakenly return to the old style. Consider Dora's experience:

When Dora accepted an offer from a more progressive firm, she was warned that as a supervisor she would need to absorb and apply the team philosophy endorsed by the new president. She accepted the challenge and immediately started to learn as much about the team approach as possible. Dora knew it would mean sharing the authority she previously enjoyed, more frequent communication, added patience so that each team member could be involved in major decisions, and a variety of other changes. In fact, she would need to revamp her behavioral patterns and style as a supervisor. For the first thirty days, things were bumpy and, on a few occasions, chaotic.

At times, Dora was tempted to fall back on her old command-and-control approach, but she resisted. She wisely recognized that she could be sending a mixed message to team members by oscillating between the two leadership styles. This inconsistency could cause confusion and lower productivity. Instead, she accepted suggestions from other team leaders (fellow supervisors), and everything started to come together. When asked by her superior how she was doing, Dora replied, "I still feel a little insecure and I still haven't been able to shed all of my previous habits, but all team members are responding and I am more excited about my job than ever before."

THE TEAM IDEA IS NOT NEW

Many books have been written about the change just presented and the need for managers to make this transition in today's business climate more than ever before. The team concept has been around for a long time and tried under many formulas. Naturally, some organizations are more suited to adopt the team approach than others. The basic trend, however, is gaining momentum. The supervisor of the future will need to be prepared as a team leader as much as a departmental manager. Why will this preparation be prevalent? Because when employees get swept up in a well-led team project, they become more involved. Personal involvement in decision making can produce higher levels of both quantity and quality. As a result, everyone benefits.

Companies require every advantage to remain competitive and can no longer afford hierarchical structures which can slow processes down to a crawl. It has become a cumbersome, inefficient model. Similarly, managers who are more comfortable with top-down management, which requires that all decision making occur by and through the manager, will not last long in this environment. To be successful, new supervisors must be responsive to these trends.

ALL TEAMS ARE NOT CREATED EQUAL

The more you explore the team concept, the more you will realize that not all teams work out. Some individuals who are excellent traditional supervisors cannot make the behavioral changes necessary to become the kind of leader required. Often it is better to work for a good traditional supervisor than to be part of a team with a weak, ineffective team leader. In other cases, a supervisor more accustomed to traditional management approaches will simply need time and support from management and patient team members to work through the transition before he or she will be able to facilitate team-based approaches at a level where true effectiveness is achieved. Similarly, team members unaccustomed to the team concept or who are just beginning to form as a group will need time and management support before realizing greater efficiency.

It is also important to recognize that not all groups that we may refer to as "teams" are, in fact, teams as that term is defined. Many organizations have working units which perform distinct functional tasks but whose members do not function cohesively as a team, nor is such functioning required to be effective. Specifically, the unit's and individual workers' tasks are structured so that members generally work on their own and independently of one another.

Rhoda is the supervisor of a credit department for a large retail department store. She supervises the second shift of 30 associates who run credit reports for credit card applications, approve or disapprove applications, and respond to phone inquiries from credit card customers and rejected applicants. At the beginning of each shift, the associates meet for fifteen minutes so that Rhoda can give them updates on policies, sales figures, and other business issues. On occasion, she invites their input regarding how to improve their work processes and customer service. Associates are generally cordial and supportive of one another.

Though this group exhibits many of the characteristics of a team, they do not, in fact, function as a team. A team generally refers to "a small task group in which the members have a common purpose, interdependent roles, and complementary skills."[1] The distinction between a working group such as Rhoda's and a team can easily be drawn by analogy to the difference between a basketball team, in which five players work interdependently and cohesively to achieve a common goal, and a gymnastics "team," in which members share a common goal—to win the meet— but who rely on individual performances and distinct roles to achieve success.

Whether you supervise a working group or a true team is less significant than the fact that, as a supervisor, you must be sensitive to individual needs and work with group members in a fashion that is most efficient and effective to achieve organizational goals. Like the gymnastics team compared to the basketball team, being classified as a working group does not make the group inferior to or less effective than a team. It will mean that the manner in which you manage the working group as compared to the team will be different, as should be your expectations for individual rather than team-based contributions from group members.

EMPLOYEE EMPOWERMENT

Empowerment is the key term when it comes to developing an effective team. Under the team umbrella you give employees more power to operate freely, more space to be creative, and more chances to contribute to productivity in their own way. Under the pyramid structure, it is the supervisor who draws the discipline line. Under the team structure, employees usually draw their own lines. In an advanced and experienced work team, members usually discipline themselves in order to achieve and maintain group acceptance and cohesion. A team that normally operates in unison can exert peer pressure on an errant member. Often the leader can remain an observer and intervene only when necessary to confront a behavioral problem that has the potential of seriously disrupting team progress. When these freedoms mesh with reality, each team member is empowered to make the team more productive. Then, rejoicing over the success of the team becomes more rewarding than making personal progress at the expense of others. Rewards are better when shared with others who have also made a contribution.

RULES OF THE GAME

What does one do to become an effective team leader? Here are a few suggestions.

- Delegate more authority and responsibility to all team members. Only in this way will they feel that they are involved and true members of the team.
- Encourage risk taking and experimentation. Within bounds, let members make mistakes without coming down hard on them. When mistakes happen, help every team member learn from them.
- Develop a shared vision. Clarify to them where they are headed. Detail the goals of the department and explain how the department goals will support the overall company goals and ultimately its mission. Make sure the resources of the department are shared equally.
- Set the stage for team problem solving. You create a problem-solving atmosphere by taking the time to bring everyone close to the problem so that they can contribute to and accept the consequences of the decision.
- Invite self-expression and open discussion even if it involves conflict. This approach can eliminate feelings of resentment that often cause members to tighten up and cooperate only superficially.
- Run team meetings regularly in order to do the preceding activities as a team. Resist the temptation to make decisions in isolation without team input simply because it seems more expedient or you are facing time pressures.

PERSONAL CHARACTERISTICS REQUIRED BY A TEAM LEADER

What are the personal characteristics of a successful team leader? We could talk about patience, having a positive attitude toward team operations, willingness to listen, flexibility, a desire to inspire, and many other traits. But ahead of those characteristics that come to mind quickly is the number one skill—sensitivity. It takes a light, delicate, and insightful touch to form a group of strangers who represent different cultures, generations, and backgrounds into a viable, productive team. It takes a perceptive individual who understands group dynamics and can lead without pushing. Such a leader must have compassion for all people and a deep desire to help each individual reach her or his potential as a team member.

It is the ability to help members develop a mutual respect for the efforts of other members that can convert a work unit into a team. Some people refer to mutual respect as the glue that keeps a good team together—like the motto of the Three Musketeers: "One for all, all for one."

A personal characteristic that should be near the top of any list is a sense of humor. A team that cannot relax now and then is a team in name only. When a team achieves a goal, a "reward party" is in order; when a team suffers a defeat, some laughter is needed to enable everyone to learn from the past and begin again. A perceptive leader (or coach) knows that sometimes it is necessary to encourage relaxation to prepare for the next effort.

Building a work team is similar to putting a winning basketball team into competition. It does not happen in a few weeks. Sometimes it takes two or three seasons. When total empowerment is accomplished, the results are obvious. The total team power is measurably greater than that previously exercised by each individual player. It is this added dimension that creates a winner.

At first, Dora didn't fully understand all the benefits of empowerment. For example, she didn't sense that being involved with a winning team could increase the self-esteem of all players and that this, in turn, would increase their contribution in new, creative ways. She didn't realize that empowerment could convert a worker into a more dynamic participant who was willing to work for the team goal with more enthusiasm and dedication.

With her new approach, Dora found herself communicating more frequently on an informal level, compromising more to accommodate team members who had demonstrated higher personal productivity. But most of all, she noticed a better learning climate emerging—everyone wanting to know how they might contribute more in different areas and what they needed to learn to make it possible. Then, when she looked over the productivity schedules, the bottom line showed that the new approach was working.

"Wow!" Dora said to herself. "By giving up some of my control and authority, I have empowered myself along with other team members."

LEADING THE CULTURALLY DIVERSE TEAM

The movement from the pyramid to the circle and team empowerment becomes more intriguing when the diverse composition of many work units is introduced. The predominantly white male team of the past is being replaced with an enticing mix of gender, age, race, and cultural backgrounds, both domestic and international. Even now, it is not unusual to find five or more different cultures represented in a team of ten workers.

What is the most important factor in creating a successful, high-producing, multicultural team? Many would say it is the attitude of the team leader. Does the leader want a team made up of persons from diverse cultures, or is it being mandated by management? Is the leader free of prejudice, so that fair treatment is guaranteed? Does the leader bring to the surface the full potential of each member, so that long-term goals can be reached? Has the leader accepted the challenge inherent in forming a model multicultural team?

When Dora took over the department in her new firm, she was not surprised about the mix of men and women or the different age levels. It did surprise her, however, to realize that she had one Asian, one Hispanic, two African Americans, and one Arab to work with. Obviously, her new company had an international flavor well beyond that of her previous experiences. Did the mix make Dora's job more difficult? At the beginning, yes. She had to remind herself that the most basic and important principle of human relationships is to treat everyone as an individual. It would be her job to ensure that each member received the full respect of all others. Building healthy, open, and compatible interpersonal relationships would be her goal.

After a full month, Dora had learned more than the identities of the members of the team she had inherited. She discovered, for example, that it was the goal of the team that really brought them together. All she needed to do was work hard herself, teach others by drawing on her greater store of knowledge, communicate a lot, compliment a lot, and keep management apprised of the progress being made.

When Dora discovered that the team concept was a top-priority goal of her new company and that all team leaders met in seminars on a regular basis, she was delighted. This environment would give her the support and skills she would need to survive as a leader in the future. All this activity confirmed that she had made the right decision to join her new corporation.

The Accommodate/Acculturate Continuum

How does the team leader manage the challenge of bringing individuals with unique talents, ideas, perspectives and contributions together to function as a cohesive, efficient unit? Specifically, how can a team leader successfully incorporate the unique contributions of team members who have not traditionally been included in the corporate structures and work culture to which the majority of team members have become accustomed?

The leader of a culturally diverse team faces essentially two challenges when working with a team that has recently brought in new or "different" team members who are unfamiliar with or whose cultural background and preferences have not previously been represented within the existing team make-up: (1) Ensuring the new or "different" member will **acculturate** to team norms, expectations, and values in order to be successful and contribute to team success; and (2) ensuring the team will **accommodate** the new or "different" team member so that his or her unique values, ideas, and perspectives contribute to team efforts and, as appropriate, influence change in how the team functions to achieve better results.

Any new team member is expected to acculturate sooner or later to team norms and expectations, particularly when these norms and expectations have proven successful for the team over time. While someone from a different culture may have different personal perspectives on some matters, some norms and expectations are non-negotiable, and the new team member should be brought to an understanding of these issues in order to be successful.

Raj comes from a culture that has a different perspective on the meaning and value of time. As a consequence, during his first week of work, he was late to work on three separate occasions because he did not fully understand the importance of reporting to work on or before 8:00 a.m. Further, he lingered during break time and caused his co-workers to be late returning from break because he did not understand the need to pay attention to the clock and viewed break time as an opportunity for building relationships with co-workers. Dora was sensitive to why Raj acted as he did. Nonetheless, she had to gently counsel him on the expectations regarding attendance and punctuality.

On the other hand, without a team leader's sensitivity to how a new team member may contribute ideas and perspectives that will truly benefit the team, even if it will change the way the team functions, the team risks loosing the synergy it might otherwise achieve. Because existing team members have formed their own dominant culture, there can be a lot of pressure on new members simply to comply and bend to the team's unspoken, yet often inefficient and ineffective, "rules." In contrast, if a team is open to new ideas that will result in positive change, it makes sense for the team to "bend" to accommodate the new member.

Raj suggested to Dora a number of changes the team could make that would greatly improve its work flow. Dora told Raj that his ideas were good and encouraged him to raise them at the next team meeting. At the meeting, three other team members engaged in a mild argument on how to improve work flow while Raj sat silently. Perceiving that Raj's ideas might greatly enhance this dialogue, she encouraged Raj to share them. The team members were resistant, but with Dora's thoughtful probing and encouragement, the team came to realize that Raj's suggestions were, in fact, the best way to improve work flow.

The team leader of a culturally diverse team is, then, challenged to manage a balance in the continuum between acculturating new members to ensure their success on the team and accommodate new members to ensure greater team success. Here are a few techniques that will help you manage this continuum:

- Learn from one another. Interteam member relationships can be strengthened as each individual learns to appreciate and enjoy the culture of another. Free and open communication encouraged by the team leader will help this happen.

- Inquire about team members' cultural backgrounds and preferences and openly discuss differences. Some team leaders may think it inappropriate to ask new members from a different culture to discuss their backgrounds and work experience in a different environment. Done properly, however, such discussions could build stronger interpersonal relationships, as well as avoid needless misunderstandings. Each culture has differences that affect work behavior. Thus, when a team member knows how a member from a different culture "sees" the world, the give-and-take can be enhanced. For example, some cultures are more patriarchal than ours, making it natural for workers from these backgrounds to sit back and wait for the boss to give orders rather than move into team efforts on their own. Knowing this will help you find ways to draw them out so their input will be considered rather than cause you to make an erroneous assumption that they don't want to contribute to team efforts.

- A new team member—especially if her or his culture has not previously been represented—needs and should receive special support and training

---

CULTURAL COMMUNICATIONS QUIZ

This exercise has been designed to help you measure your sensitivity regarding communications with recent arrivals to the United States from other cultures. Place a check under "true" or "false."

True   False

_____ _____ 1. There are more commonalities than differences among cultures.

_____ _____ 2. It is good practice to notice and discuss openly with an individual differences among cultures.

_____ _____ 3. Learning to use a few words in the language of the other person demonstrates positive intent to relate to the person.

_____ _____ 4. Nonverbal communication can speak louder than words.

_____ _____ 5. Most people from foreign cultures have more respect for authority than native-born Americans.

_____ _____ 6. It is a good idea to ask those with cultural differences whether they wish to be praised in public or in private.

_____ _____ 7. Workers from other cultures fear that their traditional values will be taken away.

_____ _____ 8. It is a good idea to reinforce positive behavioral changes with compliments.

_____ _____ 9. It is easier to understand English than to speak it.

_____ _____ 10. Some persons from other cultures speak less English than they could because they fear making mistakes.

Total _____

The authors consider all ten answers to be true.

by the team leader. This extra effort by the supervisor/leader can set the tone for other members, and everyone benefits.

- The leader should discover and value the special talents the new member brings to the team and see that those talents are made known and used, inviting collaboration between the seasoned members and the new individual.

- The team leader or supervisor plays an important role in helping those from different cultures learn team protocol and values and why the team operates by them. Until the procedures and courtesies normally practiced are accepted by newcomers, they will not find the work environment congenial. As a result, they will not make their full contribution to the team. Conversely, their inadvertent failure to follow protocols will cause undue resentment among other team members.

- Strong, productive teams are built around strong relationships that are mutually rewarding. That is, all members need to benefit from the presence of each team member. Should the leader discover that a misunderstanding or conflict exists, immediate counseling of those involved is recommended. A team is most effective when members are compatible and each relationship is mutually rewarding.

THREE TEAM ROLES IN MEETINGS

In order for teams to perform successfully, team members need to be aware of and practice the fundamentals of teamwork. First, the team should meet on a regular basis at a specified time. Teams that do not meet or miss meetings routinely do not perform well.

Research on team dynamics indicates three service roles or functions that team members must perform during their meetings. The service roles include (1) leader, (2) recorder, and (3) observer. Each role carries specific responsibilities that affect team dynamics. Except for the leader's role, having team members volunteer to fill each role is often more desirable than appointing someone who may not want it.

Role #1—Team Leader. In most cases the supervisor or manager of the department fills the leader's role. In self-led teams the leader role may rotate among the team members. In both cases, the leader of the team assumes the following responsibilities:

- Ensures that team members perform task and maintenance functions, and reduces nonfunctional behavior.
- Assists the team in choosing and focusing on its tasks and goals.
- Encourages free expression and balanced participation.
- Helps team members listen to each other.
- Helps the team manage conflict.
- Communicates concerns of the team to the next level of management.

One person or leader does not easily accomplish all these outcomes. In an effective team, each team member shares responsibility for performing tasks and maintenance behaviors and for minimizing dysfunctional behaviors. In less-mature teams the accountability for these behaviors falls on the leader. The Chart "Team

TEAM BEHAVIORS

Task Behaviors	Maintenance Behaviors	Dysfunctional Behaviors
Beginning: Proposing tasks, goals, or action; defining group problems; suggesting a procedure	**Peace-making:** Attempting to settle disagreements; reducing conflict; getting people to explore differences	**Aggression:** Lowering others' status; attacking the group or its values; joking in a nasty or hurtful way
Informing: Presenting facts; giving expression of feeling; offering an opinion	**Gate keeping:** Helping others to participate; keeping communication channels open	**Blocking:** Disagreeing and opposing beyond "reason"; resisting stubbornly the group's wish for personally oriented reasons; using hidden agenda to stop the movement of the group
Exploring others' ideas: Asking for opinions, facts, and feelings	**General agreement:** Asking whether a group is near a decision; testing a possible conclusion	
Clarifying: Interpreting ideas; asking questions in an effort to understand or promote understanding; saying things in another way	**Encouraging:** Being friendly, warm, and responsive to others; indicating an interest in others' contributions (by facial expressions or remark)	**Dominating:** Asserting authority or superiority to control the group or certain members; interrupting contributions of others; controlling by means of flattery or other forms of insincere behavior
Coordinating/ Summarizing: Pulling together related ideas; restating suggestions; offering a decision or conclusion for group to consider	**Compromising:** Giving up part of a personal idea to settle conflict; willingness to change to keep group together	**Out-of-field behavior:** Making a display of one's lack of involvement; seeking recognition in ways not related to group tasks
Reality testing: Making a critical analysis of an idea; testing an idea against some data; trying to see whether the idea would work		**Special interest:** Using the group as a vehicle for outside interests; putting one's beliefs and needs ahead of group needs

Source: Adapted from John McKinley, *Group Development Through Participation Training* (New York: Paulist Press, 1978).

Behaviors" describes task, maintenance, and dysfunctional behaviors in detail. Team members need to be confronted privately about their dysfunctional behavior when it jeopardizes the team. The supervisor or team leader usually does this. Clear expectations for what is expected and the consequences for failing to perform as expected should be explained thoroughly. If the behavior persists, the person may need to be formally disciplined or removed from the team.

Role #2—Recorder. The recorder performs an important function for the team. Primarily, the recorder is the historian for the team. The recorder is responsible for the following tasks:

- Provides the team with written documentation of the ongoing discussion by recording comments on an easel or board for all team members to see.

- Asks for clarification of ideas or statements as necessary.
- May participate in group discussion, but primarily focuses on recording team members' discussion.

Team discussion frequently ebbs and flows. Depending on the nature of the topic, the discussion may prompt many ideas, thoughts, or suggestions to roll out quickly and randomly. The recorder is responsible for capturing key words or phrases during the discussion. This transcription allows the discussion to progress to other thoughts without losing what has been said or suggested. Some team members may require more "think time" than others in order to fully express their thoughts on a subject or idea. Having a written document in front of them provides the opportunity to refer to an earlier statement on the flip chart. An illuminating thought might emerge that was missed the first time. Skills for a recorder include being a good listener and summarizer.

Role #3—Observer. The observer is like a mirror that reflects team behavior back to the team members. The reflection is open for investigation. To accomplish this task, the observer:

- Provides the team with observations of its behaviors and processes.
- Makes comments that are group directed and does not refer to the participants by name in the feedback (at least not in early discussions).
- Reports observations at times specified by the leader.
- Sits where he or she can see most team members.
- Reports what he or she observed, not what he or she thinks occurred or should have occurred.

The observer should be allotted a specified amount of time during the team meeting to discuss his or her observations. Occasionally the team should use a formal questionnaire for assessing their team behavior. Numerous team climate questionnaires are available, but using one specifically designed for your team is often the most rewarding. A typical team climate questionnaire focuses on evaluating teamwork. The "Team Feedback Form" features three example questions that often appear on a questionnaire. Your team can design its own feedback form and ask its own questions. Instructions direct each team member to individually evaluate the team's effectiveness in key areas. All individual scores can be averaged and compared to one another. All group behaviors are data for analysis.

TEAM FEEDBACK FORM				
Category		Scales (please circle)		
	Unsatisfactory		*Satisfactory*		*Excellent*
Willingness to listen to one another's views:	1	2	3	4	5
Completes assigned tasks on time:	1	2	3	4	5
Balance of participation:	1	2	3	4	5

After completing this feedback form, the team discusses its scores. Goals for correcting weaknesses can be set. The team may also wish to celebrate its strengths and accomplishments.

SEVEN NORMATIVE CONDITIONS FOR EFFECTIVE TEAMS

Being a member of a fully functioning and effective team is highly rewarding. The cohesive team, effectively led, often outproduces the same individuals working alone. This is called *synergy*. Making and keeping a team effective requires the constant diligence of each member. Your team's behaviors collectively will determine how effective your team actually is. Research has shown that teams exhibiting the following seven behaviors (or normative conditions) are most likely to be effective.

1. *Shared planning.* Group decides its goals and objectives through consensus decision making.
2. *Shared decision making through consensus.* Each member must be motivated to carry out the decisions of the group and agree that the following three conditions have been met:
   a. I have heard and understood all viewpoints expressed.
   b. My viewpoints have been heard and understood by all.
   c. I am motivated to carry out whatever decision the team makes.
3. *Shared leadership.* The special responsibility of the leader is to perform group task and group maintenance behaviors found in the "Team Behaviors" Chart. All members of a team should exhibit these behaviors, not just the designated team leader.
4. *Shared evaluation.* The group assesses the process of its discussions, not just the product of them. The observer role provides feedback to the group on the process. The group must discuss this feedback.
5. *Two-way communication.* Group members actively listen to what is said and to what is not said, as well as attend to verbal and nonverbal behavior.
6. *Mutual trust.* Participants interact in ways that support the feelings of others as worthy persons, even at times of open disagreement.
7. *Voluntary participation.* Each person must accept responsibility for his or her own actions and for maintaining group conditions that support the personal integrity of the other participants[2].

A leader must help the team address any problems it experiences. Try to be as specific as possible when describing the weaknesses of your team. You may wish to study more about team dynamics and the stages that teams go through as they develop. The leader of a group needs to hone his or her skills in team leadership. For some, these skills seem to come naturally. For the rest of us, study, practice, and help from others are necessary and desirable.

WHEN SHOULD THE NEW SUPERVISOR TRY OUT THE TEAM CONCEPT?

Some new supervisors will discover that they have joined an organization that promotes and supports the team approach. In these organizations, supervisors should, like Dora, make the transition as soon as it is comfortable to do so. For those supervisors who join firms that have had little or no experience with teams (as is often the case in small companies), the traditional or pyramid approach is recommended. This environment does not mean, however, that one cannot build a working and productive team within the pyramid structure. Many innovative supervisors have discovered that the difference between a department and a team is primarily the kind of leadership provided. You can be called a supervisor by an organization and still develop and lead a most effective team even though you receive little help and encouragement from above. If your style of supervision favors the team concept, move with confidence in that direction.

PERFORMANCE **CHECKLIST**

1. Today's business climate mandates a significant change in the way employees are organized from a traditional pyramid structure to a more circular team-based structure. Similarly, today's manager must be prepared to change management style from an approach where he or she directs all employee functions and controls decision making to one where he or she acts as a "boundary manager" and facilitates team processes and decision making.

2. A *team* generally refers to "a small task group in which the members have a common purpose, interdependent roles, and complementary skills." Not all working groups are teams, nor are they required to be depending on the organizational structure and nature of the work for which the group is responsible. Either way, the supervisor must be sensitive to the individual needs of group members and how to get the best results out of them, as appropriate, to achieve organizational goals.

3. A supervisor can become an effective team leader by delegating more authority and responsibility to team members, encouraging risk taking and experimentation, developing a shared vision among team members, setting the stage for team problem solving, inviting self-expression and open discussion, and running regular team meetings in order to accomplish these activities.

4. A team leader of a culturally diverse team is challenged to balance between acculturating new or "different" team members to group norms and expectations and accommodating them to ensure their ideas, perspectives, and contributions are fully incorporated into team efforts to achieve synergy and team success.

5. Team members fill one of three roles during team meetings: (1) The team leader ensures that tasks are properly assigned and completed, opportunities for team participation and free expression are realized, team conflicts are managed, and team concerns are communicated to upper management. (2) The team recorder maintains documentation of team meetings and decisions and clarifies ideas and statements raised by team members as necessary to ensure they are captured for future implementation. (3) The team observer serves as a mirror and observes team behaviors and processes and reports on them, when requested, to provide input on how the team is progressing and how it should change to improve team function.

6. Seven normative conditions must be present for a team to function effectively: (1) shared planning; (2) shared decision making through consensus; (3) shared leadership; (4) shared evaluation; (5) two-way communication; (6) mutual trust; and (7) voluntary participation.

TEST **YOURSELF**

For each of the following statements, check true or false.

True   False

____   ____   1. When a team is successful, members are usually more motivated than workers operating under traditional formulas.

____   ____   2. Almost all supervisors can be trained as effective team leaders.

____   ____   3. The term *empowerment* means to give an individual more authority to operate alone.

____   ____   4. Under ideal situations, team members discipline themselves.

____   ____   5. There is usually more communication under the pyramid plan of supervision.

____   ____   6. *Acculturation* means to incorporate the ideas and perspectives of employees from different cultures to change and improve team practices to achieve better results.

____   ____   7. A *team boundary* is the sphere of responsibility or work area of the team.

____   ____   8. A boundary manager is needed when a problem transcends the team's boundary.

____   ____   9. Personal involvement in decision making can produce higher levels of both quantity and quality. As a result, everyone benefits.

____   ____   10. Learning from one another is an essential component to team membership.

Turn to the back of the book to check your answers.

Total Correct _____

DISCUSSION **QUESTIONS**

1. What are some of the advantages and disadvantages to organizing employees into teams?

2. How might you implement the seven normative conditions for effective teams?

3. What are the primary benefits of a culturally diverse team and what are the challenges that such a team might face?

4. What can a work team do to create synergy?

5. Which of the following seems more challenging to you?
   a. Acculturating new team members to team norms and expectations.
   b. Accommodating team members and their ideas and perspectives, especially when they will lead to positive changes in the way the team functions.

Defend your answer.

CASE 1: **PYRAMID VS. CIRCLE**

OBJECTIVE

To assist students in evaluating the advantages of the traditional style of supervision versus the team approach.

PROBLEM

Although he is patient, Bill would like Gerald to move toward a team-based approach to managing his team from what has mostly been a traditional, pyramid approach. At a recent meeting with his supervisors, he again raised this issue with Gerald and asked what progress he was making toward changing his approach. Gerald was a little defensive about Bill's inquiry, though it wasn't Bill's intention to make Gerald un-

comfortable. Instead, Bill invited Gerald, Yolanda, and Ricardo to engage in discussion with him about these two approaches to ensure all perspectives on the issue were fully considered and, Bill hoped, so that Gerald might see the wisdom of moving toward a team-based approach. To make the discussion even more interesting and to demonstrate his full understanding of Gerald's struggle, Bill joined Gerald in his arguments for a pyramid structure against Ricardo and Yolanda's arguments for a team-based structure.

PROCEDURE

Split the class in half. Assign half the class to continue Bill and Gerald's arguments for the traditional pyramid approach and half the class to continue Ricardo's and Yolanda's arguments for a team approach. Each half of the class must convince the other of the superiority of either the traditional or team approach to organizing employees. Allow for open discussion and debate.

CASE DISCUSSION AND QUESTIONS

Both sides should focus on how the traditional approach or team approach relates to the following:

1. Employee motivation and empowerment
2. Quality and quantity of work
3. Supervisory responsibilities and challenges
4. Culturally diverse work force
5. The organization's views about worker involvement in general

After full discussion, did the class come to any definitive conclusions regarding which approach was best? If so, which approach was preferred, and what factors swayed the group to prefer it? If not, why not? Are there circumstances by which one approach is clearly superior even if the other approach is best in most other circumstances?

CASE 2: ACCULTURATE VS. ACCOMMODATE

In a team meeting, Ricardo asked Karl about his progress in updating the month's inventory control records. Karl responds that he is a little behind this month because he is having difficulty assembling the spreadsheet from the multiple sources of data he must collect. After some discussion, Ricardo learns that although the final spreadsheet Karl prepares is in electronic form, the process of compiling data is essentially an outdated manual process.

Before Ricardo has a chance to inquire about how Karl might work to change his process so that it is easier to prepare and more useful to others, Julie blurts, "I could set up an automated process in my sleep." Before Ricardo has a chance to inquire further, Julie continues, "Give me access to your databases and your system, and give me a break from some of this grunt work you keep assigning me, and I can have an inventory control system up and running in no time."

Annoyed, Karl responds, "What do you know about this process?" He then proceeds with a lengthy

description of the elaborate steps he must go through to collect and assemble data so it is presented in a meaningful format. Julie appears not to listen and finally says, "It's so silly. Whatever. I'm just a part-timer. Makes no difference to me." Karl fumes quietly.

Although he can't justify Julie's curt tone, Ricardo wonders if perhaps she can offer some solutions that would make the process more efficient and also benefit Karl in his work. At the same time, it is evident that Karl takes a lot of pride in the way he does his work and isn't at all receptive to working with an upstart like Julie.

Considering this scenario and the role profiles for Karl and Julie, how should Ricardo manage the balance in the continuum between acculturation and accommodation with respect to Julie? To the extent you feel accommodation is due Julie and that she should be utilized to assist in the project, how would you work with her and Karl to implement the changes Julie proposed? What techniques would you use?

MULTICULTURAL EXERCISE

Assume you are a successful team leader in an organization of your choice. Further assume that, with your approval, a new employee from a different culture (also of your choice) is being assigned to your team. Although

highly qualified to be a team member, this individual has some problems with the English language. List at least five steps you would take to assist the person in becoming a fully accepted, high contributor to your team.

PERSONAL GROWTH EXERCISE

Who do you know in your work or personal life from a different culture or who is simply different and doesn't fit within the majority culture or norm to which you belong? Get to know this person a little

better. Learn the struggles this individual has in understanding the majority culture and provide constructive suggestions that will help her or him better acculturate.

TO LEARN **MORE**

For more information on diversity and managing diversity, refer to these resources:

Gardenswartz, Lee and Anita Rowe. *The Managing Diversity Survival Guide: A Complete Collection of Checklists, Activities and Tips.* Boston: McGraw-Hill, 1994.

Thomas, R. Roosevelt, Jr. *Building a House for Diversity.* New York: AMACOM, 1999.

For more information on teams and leading and facilitating teams, refer to these resources:

Katzenbach, Jon R. and Douglas K. Smith. *Wisdom of Teams: Creating the High Performance Organization.* New York: HarperCollins, 1999.

Rees, Fran. *How to Lead Work Teams: Facilitation Skills,* 2nd ed. San Francisco: Jossey-Bass/Pfeiffer, 2001.

Wagner, Richard G. and John D. Farrell. *Manager as Facilitator: A Practical Guide to Getting Work Done in a Changing Workplace.* San Francisco: Berrett-Koehler Publishers, Inc., 1997.

NOTES

1. Gary Yukl, *Leadership in Organizations,* 6th ed. Upper Saddle River, NJ: Pearson Education, 2006, p. 319

2. Adapted from John McKinley, *Group Development through Participation Training.* New York: Paulist Press, 1978.

chapter **nine**

COMMUNICATING PRIVATELY

"It is the province of knowledge to speak, and it is the privilege of wisdom to listen."

Oliver Wendell Holmes

PERFORMANCE COMPETENCIES

After you have finished reading this chapter, you should be able to:

- List and explain the "Five R's" of private communications

- List and describe five steps for using the right approach when engaging an employee in a private communication

- Explain the difference between directive and non-directive communication techniques and when and how to use each

- List and describe eight techniques to use to achieve effective private communication

- Describe the Mutual Reward Theory as it applies to motivation

"**I**t's a mistake to try to teach the first-line supervisor to be a counselor," said Barbara Crane. "Counseling is for professionals only. In the hands of the regular supervisor, it could do more harm than good. Besides, the word counseling *has a negative connotation. It sounds so psychological that it scares beginning supervisors off."*

"I agree, Barbara," replied William Carroll, the director of human resources. "Although the words counseling and private communications can often be used interchangeably, we should reserve the word counseling for performance problems and disciplinary situations. It would be best to call all other one-on-one sessions communicating privately. The difference is important because in normal private communications, open, positive feedback should be encouraged."

The authors support Mr. Carroll's view. But whether you are talking about counseling, interviewing, advice giving, guiding, or coaching, communication is a major tool in your survival kit.

The supervisor is charged with the responsibility of keeping all relationships with employees healthy and productive. The best method for supporting and improving relationships is to have a sound program of preventive maintenance based on good communication, fair treatment, and other widely accepted human relations practices. But no matter how good the maintenance program may be, any given relationship can become strained, hostile, indifferent, hurt, out of balance, or weak. If it does, the supervisor must diagnose the problem, prescribe the solution, and handle it as a team leader. The best remedy for a poor supervisor–employee relationship is counseling or talking things over. Private communication, initiated and conducted skillfully, can strengthen a weak relationship when nothing else works.

WHAT IS INVOLVED IN PRIVATE COMMUNICATION?

Private communication is a controlled, two-way conversation under optimum conditions. It involves sitting down in some private place and getting job problems out in the open by talking, listening, and trying to understand the other person's point of view while avoiding actions and statements that are hurtful. It involves working out solutions that people can accept. The structure of private sessions varies widely. Sometimes a long heart-to-heart talk is needed to clear the air. Sometimes a quick exchange will clear up a misunderstanding. Perhaps the supervisor does most of the talking; the next time, it may be the other way around. Private communication is more than a casual discussion resulting from an accidental encounter. It is a serious, two-way communication initiated by either the employee or the supervisor to deal with a problem or goal. The purpose is to increase productivity by solving problems and strengthening or repairing working relationships. It is not designed to solve personal or psychological problems. As a supervisor, you are not a psychiatrist, a psychologist, or a professional counselor, but you can counsel employees in your department in order to create and maintain relationships affecting departmental productivity. All other kinds of counseling should be left to licensed professionals.

Private communication usually takes place under one of two circumstances: (1) when the employee voluntarily comes to the supervisor with a suggestion, problem, or grievance; or (2) when the supervisor intervenes to motivate an employee, correct a problem, or forestall a grievance.

The supervisor has the advantage when the employee initiates the discussion. For one thing, it means the open-door policy is working and confidence has been established. Even when the employee approaches in a hostile mood, the supervisor should welcome the communication because talking things over may be the only

safety valve available. Most of the time, employees will approach the supervisor without hostility. The climate will then be relaxed and nonthreatening to both parties. These off-the-cuff sessions can do much to strengthen relationships further. The more the employee initiates counseling, the better.

Most of the time, however, the supervisor must initiate the process. Intervention by the supervisor is necessary when situations develop that are hurting the productivity of the department. Naturally, private communication is a sensitive procedure. It takes a good sense of timing, a smooth approach, and enough personal confidence to get things started. Because of this need for sensitivity, private conversations do not occur as often as they should due to supervisors' reluctance to raise such matters with employees. The following statements express the problem:

> It's like dynamite to move in on some of these sticky human problems. No, thanks. If time can't solve 'em, don't expect me to.

> I'm always available to talk things over with the employees in my department if they come to me, but I'm not going to rock the boat by going to them and stirring up more trouble. It's hard enough to keep the lid on this department the way it is.

> I work so closely with my people that I communicate constantly on an informal stand-up basis. If I called someone into my office and closed the door, he'd be too scared to talk.

For obvious reasons, many supervisors avoid private communication even when they know that communicating in this manner might avoid problems (or resolve them before they escalate) and increase departmental productivity.

THE FIVE R's OF PRIVATE COMMUNICATION

The purpose of this chapter is to dissipate your fears about private communication and demonstrate that you can and should use the technique frequently and comfortably. It requires no magic. You can start right away without fear or misgivings if you understand and use the following principles. They are known as the five R's of private communication:

> The Right purpose, the Right time, the Right place, the Right approach, and the Right technique.

Once you learn these principles, private communication will become one of your most important supervisory tools.

The Right Purpose

Private communication as presented in this chapter should be used only for the specific purposes presented in the following list. The supervisor must not exploit the techniques to pry into employees' lives or for other non-business purposes.

1. *To strengthen, maintain, or restore a working relationship between you and one of your employees.*   The primary job of the supervisor is to keep relationships healthy, and private communication is the best tool for this task. It should be used, however, only when the break in the relationship has caused a drop in productivity. Let's look at Karl as an example.

Ricardo asked Karl to work overtime on Friday night. In the process, Karl was not given a chance to reply that he had promised to take his son to a scholarship banquet. Afterward, Karl said nothing, but his attitude changed and his productivity dropped. In talking privately with Karl, Ricardo was able to find out what was wrong, apologize, and restore the relationship.

2. *To motivate employees to achieve greater productivity.*   Private communication can sometimes help a new employee bring productivity up to standard or help more experienced employees increase their productivity. In other words, employees can be motivated to improve through the counseling process. Ricardo's communication with Julie shows how private communication can work to motivate.

   Julie had done an excellent job for four months as a part-time employee. Then she started arriving late, making mistakes, and otherwise interrupting the smooth operation of the department. Ricardo moved in with a fifteen-minute counseling session. He discovered that Julie had been so involved with a personal problem that she had lost sight of her goal, which was to earn enough money to finish college. As a result of the discussion with Ricardo, Julie was able to focus on her goal, and her part-time job became important again. Her productivity was soon back up to its normal level.

3. *To resolve personality conflicts.*   Working relationships between two employees in the same department can sometimes deteriorate, causing emotional conflicts and a drop in productivity. In order to protect both the department and other employees, it is sometimes wise for a supervisor to move in with counseling. The following incident is a case in point.

   Renee had made the mistake of badgering Giselle about her productivity, and Giselle had reacted by sulking and letting her productivity drop below standard.

Ricardo heard the rumble and invited Renee to talk it over. The basis for the approach was that he was responsible for Giselle's productivity and that Renee (because of her maturity and ability) should take the initiative (with Ricardo's help) to restore the injured relationship. The repair work took time and required much outside support from Ricardo, but this approach worked.

4. *To discipline or terminate an employee.*   Typically in an organization's disciplinary procedure, the first step is usually called a counseling session. Skillful counseling is the best possible tool to use in correcting employee violations of rules, procedures, or policies. It is a sensitive task to discipline others, but when it must be done, it requires a private setting to ensure that others do not overhear the discussion. Ricardo used this technique effectively to correct one bad habit and enabled Giselle to save face.

Giselle was socializing too much with other employees, overstaying her coffee breaks, and discussing non-business matters over the telephone with other employees. Ricardo was inclined to be tolerant until he noticed that her activities were affecting the productivity of others. Then he invited Giselle into what became a twenty-minute counseling session. Ricardo stated his concerns quickly, but was careful not to show any hostility. He also gave Giselle a chance to defend some of her actions. The period ended with a positive exchange by both parties. After two weeks, Ricardo was pleased with the way Giselle had curtailed her socializing.

Counseling is also the best approach when the supervisor must terminate someone. Companies are subject to federal EEOC laws and should adopt a disciplinary procedure. In cases where the company is accused of wrongful discharge or discrimination, the disciplinary procedure is reviewed by the courts. A company that does not have a fair and objective discipline policy that provides opportunities to correct conduct and performance problems before escalating the level of discipline (typically, oral warning, written warning, suspension, and termination) is flirting with a lawsuit. A counseling session involving termination is never easy, of course, but when handled properly, it can substantially help the employee, the supervisor, and the company.

Due to a cutback in staff, Bill was forced to terminate an employee some months ago. Pursuant to company policy, he had no choice but to terminate the employee with the least seniority. Rather than handle it on a cold, one-way basis, Bill took the time to discuss the situation at length with the employee in a counseling environment and then provided the individual with a good reference, as well as other assistance. The employee left the company in a better frame of mind, and, of course, Bill felt better too.

5. *Orientation.*   Orienting new employees is an excellent time to engage in private communication. Many supervisors set up a formal orientation period with new employees during the first day on the job, at the end of the first week, and at the end of the first month to help them adjust more fully and make it through the probationary period successfully. It is imperative that the supervisor orient a new employee. Turnover rates, job-related accidents, and satisfaction are strongly correlated to orientation. The better the orientation, the higher the satisfaction and the lower the turnover and

accidents will be. The supervisor should not delegate orientation to another employee nor assume that the company's human resources department has done the job. The supervisor is accountable for introducing new employees to co-workers; for showing them around; and for covering things such as where to eat, where the restrooms are located, when breaks are taken, starting and quitting times, when payday comes around, and so on. Company policies and procedures that affect the new employee's work should also be thoroughly covered during orientation. The supervisor should prepare an orientation manual containing pertinent information, frequently asked questions, and important phone numbers to call. The new employee can then refer to it as needed.

6. *To raise sensitive personal issues that affect job performance.* There is no easy way to call an employee's attention to the fact that she has a body odor issue, is wearing strong perfume that is bothering co-workers, or is wearing revealing clothing in violation of the dress code policy. Some issues, such as when you detect alcohol on an employee's breath, observe behavior suggesting alcohol or drug abuse, or observe lapses in an older worker's mental or physical capabilities, implicate legal concerns if not raised in the appropriate manner. Yet, these issues must be addressed in order to support the employee and, in some instances, lead the employee to seek professional help. Again, as the supervisor, you cannot play counselor or render a diagnosis, but you can address observed job-related behavior that impacts performance.

   One day, Bill observed Justin coming back from lunch and appearing shaky and slurring his speech. On two additional occasions, he detected the smell of alcohol on Justin's breath when he came into work in the morning. A co-worker also mentioned this concern to Bill. Though Bill strongly suspected that Justin had an alcohol abuse problem, it was not his purview to render such an opinion. However, Justin's behavior did impact his performance. After consultation with the HR department, Bill met privately with Justin to state the facts as he observed them. He stated how the matter was affecting Justin's work. He also offered his personal assistance to Justin if he thought it might be helpful. Finally, he provided Justin information regarding the company's confidential employee assistance program.

The Right Time

Because private communication is always a sensitive process, the timing (usually under the control of the supervisor) is vitally important to a successful outcome. If the timing is right, the results can be excellent. If the timing is wrong, little may be accomplished. Here are four suggestions that should help you choose the right time.

1. Do not intervene until you are sure it is necessary. Every employee has a few bad days or a temporary struggle with his or her attitude. Use private communication only after an employee's productivity has shown a downward trend over a period of time. You do not want to jump too early nor allow too long a time to elapse before confronting the situation. Premature intervention can do more harm than good.

2. Do not initiate a counseling period when you yourself are upset, frustrated, or angry. Counseling is a two-way affair, and if you use that opportunity to get rid of some inner hostility, it will kill any chance of a successful session.

3. Remember that certain times of the day are not conducive to counseling. Peak activity periods, just before lunch, and just before the end of the day (when employees may be anxious to get home or meet appointments) are not the most suitable. Also, try to avoid periods when the employee may be upset emotionally, unless the cause of the upset is the reason for the counseling.

4. Do not set up a private communication session too far in advance. If you invite an employee to meet you in your office at 2:00 P.M. when it is only 10:00 A.M., he or she has four hours to worry and get upset and probably will produce at a lower rate. In almost all cases, it is better to set a time with either a short gap or none at all.

The Right Place

Having the right place for private communication can be more important than you think. It is almost impossible to do successful stand-up counseling or to accomplish much in a noisy place with frequent distractions. The ideal situation, of course, is a private office. Some supervisors, however, must settle for less. One solution is coffee-break counseling, provided that outsiders are not around and do not interfere. Another alternative is to make arrangements to use somebody else's office or a vacant room.

The Right Approach

The major reason supervisors avoid counseling employees regarding their problems is that they are afraid of the first hurdle, the approach. They think about it and plan it, but not knowing how to take the first step prevents them from executing their plans. At least four primary fears cause this hesitation:

1. Fear of saying the wrong thing at the beginning, thereby causing an unpleasant confrontation.
2. Fear of invading the employee's privacy.
3. Fear of opening up a hornet's nest of other problems.
4. Fear of being disliked by the employee.

Most of these fears are not substantiated by fact. Employees like to talk to their supervisors, even about unpleasant matters. Employees do not always resent being disciplined, if it is done in the right way, and often admit that help was needed, even though they would not ask for it.

To get past these fears, supervisors need a formula or procedure to follow. The following procedure is suggested if you have a difficult employee problem to face:

1. Invite the person into your office or other designated place without advance notice, eliminating time to build fears and create a threatening climate. Maintain a calm, pleasant, subdued voice throughout your meeting.
2. Start the conversation quickly, and do not beat around the bush. Try saying something like this: "We have something important to talk about; we will

both benefit if we get at it," or "I know this issue has concerned both of us; wouldn't you agree it is best to get it out in the open?"

3. State facts as you know or have observed them. Do not make accusations or label behavior ("You're lazy," "Your work is substandard," etc.). Rather, draw your assumptions and conclusions based solely on the facts you have presented.

4. Invite the employee to offer alternative explanations for the concerns you raised and/or to offer solutions that will address these concerns. Encourage the employee to talk. Do not rush.

5. State how you would like to help the employee address the concern and the desired change you wish to see. Explain why this change is important to you, the employee, the team, and so forth. (Note: The intensity with which you insist on change and encourage the employee to participate in finding solutions will depend on the issues involved and the technique you use, as described in the next section.)

As you develop your own formula, one that fits your personality, you will find that it is not difficult to launch even a potentially unpleasant session.

The Right Technique

The two basic types of private communication are directive and nondirective. Using the directive technique, the supervisor does most of the talking and draws a rather firm line on the direction the interview will take. Although the supervisor should use this approach in a gentle and quiet manner (constructive private communication ends when an argument begins), the employee should sense that advice or direction is being given. Generally, the message sent with directive communication is that the employee must change his or her behavior, either to start doing something to improve performance or to stop doing something because it is inappropriate, non-productive, or offensive. Communication in these sessions is mostly from the supervisor to the employee. This technique is usually considered best for the following situations:

1. When a violation of company rules or policies has occurred.

2. When mistakes need to be corrected.

3. When employee hostility (toward you, others, or the company) has reached a stage where it can no longer be tolerated.

Nondirective private communication is essentially the opposite. The supervisor does less talking and encourages the employee to communicate more. It is a soft approach designed to bring hidden problems out into the open or to set a climate for free and constructive discussion on any matter important to the employee. The permissive, unstructured, or open type of counseling is often therapeutic and provides motivation for the employee. The employee should sense that you intend to be helpful and that it is not your wish to put him on the defensive. It is the only technique to use for positive communication when no problem exists; it is considered the best approach for the following situations:

1. When an employee appears to have lost her or his touch or positive attitude over a sustained period of time, resulting in lower productivity.

2. When you want to strengthen or restore a relationship.

3. When you feel you can motivate an employee to achieve greater productivity.

THE ART OF COMMUNICATING

In his book *The Art of Communicating,* Bert Decker lists nine behavioral skills that constitute the key elements of better interpersonal communication.[1] As you read through the list, notice how much more than voice is needed in effective communications.

> Eye communication
>
> Posture and movement
>
> Gestures and facial expressions
>
> Dress and appearance
>
> Voice and vocal variety
>
> Language, pauses, and non-words
>
> Listener involvement
>
> Using humor
>
> The natural self

THE NONDIRECTIVE TECHNIQUE

The Mutual Reward Theory (MRT) functions well when the rewards are sufficient and well balanced between supervisor and employee because both parties come out ahead. The employee gains rewards from the supervisor, and the supervisor receives high productivity and subsequent recognition from superiors. When such rewards are insufficient or out of balance, or the wrong rewards have been provided, MRT counseling may be the answer. When a supervisor takes time to sit down with an employee and work out a sound, reasonable reward exchange, improved motivation can be expected. This kind of resolution can happen best under the nondirective approach because the employee is more apt to state openly those rewards that are desired. The two cases that follow illustrate the technique and the approach.

Jerry had watched Mildred's productivity deteriorate for three months. In addition, her co-workers were now complaining that she was not carrying her part of the workload. Jerry called Mildred into his private office and in a quiet, non-directive manner said, "Mildred, there are certain rewards I can give you as an employee. There are also rewards you can give to me as your supervisor. Would you be willing to discuss them?" During the next forty minutes, they developed a practical reward exchange and outlined it on paper. Jerry was careful to agree to only those rewards that he could actually provide. He made certain that the rewards he requested from Mildred were reasonable. This arrangement turned out to be mutually rewarding. It was clear the following day that Mildred would quickly regain the motivation she had shown when she was first employed. By using MRT counseling, Jerry had rebuilt a relationship that improved productivity in his department.

Martin, a management trainee for a hotel chain, had been assigned to Sandra's department for thirty days as part of an extended training period. After he had been in the department two days, Sandra gave him a special assignment that involved some research and a written report. Although it was turned in on time, the report did not live up to Sandra's expectations or reflect Martin's high potential. Sandra decided to use the soft, laid-back approach of MRT counseling. After some small talk about a humorous incident that had occurred earlier in the day, Sandra said, "Martin, I realize you will be with me only for six more weeks, and I appreciate having you. I am a little concerned about your quality of work on the project you just completed. I want you to learn everything possible while you are here. Would you permit me to propose an arrangement whereby we both can benefit from your being in this department? For example, if you will write down three job-connected rewards you would like to receive from me this week, I will write down three rewards I would like to receive from you. We can then openly discuss them. Is it a deal?" Twenty minutes later they had carved out a reward exchange that was easy for Sandra to implement.

MRT conferences offer an unusual opportunity to the leader who is willing to sit down and forge a simple reward-exchange system with an employee. It could be the most motivating technique in your survival kit.

For most situations, it is more effective to use the nondirective approach more than the directive one. If you find you are not using the nondirective approach more often, you may be using counseling primarily to put out fires, instead of considering it as a way to strengthen relationships, increase productivity, and prevent problems from developing. Generally speaking, the more you use the nondirective technique, the less you will need the directive one.

Of course, the way you use either approach determines its effectiveness. Here are some techniques that will help in both situations:

1. A quiet voice is more effective and less threatening than a loud voice.
2. A good way to dissipate the employee's hostility is to let him or her talk it out first. Do not interrupt.
3. When the employee is talking (perhaps defending some action), listen instead of planning your rebuttal.
4. Periods of silence in an interview can help the employee do some important self-evaluation, so do not rush to break in on him or her.
5. Free and honest communication is restricted when a time limit is imposed or implied.
6. Because most abuse coming from employees is directed to the system, the organization, or themselves, do not take negative comments personally.
7. The resolution of a problem is not the only sign of a successful counseling period. The mere act of achieving two-way communication is worthwhile.
8. Attempt to end all sessions on a positive note and, if necessary, schedule a follow-up meeting.

LINK ALL PRIVATE COMMUNICATION TO INDIVIDUAL GOALS

For maximum effectiveness, all counseling sessions should be tied to the employee's goals. The supervisor may be required to help the employee reestablish previous goals or establish new ones.

Maggie, a registered nurse who supervised the maternity ward on the night shift, was having trouble with Melinda, a vocational nurse in charge of cleanup procedures. Melinda wanted to take over the RN's responsibilities instead of performing her own tasks. When Maggie discovered, through counseling, that Melinda was taking college courses leading to RN certification, she modified her approach. She agreed to give Melinda extra duties that would help in her advanced training, provided that she took care of her other, more mundane responsibilities first. This concession immediately improved the relationship.

Surveys made in large organizations show undisputed evidence that the further up the management ladder a person travels, the more time she or he must spend counseling others. Some company presidents spend up to 80 percent of their time in private communication with their executives. Without question, private communication is a tool the ambitious supervisor or team leader cannot ignore.

PERFORMANCE **CHECKLIST**

1. Private communication is a controlled, two-way conversation under optimum conditions. It involves sitting down in some private place and getting job problems out in the open by talking, listening, and trying to understand the other person's point of view while avoiding actions and statements that are hurtful. It involves working out solutions that people can accept.

2. The five R's of communicating privately are:
   a. The Right Purpose: The purpose must relate to job-related issues, such as to further develop your relationship with an employee, to motivate the employee to greater productivity, to resolve personality conflicts, to discipline or terminate the employee, to orient the employee to the department, or to raise highly sensitive personal issues that impact performance.
   b. The Right Time: A supervisor should engage in private communication only when he or she is sure that intervention is appropriate. The supervisor should also engage in such communications when he or she is not upset, frustrated, or angry with the employee. She should also be careful to choose the right time of day and to not give too much advance notice of the desire to communicate privately to minimize worry on the part of the employee.
   c. The Right Place: Generally, a private office or other private area is best to meet to engage in private communication where there are no outsiders around who may interfere.
   d. The Right Approach: The supervisor should invite the person to his or her office to discuss the matter in a calm, supportive manner; be upfront about the purpose of the meeting; state facts on which he or she relies to support her reason for meeting; invite the employee to offer alternative explanations for the issues that the supervisor raises or solutions on how to address the concern; and state the desired change he or she would like to see the employee make and why such change is important.
   e. The Right Technique:
      i. The directive private communication is intended for rules violations, clear mistakes that must be corrected and hostile behaviors that can no longer be tolerated. The directive style makes clear that there are matters that the employee must change with little or no leeway. It should be used less than the nondirective style.
      ii. Nondirective private communication is intended for conversations where the supervisor wants to help an employee return to a higher level of productivity, strengthen or restore a relationship with an employee, or help an employee regain a positive attitude that may explain a lower level of productivity over a period of time.

TEST **YOURSELF**

For each of the following statements, check true or false.

True   False

____ ____   1. It is a good idea to link all private communication to the goals of the individual being assisted.

____ ____   2. Mutual Rewards Theory (MRT) and private communication constitute the best approach to use in the repair of a broken relationship.

____ ____   3. *Private communication* is best defined as talking things over in a relaxed climate in which both parties express themselves freely.

____ ____   4. A supervisor is in a good position to counsel an employee on psychological problems.

____ ____   5. Private communication is most effective near the end of the working day.

____ ____   6. The directive technique is best when a company policy has been frequently violated.

____ ____   7. The nondirective technique is best to use in an attempt to motivate an employee.

____ ____   8. The five R's of private communication are the right purpose, the right time, the right place, the right approach, and the right technique.

____ ____   9. Disciplining an employee should be done in a private setting.

____ ____ 10. Use private communication as soon as an employee's productivity takes a down turn.

Turn to the back of the book to check your answers.

Total Correct____

DISCUSSION **QUESTIONS**

1. What additional reasons might explain why supervisors are reluctant to initiate private communication sessions with their employees? What would you suggest to a supervisor who has this problem?

2. Some management and personnel people claim that young supervisors today find it more diffi-cult to do counseling, especially for discipline or termination, than their older counterparts. Do you agree or disagree? Why?

3. Does frequent stand-up or informal communication between a supervisor and an employee eliminate the need for private communication? Build your case one way or the other.

CASE: **TECHNIQUE**

Ricardo is upset over the night watchman's written report (sent through Bill's office) accusing Julie of goofing off on the job and (on one occasion) of having a male friend at work with her. The situation is aggravated by the fact that Ricardo recently defended Julie in front of Bill, who had used her as an example when he suggested to Ricardo that he wasn't as firm with employees regarding certain performance issues as he should be. In checking further, Ricardo also discovers that the stockroom (one of Julie's responsibilities) is in poor condition. Ricardo concludes that Julie is taking advantage of him. He decides to have a serious talk with Julie this afternoon when she reports to work after her class at college. Ricardo is aware that Julie is highly sensitive, impatient, and sometimes explosive.

He also recognizes that Julie has been a productive employee in the past and has high potential. His problem is deciding between the two counseling techniques.

Technique 1: Directive private communication. Under this firm approach, Ricardo would force an unpleasant confrontation by laying all the cards on the table in a stiff warning designed to shake up Julie. It would leave no possibility of misinterpretation. Julie would know exactly where she stands, and the session would amount to a first warning that could lead to termination if Julie's behavior does not change.

Technique 2: Nondirective private communication. Under this softer approach, Ricardo would try to avoid an unpleasant confrontation by talking things over easily and quietly, so that in the end Julie would discipline herself. Ricardo would try to listen more than talk; he would be sensitive to Julie's explanation. In this manner, Ricardo would gain better results in the end and avoid harsh words that would be mutually disturbing.

Which technique would you use? Why? If you select an alternative approach or a combination of the two, defend your position.

TECHNIQUE ANALYSIS **EXERCISE**

Directive communication is usually best when the employee needs to receive a clear, unmistakable signal that he or she has violated the supervisor's discipline line and that similar behavior will not be tolerated in the future. Nondirective communication (a much softer approach) is usually best in all other cases of intervention. Listed below are ten hypothetical situations. Place a check under the technique you would use in each case.

TYPE OF COUNSELING SITUATION

Directive   Nondirective

Directive	Nondirective	
____	____	1. Employee comes to work intoxicated
____	____	2. Employee is repeatedly impolite to customers
____	____	3. Substantial drop in personal productivity
____	____	4. Employee absent two days without calling in
____	____	5. Worker has been creating disturbances that influence productivity of others
____	____	6. Employee is in violation of dress code
____	____	7. Employee is parking in wrong area repeatedly
____	____	8. Safety rule violation by employee endangers co-workers
____	____	9. Employee makes excessive personal telephone calls
____	____	10. Employee fails to report equipment damage that caused you embarrassment in front of your superior

To compare your answers with those of the authors, please turn to the back of the book.

PERSONAL GROWTH **EXERCISE**

Ask someone who's opinion you respect what they think makes someone an effective listener. You might consider asking (a) your spouse or significant other; (b) a fellow supervisor; (c) your boss; (d) your religious leader.

NOTE

1. Bert Decker, *The Art of Communicating: Achieving Interpersonal Impact in Business.* Menlow Park, CA: CRISP Publications, 1988.

chapter **ten**

THE PROBLEM EMPLOYEE

"Happy is he who has been able to learn the causes of things."

Virgil

Improving Productivity
Leading Teams
Communicating Effectively
Managing Conflict
Improving Performance
Managing Time
Benefiting from Change

PERFORMANCE COMPETENCIES

After you have finished reading this chapter, you should be able to:

- Describe four steps to take when facing disagreement or conflict

- Describe corrective and non-corrective interviews

- Describe typical forms of sexual harassment

- Explain five things to do when sexual harassment occurs

- Explain how to address typical difficult employee behavior situations, such as when an employee is not meeting standards, has a chemical dependency problem, or has the potential to become violent

A problem employee is one who repeatedly violates a departmental discipline line, frequently causes disturbances among other personnel, or lowers productivity through some form of unacceptable behavior. Sooner or later, every supervisor must deal with such an employee. Problem employees can quickly destroy the effectiveness of a team. Managers and team leaders do not have the luxury of letting time take care of such individuals and cannot sweep the problem under the carpet.

Private communication is the answer, and the techniques covered in Chapter 9 will come to your rescue. A skillful supervisor is often able to turn a problem employee into a superior employee by discovering the cause of the problem and coming up with the right answer. Sometimes, however, the best a supervisor can do is alleviate the problem so that everyone can live with it and productivity is not damaged. In some cases the only acceptable solution is to take corrective measures, which may end with the dismissal of the employee. Every case deserves individual analysis and treatment.

Diane, a single parent, was demonstrating an increasing amount of hostility toward her fellow employees—so much so that departmental productivity was measurably down. After two counseling sessions, the problem was narrowed down to an imbalance between home and career. Diane was unable to separate the two and, as a result, she was adding home problems to job demands. This behavior irritated coworkers, created customer complaints, and put unreasonable demands on her supervisor. Once the situation was isolated and discussed, Diane was able to discipline herself to achieve a better home–career balance. She was no longer a problem employee.

Chris was a classic example of how the frustration–aggression hypothesis can create a problem employee. A recent graduate from an MBA program, Chris had set excessively high career goals for himself.

As a result, he became frustrated over his slow progress; this frustration, in turn, resulted in aggressive behavior. For example, Chris would lose his patience in working with others and walk away in a huff. During staff meetings he would seek controversy and spill out his feelings. After two counseling sessions, Chris recognized his own problem and found employment in a new environment where his talents and education could be put to more immediate use.

A PROFESSIONAL PERSPECTIVE

What are some of the fundamental concepts involved? What are the mandated corrective steps? And, most important, how can you prepare now to handle such individuals?

First, you should keep the following five fundamentals in mind, so that you view the individual—and the problems he or she is creating—in professional perspective.

Expect Good Results

Have faith in your ability to resolve the problem and build a better relationship with the individual. You must initiate communication with the problem employee if the problem itself is to be dealt with openly and a solution reached. If you fear the process, you are already at a disadvantage.

Everyone Can Come Out Ahead

Accept the premise that you can find one solution that is best for the individual, you, and the organization. The only way you can achieve this elegant solution is through open, two-way communication. Your goal is to save the employee, keep him or her in your department, and convert the individual into a productive, cooperative member of your team. The more you anticipate good results, the more they are apt to occur.

The Nondirective Approach Is Usually Best

Recognize that heavy discipline at the beginning often intensifies an existing problem. Both you and the employee may have a tendency to be defensive. If you create a threatening climate, the employee may become emotional. The problem employee becomes more of a problem and a solution becomes impossible. Another reason a heavy hand at the beginning can backfire is that heavy discipline can, perhaps through misinterpretation, cause other employees to feel uncomfortable.

Waiting Is Usually a Mistake

The longer one waits to correct unacceptable behavior of a serious nature, the more explosive the situation may become. Most supervisors who delay taking action permit the behavior of the problem employee to get under their skin, where it festers until the supervisor can no longer deal with it objectively. The sooner you deal with a problem, the less emotional you will be. Waiting is often unfair to other employees who are working responsibly and perceive that the supervisor's inaction connotes acceptance of unacceptable behavior and allows the irresponsible co-worker to "get away with it."

Jason tolerated Rosemary's disruptive behavior for six weeks without saying a word. Each time she violated his discipline line, his dislike for her increased; each time she was insensitive to customers and co-workers, he became more frustrated. Finally, one morning he reached his tolerance level, invited her into his office, and exploded. The moment the interview was over, Jason knew he had made several mistakes. His relationship with Rosemary worsened, and he could not see any chance in the future to restore it. He had a guilty feeling about his behavior, and he knew it had hurt his relationships with her co-workers. He was ineffective for the rest of the day. As a result, Jason resolved to deal with such problems in the future as soon as they surfaced.

Protect Yourself

Accept the fact that a single problem employee can cause your downfall as a supervisor. The following case illustrates this fundamental.

Some co-workers did not think that Marge was ready for her promotion to operations officer of her busy savings and loan establishment. But management thought differently, and their confidence in her seemed justified, at least during the first months. A serious cloud appeared when Susan, a teller, became a problem. It started when Susan violated the acceptable dress code; it intensified when she became sullen with some customers; it became intolerable when it affected the productivity of others. Although Marge had no experience in handling such a situation, she knew she had only three alternatives. She could delay action, she could go to her boss, or she could initiate a one-on-one talk today. She decided on the last alternative and immediately called Susan into her office.

Marge was careful not to create a threatening climate. She did not overplay her hand, but she quickly led into the problem and made it clear that she was in charge and was going to stand her ground. Although she experienced some difficult moments, eventually some healthy two-way communications took place. Susan decided that the work environment in a savings and loan institution was not for her, and one week later she resigned. Susan departed without hostility, and Marge had solved her problem. From that moment on, all of her employees seemed to respect her more, and productivity increased. Best of all, management was most complimentary. Her immediate supervisor said, "We were monitoring the situation carefully and sensed that your future depended upon how you handled Susan. We are extremely pleased."

OBJECTIVITY REQUIRED

Even if you accept these fundamentals and practice them, solving employee problems will not be easy. Many, however, are less difficult than they appear. One reason is that an employee may become a problem in your eyes, but not in the opinion of others. The employee is irritating you, but not co-workers or other management personnel.

Roger had a solid reputation as a superior manager, but he became irritated with Tony, a management trainee, the first day Tony was assigned to his department.

Roger thought Tony was too aggressive. He immediately disciplined Tony in unfair, unprofessional ways—not his usual approach. Then, by chance, he overheard two of his regular employees defending Tony. Roger took stock of himself, admitted he had been unfair, and made a complete turnabout. As a result, he built an excellent relationship with Tony. What he had interpreted as aggressiveness was assertiveness that others appreciated.

Your discipline, or authority line, is essential for employees not only to respect you but also to keep their productivity at a high level. Discipline must be maintained at all costs. But the supervisor must be careful to treat all employees fairly and consistently. Maintaining productivity leaves no room for personal vendettas between a supervisor and an employee.

The supervisor must protect his or her discipline line in quiet, effective ways or eventually lose the respect of those who must live with it. To permit one employee to cross the line is to lose the respect of those who still honor it. When the supervisor loses authority, productivity can drop drastically.

Joel had been able to maintain a relaxed, comfortable discipline line for almost six months. Not a single employee was taking advantage of him. Then Victoria, who was having personal problems, started testing the line from all directions. She not only challenged traditional procedures she had previously honored, but she started to make complaints to Joel's boss. The conflict came to a head when she challenged Joel openly on a procedural matter in a staff meeting.

Joel initiated a long interview the following day to discuss her recent behavior in relationship to departmental productivity. The atmosphere was tense until, near the end of the interview, the conversation turned to Victoria's career goal, and Joel stated that he would like to help her reach it. Eventually, a kind of trade-off took place: Victoria promised to be more sensitive to Joel and to departmental objectives, and Joel agreed to do what he could to prepare her for her career goal without favoring her over others. The compatibility contract lasted until Victoria earned a promotion, six months later.

EXPLORATORY INTERVIEWS

The purpose of the exploratory interview is to lay the problem on the table in a nonthreatening manner. Both parties should have an equal chance to communicate; both old and new facts should be introduced; if possible, the roots of the problem should be revealed. Sometimes the exploratory interview can do it all. It offers the supervisor the opportunity to put forth her assumptions and conclusions based on the facts and observations as she understands them and give the employee the chance to address and clarify any misunderstandings and misinterpretations the supervisor may have made. After an open and frank dialogue to correct misunderstandings, the air is cleared and no further action may be necessary.

Sally took Jennifer out to lunch to discover, if possible, what was causing her hostility. She found a private place, made certain that the environment was relaxed, and then introduced the subject. The discussion that followed showed that Jennifer thought Sally had been unfair to her and that her resentment had created a barrier between them. As a result, she had violated the departmental discipline line to show her independence. When Sally convinced Jennifer that the unfair treatment had not been intended, they both agreed to start from scratch. The exploratory interview had solved the problem. No further action was necessary.

Construction superintendent Rich had received two reports that Betty, the woman who did cleanup work in the completed buildings, had violated safety regulations. He called her into his mobile office and quickly introduced the subject. It turned out that Betty was uninformed about the safety regulations and had not been aware that she was breaking them. When he received no further complaints, Rich figured the exploratory interview had corrected the problem.

If an employee's behavior is not appropriate, the reason may be caused by inadequate training. Be sure to check to see whether the employee knows how to perform correctly before taking disciplinary action.

CORRECTIVE INTERVIEWS

When the exploratory interview tells the supervisor that the problem is deeper than a basic misunderstanding, a follow-up is indicated. Such a follow-up can take one of two forms. In cases that show evidence that firm rules have been broken, the supervisor initiates a series of corrective interviews. In cases where the human relations problems are complex, one or more non-corrective follow-up discussions may be necessary to resolve the problem. The decision to conduct follow-up interviews can be made during the exploratory interview or later. The supervisor can discuss it with the employee in advance or use the wait-and-see approach. Each case requires individual analysis. Sometimes the exploratory interview is interpreted by the employee as a warning; sometimes it is not.

Assume that during an exploratory interview, you suspect that a problem employee is violating a rule, but you have no evidence. Later, however, you discover the evidence. At that point you set up Corrective Interview 1.

Corrective Interview 1.   The purpose of this first follow-up step is to verify the violation and warn the employee. *Verification* means critical documentation. Although required documentation varies among organizations, basically it

should include the following: (1) a specific description of the violation; (2) the name of the violator, the date it occurred, and the date of the corrective interview; and (3) the written acknowledgment or rebuttal of the employee. A corrective interview 1 is, in effect, a documented first warning.

Corrective Interview 2.   This interview need not take place unless a further violation is reported. If a second incident (even a different violation) is reported, the second interview should take place with the same documentation procedure. This meeting becomes a second warning.

Corrective Interview 3.   This interview is necessary only if a third violation occurs. The procedure will vary according to each organization (and legal counsel) but generally will include (1) a third person (upper management person, representative from the human resources department, or staff lawyer); (2) a review and presentation of previous documented warnings; and (3) notice of termination. Whatever the procedure, the supervisor should permit two-way communication and attempt to show the employee that he or she has been treated fairly. The rights of the employee must be protected at all costs.

Note that this is a typical progression that organizations use to correct employee behavior and performance problems. The precise process used for your organization should be outlined in its human resources policies. Consult your human resources department regarding the precise process to follow and for advice on how to proceed in a way that is consistent with these policies. When a procedure like the one described above is followed carefully, most employees will improve their performance or submit their resignation voluntarily before Corrective Interview 3 takes place. If not, then the groundwork has been laid to justify termination.

FACING DISAGREEMENT OR CONFLICT

As a supervisor, you may run into a conflict with an employee, a peer, or your own boss. Four steps will help guide you through such an experience so that the best solution is found and both you and the other party maintain a healthy relationship.

Step 1.   Don't put the other person down. It is important to preserve the integrity and self-respect of all parties. In a heated discussion, it is easy to say something demeaning. To avoid this trap, keep your focus on the issue, not the person.

Step 2.   Search for common ground. Try to see things from the other person's perspective so that you can discover a basis to resolve the matter. In order to better understand the other person's position, you must listen with empathy and be flexible.

Step 3.   Do not expect behavioral changes. The purpose of resolving conflicts is to find agreement on what must be done, not whether a behavioral change is required of you or the other party.

Step 4.   Compromise is not throwing in the towel. The goal is to find the best solution to improve productivity (reach agreed-on goals), not to discover who might be right or wrong. Thus a compromise—especially after an open discussion— can be the best solution for both parties and the company.

Agreeing to a compromise does not mean you have given up your individuality. It simply means you understand the situation.

NON-CORRECTIVE INTERVIEWS

Assume that during an exploratory interview you discover a deep-seated human relations problem. Perhaps a personality conflict between two co-workers is damaging productivity. Maybe one employee's attitude is so negative that it is hurting the productivity of others or causing customer complaints. Possibly a conflict has arisen between you and the problem employee. Situations of this nature call for one or two follow-up interviews.

Non-corrective Follow-up 1. A single exploratory interview will not solve most human relations problems. It takes time to dissipate misunderstandings and misinterpretations. When an exploratory interview reveals hostility between the supervisor and an employee, for example, the conflict may never be solved. But holding one or two follow-up interviews is more effective than trying once and giving up.

Jane was disturbed to discover that Carol was upset and hostile toward her. About all she was able to accomplish during the exploratory interview was to listen and let Carol get her inner anxieties and frustrations out in the open. Three days later Jane conducted a follow-up interview that was less volatile, with more of a two-way discussion. At this stage both individuals admitted to some mistakes and misinterpretations. The relationship was beginning to be rebuilt. Later Jane initiated a third interview in which mutual rewards were discussed. Eventually the relationship was fully restored, and all hostility dissipated.

Non-corrective Follow-up 2. As just illustrated, more than one follow-up interview is often necessary to solve a human relations problem. The process of restoration is not easy or fast. In most cases, some give-and-take is necessary to build a new foundation for mutual respect. Normally some behavioral changes must take place on both sides in the interim between interviews. The supervisor should not expect to be able to solve all human relations problems, but in most cases the combination of good exploratory techniques and one or more follow-up interviews is an excellent way to ensure harmony and high productivity in a department.

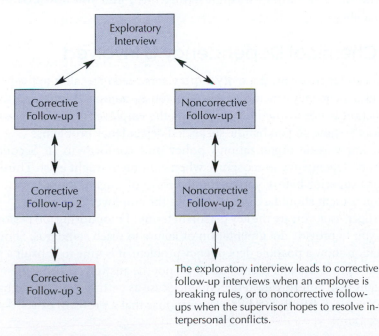

The exploratory interview leads to corrective follow-up interviews when an employee is breaking rules, or to noncorrective follow-ups when the supervisor hopes to resolve interpersonal conflicts.

SOLVING PROBLEMS: AN ONGOING PROCESS

Give the interview process a chance to work. Inexperienced supervisors sometimes become discouraged if they do not see immediate results. Resolving conflicts, helping others change their attitudes, and dissipating hostility take time. Remind yourself that although the process does not always work, it works often enough to be worth your effort. Even if you fail, you will have had the satisfaction of trying.

When Your Image Is Being Tested

Your image as a supervisor is important. A problem employee can cause a great deal of conversation both inside and outside your department. If you wind up with such an employee, you can rest assured that others will be watching how you respond. The non-problem employees on your staff will be watching even more closely than management. Studies show that most co-workers have a lower tolerance of problem employees than supervisors expect. Your employees want you to solve the problem to make life easier for them. Obviously, the supervisor who has enough leadership ability to solve the problem will enhance her or his image in all directions.

When the Employee Is Unable to Reach Standards

You may have to learn to live with certain low-level employees. You may discover one or more employees in your department who do not, and never will, live up to your expectations. These individuals do not influence the productivity of others or cross your discipline line, but they contribute less than other workers. For example, you may have a mature employee who has seniority but cannot adjust quickly to dramatic changes, or an employee who refuses to communicate but produces better than average work. Such employees can make your job as a supervisor more difficult, but they are not troublemakers.

Sometimes counseling will strengthen these employees; sometimes it won't. When you have done your best to change their behavior, you must continue to be positive with these employees without letting them pull you down or hurt your leadership ability.

When Chemical Dependency Is Involved

To maintain and increase productivity, supervisors need to be alert to the possibility of chemical dependency (including alcohol abuse) among employees. Tolerating abuse/addiction is not in the best interest of the employee, the supervisor, or the organization. So how do you handle suspected dependency problems?

First, know your organization's policy and conform to it. Second, learn enough about dependency to recognize when a problem might exist. Third, always consult your superior before you begin any form of intervention. Fourth, have a third person present should a discussion with the employee take place.

As a supervisor, you are the key person in terms of monitoring job performance. It is up to you to provide documentation of failure to reach standards. Should such documentation show a possible dependency problem, it is time to consult a superior and bring in a professional. Procrastination is not the answer.

It might help you to view a dependency case as getting around the bases in a ballgame. You reach first base when you recognize that a problem exists, document your observations, and schedule a discussion with the employee. You arrive at second base when you create an open atmosphere for the discussion of reasons for non-performance, and let it be known that you will support bona fide efforts to correct it.

You get to third base when the employee recognizes the jeopardy his or her job is in, takes responsibility for the problem, and commits to improving performance. You reach home plate (and score) when the employee seeks professional help from either internal or external sources and undertakes treatment.

Keep in mind that you are probably more important to your organization than the problem employee in question, so do not let the individual destroy you. It means you must deal with the employee in legal ways so that both you and the organization are protected. If you need backup assistance, do not hesitate to ask for advice and support from your supervisors. As a beginning supervisor, you are not supposed to know all the answers, so do not let personal pride keep you from seeking support. In dealing with problem employees, it can be a serious mistake to act prematurely on your own.

When Sexual Harassment Occurs

Sexual harassment is unwelcome behavior of a sexual nature that interferes with an individual's work performance or that creates an intimidating, hostile, or offensive working environment for the individual. In most cases, sexual harassment is more than a single incident. Rather, it is typically a deliberate pattern of severe and pervasive activity that occurs over a period of time.

Sexual harassment violates federal law under Title VII of the Civil Rights Act of 1964, as well as most state laws. Victims can be male or female, a manager or subordinate, a vendor or customer. Perpetrators can be male or female, and their victims can be of the same sex or the opposite sex. It is the responsibility of the supervisor or team leader to create and maintain a working environment where no form of harassment from any source is permitted. The following steps are recommended:

TYPICAL FORMS OF SEXUAL HARASSMENT

Verbal	Visual	Physical
Telling risqué jokes	Wearing suggestive clothing	Touching, making physical contact
Asking for sexual favors	Staring at someone's anatomy	Standing too close
Commenting on one's anatomy	Flirting	A too lengthy handshake or hug
Pursuing an unwanted relationship	Using vulgar hand gestures	
Giving compliments with sexual overtones	Displaying lewd or obscene pictures	

1. The topic of harassment should be discussed openly in a staff meeting, and the supervisor should describe the legal parameters of sexual harassment and encourage employees to come forward with complaints. If available, the supervisor should attend his or her company's sexual harassment training and arrange for similar training for all staff.

2. Upon receiving a complaint, the supervisor should listen and record the specific conditions under which the alleged harassment took place. He or she should make no conclusory statement about whether or not sexual harassment has occurred. Rather, the supervisor should assure the employee that the matter will be addressed and corrective action taken, if warranted.

3. The supervisor should then take up the matter with the director of human resources or another superior for verification and possible action. Typically, an HR representative or legal counsel will conduct an investigation. The supervisor should cooperate with this investigation, but should not conduct the investigation beyond obtaining basic information as described above.

4. In counseling an individual who may be guilty of sexual harassment, the supervisor is advised to have a third-party specialist present. Unless there is a concern that the alleged offender may engage in similar acts before the investigation is complete, such counseling should not occur any earlier. The supervisor should consult with the appropriate organizational authorities before counseling the individual and instituting any discipline.

5. The individual who initiated the complaint should be advised on the action taken and encouraged to return should any further harassment occur.

Beyond these basic steps, the supervisor should become fully apprised of his or her organization's policies and procedures for responding to sexual harassment and consult with HR or legal counsel whenever an incident of possible sexual harassment has occurred.

When Concerns about Workplace Violence Are Raised

Concerns about workplace violence occur when there is a threat, expressed or implied, that causes an individual to be reasonably apprehensive that harm to his or her health or safety is about to occur, or when physical force or violence has occurred that has caused such harm to a person's health or safety. Clearly, in the latter circumstance, there is no question that a supervisor, with the full support of the organization (security personnel, HR, legal counsel, etc.) must act quickly to respond to eliminate the possibility of further harm. Termination is generally the outcome of such actions, though criminal action against the perpetrator is also possible.

Yet, a supervisor must be vigilant when an employee makes comments or takes actions that may be interpreted as threatening and potentially violent. The supervisor cannot wait for these behaviors to result in violent action and must, with the advice and support of appropriate authorities, address the situation with the offending employee. While discipline may be recommended, meeting with the employee may also present an opportunity, as appropriate under the circumstances, to surface any personal problems the employee is experiencing so that he or she can be directed to seek professional help.

When a Reduction in Staff Is Mandated

Sometimes a non-problem employee must be released because of a cutback in personnel. In such cases, the supervisor must work closely with the department of human resources to make certain that no age or other type of discrimination is involved. Releasing a good employee may be the most difficult action a supervisor must take. Everything possible should be done to assist the individual in finding another position of equal or higher status.

This chapter has been designed to give you the confidence, techniques, and procedures that will help you either prevent employee problems or handle them gracefully and legally when they emerge. If you can handle problem employees effectively without continually turning to your superiors for help, you will not become their problem employee.

PERFORMANCE **CHECKLIST**

1. A skillful supervisor is often able to turn a problem employee into a superior employee by discovering the cause of the problem and coming up with the right answer. Sometimes, however, the only acceptable solution is to take corrective measures, which may end with the dismissal of the employee. Every case deserves individual analysis and treatment.

2. When preparing to address a problem employee and take corrective action, the supervisor should take into consideration these fundamentals: (1) expect good results; (2) everyone can come out ahead; (3) the non-directive communication approach is usually best; (4) waiting to raise the concern is usually a mistake; and (5) take measures to protect yourself when addressing problem employees.

3. Absolute objectivity is required when addressing a problem employee with corrective action.

Therefore, a supervisor must ensure his or her approach is consistent with what he or she would do in similar circumstances with other employees. He or she must ensure that emotion and bias do not come into play and that he or she understands the employee's perspective fully before pursuing corrective action.

4. Often an exploratory interview with a problem employee is all that is needed to clarify any misunderstandings the supervisor may have about performance problems and to give the employee the opportunity to fully explain and clarify these misunderstandings. Once the air is cleared, no further action may be required.

5. If further action is required after the exploratory interview, the supervisor must then engage in up to three corrective interviews: (1) to verify the violation, warn the employee, and document the concern, which becomes the first warning; (2) if a

second incident occurs, to engage in a similar process as the first interview and document the meeting as a second warning; and (3) if a third violation occurs, to proceed to a notice of termination or allow the employee to resign in lieu of termination. The precise process utilized by the supervisor's organization may vary somewhat from this process; the supervisor should become familiar with these policies and consult with the HR department to ensure he or she follows the process correctly.

6. Often, non-corrective exploratory interviews involving deep-seated human relations problems will require follow-up interviews until matters have been fully addressed and resolved.

7. Utilizing exploratory and corrective and non-corrective interviews to address employee problems is an ongoing process and is especially useful when your image as a supervisor is being tested, an employee is unable to reach standards, chemical dependency is involved, a reduction in staff is mandated, or sexual harassment or workplace violence concerns arise.

TEST **YOURSELF**

For each of the following statements, check true or false.

True   False

1. Private communication is the best practical tool a supervisor can use in dealing with a problem employee.

2. The fears some supervisors have of initiating private communication with problem employees are fully justified.

3. If the supervisor takes no action, a problem employee can cause that supervisor's downfall.

4. After an exploratory interview in which corrective counseling is initiated, termination should occur immediately.

5. Agreeing to a compromise means giving up some of your individuality.

6. Studies show that co-workers have a lower tolerance (less patience) for problem employees than most supervisors imagine.

7. An employee who consistently produces less than others is a problem employee.

8. Tolerating abuses/addiction is not in the best interest of the employee, the supervisor, or the organization.

9. Supervisors who adjust their discipline lines to accommodate problem employees are usually successful.

10. If an employee's behavior is not appropriate, the cause may be inadequate training.

Turn to the back of the book to check your answers.

Total Correct _____

DISCUSSION **QUESTIONS**

1. In what specific ways might a new supervisor build sufficient personal confidence to deal with a problem employee on a one-on-one basis?

2. Assuming that the supervisor is a skillful communicator, what odds would you give counseling to convert a problem employee into a superior one? (a) Greater than 50 percent; (b) 50 percent; (c) Less than 50 percent. Defend your answer.

3. If a problem employee resigns voluntarily between corrective private communication sessions 1 and 2, has the attempt failed? Explain your views.

4. What are some forms of sexual harassment that have taken place in your workplace? How have they been handled? In your view, were they handled effectively? Why or why not?

CASE: **CONFRONTATION**

OBJECTIVE

To evaluate the nature of conflicts between traditional supervisors and assertive employees.

PROBLEM

The relationship between Ricardo and Renee has deteriorated. Renee is hostile, taking potshots at Ricardo in conversations with co-workers, openly confronting him in staff meetings, and generally being disruptive. The situation is hurting the productivity of the department and rendering Ricardo ineffective. Readers not involved in role-playing should study and evaluate the conflict between Ricardo and Renee located in the Role Profiles section in the back of this book, as well as the additional information that follows.

PLAYERS

Ricardo and Renee.

PROCEDURE

The players should read and become familiar with the additional information regarding Ricardo and Renee, as well as re-familiarize themselves with the Role Profiles section in the back of the book. The players rehearse their own roles over and over, until they are deeply into the characterization. Neither party is to communicate with the other. Renee is to enter Ricardo's office determined to come out ahead; Ricardo is equally determined to resolve the problem to his satisfaction. After a ten-minute confrontation—no holds barred—both individuals are to relax and switch roles, each playing the other.

ROLE OF RICARDO

You are disturbed by Renee's hostility. You recognize that she is extremely capable and a high producer. You recognize that she may become a supervisor eventually, but first you feel she should "pay her dues." She is criticizing you before your superiors and showing disrespect for you and your position among co-workers. You recall a constructive talk with her sixty days ago when you stated that you would give her the training she needs to become a supervisor, which you feel you have done. You do not feel her impatience is justified. In the next few minutes, you intend to listen carefully and keep an open mind, but under no circumstances will you bend your discipline line. You would be happy if Renee moved to another firm.

ROLE OF RENEE

You feel your assertiveness is justified because Ricardo has you boxed in. He refuses to recommend you for a higher position outside his department. He does not appreciate your high productivity and generally fails to understand you. You recall a meeting sixty days ago when he promised to help you win a promotion to supervisor in another department. He has not fulfilled this promise. He seems to feel you should "pay a price" to him before he will go to bat for you. You have no intention of being subservient. Because you have an outstanding record within the department, you feel that any pressure you put on Ricardo is justified. As you enter his office, you intend to listen and keep an open mind, but if Ricardo doesn't handle things to your satisfaction, you intend to resign on the spot.

CASE DISCUSSION AND QUESTIONS

Discuss the nature of such conflicts and the possibility of dissipating them through the interview process. What might Ricardo have done differently to eliminate the problem in the first place? Is Renee justified in her assertiveness? What might she have done differently to get the result she desired?

MUTUAL REWARD THEORY (MRT) **EXERCISE**

MRT guidance occurs when the supervisor sits down with an employee and explores, in a non-directive manner, the reward exchange between the two people. If rewards can be balanced so that both people get the primary rewards they desire, the problem employee can become a reliable, high-producing worker. Although MRT is not a surefire solution to all employee problems, it frequently works and may be the best tool available to the supervisor.

Assume that you have a problem employee who has been violating your discipline line in subtle ways, creating disturbances that affect the productivity of his co-workers; and showing hostility toward you. You invite this individual to sit down with you and write out three rewards he or she would like to get from the job. The individual writes the following:

1. Give me more responsibility so I can learn more.
2. Help me get a promotion when I demonstrate I am ready.
3. Get off my back.

1. Which of the requested rewards will you agree to provide? 1. _____ 2. _____ 3. _____

2. What rewards will you want in exchange? 1. _____ 2. _____ 3. _____

3. If an agreement is reached, what follow-up arrangements will you insist on?

4. How do you rate your chances for success? No chance _____ 50 percent chance _____ Excellent chance _____

5. How would you react to MRT counseling if you were a problem employee, and the technique was used in a skillful manner by your superior?

6. As a supervisor, do you feel you have the right to initiate the MRT idea with your superior in an attempt to gain a better reward exchange so that both parties can come out ahead? Explain your answer. Compare your answers with those of the authors in the back of this book.

PERSONAL GROWTH **EXERCISE**

Identify a bad habit you have that potentially affects your performance at work and that you wish to change. Identify three possible things you can do to change or eliminate the bad habit. If your supervisor were to approach you to discuss this bad habit and offer support, would you be receptive or resistant? What approach would he or she need to take so that you would be receptive? If you are comfortable, discuss this issue with your supervisor for the purpose of eliciting his or her support to address the bad habit in order to improve your performance.

TO LEARN **MORE**

To learn more about approaches to confronting individuals in supportive ways to bring change in behaviors and relationships, refer to the following resources:

Goodwin, Cliff, and Daniel B. Griffith. *The Conflict Survival Kit: Tools for Resolving Conflict at Work*. Upper Saddle River, NJ: Pearson Education, 2007.

Pachter, Barbara. *The Power of Positive Confrontation: The Skills You Need to Know to Handle Conflict at Work, Home, and in Life*. New York: Marlowe and Company, 2000.

Patterson, Kerry, Joseph Grenny, Ron McMillan, and Al Switzler. *Crucial Confrontations: Tools for Resolving Broken Promises, Violated Expectations, and Bad Behaviors*. New York: McGraw-Hill, 2005.

Patterson, Kerry, Joseph Grenny, Ron McMillan, and Al Switzler. *Crucial Conversations: Tools for Talking When Stakes Are High*. New York: McGraw-Hill, 2002.

Stone, Douglas, Bruce Patton, and Sheila Heen. *Difficult Conversations: How to Discuss What Matters Most*. New York: Viking, 1999.

chapter **eleven**

STAFFING

"Team players are the leaders of tomorrow."

Dale Carnegie

Improving Productivity

Leading Teams

Communicating Effectively

Managing Conflict

Improving Performance

Managing Time

Benefiting from Change

A s a new supervisor, Virginia set out to hire a qualified replacement for an employee who had left. Without any background in interviewing, Virginia selected an individual with a persuasive personality but also with psychological problems. Further investigation would have revealed that the applicant had been a problem employee in all of her previous jobs. Virginia lived with the situation for six months. Finally, after the conflicts created by the situation rendered the new employee so ineffective that Virginia's own job was on the line, the individual resigned on a voluntary basis after a serious discussion with Virginia regarding the likelihood of termination if matters did not improve. Inexperience caused Virginia to hire a problem rather than solve one.

As a manager, you may or may not become deeply involved in the staffing process. Some managers have complete control over who is hired or transferred to their departments; others are assigned new employees from the human resources department, with or without refusal power. The more your role as a manager involves you in the staffing process, the more important this chapter will be to you.

EMPLOYEE TURNOVER

In some respects, the lower the personnel turnover in a department, the better. Employee stability and high productivity often go together. But frequent personnel turnover is a fact of life. No matter how effective you become as a supervisor, now and then a key employee will shock you with a resignation. A promotion or lateral move that is good for the firm can create a problem for the supervisor.

PERFORMANCE COMPETENCIES

After you have finished reading this chapter, you should be able to:

- Explain four tips to follow when preparing to conduct an interview

- Design a new employee orientation program

- Describe at least five good interview questions

- Explain the six rules to follow when rotating your staff

- Explain the differences between full- and part-time employees and independent contractors, as well as how each contributes to achieving organizational goals

- Demonstrate a basic understanding of the federal laws that govern the employment relationship

Mary was pleased that management had selected Carla to supervise a newly created department. It was a high compliment to Mary, who had trained Carla as her assistant. But the decision would mean screening, employing, and training a replacement. Other factors were involved. Which of her current staff could best fill Carla's shoes? Would now be a good time to reorganize the entire department? How could she turn the vacancy into an advantage?

Personnel changes present major challenges to all supervisors—challenges that must be approached with sound planning and vision.

THE STAFFING PROCESS

The workforce is changing. The number of working single parents has increased and will continue to grow. People are living longer; therefore, employees are concerned with elder care. New fathers, as well as new mothers, see the value of bonding with new babies and want time off for this purpose.

Staffing includes much more than simply filling a vacancy. It also involves determining long-term personnel needs, orientation and training, transfers and reassignment, rotation, performance evaluation, and terminations. It involves ensuring that you, as the supervisor, and your company, as the employer, are fulfilling your obligations in the employment relationship with each employee throughout his or her career with your organization. The moment a vacancy or personnel change becomes a reality, experienced supervisors ask themselves these questions:

- Is the function performed by the employee who is leaving absolutely necessary?
- Could the tasks be divided among other employees?
- What skills are missing among the staff?
- What kind of new person will contribute to greater productivity?
- Is someone being trained to eventually take my job as supervisor?

The goal of every supervisor should be to hire, develop, and maintain the most cohesive and productive staff possible. It is not a goal easily reached.

Preparation for the Interview

It is impossible to hire the best available applicant for a given job unless the skills and duties required are known ahead of time. If a printed job description is available, it should be carefully reviewed and brought up-to-date. If not, the competencies required should be written out by the supervisor. Only with such data at hand can the best match between applicants and job be achieved. Following are four additional tips:

Tip 1: Federal and state civil rights laws must be upheld in hiring decisions. Sex, race, national origin, age, and religion have nothing to do with how an individual will perform and cannot play a part in the selection process. You must seek and hire the best-qualified person for the job. People with disabilities should be considered equally by focusing on what they can do and how they can contribute to productivity. Sexual orientation should also not play a factor, even though federal and many state laws do not explicitly protect this category.

Tip 2: Avoid the practice of "First come, first hired." You cannot find the best applicant without taking the time to discover what the market has to offer. Employers should "cast a wide net" to create the most comprehensive list of qualified applicants possible.

Tip 3: Screening written applications and interviewing should be done studiously. The more one rushes the process, the more subjective one becomes, and the more mistakes are made.

Tip 4: As an interview approaches, review the competencies you seek in an applicant (a *competency* is a skill that can be observed or measured); have a list of questions you intend to ask that will tell you about the applicant's prior related experiences; know what information you need to provide each applicant regarding the organization and the job—both advantages and disadvantages; and have a pad available for taking notes.

Interviewing Techniques

Interviewing a prospective new employee is a form of counseling. Generally speaking, it is a good idea to follow these steps:

Step 1. Put the applicant at ease so that you can get the most realistic view of how the applicant would perform on the job to be filled.

Step 2. Encourage the applicant to talk through appropriate questions so that you will learn about her or his potential ability to contribute to your department.

Step 3. Provide the applicant with an opportunity to ask questions.

Step 4. Verify the data on the application form, especially those pertaining to training and skills.

Interview Questions

Listed here are some typical questions that interviewers often ask job seekers. Their purpose is to generate a dialogue so that a decision can be based on as much information as possible.

- Why do you want to work here?
- What are your skill levels?
- What can you contribute?

INTERVIEWER'S SELF-ASSESSMENT EXERCISE

This exercise is designed to help you prepare for an interview with a prospective employee for your department. Circle the number that best reflects where you currently fall on the scale. The higher the number, the better. In those areas where you rate yourself a 3, 2, or 1, strive for measurable improvement over your past techniques.

	5	4	3	2	1
1. I analyze job requirements before beginning the selection process.	5	4	3	2	1
2. I study the qualifications of applicants in light of the job requirements.	5	4	3	2	1
3. I begin each interview by establishing a relaxed climate conducive to good communication and use open-ended questions to draw out essential information.	5	4	3	2	1
4. I avoid preconception, personal bias, and prejudice.	5	4	3	2	1
5. I adhere to equal employment opportunity guidelines.	5	4	3	2	1
6. I record key points.	5	4	3	2	1
7. I provide information about the job and the organization and answer the applicant's questions.	5	4	3	2	1
8. I make selection decisions on the basis of job requirements.	5	4	3	2	1
9. I document my selection decisions.	5	4	3	2	1
10. I let all candidates know the outcome of their interview at the appropriate time.	5	4	3	2	1

Total _____

A score between 40 and 50 suggests that you probably conduct successful interviews. A score between 30 and 40 indicates some significant strengths, as well as some improvement needs. A score below 30 calls for a serious effort to improve in a number of areas. Make a special effort to improve in any area where you scored 3 or less, regardless of your total score.

- Why should we hire you?
- Why did you leave your last job?
- What are your strengths that would contribute to your success in this position?
- What areas needing improvement do you have that would challenge you in this position?
- Tell me about your work experience.

- Tell me about a time when you had to
  - solve a problem quickly.
  - make a decision.
  - deliver bad news.
  - make an unexpected change.
  - meet a deadline.
  - organize an event.
  - resolve a conflict with your supervisor.
  - handle an ethical dilemma.

Special note should be taken to avoid, as much as possible, questions that lead to "yes" or "no" responses. While you might ask an occasional question like, "Have you ever been reprimanded?" or "Have you ever received special commendation for your work?" you will want to follow up a "yes" or "no" answer (particularly a "yes" answer) with a request for additional explanation. Most of the questions in this list are open-ended and require the applicant to provide more detailed responses. If sufficient detail is not given at first, then you can ask specific follow-up questions to encourage further elaboration.

An important technique related to open-ended questions is behavioral interviewing. The questions under the heading, "Tell me more about a time when you had to . . ." are good examples of this technique. Rather than suggesting the answer to the interviewee through the way you ask the question, behavioral questions require the applicant to reflect on how he or she would act or behave under specific circumstances. This will give you a better perspective on how the interviewee's behaviors and experiences will fit within the context of your work environment.

Care should be taken to ask the same questions of all applicants so that each individual is given the same opportunity to respond to the same questions and more objective comparisons can be made. Questions of a highly personal nature or those that will embarrass or confuse the applicant should not be used. Do not ask questions that are discriminatory in nature. For example, questions about religious affiliations or an applicant's family or marital circumstances are not proper. In addition, while it is appropriate to ask employees how they would perform a particular task, provided it is asked of all applicants, it is improper to ask a person with a known or suspected disability how he or she will perform a task given the existence of such a disability. For a complete list of questions you should not ask, contact your local Equal Employment Opportunity Commission (EEOC) office and request information, or access EEOC's website at www.eeoc.gov. The material they provide is free of charge and indispensable. The section at the end of this chapter regarding legal obligations provides additional guidelines.

Employment interviews are normally divided into two approaches. One is a guided pattern (directive) in which the interviewer has a precise list of questions—a script—and does not deviate from it (or very little) for each applicant. The other is less structured or unguided (non-directive) and is more free-flowing, allowing the interviewer and interviewee to build off questions asked and comments made in a more conversational manner. For an inexperienced interviewer, a guided pattern is often best. For example, a novice might consider using the following Job Qualification Checklist. The acronym CASSI (i.e., Cooperation, Attitude, Skills, Stability, and Interest) is designed to help the supervisor remember to rate all five categories in each interview.

JOB QUALIFICATION CHECKLIST		
	Yes	No
C COOPERATIVENESS (Will the applicant make an effort to work well with the staff?)	_____	_____
A ATTITUDE (Does the applicant have a good work attitude? Does he or she really want to produce?)	_____	_____
S SKILLS (Does this person have all the specific skills to match the job opening?)	_____	_____
S STABILITY (Is the applicant seeking a permanent or interim job?)	_____	_____
I INTEREST (Has the applicant expressed high interest in the job?)	_____	_____

Although no system is perfect, any guided pattern has the advantage of providing at least some objectivity. Of course, guided or unguided, the interviewer must ensure that all the right questions are asked so that the characteristics stated in the checklist surface and all intended areas of inquiry are covered for each applicant.

Ending the Interview

It is important to terminate the interview in a friendly manner, without making a false commitment. A suitable closing comment might be: "We will make a decision this Friday. If you do not hear from us by next Monday, we still appreciate your interest in our organization and we will keep your application on file."

Even under ideal circumstances, a final choice is difficult to make. It is usually advisable to talk to a superior—especially if two or more candidates appear to be equally qualified.

Reference and Background Checks Prior to Extending an Offer

Prior to extending an offer, your employer will likely require you, or appropriate authorities on your behalf, to conduct reference and background checks. Employers have an obligation to not only ensure prospective employees are qualified and have a good work record, but that there are no concerns regarding their criminal history. Failure to do so could result in liability for negligent hiring if harm occurs as a result of the new employee's actions that could have been avoided by conducting such checks. Further, checks should be done to ensure the applicant is truthful with respect to the representations made in the resume and application and during interviews. Background checks may include, as relevant to the position and permitted by law, checks on criminal history, driving records, credit, education credentials, and basic employment verification.

While doing a routine reference check with a former employer, the former employer's representative may only provide limited information regarding the former employee's position, title, salary, and start and end dates. Generally, this should not necessarily be taken as a negative, because many employers are reluctant to give more information due to liability concerns such as claims of retaliation or false misrepresentation from the former employee. However, if the former employee is aware of circumstances where the applicant's conduct did or could have caused harm, such as an incident of sexual harassment or workplace violence, the employer may be liable if it does not disclose such information and the individual subsequently engages in similar actions at the new company that cause harm.

Many companies obtain the applicant's consent by having him or her sign a form authorizing the former employer to provide relevant information, which may alleviate the former employer's concerns somewhat about disclosing information. While you may be responsible for doing some of the reference checking, such as contacting specific individuals the applicant provided you as character references, company representatives may follow up with other reference checks relating to criminal history, standard education and employment verification, and so forth, or utilize third party vendors to collect such information. You should check with your human resources (HR) department or superiors regarding your organization's policies and procedures and follow them closely. By all means, do not extend an offer until the appropriate checks have been made and prove acceptable.

ORIENTATION AND TRAINING

All of the time and energy devoted to finding the best available candidate can go down the drain if the newcomer is not made a full member of the team. Chapters 8 and 13 provide suggestions in accomplishing this goal. The following suggestions can also be helpful:

- See that the new member is introduced personally to all members of the staff.
- Check out the use of any equipment the new employee will operate.

- Assign a regular employee as a sponsor to answer questions and help the new employee adjust.
- Make sure that basic department rules and company policies are understood.
- List and discuss specific responsibilities.
- Follow up at the end of the first day or shift to see whether the new employee has questions to be answered or whether any adjustments need to be made.

Studies have shown that poor orientation leads to higher turnover rates and, worse, to industrial accidents. Some supervisors prefer a checklist to follow. A typical form is printed on page 163. As noted on the checklist, blank spaces are provided to add items that are specific to your unit, such as basic workplace culture issues like pitch-ins and holiday celebrations or specific details about phone usage, break room use and clean-up, copiers, and so forth. If it would have been helpful to you to know on your first week of employment, include it on this list to be sure you cover it.

A supervisor should monitor the progress of a new employee until she or he has become a relaxed, full partner in the team and is making satisfactory progress toward maximum productivity. If additional training or counseling is required to reach this goal, it should be done quickly. With help, most new employees can make a complete adjustment within one week to a month.

STAFF SHIFTING AND ROTATION

Moving staff members into different roles for both training and motivational purposes is an excellent practice and can measurably improve departmental productivity. Sometimes the employment of a new staff member precipitates such action. Even without personnel turnover, rotating employees from job to job is a good idea in many work environments. Employees who are allowed to stay in the same job too long often fall into a low productivity rut. When given a new challenge, their attitudes improve and they make a bigger contribution. Frequently, a simple job exchange can help both employees because the more experience one obtains, the better prepared one becomes for future advancements—including that of supervision. In rotating or shifting employees, the following rules may apply:

Rule 1: Discuss proposed changes ahead of time with all parties involved.

Rule 2: Avoid forcing new assignments, especially if the individual is insecure about having the ability to perform in the proposed role.

Rule 3: If necessary, provide additional training.

Rule 4: Give all staff members a fair chance.

Rule 5: Avoid changes unless they are beneficial to both employees and the department as a whole.

Rule 6: Compliment those who make adjustments gracefully.

Advanced planning accompanied by personal counseling is the key to staff shifting and rotation. Spur-of-the-moment decisions can often do more harm than good.

SUPERVISOR'S ORIENTATION CHECKLIST

The new supervisor who has not been provided with more sophisticated materials by the company may find this checklist helpful.

ADMINISTRATIVE PAPERWORK

- ☐ I-9 form
- ☐ State and federal withholding forms
- ☐ Direct deposit
- ☐ Computer use agreement
- ☐ Security authorizations (keys, etc.)
- ☐ _____
- ☐ _____

PREPARE WORK AREA (PRE-ARRIVAL)

- ☐ Name plate for desk
- ☐ In-box and mailbox
- ☐ Scissors
- ☐ Clean trash can
- ☐ Notebooks
- ☐ Calendar
- ☐ Pens/pencils/highlighter
- ☐ Tape dispenser
- ☐ Stapler
- ☐ Post-its
- ☐ Order business cards
- ☐ _____
- ☐ _____

COMMUNICATE TO DEPARTMENT (PRE-ARRIVAL)

- ☐ Schedule department tour
- ☐ Assign mentor (if applicable)
- ☐ Announce arrival via publication or e-mail
- ☐ Schedule lunch for day one
- ☐ Schedule necessary training
- ☐ _____
- ☐ _____
- ☐ _____

DEPARTMENTAL ORIENTATION

- ☐ Welcome letter from department head
- ☐ Copy of job description
- ☐ Department's mission and values statements
- ☐ Department policies
- ☐ Time reporting procedures
- ☐ Time off procedures
- ☐ Leave procedures (FMLA, etc.)
- ☐ ADA and other accommodation procedures
- ☐ Overtime procedures
- ☐ Dress requirements
- ☐ Emergency and security procedures
- ☐ Departmental standards
- ☐ Performance expectations and evaluation process
- ☐ Daily, weekly interaction with supervisor
- ☐ Who to go to for help
- ☐ _____

GENERAL COMPANY ORIENTATION

- ☐ Welcome to CEO
- ☐ Company mission, values, history, organization chart
- ☐ Safety training
- ☐ Employee policies and receipt of employee handbook
- ☐ Benefits enrollment
- ☐ _____

TECHNOLOGY SET-UPS

- ☐ Passwords
- ☐ Workstation
- ☐ Telephone and voicemail
- ☐ Phonebooks, contact lists
- ☐ E-mail
- ☐ Printers path set up
- ☐ Other resources
- ☐ Pagers
- ☐ Cell phones
- ☐ Laptops
- ☐ Copier
- ☐ Fax machines
- ☐ Websites
- ☐ _____
- ☐ _____

TOURS AND INTRODUCTIONS

- ☐ Office
- ☐ Cafeteria
- ☐ Coffee, break areas
- ☐ Parking
- ☐ Supply room
- ☐ Mail room
- ☐ Introductions: _____
  _____
  _____
- ☐ _____
- ☐ _____

Transfers

When a supervisor senses that he or she has a problem employee, the first thing that often comes to mind is a transfer to another department within the same firm. In exceptional cases, such as an irreconcilable conflict between a supervisor and an employee, an in-house transfer may be feasible. Perhaps it will give the individual a new, fresh opportunity; perhaps she or he will be happier under a different management style. But to initiate a transfer as a ploy to get rid of a problem employee who you know will give the next supervisor a similar problem is not professional. If you are truly dealing with a problem employee, you must either set and enforce clear expectations for a change in behavior or take actions leading to termination. If the request comes from a non-problem employee, it is another matter. It is possible, for example, that some time in the future an employee of yours will ask for a transfer so that she or he will be free from your style of supervision. If it happens, do not take it personally. You cannot be expected to have the kind of style that will please everyone. In such cases, a transfer might be advantageous to all the parties involved.

Justifying a Larger Staff

You will hear certain supervisors complaining about departmental workloads.

- "There is no way to catch up around here."
- "The more we do, the more they pile it on."
- "Too much work—too few people."

Sometimes such complaints are justified. Often they are not. Only when all employees—and the supervisor—are working close to their productivity potentials and the workload continues to increase should a supervisor take an overload problem to his or her superior. In doing so, consider the following suggestions:

- Demonstrate your overload position with facts. Quote comparative labor cost figures with a similar operation.
- Compare today's heavier workload with that of past periods in an objective manner.
- If you cannot justify hiring a full-time employee, consider someone part-time.

Whenever a supervisor seeks to increase her or his staff, management will automatically pry into the operation with a sharp eye. Only when such scrutiny produces a well-run department is such a request given serious consideration. If increased staff is not justified, you may need to take a closer look at other causes for your workload problems such as problems in delegation, inefficient use of time, clear behavior and performance problems on the part of one or a few employees, and bottlenecks in workflow—all problems that are addressed in other chapters of this text.

THE PART-TIMER

Federal legislation defines a part-timer as an employee who works less than 1,000 hours per year (17½ hours per week). Organizations generally view a part-timer as an individual who works twenty-nine hours per week or less. The average is about twenty.

Part-time jobs normally have these characteristics:

- Wages are typically lower.
- Only the basic or required benefits are provided.
- Some organizations use part-timers as a pool from which to select full-timers.
- Part-time jobs usually offer less job security.
- Part-timers give many types of organizations flexibility and lower labor costs.

The Core-Ring Approach

To determine the best mix of full-time versus part-time workers, organizations are turning to the core-ring approach. As illustrated, core employees constitute the full-time, regular workforce. They are the heart of the organization and usually receive comprehensive benefits.

Part-timers, in contrast, make up the outer ring of employees. Typically, they do not earn pensions, participate in profit-sharing plans, or receive paid vacations. Some sources estimate that more than 25 million part-timers participate in the labor force.

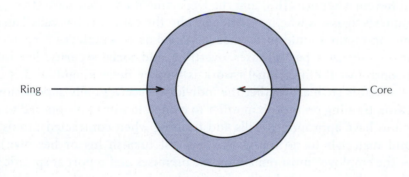

Popularity of Part-Timers

Some experts claim that full-time, core employees are paid for eight hours of work, but actually work closer to six or seven. This discrepancy is because it may take ten minutes or more for them to get ready to work, two fifteen-minute breaks are required, and often employees start getting ready to leave before the end of their workday. In contrast, part-timers employed for four hours may actually work at top performance for almost the entire period.

Part-time workers can be divided into three classifications: (1) full-time students who seek "peak period" jobs for approximately twenty hours per week to help with educational expenses, (2) homemakers who seek part-time work so they can devote more time to children, and (3) retired people who wish to supplement their retirement incomes.

Many supervisors claim that part-timers are a welcome challenge when it comes to weaving them into the general mix of employees. They like the enthusiasm, energy, and flexibility they bring with them. Others claim that the high turnover rate of part-timers negates their advantages. All agree that it takes additional time and energy from the supervisor to convert part-timers into productive members of a work team.

INDEPENDENT CONTRACTORS

Another way that employers balance productivity demands with payroll and benefit cost issues and immediate workforce needs is through the use of independent contractors. While independent contractors may sit side-by-side full- and part-time employees, they are not "employees." Typically, an independent contractor is someone who is contracted to provide specific services for a company in exchange for a fee, which may be paid either at the completion of all work or in installments as portions of the work are completed, rather than on an hourly wage or a salary basis.

The key distinction between independent contractors and employees is that independent contractors generally control the manner in which the work is performed and are responsible to the organization that contracted with them for the product, as agreed by contract. In contrast, employees are subject to the control of their employers, not just for the product, and for how, where, and when the work is done. This distinction is important under law, because both the Internal Revenue Service (IRS) and the Department of Labor have strict guidelines and tests to assess whether someone who the company has called an independent contractor should instead be classified as an employee for which the company is subject to payroll taxes, overtime, and social security. The issue of overall control of the individual's work is the key determinant, and is determined by factors such as whether the individual receives daily supervision and instruction; training on the job in order to complete work (as opposed to being expected to have appropriate skills and training when contracted); tools, supplies, and materials to do the work (or must furnish his or her own); and whether the employee must remain on the premises and report at specific times to do the work (as opposed to having freedom to come and go and work off premises).

Advantages and Disadvantages

Engaging independent contractors makes sense when there are specific short-term projects that must be completed that require specific and often higher-level skill sets to complete. Even though the cost of these services may be more than what the company may pay for the same work done by a full-time employee, it is cost effective because payroll and social security taxes, overtime wages, and standard company benefits are not due. Some of the drawbacks are that independent contractors are not easily integrated into the work setting, which may result in communication and relationship problems and may also affect the morale of employees. Further, if you need the ongoing knowledge and expertise of workers for future projects, as well as some level of commitment and loyalty to the organization and its goals, you will not benefit as greatly as you would by utilizing full-time employees.

THE ART OF SCHEDULING

Flex-scheduling, peak periods, and the need to customize "job hours" for people with special skills is an increasing challenge. Most supervisors, especially those who utilize part-timers, often prepare weekly printed schedules and post them on a bulletin board or electronic calendar. Once posted, the schedule becomes set. Changes are permitted only under exceptional circumstances.

Obviously, restaurants, fast-food operations, retail stores, and organizations that are open extended and irregular hours are presented with the greatest challenge.

Frank operates his highly successful cafe with five full-timers and twenty part-timers. To simplify his scheduling, Frank posts a weekly schedule listing the hours to be worked by each employee. If a part-timer needs to be absent for a shift, it is the employee's responsibility to get a replacement from the total list of available part-timers provided, with telephone numbers, by Frank. Frank claims his system works 95 percent of the time and requires a minimum amount of supervision.

Like Frank, most organizations, using their computer capabilities, develop and execute work schedules and patterns to meet their own particular needs. Although some supervisors delegate this function, they recognize that the responsibility remains with them and that some flexibility is necessary to keep motivated employees.

SUPERVISOR'S RELATIONSHIP WITH THE HUMAN RESOURCES DEPARTMENT

Supervisors who work for large organizations that have professional human resources (HR) departments (personnel and training) have a big advantage when it comes to staffing. Most of the work of recruiting, testing, interviewing, orientation, training, and terminating is done for them by professionals. In some cases, all the supervisor needs to do is accept or reject a possible staff member sent for consideration.

It is important, however, that the supervisor do everything possible to maintain good relationships with human resources experts. Fostering such a relationship includes the following:

1. Informing human resources and training specialists of the exact skills and competencies you need for maximum productivity.
2. Accepting the fact that human resources departments do their best to attract the most qualified applicants. (Employment people cannot change market conditions.)
3. Abiding by equal opportunity laws and other legal restrictions.
4. Paying compliments and offering feedback to those who get the right people properly trained to you.
5. Making sure the new hire is oriented into her or his particular work area. Remember, orientation should be done by the supervisor, and not delegated to anyone else.
6. Maintaining an ongoing relationship with HR representatives and continuing to seek advice as needed to ensure you remain in compliance with laws and policies and consistent with organizational practices as you manage employees throughout their work in your department.

MEETING ONGOING LEGAL OBLIGATIONS TO YOUR EMPLOYEES

All employment decisions including hiring must follow Equal Employment Opportunity (EEO) guidelines. EEO laws are enforced by the Equal Employment Opportunity Commission (EEOC). The supervisor must become acquainted with how EEOC impacts the organization and the supervisor. Employment decisions that ignore or violate EEO guidelines may result in costly litigation fees. Your human resources department can help explain these guidelines to you.

In addition to EEOC regulations, there are numerous other laws you must pay attention to as you manage your staff. While this text provides a wealth of tools and information for doing this, along the way you must be sure you are honoring your end of the employment relationship by adhering to all relevant HR policies and federal and state laws. Ensuring that you fairly and objectively make decisions affecting your employees not only protects you and your employer, but is also part of your responsibility to provide a safe, equitable, and supportive work environment.

The most significant federal laws pertaining to the employment relationship are described briefly in the next sections. As you consider them, here are a few basic considerations to keep in mind to ensure you are managing employees within appropriate legal parameters:

1. Know and understand these laws, what they are intended to cover, the rights and protections they afford, and your employer's specific legal obligations. Participate in your organization's legal compliance training to learn more about these laws and responsibilities. If no training exists, ask the appropriate authorities to provide this information to you, and consider attending outside training seminars or classes at your local community college.

2. Have sufficient knowledge of these laws and regulations to be able to identify when your legal obligations are triggered as a result of specific situations that arise. For example, you should be able to identify when a sexual harassment concern has been raised, when an FMLA request is being made, or when an employee may need a disability or religious accommodation. You should also be able to recognize when potential inequities may exist in employment decisions based on race, gender, or other inappropriate considerations, such as in hiring, terminations, discipline, or other areas, and seek to avoid them.

3. Understand your organization's standard process for responding to these matters. Learn how you must respond to specific situations and the extent to which you may intervene to address them immediately and the extent to which your organization expects you to seek assistance from other authorities, such as HR, legal counsel, the EEO office, your superiors, and so on.

4. Take the proactive approach. Take affirmative steps to recruit qualified candidates, particularly minorities, women, and people with disabilities. Seek to support their career, growth, and advancement opportunities. Create and maintain a working environment that supports them and that is fair, equitable, and respectful to all. Continually affirm to employees your commitment to affording equal opportunity and valuing differences.

5. Ensure all employment decisions you make are objective, free from bias, and based on non-discriminatory criteria. Ensure that hiring and promotional decisions are based on bona fide job qualifications and not subjective criteria. Implement disciplinary action evenly among all workers for similar offenses, and be prepared to justify your decisions with appropriate, thorough documentation that supports your decisions with concrete, factual data and observations.

6. When in doubt, consult with the appropriate organizational authorities to be sure these issues are properly handled. Ideally, you should not be in a position where you must act alone to address these matters.

Title VII of the Civil Rights Act of 1964

Title VII of the Civil Rights Act of 1964 prohibits discrimination on the basis of race, color, gender, religion, or national origin in virtually any employment decision, including hiring, firing, training, discipline, compensation, benefits, classification, or other terms and conditions of employment. This law applies to employers with fifteen or more employees as well as unions and employment agencies that make referrals for employment. Title VII is enforced by the Equal Employment Opportunity Commission. Violations of this law can result in actual damages to the complaining employee (back pay, front pay, value of other benefits, etc.) as well as potentially punitive and compensatory damages.

Pursuant to regulations and U.S. Supreme Court decisions regarding "gender," the EEOC has authority to receive and investigate complaints involving sexual harassment. which includes "quid pro quo" harassment involving conduct by a supervisor or other responsible authority toward an employee where a tangible employment benefit is threatened or promised. It also includes "hostile environment" harassment involving conduct and statements of a sexual nature that are pervasive, repeated, and severe, and impact the work environment and employees' ability to perform their jobs. Similar provisions prohibit harassment based on race and national origin. Under the definition of "gender," Title VII, by amendment, also covers pregnancy discrimination. Finally, Title VII requires employers to provide accommodation for various employees' religious practices and also exempts some employers (churches, schools with religious affiliations, etc.) from coverage under the law.

Age Discrimination in Employment Act (ADEA)

The Age Discrimination in Employment Act (ADEA) protects employees who are 40 years of age or older from the same broad list of employment decisions that are covered under Title VII. While the law also prohibits practices and policies that have the tendency to discriminate against a class of older workers, it exempts from coverage employers' actions "to observe the terms of a bona fide seniority system or any bona fide employee benefit plan such as a retirement, pension, or insurance plan." The law also prohibits mandatory retirement, except that employers can require compulsory retirement at age 65 of its high-level employees with substantial executive authority, provided certain requirements regarding pensions and income levels are followed. The ADEA also covers, by amendment, early retirement incentive programs and requires that employers follow specific procedures to ensure employee's decisions to accept such agreements are voluntary and not coerced. The ADEA is enforced by the EEOC.

Americans with Disabilities Act of 1990 (ADA)

The Americans with Disabilities Act of 1990 (ADA) prohibits discrimination in employment against people with disabilities. This law and its accompanying regulations provide a comprehensive list of disabilities that apply and includes both physical and mental disabilities, both known (e.g., person with impaired vision or in a wheelchair) and "hidden" (e.g., person with heart trouble, diabetes) as well as situations where an individual is "regarded as" disabled, such as when a disability is suspected but is not job-related or does not "substantially limit" the person's ability to perform the job. A significant area of protection under the ADA is the requirement that employers provide "reasonable accommodation" to individuals with disabilities to enable them to perform their jobs, provided the accommodation does not create an "undue burden" on the employer or constitute a "direct threat" to the employee or others. The ADA is also enforced by the EEOC.

Family and Medical Leave Act (FMLA)

The Family and Medical Leave Act (FMLA) provides up to 12 weeks of leave per year, which may be used in full blocks or intermittently, for certain qualifying events, including birth of a child or to care for a newborn, adoption or foster care, and a serious health condition of the employee or the employee's spouse, son, daughter, or parent. Employees do not qualify for FMLA leave until they have worked one year or at least 1,250 hours in the preceding 12-month period. Employees must generally give 30 days' notice of the need for leave, where practical. FMLA regulations further allow employers to require medical certifications for serious medical conditions. FMLA applies only to employers with 50 or more employees within a 75-mile radius. It is enforced by the U.S. Department of Labor.

Immigration Reform and Control Act of 1986 (IRCA)

The Immigration Reform and Control Act of 1986 (IRCA) prohibits employers and other entities from hiring, recruiting, or referring for a fee unauthorized aliens. Through use of the I-9 form, it requires employers to verify that the employees they hire are U.S. citizens or aliens authorized to work in the United States. IRCA also provides some protection for U.S. citizens and authorized aliens from discrimination in hiring, recruitment, or referrals for a fee. The Immigration and Naturalization Services (INS) has oversight authority of IRCA.

Fair Labor Standards Act of 1938 (FLSA)

The Fair Labor Standards Act of 1938 (FLSA) covers three areas: (1) child labor; (2) minimum wage; and (3) overtime provisions. With respect to overtime, employers must be attentive to extensive regulations concerning classifying its employees as "exempt" from the overtime provisions and those that are "non-exempt." The distinction between these is determined by examination of how employees are paid (salary or hourly wage) and the duties that employees perform. While many positions with management and decision-making authority are typically exempt from overtime coverage, the analysis is not always so clear-cut. Generally, HR classification specialists should be called on to ensure employees are properly classified and paid. For positions that are "non-exempt," employers generally must pay time and a half for every hour over 40 in a workweek. FLSA regulations provide additional specificity in determining what is "work" and what is not to determine the hours worked for which overtime is due.

Other Federal Laws That May or May Not Impact the Supervisor's Area of Responsibility

There are many other federal laws influencing employment. Your employer may or may not be subject to them depending on the nature of its workforce and the work involved. Among these laws are: (1) the National Labor Relations Act, which governs labor relations and union activities; (2) the Uniformed Services Employment and Reemployment Rights Act (USERRA), which provides protections for employees on leave and returning from leave due to military service; (3) the Health Insurance Portability and Accountability Act (HIPPA), which provides strict guidelines concerning the use and release of an employee's personal medical information; and (4) the Worker Readjustment and Retraining Act (WARN), which generally requires employers to give 60 days' advance notice to employees regarding plant closings and mass layoffs.

State Laws

In addition to federal law, employers must be attentive to state laws that protect employees. For example, although federal law does not currently provide protection to employees for discrimination based on sexual orientation, familial status, marital status, or other categories, many states do. Further, laws concerning employees' privacy rights, jury duty, and protection against whistle blowing (if any) are generally covered under state law. Finally, the regulation of matters like workers compensation and unemployment insurance come under state jurisdiction.

PERFORMANCE **CHECKLIST**

1. Staffing includes much more than simply filling a vacancy. It also involves determining long-term personnel needs, orientation and training, transfers and reassignment, rotation, performance evaluation, and terminations.

2. When preparing for the interview process, four basic tips will help you: (1) Be sure to uphold all relevant federal and state laws pertaining to the hiring process, particularly those pertaining to non-discrimination; (2) "cast a wide net" to create the most comprehensive pool of qualified candidates possible; (3) perform screening of applications and interviewing in a studious manner; and (4) know the competencies required and the questions you will ask before beginning the interview process.

3. When conducting interviews, ask open-ended questions and questions that help you determine how an applicant will act under certain circumstances relevant to the position based on previous experience. These will give you a better sense of how the applicant will perform in the position than asking questions that require only "yes" or "no" responses.

4. There are two approaches for conducting interviews: (1) guided (directive) pattern, in which the interviewer has a precise list of questions—a script—and does not deviate from it (or deviates very little); and (2) unguided (non-directive) pattern, which is more free-flowing, allowing the interviewer and interviewee to build off questions

asked and comments made in a more conversational manner. Inexperienced interviewers may prefer guided pattern.

5. Before extending an offer, supervisors should ensure that all appropriate background checks are conducted, including, as required for the position, checks on criminal history, education credentials, driving records, employment verification, credit, and truthfulness of matters asserted in the applicant's resume, application, and in interviews. Failure to conduct appropriate checks could result in liability for harm caused by the newly hired employee that could have been prevented had appropriate checks been made.

6. When bringing a new employee on board, the supervisor should ensure that he or she is made to feel welcome and has been provided all the resources, training, supplies, introductions to staff, and other matters typically associated with orientation of new employees. The supervisor may wish to use a checklist to ensure all appropriate matters have been addressed.

7. When assessing issues regarding transfers, job rotation, and increasing staff, the supervisor should assess the need for such measures and the benefits and impacts for taking such measures. Transfers may be appropriate if it will help develop an employee or the employee is not the right fit within his current department, but it should not be done simply to move a problem employee to another department. Job rotation may be appropriate to provide variety and job development for staff. Increasing staff should be done carefully and only if justified due to increased workload rather than due to inefficient use of time, poor delegation, bottlenecks in workflow, or other issues that could be addressed without increasing staff.

8. The use of part-time employees and independent contractors may make sense in some instances. Part-timers are often more productive within their time at work relative to full-time workers, for whom break time, lunch time, and other factors must be considered. Using part-time workers can, however, present a challenge when scheduling. Independent contractors may be beneficial when specialized short-term projects require specialized skills and their work would help the company reduce costs associated with payroll and social security taxes, overtime, and standard company benefits. They are less beneficial if there is a need for commitment, loyalty, and institutional knowledge over time.

9. Supervisors must continue to hold up their end of the employment relationship beyond the process of hiring and orientation. They must maintain their relationship with HR to receive advice as needed to manage the employment relationship throughout their employees' careers within the organization. They must also become familiar with the laws and regulations affecting the employment relationship and ensure they and the organization meet their obligations regarding employees' rights and protections under these laws.

TEST **YOURSELF**

For each of the following statements, check true or false.

True   False

1. One reason for a professional interview is to avoid hiring a problem employee.

2. Orientation of the new employee is not a function of the staffing process.

3. If not available elsewhere, supervisors should write their own job descriptions.

4. It is not important to ask each applicant the same series of questions.

5. A job qualification checklist helps a supervisor follow a guided interview pattern.

6. Most new employees make a complete adjustment within two days.

7. Job rotation should be used only when employees are highly motivated.

8. It is acceptable professionally for a supervisor to initiate a transfer for a problem employee.

9. Interview questions that inquire about how applicants would respond to specific work situations will elicit more information about their abilities than closed-ended questions.

10. In large organizations, staffing should be a cooperative undertaking between the human resources department and the involved supervisor.

11. Hour for hour, part-timers are often more productive than full-time workers.

_____ _____ 12. When interviewing potential employees, questions about religious affiliations are proper.

_____ _____ 13. EEOC provides material free of charge on what questions should and should not be asked in interviews.

_____ _____ 14. A poor orientation program leads to increased turnover rates.

_____ _____ 15. The supervisor should orient a new employee to the work area, not anyone else.

Turn to the back of the book to check your answers.

Total Correct_____

DISCUSSION **QUESTIONS**

1. Are the advantages of job rotation within most departments worth the effort? If so, why do the majority of supervisors avoid the process?

2. If you were a supervisor for an organization that assigned new employees to your department without giving you the opportunity to interview or reject applicants, would you make an attempt to change the procedure? If so, how would you go about it?

3. In addition to reviewing the material in this chapter, what might a supervisor do to obtain additional information and insights into staffing problems and interviewing techniques?

CASE 1: STAFFING, **PART 1**

In a regular staff meeting, Bill announced that the company has acquired a new account that will increase business. The new business will require the hiring of two new employees within the next six weeks. Bill expects you to be involved in the staffing process. You will interview and select from a short list of applicants provided to you by human resources. How will you prepare for the interview? What criteria will you use to select the best applicants?

CASE 2: STAFFING, **PART 2**

After you've completed your analysis from Part 1, Bill returns and suggests that perhaps one of the two employees you must hire need not be full-time. Perhaps filling a part-time position will be sufficient, or perhaps the work involved is the kind that can be assigned to an independent contractor. Then again, Bill is not sure, which is why he has returned to ask your advice.

How will you decide whether Bill's speculation on the second position has merit? What criteria will you use to determine if the second position should be full- or part-time or should instead be filled by utilizing an independent contractor?

Turn to the back of the book to compare your thoughts to those of the authors.

JOB QUALIFICATION **CHECKLIST**

Based on what you have learned in this chapter, devise a ten-point "Job Qualification Checklist" that will help you be more objective. Consider all factors that build a more harmonious and productive staff without violating any EEO laws. In considering this assignment, list these points in order of importance based on the following statement: "I would seek the following ten qualifications in any applicant that I would add to my staff:"

PERSONAL GROWTH **EXERCISE**

Prepare a personal skills inventory by listing all the skills that you feel you possess that are job related. List skills that you feel you need to improve.

chapter **twelve**

DELEGATION

"Gold is where you find it."

American saying

PERFORMANCE COMPETENCIES

After you have finished reading this chapter, you should be able to:

- List five reasons why supervisors don't delegate responsibilities and duties often enough

- Describe the conditions under which a supervisor should delegate more

- Describe in specific terms how to delegate

"For Pete's sake, Harry, turn some of that stuff over to your employees and relax a little."

"Good grief, Sally, it's ridiculous for you to kill yourself doing such routine work when you have nine people in your department who need the experience."

"Come off it, Frank. You'd have plenty of time for more important things if you'd delegate some of those jobs you shouldn't be doing in the first place."

Sound familiar? Yes, it's easy to tell others to delegate and it's true that most supervisors should delegate more, but most of us have to learn the lesson the hard way. Take Dee as an example.

Dee was a new, young, capable, and highly enthusiastic manager. She had five full-time and three part-time employees. Despite advice from all sides, she could not learn to assign responsible work to others. Instead of delegating more, she simply pushed herself harder. Dee was so eager to be a successful supervisor that she was blind to what was happening. One of her best friends told her to manage more and do less. Her boss took her aside and gave her a heart-to-heart talk about the problem, but with little success.

Then one afternoon, Dee passed out on the job and was taken to a local hospital by ambulance. The diagnosis was complete exhaustion. Dee hadn't received the message from her friends or boss, but she heard it loud and clear from her doctor. He put it very simply: She had to learn to reduce her workload.

Delegating can, of course, mean many things to many people, but primarily it involves turning important work over to someone else. It means giving others the authority to do an assignment, with expected results mutually understood, but retaining for yourself the ultimate responsibility for ensuring tasks are done. It means having sufficient faith in others to let them do important work for you.

When it comes to delegating, most inexperienced supervisors make two big mistakes: (1) They fail to do it skillfully, and (2) they fail to delegate enough. Delegation of duties is difficult to put into practice, yet delegating responsibilities and duties to others is a must. Unless you learn to do it often and skillfully, your future as a manager may be seriously limited.

FAILURE TO DELEGATE

Why do some supervisors fail to delegate as much as they should? The four basic reasons are psychological in nature.

No Faith in the Employees They Manage

Many supervisors do not see enough potential for success in the people who work for them, and as a result, never give their employees important and difficult assignments. Sometimes this kind of withholding happens because the supervisor has been burned in the past by poor performance; sometimes it is caused by unrealistic standards set by the supervisor. Most supervisors, however, simply lack confidence in the performance possibilities of employees. Unfortunately, this lack of confidence often results in poor performance when the supervisor is forced to delegate. To delegate successfully, you must have confidence in the results you anticipate and transmit this feeling to the employee.

Fear of Superiors

Every time you delegate important work to others, you risk failure and possible criticism from your superiors. You lay your personal reputation on the line, which is as it should be. If you are not sufficiently secure in your job and with your company to risk a few failures, then you should not be a supervisor in the first place. Fear is a powerful emotion that can tie you up in knots and cause you to be too cautious. You must conquer fear before you can delegate freely and effectively.

Desire for Personal Credit

Some supervisors with a strong need for ego fulfillment try to do all the important work themselves so that they will receive personal credit from their superiors. In taking this narrow perspective, they fail to see that by relinquishing personal credit to their employees, they can (through motivation of individuals) increase productivity, which in turn will improve the reputation of the department. It is shortsighted for a supervisor to want personal credit when departmental success will ultimately be more beneficial.

Misjudgment of Time

Many supervisors are also shortsighted about time. They refuse to take time to delegate responsibility today to free themselves for more important work next week. Time is the supervisor's most important commodity. If you refuse to delegate because doing it properly takes too much time, you are guilty of poor planning. Skillful delegating saves time.

QUESTIONS TO ASK YOURSELF BEFORE DELEGATING

Before turning your desire to delegate into an action plan, you must seriously consider whether you and the employee to whom you would delegate the work are prepared. You must decide if the delegation makes sense. In short, you must put some thought into the who, what, when, where, why, and how of the delegation. Delegation involves more than a hand-off; preparation is required. For starters, consider the following questions:

- Have you clearly identified the work that you should delegate? Can it be readily explained to the person to whom you plan to delegate the work?

- Does the work need to be delegated? Is it a meaningful or necessary aspect of unit operations? Will it make your workload easier? Will it provide a growth opportunity for someone else? Or is it merely busy work?

- Have you chosen the right person? Does the employee want new assignments? Does he or she possess the appropriate level of competence and initiative needed to complete the assignment?

- Knowing that you keep the ultimate responsibility for ensuring the work is completed, how much authority to make decisions are you willing to grant?

- Will the employee be sufficiently empowered to perform the work, or will he or she become frustrated because there are elements of the work that are beyond his or her control, such as decision-making authority he or she doesn't possess?

- What standards of performance will it take for you to be satisfied? How will you know if this standard has been met? How will you oversee progress and monitor the work?

- What obstacles (if any) exist? How can they be overcome?
- Are you willing to spend the time required to train the person so that he or she produces at an acceptable level?
- Do you have an employee who has asked for more authority? Is he or she ready for additional responsibilities?

WHEN AND HOW TO DELEGATE

When should the leader delegate? You might wait forever for the perfect time to delegate, but some delegation should take place under the following conditions:

1. When you need more time for work that only you can do, especially planning responsibilities that will contribute more to departmental productivity than the job being delegated.
2. When delegating will help involve employees, improve their morale, and cause them to work closer to their potential.
3. When it will not show undue favoritism or seriously damage relationships with other employees.
4. When you are willing to take the time and effort to do a skillful job of delegating.
5. When you are under pressure and must relinquish some responsibilities in order to protect your physical and mental health.

How can you delegate skillfully? Everyone agrees that surfing, sky diving, and water skiing take skill, but few people acknowledge that the same is true of delegating. Yet delegating has its own special procedures. If you follow the following steps, you will greatly improve your skill in delegating.

Select the Task Carefully

Make up a priority list of assignments you might delegate. For a job to qualify for this list, it should be taking too much of your time, should be rather low in responsibility compared to your other duties, and should be motivating for your employees. Do not delegate tasks simply because you are bored with them, but you can consider delegating tasks that may bore you because they have become rote but may be viewed as opportunities to learn and develop or to have greater variety in the work your employees do. Also, you should not delegate tasks that should properly remain within your purview as a manager, if only because your superior expects this. For example, you may not enjoy doing weekly scheduling, budgeting, and payroll duties, but if it is expected that you retain them, even if others are capable, you must not delegate them. Finally, be careful to choose those assignments that you know employees will have sufficient information, access to others who share some responsibility for completing the assignment, and empowerment to make decisions, as you deem appropriate, so that they will not become frustrated.

Once you have your list, start from the top and delegate one task at a time. Try to spread them out over all your employees until you sense you are reaching a saturation point.

Select the Person Carefully

Consider all factors involved before selecting the person to whom you will give a specified task. Which employees have too much or too little work to do? Does any particular individual need a special challenge? Will the individual you select accept it with enthusiasm? Does the person have the training and talent to execute it well? If not, are you prepared to spend the time necessary to ensure the individual receives proper training and support? How will co-workers react? Will it increase departmental productivity? Obviously, you must know your employees well if assignments are to fit the special needs and talents of each.

Prepare All Individuals for Change

Because sudden unannounced changes can disturb people and hurt productivity, announce your decision carefully in order to protect your relationships with all employees and to give the employee receiving the assignment all possible assistance. In most cases, a group announcement is best so that everyone is informed, misunderstandings are minimized, and an opportunity to ask questions is provided. In delegating, you must be concerned with the feelings of all employees, not just those of the person to whom you are delegating.

Turn Over the Assignment

Consider the following steps in turning over new responsibilities to an employee:

1. Meet in private where you will not be interrupted and allow sufficient time to delegate carefully and thoroughly.
2. Go over the new job step by step. Break big tasks into smaller, more manageable ones. Illustrate or demonstrate whenever possible.
3. Instill vision regarding the value and importance of the task. Explain why the task matters and how it contributes to broader organizational goals.
4. Establish, as relevant, clear goals, acceptable levels of performance, timelines, and benchmarks for completion.
5. Clarify how much authority you are granting and how much you are retaining. Further, clarify the amount of autonomy you are granting (or not) to function independently without need to consult you.
6. Explain the level of support that is available to assist the employee, including from you, co-workers, and managers and employees outside the work unit who share responsibility for completing the task. Note: Be sure to communicate with these individuals so they will anticipate contact from the employee instead of from you.
7. Ask the employee for verbal feedback on all details presented to eliminate future misunderstandings. Give the employee full opportunity to ask questions.
8. Compliment the employee on previous work and transmit your confidence in the way she or he will perform the new responsibility.
9. Establish how you will monitor progress, including the form of reporting required (verbal, written summary, checklist, spreadsheet, etc). Set a time and date for follow-up. Prior to this time, give the employee freedom to

perform the task without appearing to hover or second-guess. Affirm that you remain accessible at any time prior to this time if the need arises. However, if you sense the employee is struggling and hasn't come to you for support, it may be best to check in before the due date.

10. Continue to monitor task progress, but soon let the employee do the task without your interference or control.

Provide Follow-Up

Soon after delegating, make yourself available to answer further questions and provide additional training. Questions similar to these often facilitate communications:

- How are you doing on the new equipment?
- How do you feel now about your new assignment?
- Do you need any help I have not provided?
- Do you have any suggestions for me or other employees?

To delegate without follow-up is to ask for trouble and disappointment. You can delegate authority—power to get things done—but not your responsibility. The final responsibility for results is shared by all employees, but the supervisor must take the greatest percentage. If you learn to delegate frequently and skillfully, you will eventually worry less, feel less pressured, have more time to plan and organize, build better relationships with your employees, and motivate greater productivity in your department.

DELEGATING AS PART OF A LARGER PLAN

To become more efficient and make better use of your time, you must do both a departmental and a job analysis. That is, you must step back and look at how your department is operating to reach your productivity goals; you must then analyze all positions (including your own) to see how they can blend in better with the total operation. As you do this analysis, consider the following:

Discontinue low-priority tasks or non-therapeutic time wasters.   As with most situations, a few little things will not contribute to productivity or employee morale and can be eliminated. The same is true with time wasters that do not contribute to a happy working environment or your own positive attitude.

Delegate more of what is left.   To free yourself for more important tasks, set up a running policy (utilizing the techniques presented in this chapter) of continuous delegation so that employees' abilities expand as you become more effective as a supervisor.

Be more efficient at what you do.   Chapters 13–19 will come into play here. As you prioritize your work and improve your own job skills, you will cut down on the time devoted to various aspects of your job. If such time and task management require additional training on your part, enroll in whatever program will help. Ask your superior to recommend worthwhile training. Seek a mentor—a person who can coach you personally.

SPEND TIME TO DELEGATE NOW TO SAVE TIME LATER

If you are not used to delegating and have considered all that is involved after reading this chapter, you may feel overwhelmed and be wondering whether it is worth it. Indeed, if you and your staff are unfamiliar with delegation, you will likely spend more time up-front with the process of delegation than you did formally doing the tasks on your own.

Stick with it. Once you've developed the habit of delegation and instilled an expectation for delegation among your staff, you will increase overall effectiveness and efficiency within your work unit and find you have much more time to address those high-priority tasks that only you can handle as a manager and are, presumably, why you were hired to be the manager in the first place.

What will you do with the time you save? Here are three suggestions: (1) Spend more time improving relationships; (2) start solving problems before they occur; and (3) do even more departmental planning.

PERFORMANCE **CHECKLIST**

1. When it comes to delegating, most inexperienced supervisors make two mistakes: (1) They fail to do it skillfully, and (2) they fail to delegate enough. Yet delegation is a must. Unless you learn to do it often and skillfully, your future as a manager may be seriously limited.

2. Supervisors often fail to delegate because they lack faith in their employees, fear their superiors and their expectations, desire the personal credit that comes from doing tasks themselves, and misjudge the time needed to delegate and complete tasks.

3. Effective delegation requires preparation and involves asking yourself a number of questions, such as what needs to be delegated; to whom will you delegate; does the person to whom you delegate have sufficient competence, initiative, and desire to accept the delegation; what are your expected standards of performance; what level of authority are you prepared to delegate; what

obstacles exist to the delegation, and how will you overcome them; and are you prepared to spend the time needed to train the employee to perform the delegation as expected?

4. Delegation is appropriate when you, as the supervisor, need more time to engage in higher-priority matters such as departmental planning; when delegation will help involve and develop employees and improve their morale; when delegation to one employee won't result in favoritism or damaged relationships among other employees; when you are willing to take the time to skillfully delegate; and when delegation becomes necessary to protect your physical and mental health.

5. When delegating, you must select the task and person carefully; prepare individuals in your department carefully, particularly if you and they are unaccustomed to delegation; engage in a well-thought out meeting with the employee to ensure that all details regarding tasks, levels and amount of authority, autonomy, and support, and the process for monitoring and follow-up are fully explained; and provide for follow-up to ensure the task is completed properly.

6. The supervisor should consider delegation as part of a larger plan to improve productivity by discontinuing low-priority tasks and non-therapeutic time wasters, delegating more of the meaningful work that is left, and becoming more efficient at what he or she does.

7. While more time may be spent upfront with the process of delegation, particularly if the supervisor is unfamiliar with delegation, it is time well spent so the supervisor can then spend more time improving relationships, solving problems before they occur, doing more departmental planning, and essentially doing those higher-priority tasks for which he or she was hired in the first place.

TEST YOURSELF

For each of the following statements, check true or false.

True   False

1. You can delegate responsibility but not authority.
2. Skillful delegating takes more time now but saves time later on.
3. Favoritism may be uncovered by looking at a supervisor's delegation habits.
4. Delegating should eventually involve all employees, not just those who are the most capable.
5. It is a good idea to keep matters of delegation (what is delegated to whom) confidential.
6. Most successful supervisors prefer to do things themselves rather than delegate.
7. It is okay for supervisors to keep a few therapeutic chores for themselves.
8. Skillful delegating can help significantly in motivating all employees to close their productivity gaps.
9. Delegate only those tasks that you are bored with.
10. Monitor the progress of the employee with the delegated task, but let the employee complete the task without your interference or control.

Turn to the back of the book to check your answers.
Total Correct _____

DISCUSSION QUESTIONS

1. Draw up a profile of an individual who, because of certain personality traits, might not be able to delegate and therefore should not be a supervisor.

2. Would most employees be happier and produce more if they were given more authority by their managers? Why or why not?

3. Why do so many supervisors use the lack of time as an excuse for not delegating? How would you convince such a person that spending time now could save time later?

4. What tasks could your supervisor delegate to you or others that would reduce her or his workload and provide you with the opportunity to learn?

CASE: TO DELEGATE OR **NOT TO DELEGATE**

OBJECTIVE

To provide simulated practice in delegating.

PROBLEM

Ricardo has taken a close look at himself and his department and has decided that he must delegate more of his duties to his employees for the following reasons: (1) He has been working sixty hours a week for more than six months. (2) The pressure of trying to get everything done has put him on edge with some of the staff. (3) He has not been sleeping well because of worry. Last night he spent two hours formulating the following list of responsibilities he might delegate to his five employees:

1. A weekly report that takes fifty minutes to prepare. This report could easily be delegated to Renee, but it would reveal certain departmental figures that have not been revealed to employees in the past. Nothing about the data is secret, but Ricardo feels he might lose control if everybody knows what goes on.

2. A weekly job that Ricardo has always enjoyed doing. Giselle would love to do the job (she would probably do it better than Ricardo), but Ricardo wants to keep it because it keeps him closer to his employees and facilitates communication. This job usually takes about one hour.

3. A routine weekly stock or supply room count that takes an hour and a half. Ricardo has delegated this job before, but he always ends up taking it back because the grumbling from the employee disturbs him more than doing the job

himself. Besides, sometimes the count is wrong, and he ends up doing the job himself anyway.

4. Sending, via e-mail, a fifteen-minute report to the computer center each afternoon at 4:00. Ricardo has refused to delegate this task because, if it is not done accurately, he fears he will be reprimanded by Bill. Karl would be able to do the job and not be overloaded.

5. A weekly (thirty minute) delivery job of a special report to top management. Ricardo has kept this task to do himself because it gives him a chance to have a cup of coffee and play a little politics with middle (and sometimes top) management executives.

6. A routine meeting each month, which many supervisors already delegate to a subordinate. It would be excellent training for Marty to have this assignment. Ricardo has kept it to himself, however, because he is afraid that something will happen at the meeting that he won't know about.

PROCEDURE

Have the class number off from one to five to form five small groups. Each group selects a group leader. Each group is to find a quiet location where they can discuss Ricardo's list of six tasks that could be delegated. Which should be delegated first? Which last? Each group should assign a priority number from 1 to 6 to each possibility. The leader of each group should try to get complete agreement on the allocation of priority numbers within a fifteen-minute period. The following factors should be taken into consideration: Try to

	MASTER SCHEDULE					
Responsibility	**Grp. 1**	**Grp. 2**	**Grp. 3**	**Grp. 4**	**Grp. 5**	**Class Choice**
1. Weekly report						
2. Fun job						
3. Stock room count						
4. E-mail						
5. Delivery job						
6. Routine meeting						

(1) save Ricardo as much time as possible, (2) relieve him of menial tasks, (3) improve departmental productivity, (4) train others for future supervisory roles, and (5) improve Ricardo's image as a supervisor. Once each group has completed its priority list, the results should be recorded on a master schedule on the blackboard.

After each group has recorded its choice, the points should be added horizontally and the total put in the last column under "Class Choice." The lower the number, the higher the priority given by the class.

ALTERNATIVE PROCEDURE

Instead of forming groups, have students do their own prioritization as instructed in the "Delegation Exercise" that follows this case and then engage in full class discussion.

CASE DISCUSSION AND QUESTIONS

Should Ricardo delegate all six possibilities? Which, if any, should he keep to himself? What other factors should he take into consideration?

DELEGATION **EXERCISE**

Read the case *To Delegate or Not to Delegate*. Assign a priority to each of the responsibilities listed next (from most important to least important) and give the reasons for your rankings. Which, if any, would you keep?

Weekly report   Priority _____
Rationale for assignment:
Fun job   Priority _____
Rationale for assignment:
Stock count   Priority _____
Rationale for assignment:
E-mail   Priority _____
Rationale for assignment:
Delivery job   Priority _____
Rationale for assignment:
Routine meeting   Priority _____
Rationale for Assignment:

You can match your priority assignments (and your rationale) with that of the author by turning to the back of this book.

PERSONAL GROWTH **EXERCISE**

Identify three tasks that you really enjoy doing in your job. List the things that make these tasks enjoyable. Then, consider whether these tasks can be delegated to others readily and, if you are currently a supervisor, whether you should go ahead and delegate them. While you may like these tasks, are they tasks that others can do, if properly delegated, so you can perform other higher-priority matters? If you feel unwilling to delegate them, no matter how much you like them and know you need to delegate them, what does this tell you about the challenges of being a supervisor? What does this tell you with respect to your commitment to being a supervisor who must be willing to let some things go in order to achieve overall departmental productivity?

TO LEARN MORE

The following references provide further information and instruction regarding the delegation process:

Blanchard, Ken, John P. Carlos, and Alan Randolph. *The 3 Keys to Empowerment: Release the Power within People for Astonishing Results.* San Francisco: Berrett-Koehler Publishers, 1999.

Huppe, Frank F. *Successful Delegation: How to Grow Your People, Build Your Team, Free Up Your Time and Increase Profits and Productivity.* Hawthorne, NJ: Career Press, 1994.

Maddux, Robert B. *Delegating for Results: An Action Plan for Success.* Menlo Park, CA: Crisp Publications, 1997.

Nelson, Robert B. *Delegation: The Power of Letting Go.* Glenview, IL: Scott, Foresman and Company, 1988.

Staub, Joseph T. *The Agile Manager's Guide to Delegating Work.* Bristol, VT: Velocity Business Publishing, 1998.

Tepper, Bruce B. *Delegation Skills.* Burr Ridge, IL: Richard D. Irwin, 1994.

chapter **thirteen**

USE YOUR KNOWLEDGE POWER

"Knowledge advances by steps, and not by leaps."

Lord Macaulay

Improving Productivity
Leading Teams
Communicating Effectively
Managing Conflict
Improving Performance
Managing Time
Benefiting from Change

A leader has three sources of power. First, considerable power goes with the job itself. It is called *position power*. It must be used wisely. The second source is *personality power*—encouraging greater productivity through the force of your personality and character. The third source is the most underestimated of all—*knowledge power*. You may not have viewed it this way in the past, but teaching your staff new ideas, skills, and competencies gives you increased influence and credibility in their eyes. This chapter will assist you in making the most of your knowledge power.

Employees usually take pride in learning something new and doing it well. When you make learning possible, you earn their respect and build enduring, productive relationships. As a supervisor, you have daily opportunities to use your knowledge power.

The supervisor is frequently the only person who teaches the many skills that new employees need to learn: how to operate machines, complete forms, understand procedures, work skillfully with difficult customers or patients, complete reports, maintain equipment, and so on. Permanent employees need to learn how to operate new generations of equipment, follow changing procedures, and perform tasks more effectively. On-the-job training never stops.

HOW TO TEACH BY NOT TEACHING

You can become an outstanding on-the-job instructor without employing any of the formal methods we usually associate with the traditional classroom teacher. All supervisors are models, and to a

PERFORMANCE COMPETENCIES

After you have finished reading this chapter, you should be able to:

- Apply the four-step teaching formula when providing on-the-job training

- Explain three errors to avoid when training new employees

surprising extent, your employees will adjust their behavior to the model you set. They will learn a great deal from you without your knowing it. But they also need specific help from you, and you want to provide this help in your own style without being labeled a "teacher." Instead of saying to a new employee, "Let me teach you how to do this," it might be better to say, "Let's figure out how you can do this quickly, comfortably, and correctly." Instead of saying to a regular employee, "Let me teach you to do it right the first time," it might be better to say, "Let me show you how I do this, and then you can figure out the best way for you to do it." It is one thing to be an effective classroom teacher; it is something else to be an effective on-the-job instructor.

YOUR ATTITUDE TOWARD TEACHING

What is your personal attitude toward sharing your knowledge with employees? Are you willing to set aside enough time to do it professionally? Do you desire to build a good reputation as a patient, caring instructor? Are you more like Marvin or Mary?

Marvin accepts a new employee into his department regardless of how much experience the individual has. When assuming his teaching role, he is patient, positive, and thorough, even if the learner is slow to catch on. As a result, Marvin develops a cohesive, productive, and loyal staff. His patient teaching attitude is admired and respected, especially by those from other cultures.

Mary consistently complains that new employees should have learned more in school. She shows little patience in teaching others. As a result, her staff makes more mistakes and personnel turnover is high. New workers are often forced to go to co-workers for help they need. Mary's negative attitude toward teaching others creates problems instead of solving them.

THE FOUR-STEP PROCESS

For years, professional instructors have followed the four-step teaching process that is best used in practical on-the-job situations. You may wish to view this process as a baseball game, in that you have four bases to cover before you can score. In other words, you (the instructor) will take the employee (learner) around four bases, one at a time. What follows will show you the moves you should make, the dangers you face, and the signals you should follow.

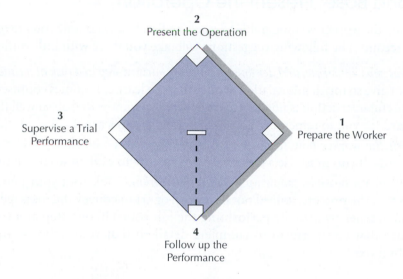

2
Present the Operation

3
Supervise a Trial
Performance

1
Prepare the Worker

4
Follow up the
Performance

First Base: Prepare the Worker

Because it is difficult to learn until one is psychologically and emotionally ready, your first responsibility is to help the new employee prepare for what you will teach. Here are four tips:

Put the learner at ease.   Give the employee time to adjust to you as a person before you move into teaching the job itself. Find out a little more about the employee, make small talk, and try to put the person at ease. Make the effort to establish a relaxed learning climate. It is time well spent.

State the job you are going to teach and find out what the employee already knows about it.   Do not waste time (or insult the employee) by teaching something he or she already knows. You may discover that a quick review is all that is necessary.

Motivate the person to learn the job.   Give the worker some reason to learn. You might suggest that it could help the individual earn the respect of others, or you might talk about the personal satisfaction and pride that can come from learning something new. Make it sound exciting. Your job as a teacher will be much easier if the worker wants to learn.

Place the worker in the correct learning position.   Just as a baseball player must have the right stance to hit the ball, it might be best for the worker to be at your left side instead of your right or to stand instead of sit. Determine the best physical position for the learner in each job you teach and be certain that he or she is located properly before you start. Attention to this factor will make the job easier for both parties. The correct learning position also means learning style. Do you know if the employee learns best by having things explained (auditory); by touch, feel, and doing (kinesthetic); or by demonstration first before attempting to do it (visual)? These are the three primary ways we learn. Knowing the way the employee learns best and seeking to accommodate it will prove your quickest, most efficient strategy.

Second Base: Present the Operation

Preparing the worker is comparable to reaching first base, and now you are ready to try for second. The following suggestions will take you there with little difficulty:

Describe, illustrate, and demonstrate one important step in a task at a time. Do not give so much information at once that the learner becomes confused. This careful instruction is not easy to do because you know the job so well that it is hard for you to remember how long it took you to learn it.

Tell the worker how to do the job, speaking clearly and slowly. Use simple words. If you must use a technical term, be sure to explain what you mean.

Whenever possible, follow up with an illustration. Take out your pencil and sketch the process; it need not be a work of art to convey the message. Show the learner by actually performing the job yourself, one step at a time. Be sure that you perform in complete detail so that your actions are easily observed.

Stress each key point.   Determine and then stress the one key point in each step of the operation as you go through the process. This emphasis will help the learner recall each step later by remembering the key points, and the process will thereby become easier. When a given job takes more than five steps, this procedure becomes increasingly important.

Instruct clearly, completely, and patiently, but do not give the worker more than can be mastered.   The greatest error that most supervisors commit is trying to teach too much too fast. They overestimate their teaching abilities and the employee's learning ability. If you try to teach too much at one time, you will only confuse the learner, and you will have to start over. Break the total job into separate steps and present them in sequence. Do not start the second step until the first has been mastered. If necessary, permit a lapse of time between steps. Focus on teaching the material thoroughly, even though time is at a premium.

Third Base: Supervise a Trial Performance

Give the new worker an immediate opportunity to do the job on a trial basis following this three-step procedure:

Have the learner do the job so that you can correct errors quickly.   Few new workers perform jobs perfectly the first time, and the only way to spot errors is to have the worker try out the process under your direction. Of course, errors should be pointed out and corrected quickly without showing impatience.

Have the employee explain the key points of the job.   It is important that the key points learned in the second step be repeated verbally by the learner during the first performance. Explaining each one makes it easier to remember.

Make sure the worker understands.   It is vital that the learner understand why it is best to do a job in a certain way and why the job is important to the total efficiency of the department. Give the employee the opportunity to ask questions.

The idea of this third step is to continue until you know the learner knows. If necessary, continue the dry runs until the skill is mastered.

Home Base: Follow Up the Performance

Tell the worker where to go for help. If you are not easily accessible to the new worker, find a co-worker to help the employee achieve and keep a high level of productivity. In short, appoint a co-worker who will be compatible with the new employee and willing to help when needed.

Check frequently to see if all is going well. Take time to check with the worker as well as the sponsor. Nothing can replace your own interest during the employee's first critical days of learning.

Taper off coaching so that the worker does not feel oversupervised. After a certain point, the employee deserves the satisfaction and freedom of going it alone. Stepping back will provide the worker with the confidence needed to assume further responsibility at a later date. Oversupervising can destroy initiative. Pull away when your job performance standards have been met.

If you follow these steps, your chances of success will be greatly enhanced. The new worker will know how to do the job, will do it right the first time, and will have the confidence to be a long-term, productive member of your department. You will have begun to establish a solid relationship with the new worker.

If You Strike Out

If you have tried the four basic steps and still feel that you have failed in your efforts to train a new employee, the cause could be one or more of the following three errors:

1. *Failure to devote enough time to training.* You must allow sufficient time to do the teaching job properly, even if it means putting aside some of your other responsibilities temporarily. It will not be easy to do, but the long-range productivity of your workers will prove that you have spent your time well.

2. *Failure to follow the system step by step.* The system provided in this chapter takes time, but it works. If you skip a step, the system will break down.

3. *Failure to show enough patience with the slow learner.* Few new workers will be as smart as you would like them to be. Some may learn more slowly than employees you have trained in the past. When you must teach a slow learner to do a job, you must slow your own pace or the results will be most disappointing. Cover each of the four bases with special patience and consideration, even if it means taking twice as much time as you had devoted in the past. Keep in mind that slow learners can become excellent producers once they master the job, so the extra time you devote will not be wasted.

DELEGATING TRAINING RESPONSIBILITIES

Professional educators frequently admit that the best way to learn to do something well is to teach it. At times you may wish to delegate the training of a new employee to a regular employee who fully understands and practices the four-step process effectively. By delegating, you will give recognition to the regular employee, provide excellent training to the new employee, and save yourself time. It may be wise, however, for you to retain the follow-up responsibility to make certain that the employee you selected as a coach does the job correctly.

GROUP INSTRUCTION

As a supervisor, you may be invited to make a presentation to other supervisors and your superiors. You can prepare for the event by making one or more group presentations to your own employees. Follow the same basic steps you use in individual instruction. That is, prepare the group (audience), present the new material (knowledge), gain involvement through questions, and summarize (follow through) by repeating the goal of the meeting.

As you follow these basic principles, you might also consider the following:

1. The more visual aids (keeping them simple) you prepare in advance, the more confidence you will have in your presentation and the more effective you will be.
2. Generally speaking, lecturing is the least effective teaching method, so strive for as much group interaction as possible.
3. Cover your subject carefully by outlining your instructions from start to finish.

Training never stops. As long as you must cope with an ever-increasing number of changes, you must accumulate new knowledge and pass on what you have learned to those who work for you. Everyone, including your superiors, finds it stressful to keep up with changes both in the environment in general and within the organization in particular. You will need to train yourself to deal with the impact of change, which means you will need to learn new ways to perform responsibilities. The greater the changes, the more you must learn; the more you learn, the more time you must spend instructing others and preparing them for change.

Changes manifest themselves in different ways: new procedures, new techniques, new generations of computers, new skills, and new ways of dealing with problems. As changes occur, you should occasionally search for new ideas and procedures to put into your own personal "knowledge bag." You should continue to educate yourself through both self-instruction and formal course programs. When you learn something that will improve the productivity of your department, you should pass it on, using the four-step method, to your staff.

Use your knowledge power wisely.

PERFORMANCE **CHECKLIST**

1. Employees take pride in learning something new and doing it well. When you make learning possible, you earn their respect and build enduring, productive relationships. As a supervisor, you have daily opportunities to use your knowledge power.
2. You must have the right attitude about teaching others, which means a willingness to set aside enough time to do it professionally and the desire to build a good reputation as a patient, caring instructor.
3. Effective on-the-job instruction involves a four-step process, much like the four bases in a baseball game:
   a. First base: Prepare the worker. Put the learner at ease. State what you are going to teach and find out what he or she already knows. Motivate the person to learn, and place him or her in the correct learning position.
   b. Second base: Present the operation. Describe, illustrate, and demonstrate one step at a time.

   Speak clearly and slowly when explaining how to do the job. Use illustrations when possible. Stress each key point. Instruct completely, but not more than the worker can master.
   c. Third base: Supervise a trial performance. Have the learner do the job so you can correct errors quickly. Have the employee explain key points. Make sure the worker understands.
   d. Home base: Follow-up the performance. Check frequently to see how the worker is doing, but taper off as he or she develops confidence to do the job on his or her own.
4. Delegating training responsibilities to an experienced employee is a great way to give recognition to the employee, provide excellent training to the new employee, and save yourself time.
5. When providing group instruction, use visual aids as much as possible, provide more opportunities for group interaction than lecturing, and cover your subject carefully by outlining your instruction from start to finish.

TEST **YOURSELF**

For each of the following statements, check true or false.

True   False

_____ _____   1. Employees take pride in learning to do something difficult.

_____ _____   2. Employees in training want their supervisors to act like classroom teachers when giving instructions.

_____ _____   3. Sharing your knowledge is one of the best ways to build a good relationship with a new employee.

_____ _____   4. Most supervisors are too slow and deliberate when it comes to teaching an employee a new skill.

_____ _____   5. Most learners are not interested in why it is better to do something one way rather than another.

_____ _____   6. For group presentations, one should not follow the same basic steps used in individual instruction.

_____ _____   7. Step 2 (present the operation) is the most critical step in the four-step process.

_____ _____   8. The primary reason for step 3 (try-out) is to discover errors quickly so corrections can be made.

_____ _____   9. Having the learner repeat key points verbally is not a part of the four-step process.

_____ _____   10. When making a presentation, ensure you cover your subject by outlining your instructions from start to finish.

Turn to the back of the book to check your answers.

Total Correct _____

DISCUSSION **QUESTIONS**

1. Assume that you are going to start training a new employee on your computer system tomorrow. How would you implement the four-step system?

2. From your experience as a non-supervisor (learner), do you feel that supervisors, generally speaking, are good instructors? Cite examples to support your view.

3. How can supervisors or team leaders train themselves to spend sufficient time on quality instruction that will earn respect from all employees? Be specific.

CASE: **TRAINING**

Bill has become increasingly disturbed over high personnel turnover, low productivity, poor quality standards, and the increasing number of mistakes made by new employees in all the departments under his management. As a result, he has designed a new orientation plan based on the premise that the quality of on-the-job training has not been up to standard. The supervisor will be totally responsible for the implementation and success of orientation.

The new plan specifies the following:

1. The four-step teaching method is mandated.

2. At the end of two weeks, the new employee and his or her supervisor will meet in Bill's office for a short evaluation and progress report.

3. Those supervisors who receive high marks from new employees will receive, as a reward, a one-time three-day weekend.

How do you respond to this plan? Do you feel the supervisor has been given a proper role in the plan? Will it reduce turnover, increase productivity, and curtail mistakes? What negative side effects might it generate? Is the plan too ambitious? Would Bill have time to follow through on all evaluations? Is Bill being too heavy-handed in his approach?

KNOWLEDGE TRANSFER **EXERCISE**

There is an old saying that the best way to learn something is to teach it. In this exercise, you are to select a special skill (if possible, one you have competence in) and teach it to a second party. The skill can be how to use the metric system or a calculator, or how to fill out a form—anything, in fact, that needs to be taught to a beginner. The learner can be an employee, a friend, a spouse, a child, or a fellow supervisor. Before you actually teach, prepare yourself by writing out how you intend to employ the various steps.

1. Prepare the learner:
2. Present the operation:
3. Try out performance:
4. Follow-up:

Once you have prepared yourself to teach the skill selected, and have actually taught it to a learner of your choice, evaluate your performance by writing out improvements you would make the second time around.

See the authors' comments in the back of the book.

PERSONAL GROWTH **EXERCISE**

How do you like to learn? What is your preferred learning style? Do you like to learn by doing, by seeing how something is done first, or by having things explained verbally or in writing before doing it? Think about how you like to learn and why. Then, think about someone you work with or that you know personally who likes to learn in a different way than you. Consider how you would adapt your preferred learning style in order to teach that person. Find an opportunity to teach something to that person and adapt your style to help him or her learn.

TO LEARN **MORE**

The following references provide information for managers on how to provide on-the-job training:

Jacobs, Ronald L., and Michael J. Jones. *Structured On-the-Job Training: Unleashing Employee Expertise in the Workplace.* San Francisco: Berrett-Koehler Publishers, 1995.

Nilson, Carolyn. *Training for Non-Trainers: A Do-It-Yourself Guide for Managers.* New York: AMACOM, 1990.

Improving Productivity

Leading Teams

Communicating Effectively

Managing Conflict

Improving Performance

Managing Time

Benefiting from Change

chapter **fourteen**

MANAGING PERFORMANCE

"Achieving good performance is a journey, not a destination."
Kenneth Blanchard

PERFORMANCE COMPETENCIES

After you have finished reading this chapter, you should be able to:

- Explain the purpose and goals of performance management and performance evaluations

- Explain five benefits that management receives from conducting performance evaluations

- Explain five benefits that employees receive from performance evaluations

- Describe the two parts of a performance evaluation

In most sizable organizations, supervisors evaluate each individual in their departments every six months or once a year. If you have been on the receiving end of such an evaluation, you probably still remember the supervisor, the printed instrument, the interview, and the results. For some, this may have been a completely rewarding experience in which you felt you received support, meaningful feedback, an objective assessment of your work that was fairly rewarded, and clear guidance on how to improve or continue good performance for the next evaluation cycle. For others, it was likely a frustrating, negative experience that left you feeling that your supervisor had no true understanding of the work you performed, and that the evaluation was unfair because it was not the product of meaningful feedback you could have received during the review period so you could correct performance deficiencies. As a result, the process left you feeling generally distrustful of your supervisor and the organization. The challenge as a supervisor is to engage in a performance evaluation process that meets your organization's purposes for conducting performance evaluations and also provides employees the former rather than the latter experience.

The primary purpose of this chapter is to prepare you to administer such evaluations for the first time or to help you improve on the way you have handled them in the past. The secondary purpose of this chapter, which we cover first, is to provide a context for conducting performance evaluations as part of a cycle of activities that must occur within the evaluation period, generally referred to as **performance management,** so that the evaluations you conduct will be meaningful and supportive for employees.

WHAT IS PERFORMANCE MANAGEMENT?

Performance management is a continuous process of identifying, measuring, and developing individual and group performance in organizations. It involves more than the process of reviewing an employee's performance, documenting it, drafting a form, and meeting to discuss the form before finalizing it and placing it in the employee's permanent file. These activities constitute the performance evaluation process, which as noted below is only a portion of five basic activities in which an organization and its supervisors typically engage as part of a comprehensive performance management regime. These five activities are:

1. Planning performance, including defining major job duties, developing performance standards for how these duties will be performed and evaluated, and establishing job and developmental goals and objectives.
2. Monitoring performance, including providing ongoing coaching and feedback to the employee as needed throughout the cycle period.
3. Evaluating the employee's job performance in fulfilling performance standards and meeting job and developmental goals and objectives.
4. Reviewing performance with the employee, including discussing what the employee accomplished, how well the employee performed those accomplishments, and progress in meeting job and development goals and objectives.
5. Renewing the performance plan for the next cycle, including establishing new performance expectations and job and developmental goals and objectives.

Clearly, if all your organization emphasizes are the steps involved with the evaluation alone, then it may be ignoring or seriously undervaluing the importance of this cycle of activities to support and render meaning to the review, evaluation or appraisal you ultimately perform. Yet, even when an organization implements a comprehensive cycle of such activities, it must give careful attention as to how it does this and not simply go through the motions. Otherwise, its results will be no better than simply focusing on the evaluation alone or doing no evaluation at all.

EFFECTIVE PERFORMANCE MANAGEMENT

Many books are in print regarding how to conduct performance evaluations and develop performance management processes and systems. Consultants can be retained to assist organizations to develop workable approaches to managing performance. Yet, there remains wide variance and disagreement on the best approach, with management practitioners at one extreme who wholly embrace formal evaluation methods, practitioners at the other extreme who would essentially advise throwing out evaluation and performance management processes altogether, and practitioners who recommend variants somewhere in between. Despite all the literature and expertise available on the subject, about all that is certain is that there is no one-size-fits-all approach and no approach that is perfect.

Nonetheless, if we could suggest a broad distinction between approaches that are ineffective and approaches that are more effective, it would break down this way:

1. *Approaches that are process- and form-driven are generally ineffective.* You can purchase books that provide standard forms and suggest specific

terminology and phrases to use to evaluate specific jobs and job duties. Organizations that are careless or simply feel pressured to implement something, if only for the sake of saying they have a system, might simply do a "cut and paste" job with such information and, suddenly and magically, have a process and forms in place. Such organizations typically take a top-down, command and control approach by creating a process with minimal or no input from employees or even front-line supervisors or concern about whether they will "buy in" to it. As the process is implemented, the associated cyclical activities typically involve a one-way supervisor-to-employee communication process where the employee is not engaged in conversations with the supervisor regarding performance expectations and does not receive appropriate feedback and coaching needed to improve performance prior to the evaluation. These organizations then expect better outcomes in the form of improved performance and the more efficient achievement of organizational goals.

2. *Approaches that are relationship- and communication-driven between supervisor and employee are generally more effective.* Other organizations recognize that implementing a performance management process involves a change process. When creating it, employees and managers at all levels are consulted to ensure they will buy in to it so that the process implemented fits within unit and organizational goals and strategies. Once it is implemented, the semi-annual or annual cycle of activities involves meaningful dialogue regarding establishing performance expectations, identifying work and career goals for the evaluation period, and consistent feedback and coaching directly relevant to the performance expectations identified. It also involves continual renegotiation of expectations as goals are accomplished or business demands change, and give-and-take during the evaluation period that generally is positive and presents no surprises because of

all that has preceded it to ensure the employee is supported. To be sure, processes and forms are utilized in such approaches, but they are used in service to these larger purposes.

It may be obvious at this point that one key distinction between these two approaches focuses on the underlying assumptions that organizations make about them. The first approach represents a more traditional, industrial-age model that doesn't fit well within the knowledge-worker era in which we live that emphasizes empowerment and choice for employees. Some of these distinctions are dramatic:

	TRADITIONAL, INDUSTRIAL-AGE MODEL	MODERN KNOWLEDGE-WORKER MODEL
Focus	Control employees and their work methods	Provide freedom and empowerment to employees to make decisions and participate in the process
Trust	Process instills distrust through "inspection" to find deficiencies	Process establishes trust through finding ways in which employees can maximize their contributions to achieving organizational goals
Evaluations	Focus on past results and tend to offer criticism about past performance	Future oriented and emphasis on establishing work objectives that can be achieved moving forward
Purpose	Often limited to determining "pecking order" and annual compensation	Improve performance, reinforce good performance, provide feedback, and support job and career development; compensation discussions held separately
Feedback	One-time, one-way communication process from supervisor to employee	Ongoing two-way feedback loop in a supportive climate designed to foster the supervisor–employee relationship

The transition from former to current models for performance management does not occur overnight, and many organizations continue to struggle with making the transition successfully. You may find in your organization, as in many organizations, aspects of both. For the transition to be complete, the following elements will generally exist.[1]

1. *Congruence with strategy:* Employees should have a clear understanding of how the behaviors on which they are being evaluated connect to organizational goals rather than feel they are being measured purely for arbitrary or irrelevant purposes.

2. *Thoroughness:* The employee should be evaluated on the key job responsibilities for his or her position. This is typically between four and seven such responsibilities. Ideally, the process should encompass a cycle of activities over the course of a year, rather than a shorter period, so that the full picture of performance can be observed, rather than merely a "blip" that may provide an inaccurate measure.

3. *Practicality:* Though forms are involved, if there are too many of them or if they are lengthy and complex, they will not be embraced by supervisors and employees alike. If the processes used do not facilitate the two-way communication process between supervisor and employee effectively, they should probably be rejected in favor of simpler, more flexible methods.

4. *Meaningfulness:* The performance management process should have deeper purposes beyond compensation considerations alone, including full opportunity for discussion of challenges and barriers affecting performance, rene-

gotiation of goals as business needs change, training and professional development needs to meet job goals and future growth opportunities, and other issues that will support the employee's success.

5. *Specificity:* The system should provide specific and clear guidance, coaching, and feedback regarding expectations. Effective communication is the foundation for this to occur. This includes constructive as well as positive feedback. Discussions about performance problems should be solution oriented.

6. *Inclusiveness of employee "voice":* Research has demonstrated the more involved the employee is in the performance management process, including not just the feedback loop but in the actual design of the process and the opportunity to develop in partnership with the supervisor performance expectations, job design, and job and career goals, the more likely the employee will experience increased satisfaction and value in the system, become increasingly motivated to improve performance, and perceive increased fairness in the system's ability to evaluate his or her performance and provide appropriate, fair rewards.

This last item regarding employee voice is perhaps the single most important element that is different from traditional approaches. It is also something over which supervisors can have the greatest influence, despite inherent limitations and flaws that may exist within the organization's processes otherwise.

PERFORMANCE EVALUATION INSTRUMENTS

When done effectively as part of a performance management process, performance evaluations give you an opportunity to improve your counseling techniques. They permit you to apply the five Rs of counseling you learned in Chapter 9. As such, they should be viewed as a positive experience—something you can learn to do well that will put you in good stead as you move into higher management roles.

A formal evaluation usually requires that the evaluator make use of an evaluation form. This form documents the results of the evaluation and is placed in the employee's employment file. There are almost as many different evaluation instruments as there are organizations that use them. Few, if any, fully satisfy the people who design them or the supervisors who use them. Almost any form, however, can be used effectively if your attitude toward it is positive and you take seriously your obligation to provide coaching, feedback, and other support throughout the review period leading up to preparing the form and meeting to discuss it. Without this commitment, any form, no matter how carefully prepared, will be meaningless.

Three examples of evaluation instruments are provided for your consideration as you read the remainder of this chapter. Study them closely and think about how each form could serve you when evaluating an employee's performance. The first two forms provide specific pre-determined criteria on which to evaluate employees. The third form is divided into two segments. The first segment is the behavioral performance standards form, which is filled out at the beginning of the performance management cycle, ideally through conversation and agreement between supervisor and employee. Unlike the previous two forms in which pre-set evaluation criteria are provided, the supervisor must create this criteria based on the key job responsibilities for the position (usually between four and seven). The second segment is the actual evaluation form in which the supervisor must determine for each job responsibility whether the employee met, exceeded, or did not meet expectations as originally identified.

SHORT-FORM APPRAISAL*

EVALUATION OF WORK PERFORMANCE

QUANTITY of Individual's Work	LOW	LESS THAN ACCEPTABLE	COMPLETELY ACCEPTABLE	MORE THAN ACCEPTABLE	HIGH

SUPPORTING COMMENTS: _____
_____
_____
_____
_____

QUALITY of Individual's Work	LOW	LESS THAN ACCEPTABLE	COMPLETELY ACCEPTABLE	MORE THAN ACCEPTABLE	HIGH

SUPPORTING COMMENTS: _____
_____
_____
_____
_____

CONTRIBUTIONS to Work Group's Performance	LOW	LESS THAN ACCEPTABLE	COMPLETELY ACCEPTABLE	MORE THAN ACCEPTABLE	HIGH

SUPPORTING COMMENTS: _____
_____
_____
_____
_____

SIGNATURE OF EMPLOYEE _____ PREPARED BY _____

Manager's Signature _____ Human Resources approval _____

*Supporting comments must be specific and must include examples of performance that have been demonstrated to be in harmony with the rating.

LONG-FORM APPRAISAL*

PERFORMANCE EVALUATION AND
DEVELOPMENT PLAN

General

Name: _____   Date of Evaluation: _____

Date Hired: _____   Division and Dept.: _____

Job Title: _____   Evaluating Manager: _____

Time in Present Position: _____   Reviewed By: _____

The purpose of this evaluation is to:

1. **Set Goals.** The manager and the employee establish mutually agreed-upon goals for future progress and development.

2. **Inform.** The manager and the employee communicate openly and honestly about performance.

3. **Develop.** The manager and the employee identify actions the employee can take to enhance his or her development.

4. **Evaluate.** The manager and the employee evaluate results based on pre-established goals and performance measures.

I. POSITION OBJECTIVES AND MAJOR RESPONSIBILITIES. Summarize specific responsibilities of the job.

_____

_____

_____

_____

_____

II. ACCOMPLISHMENTS AND/OR IMPROVEMENTS: What specific accomplishments and/or improvements has this individual made since the last review? What progress has been made toward meeting established performance goals?

_____

_____

_____

_____

*Reproduced by permission of Hewlett-Packard, Inc.

Please consider the employee's demonstrated performance and mark the circle which most clearly describes that performance.

EXCEPTIONAL: Performance consistently far exceeds expectations.

VERY GOOD: Performance consistently exceeds normal expectations and job requirements.

GOOD: Performance consistently meets expectations and job requirements.

ACCEPTABLE: Performance usually meets expectations and minimum requirements for the job.

UNACCEPTABLE: Performance is below the minimum acceptable level.

WORK QUALITY: The reliability, accuracy, and neatness of work produced.

○ Exceptional   ○ Very Good   ○ Good   ○ Acceptable   ○ Unacceptable

_____
_____
_____
_____
_____

WORK QUANTITY: The amount of volume of work turned out.

○ Exceptional   ○ Very Good   ○ Good   ○ Acceptable   ○ Unacceptable

_____
_____
_____
_____

JUDGMENT: The ability to make well-reasoned, sound decisions that affect work performance.

○ Exceptional   ○ Very Good   ○ Good   ○ Acceptable   ○ Unacceptable

_____
_____
_____
_____
_____

INITIATIVE: The combination of job interest, dedication, and willingness to extend oneself to complete assigned tasks.

○ Exceptional   ○ Very Good   ○ Good   ○ Acceptable   ○ Unacceptable

_____

_____

_____

_____

_____

TEAMWORK: The working relationship established with fellow employees in the working environment.

○ Exceptional   ○ Very Good   ○ Good   ○ Acceptable   ○ Unacceptable

_____

_____

_____

_____

_____

DEPENDABILITY: The reliance that can be placed on an employee to persevere and carry through to completion any task assigned. This also applies to attendance and punctuality.

○ Exceptional   ○ Very Good   ○ Good   ○ Acceptable   ○ Unacceptable

_____

_____

_____

_____

_____

_____

PERFORMANCE SUMMARY:

_____

_____

_____

_____

_____

_____

III. DEVELOPMENT PLAN: What specific action can you suggest to help the employee improve his or her performance? How can you, as manager, help?

_____

_____

_____

_____

_____

_____

_____

_____

IV. NEXT YEAR'S GOAL STATEMENTS: Establish with your manager goals that may include new and better ways to carry out job responsibilities, as well as plans for personal development. Stated goals should be included as a basis for the next formal performance evaluation.

_____

_____

_____

_____

_____

_____

_____

V. EMPLOYEE COMMENTS: Each individual evaluated is encouraged to add any comments to this review. If additional space is needed, attach a separate sheet.

_____

_____

_____

_____

_____

I am signing this evaluation to indicate that my manager and I have had a discussion of the above comments.

_____   _____
Date   Employee Signature

BEHAVIORAL PERFORMANCE STANDARDS FORM

Performance standards for job responsibilities for:

Employee: _____ Job Title: _____ Date: ___/__/__
Supervisor: _____ Review period: From __/__/____ To __/__/____

Identify primary job responsibilities from position description (typically 4-7)

1.
2.
3.
4.
5.
6.
7.

Identify performance standards for each job responsibility with behavioral standards descriptors for "meets", "exceeds" and "does not meet" expectations indicating:

➢ **Quantity:** How much or how many must be done
➢ **Quality:** How well the job responsibility must be done
➢ **Timeliness:** How fast or by what deadline the job responsibility must be done
➢ **Expense:** Under what cost constraints the job responsibility must be done
➢ **Other:** Customer satisfaction; independent intiative required; other relevent, verifiable measures

1. Job Responsibility: _____
(add additional lines as necessary)

Behaviors typical of "Exceeds Expectations:"

Behaviors typical of "Meets Expectations:"

Behaviors typical of "Does Not Meet Expectations:"

(Continue to identify behavior performance standards for up to 7 job responsibilities)

7. Job Responsibility: _____
(add additional lines as necessary)

Behaviors typical of "Exceeds Expectations:"

Behaviors typical of "Meets Expectations:"

Behaviors typical of "Does Not Meet Expectations:"

Additional comments for supervisor and employee _____

_____

Employee's Signature _____ Date _____

Supervisor's Signature _____ Date _____

PERFORMANCE EVALUATION

Employee: _____   Date: ___/__/__
Supervisor: _____   Job Title: _____
Review period: From __/__/____ To __/__/____

List primary job responsibilities (These should be the same 4-7 responsibilities from the position description that you listed on the "Behavioral Performance Standards Form".)

1.
2.
3.
4.
5.
6.
7.

For each job responsibility,

1) Make a statement of evaluation based on the previously agreed upon standards. Indicate whether the employee:

   * Generally "Exceeds Expectations"
   * Generally "Meets Expectations"
   * Generally "Does Not Meet Expectations"

2) Describe the behavior or incidents that you have observed or verified that led to this evaluation.

3) State the outcomes or results of the behavior.

1. Job Responsibility: _____

With respect to this job responsibility, this employee generally:
a. exceeds expectations ___; b. meets expectations ___; c. does not meet expectations ___

Please describe the behaviors the employee demonstrated related to this job responsibility.

What are the outcomes or results of the behaviors?

2. Job Responsibility: _____

With respect to this job responsibility, this employee generally:
a. exceeds expectations ___: b. meets expectations ___: c. does not meet expectations ___

Please describe the behaviors the employee demonstrated related to this job responsibility.

What are the outcomes or results of the behaviors?

3. Job Responsibility: _____

With respect to this job responsibility, this employee generally:
a. exceeds expectations ____; b. meets expectations ____; c. does not meet expectations ____

> *Please describe the behaviors the employee demonstrated related to this job responsibility.*

> *What are the outcomes or results of the behaviors?*

(Continue to evaluate performance for up to 7 job responsibilities as identified above and on the Behavioral Performance Standards Form.)

Goals for next review period:

> *State the specific areas of performance needing improvement and/or knowledge, skills and abilities to be developed:*

> *What specific development opportunities does the employee need to pursue for the next review period?*

Overall Performance:

With respect to overall performance, this employee:

a. _____ exceeds expectations
b. _____ meets expectations
c. _____ does not meet expectations

Comments

Employees's Comments (optional) _____

_____

_____

Employee's Signature _____ Date _____

Supervisor's Signature _____ Date _____

WHY EMPLOYERS EVALUATE PERFORMANCE

Organizations generally seek to fulfill a number of goals when they institute performance evaluation processes:

1. *Link evaluations to departmental objectives.*   For example, your superior (evaluating you as a supervisor) might tie your evaluation to the success you have had in reaching the objectives you submitted at an earlier time. If you have made excellent progress toward the goals approved earlier, chances are good that you will receive a positive report. Other factors that may be considered include human relations skills, dependability, and the ability to handle problem employees.

2. *Accountability.*   Through the evaluation process, the employee is asked to account for past performance based on performance standards identified and agreed on through discussions with his or her supervisor that are then included in the evaluation instrument.

3. *Compensation.*   In a majority of organizations, salary increases, bonuses, and other forms of compensation are tied to the performance rating. The evaluation also provides a record justifying the compensation given. Results are therefore critical to those being evaluated.

4. *Job and career development.*   It is inevitable and fortuitous that going through the evaluation process frequently causes employees to review their own career progress or master plans. More than anything else, an evaluation tells you how you are doing, and whether you should make adjustments to your long-term career path and accept new challenges to get there. It is a time of self-evaluation.

5. *Feedback on performance.*   Ideally, the evaluation instrument is a culmination of a year-long conversation between supervisor and employee. If done appropriately, there should be no surprises. The evaluation is essentially a communication tool confirming the performance achieved and identifying areas needing improvement or in which to continue good performance.

6. *Performance improvement.*   As a front-line supervisor, you will want to tie your evaluations to the future planning for your employees. If they receive weak evaluations that do not reflect performance accurately, what can they do to make improvements before the next period arrives? What self-improvement projects might they undertake to eliminate deficiencies? This is Mrs. Petronzio's principal reason for evaluating performance:

Mrs. Petronzio is the director of a convalescent home with a staff of thirty-six. Three years ago, she was required by new management to do evaluations on all employees. She viewed the new responsibility as a challenge that could increase staff productivity and spent considerable time reading about performance evaluation techniques and getting acquainted with the form.

Her first evaluation was with Maisie, a vocational nurse, who was highly dependable and capable of taking over any position that did not require the presence of a registered nurse. Mrs. Petronzio rated Maisie excellent in every category but cooperativeness because Maisie had become irritated with others in a variety of situations.

Under Mrs. Petronzio's gentle probing, Maisie admitted that she was frequently upset over the poor attitudes and performance of registered nurses who were paid substantially more than she. When Mrs. Petronzio suggested that Maisie could qualify as a registered nurse with special training at a local college, she was interested. Eventually, she undertook the program. Not only did Maisie receive an excellent rating in all factors the next time around but, after three years of training, she became a registered nurse—something that might not have occurred without engaging in this evaluation process.

BENEFITS TO MANAGEMENT

Who benefits from these formal performance evaluation programs? Why are they used so often? Are they truly helpful to employees?

Management has good reason for supporting the program and insisting that all people (including themselves) be measured occasionally under a standardized procedure.

1. It is the best way to make sure that the high-production employee is identified and recognized and that the low-production employee is located and counseled.
2. When properly administered by the front-line supervisor, the system builds a stronger working relationship between the supervisor and the employee, and thus helps improve performance.
3. The policy produces a more objective basis for salary increases and promotions.
4. A formal system, although never perfect, will provide better and more uniform treatment of individuals by supervisors than having no system.
5. Employee evaluations provide organizations with the help they need to maintain and improve quality as well as quantity standards.

Management, however, is the first to recognize that the key to the success of the evaluation system is its administration. For this reason, supervisors are being given more training to make the system work. (It is also why you are reading this chapter.)

BENEFITS TO EMPLOYEES

It is easy to see why management endorses a good evaluation system that is administered properly, but what about its benefits to employees? Do they really come out ahead? In many cases, the answer is yes for the following reasons:

1. The procedure clarifies what is expected of the employee.
2. It provides a system of recognition and prevents employees from being ignored or lost.
3. It allows the supervisor the opportunity to praise good work.
4. The evaluation helps the employee pinpoint weak areas so that improvements can be made.
5. It forces periodic communication between the supervisor and the employee.

6. It provides the employee with a work record that can be used for making decisions about promotions and bonuses.

USING A POSITIVE APPROACH

These benefits to managers and employees for evaluating performance all seem good. Why, then, are rating systems unpopular with many supervisors and employees? Many employees complain every time their review period comes along, and some supervisors dread the process just as much. If the process is so beneficial, why do supervisors and employees react this way?

Supervisors usually take one of two positions when it comes to formal reviews. Those who choose the first position see the value in the process and turn it into a positive tool. Their employees look forward to it. Even in organizations that are more process-driven and have not implemented an effective performance management process, these supervisors do not make excuses and find ways to provide meaningful support throughout the process and to ultimately make the resulting evaluation process a positive experience. Those who take the other position refuse to see the purpose and fight the process most of the way. Their employees resent the procedure as much as their supervisors do. In other words, you, as the administrating official, determine the success or failure of any evaluation system regardless of any deficiencies in the process; you can look forward to every review situation, or you can try to avoid it. How you handle the procedure will determine whether your employees consider it an opportunity or a disagreeable chore.

The positive approach pays off for professional supervisors because they use the evaluation system to improve productivity in their departments. They take advantage of the procedure to build better relationships with their people. They make it a vehicle to get raises and promotions for their better employees. Here are some suggestions to help you turn formal reviews into a positive rather than a negative force.

Use the System with a Positive Attitude

Use whatever evaluation form the company provides with a positive attitude. Do not complain to your employees about the form's shortcomings; all forms have them. If you have suggestions on how to improve the form or the process, communicate them directly to your supervisor or to the company's human resources department. If you spend your time complaining and trying to change the system, you won't have enough time left to make it work.

Do Not Take the Easy Way Out

With all your other responsibilities, you may be tempted to back away from an honest evaluation of your people by giving them a better rating than they deserve, sometimes referred to as the *error of leniency*. Employees know how they perform better than you do, and may lose respect for you if you are too soft or permit intimidation. Most employees want an accurate evaluation and may feel shortchanged and disappointed if you do not give it to them. However, be sure to be fair. A minimal rating or a grudgingly given high mark may leave the employee feeling unappreciated. Motivation to produce can drop dramatically if employees

sense that you are not objective. As you complete the evaluation form, try following these suggestions:

1. Remember that you are appraising the employee's work, not his or her personality. Base your evaluation on objective data such as production figures, competence, attendance records, or mistakes.

2. Avoid basing your evaluation on the potential of the employee rather than on actual performance. Evaluate what the employee contributed to the department's productivity, not what he or she is capable of contributing.

3. Base your evaluation on the employee's average performance during the period covered, not on isolated examples of extremely good or bad work. One good or bad day, week, or month shouldn't necessarily result in a corresponding high or low rating.

4. Avoid the *halo effect.* In other words, rather than permit one prominent, typically positive quality to influence your rating of other factors, include all important productivity factors. Similarly, avoid the *horn effect,* by which one prominent, typically negative quality influences the overall rating.

5. Avoid the *error of central tendency,* in which you select the middle rating on all factors. Supervisors can fall into this trap when they are in a hurry or want to play it safe because they do not want to accept the responsibility of justifying a high rating or a low rating.

Always Discuss the Evaluation Openly with Employees

Different organizations follow different procedures. Some require that employees evaluate themselves first and then let the supervisor react. Some require that the supervisor rate the employees first and then let them react. Some leave it up to the supervisor.

Regardless of the system (and each has advantages), you should discuss the evaluation openly with the employee, explaining and, if necessary, defending your position on all factors rated. Try to establish two-way communication in which the employee has a free and fair chance to present his or her case. An employee rating without an unhurried discussion may be in compliance with the system, but it is a mockery of its purpose. Important employment decisions are based on documented performance. Pay raises, promotions, transfers, and keeping one's job when a layoff is coming are serious matters and often determined by one's performance. Supervisors need to know how to evaluate performance and how to conduct the evaluation conference so that the evaluation is accurate. If your company has a training program on this topic, take advantage of the opportunity and attend. Many times local colleges put on seminars related to management or supervision, and performance evaluation is generally included as a topic.

TWO PARTS OF THE PERFORMANCE EVALUATION

The two parts to the performance evaluation are *content* and *process*. Let us consider content first. The content is the evaluation form itself. A typical form, like the ones in this chapter, includes its purpose, instructions on how to fill it out, and where copies are to go. It contains the behavior categories being assessed and the rating scales by which performance is measured.

The supervisor should give the employee a copy of the form at the beginning of the evaluation period so they both may refer to it from time to time. Together they can focus on defining the categories of behavior. For example, for the first two forms provided in this chapter, the employee may need a more complete definition or clarification of exactly what behaviors the supervisor sees in the category labeled "Dependability." Of the many behaviors that could fall into this category, those behaviors the supervisor thinks fall in this category need to be communicated to the employee throughout the performance management cycle, not just at the end when employees receive their performance evaluations. If the supervisor does not convey clear behavioral expectations of dependability, then employees have to guess as to what the supervisor thinks dependability is; they may guess wrong. Supervisors may find it necessary to include the employees in defining terms.

With respect to the third form in this chapter, the precise behaviors and responsibilities on which the employee will be evaluated should be defined at the beginning of the performance management cycle through two-way discussion and preparation of the behavioral expectations form.

The rating scale should also be considered carefully because it has serious pitfalls. In our example from the first two forms, notice that the rating scale is as follows:

○ Exceptional   ○ Very Good   ○ Good   ○ Acceptable   ○ Unacceptable

Most supervisors find it easy to explain the differences between "Exceptional" performance and "Unacceptable" performance because they are the extremes. But many experience difficulty explaining the difference between, say, "Acceptable" performance and "Good" performance. Trouble brews when an employee asks what exactly they have to do to move from the lower rating of "Acceptable" to the higher rating of "Good." If the supervisor cannot tell employees what they must do to improve, one may wonder exactly how the supervisor arrived at that rating in the first place.

Similar challenges exist with the third form provided in this chapter, which reduces the number of ratings from five to three: (1) Meets expectations; (2) Exceeds expectations; and (3) Does not meet expectations. At a minimum, the supervisor must be clear upfront how "Meets expectations" is defined when preparing the

Behavioral Performance Standards Form so that employees will see how their actual performance compares to this standard when they receive the actual evaluation form.

CONDUCTING THE EVALUATION

The second part of the performance evaluation is the process. The process is how the performance review or conference is conducted. It is the who, what, where, how, and when of the evaluation. Many employees complain that their evaluation is completed by their supervisor and merely handed to them for their signature without a personal or private review conference. The employee is left out of the process entirely. Leaving the employee out is a big mistake. As mentioned earlier, performance evaluations have enormous effects on employees, and they expect and deserve a professionally conducted review. This process takes time, and a professional review would have the following characteristics:

Who does it?   One's immediate supervisor is usually the person who is in the position to observe directly the performance of an employee. Employees are skeptical of a review done by someone who does not see their work.

What is done?   During the review, the supervisor allows time for questions and an opportunity for the employee to provide input into her or his final rating. This process takes open two-way communication. The supervisor needs to listen and be open to changing the rating during the discussion. Hurry through the formal evaluation and it will not accomplish its purpose. To rush the procedure is to destroy it. You must make time to do it properly.

Where is it done?   The evaluation is a confidential matter between the supervisor and employee. It should be done in a quiet, private place.

How is it done?   The review meeting deserves time, giving the employee the opportunity to thoroughly discuss her or his performance. The talk–listen ratio should be balanced or in favor of the employee, meaning that the supervisor should do most of the listening and the employee most of the talking. You must be sure of your ground when you rate an employee in a way that will affect the individual's future. When you must give an unsatisfactory rating, make sure you follow these steps: (1) Have all the facts at your disposal; (2) discuss the problem with the employee; (3) take your decision to both your superior and the human resources director; and (4) be ready to recognize an improvement in productivity if and when it happens. Of course, if you have engaged in ongoing conversation about these issues through the performance management cycle, these matters should not come as a surprise during the evaluation meeting.

When is it done?   Do not be late giving the evaluation. Late evaluations may cause a delay in a raise, promotion, or other important employment decision for the employee. Do it on time or before the last possible due date. If evaluations are routinely late in coming, the employees may conclude that performance does not matter to the supervisor and may result in lower productivity or job dissatisfaction. Do not convey to the employee that once the regular evaluation is over, no further help or counseling will occur until the next time. If the evaluation was positive, the employee may feel you will ignore future problems. If it was negative, he or she may feel that you will not be available for more help until the next evaluation session. Good follow-up procedures are essential to the success of the system.

USING THE EVALUATION PROCESS AS A POSITIVE TOOL

The first time an employee is formally evaluated can be extremely important to both the individual and the organization. Take extra time to (1) explain the purpose and procedure, (2) go over the form in detail so that no misunderstandings remain, and (3) make sure the employee has an opportunity to ask questions and feel at home with the procedure.

Introspective self-evaluation is the primary purpose of any evaluation program. It is not a tool to embarrass, intimidate, dispose of, annoy, or harass an employee, but rather to help the employee gauge his or her progress and future with the company. Geared to the needs of the employee, the system cannot fail; geared exclusively to the needs of the organization, it becomes suspect and loses its value.

Many evaluation systems seem overcomplicated with too much detail. Even so, try to work within the system by following the instructions carefully. Follow the necessary red tape without griping. The system depends on you to make it effective.

Sometimes you may be so enthusiastic over an outstanding evaluation that you either make or imply a promise that you cannot keep in a reasonable length of time. Nothing destroys morale more than a broken promise; therefore, you must protect everyone by making only clear statements that cannot be misinterpreted.

To judge, measure, or evaluate the performance of another person fairly is a sensitive, difficult process. Realizing that it is never easy to separate performance from personality, accept all available help to keep the procedure from backfiring and causing serious human problems. The suggestions presented will help you stay on the right track, but they cannot remove the responsibility of the ultimate rating decision from your shoulders. You are the only one close enough to the employee to have all the necessary facts and data, who can provide the quality counseling that must accompany the process, and who can translate the theory into reality.

PERFORMANCE **CHECKLIST**

1. Performance management is a continuous process of identifying, measuring, and developing individual and group performance in organizations. It involves a cycle of activities, including (1) planning, (2) monitoring, (3) evaluating, (4) reviewing performance, and (5) reviewing the performance plan for the next cycle.

2. The most effective organizational performance management regimes are those that are relationship- and communication-driven rather than process- and form-driven. This means that rather than simply being a process where supervisors complete annual performance evaluation forms to satisfy organizational expectations, the organization promotes annual activities such as coaching, feedback, conversations regarding job and career development, and opportunities for renegotiating performance expectations and goals so that the year-end performance evaluation is meaningful, objective, and more likely to be supported by the employee.

3. More organizations are developing performance management systems that involve more of a partnership between supervisor and employee rather

than the traditional top-down, command and control approach. Elements of an effective performance management system that embraces this more supportive approach include (1) congruence with organizational strategy, (2) thoroughness, (3) practicality, (4) meaningfulness, (5) specificity, and (6) inclusiveness of employee "voice." As a supervisor, even if the system in your organization doesn't incorporate these elements, you can have the greatest influence in the process by doing more to include the employee's voice in the process.

4. Standard goals that organizations hope to accomplish when evaluating performance are to (1) link performance to departmental objectives, (2) ensure accountability to performance standards identified, (3) determine compensation, (4) identify job and career goals and development strategies, (5) provide feedback on performance, and (6) conduct future planning to determine areas needing improvement or areas to continue good performance.

5. Despite clear benefits to supervisors and employees, many are resistant to the performance evaluation process. While no performance evaluation process is perfect, as a supervisor, you must have a positive attitude about it, not criticize it openly before employees, and ensure that you engage in appropriate activities such as coaching and feedback throughout the performance management cycle. If you do this, you will better ensure that employees will support and find value in the year-end evaluation process.

6. In addition to conveying a positive attitude to employees about the performance evaluation process, you will also be more effective in evaluating performance if you (1) avoid common rating errors such as the halo effect, the central tendency error, and evaluating performance based on isolated incidents; (2) discuss the evaluation openly with employees; (3) ensure that the "content" of the evaluation, including all rating criteria, is objective, concrete, not subject to interpretation, and fully explained; and (4) ensure that the "process" for performing the evaluation and conducting the evaluation meeting provides full opportunity for the employee to ask questions, raise concerns, and be treated fairly and objectively when performance deficits are addressed.

TEST YOURSELF

For each of the following statements, check true or false.

True False

1. There is no such thing as a perfect evaluation form.
2. There is no relationship between formal evaluations and motivation.
3. Most supervisors are overly critical in their evaluations.
4. Evaluate the worker's personality along with his or her productivity.
5. Always base an evaluation on the employee's potential.
6. Evaluations should center on typical or average performance, not high or low spots.
7. The halo effect occurs when good or bad performance in one area is permitted to influence ratings in other areas.
8. The error of central tendency is to rate central factors (characteristics) extremely high.
9. Final results from evaluations should never be discussed with the employee.
10. The evaluation and the interview that follows should deal with past performance and not future goals.

Turn to the back of the book to check your answers.
Total Correct____

DISCUSSION QUESTIONS

1. If you were the owner of a firm with fifty employees, would you initiate a formal evaluation program? Would you tie pay raises to the results? Would you develop your own instrument?

2. Can you explain why so many supervisors dread formal evaluations? Does their attitude keep them from doing a good job of reviewing? Why is it so difficult to judge or evaluate others?

3. Do you agree that employees should complete their own evaluation forms and then let the supervisor react and make changes before submitting the forms to the human resources department?

4. Recall the details of your last performance evaluation. How was it handled? What could have been done to improve it, to make it more accurate and beneficial to you?

5. Often, supervisors and employees remark that categories of performance are vague, that their definitions of performance are unexplained. For example, review the Short-Form Appraisal and define what exactly is meant by "Quality of Individual's and Work." Explain the difference between "Less than acceptable" and "Completely acceptable" in one's quality of work.

CASE: OPTION

OBJECTIVE

To discover the advantages and disadvantages of two different approaches to formal evaluation of employees.

PROBLEM

Yolanda and Gerald are in complete disagreement regarding the best way to evaluate their employees. Bill, tired of the conflict, must intervene to help resolve the dispute.

PROCEDURE

Everyone in the class or seminar reads the following material and then discusses the advantages and disadvantages of each approach from their point of view as employees being evaluated. After the discussion, they vote on the approach (that of Yolanda or Gerald) they prefer.

YOLANDA'S TECHNIQUE

Yolanda prefers the non-directive, soft approach. She likes to sit down in a non-threatening manner and quietly discuss and settle on the rating of each factor without any advance preparation from either party. She feels that when employees fill out their own evaluation forms in advance, they tend to defend each rating they give themselves, and the interview may turn into an argument. Her approach is to ask the employee what rating she or he feels is right. If she agrees, they move on quickly; if not, they talk it over. Yolanda frequently gives in, but she argues that her concession is not a "whitewash" job. She believes that through open discussion, employees sense their own shortcomings. Other pressures are not necessary. Her ratings are consistently higher than those of Gerald.

GERALD'S TECHNIQUE

Gerald takes a more direct, hard approach. He follows the procedure of giving the evaluation instrument to each employee a few days in advance, asking that it be completed and brought to the interview at the scheduled time. In the meantime, he spends considerable time completing the same form independently. The interview consists of comparing forms and adjusting differences. When Gerald feels he is right, he takes a firm stand and presents all possible data to back up his lower or higher rating. He does, however, make some adjustments when justified. He is always complimentary on high ratings, strives to be fair, and takes time to tie the procedure to long-term career plans.

CASE DISCUSSION AND QUESTIONS

Which supervisor would you prefer to rate you? Why? Discuss how each technique might be improved or how a combination of both could be more effective.

RATE YOURSELF EXERCISE

The purpose of this exercise is to introduce you to formal evaluations by having you *evaluate yourself*. In doing this, consider your performance on either a current job or one you have had in the past. Rate yourself excellent, good, fair, or poor on the following factors, or if you prefer, whether you meet, exceed, or do not meet expectations.

Factor	Rating
Attitude	
Productivity	

Reliability

Job knowledge

Relations with others

Self-motivation

Improvement since
   last rating

Initiative

New ideas submitted

Willingness to listen

Now that you have rated yourself, please do one of the following:

1. Have your present superior actually complete the same rating form on you for matching and discussion purposes.
2. Complete the evaluation form the way you *think* your supervisor would do it, then match with your previous self-evaluation.

In doing this, be 100 percent honest with yourself.

Factor	Rating
Attitude	
Productivity	
Reliability	
Job knowledge	
Relations with others	
Self-motivation	
Improvement since last rating	
Initiative	
New ideas submitted	
Willingness to listen	

PERSONAL GROWTH **EXERCISE**

This exercise is designed to help you look at yourself to determine whether you are an objective evaluator. Consider five people you know reasonably well. Choose at least one person who is a close friend and at least one person who is only an acquaintance to whom you are not particularly close. Now, using whatever *five* criteria you choose regarding personal characteristics (honesty, integrity, friendliness, loyalty, trustworthiness, sense of humor, etc.), take a step back and evaluate them based on the scale of excellent, good, average, and poor. How do these five people rate? Have you been objective, or is there any bias one way or the other toward those who are friends and those who are acquaintances? What does this tell you regarding the difficulties of evaluating employees objectively?

TO LEARN **MORE**

For more information on performance management and various philosophies on performance management, refer to the following resources:

Coens, Tom, and Mary Jenkins. *Abolishing Performance Appraisals: Why They Backfire and What to Do Instead.* San Francisco: Berrett-Koehler Publishers, 2000.

Grote, Dick. *The Complete Guide to Performance Appraisal.* New York: American Management Association, 1996.

Lee, Christopher D. *Performance Conversations: An Alternative to Appraisals.* Tucson: Fenestra Books, 2006.

NOTE

1. Herman Aguinis, *Performance Management.* Upper Saddle River, NJ: Pearson Education, 2007, pp. 16–18.

MANAGING YOURSELF

"The fault, dear Brutus, is not in our stars,
But in ourselves, that we are underlings . . ."

WILLIAM SHAKESPEARE, *Julius Caesar* (Act I, Scene ii)

chapter **fifteen**

LEARNING HOW TO CONCENTRATE AND MANAGE YOUR TIME

"I must govern the clock, not be governed by it."

Golda Meir

Most beginning supervisors discover that their new and demanding responsibilities cause them to move, physically and mentally, in too many directions at the same time. Under these conditions, it is easy to start operating off the top of your head. When this sort of behavior occurs, it is a signal that you are not doing enough concentrating or organizing your time effectively. The results can be confusion, frustration, and possibly a drop in departmental productivity.

WHAT IS CONCENTRATION?

Concentration is being able to focus your mental attention on a chosen project while you temporarily set aside matters of less importance. It is devoting your mind exclusively to one problem until you have the best solution you are capable of reaching. It is also getting the full message from a chapter you are reading in less time. The nice thing about concentration is that it is a mental discipline anyone can learn.

ELIMINATING DISTRACTIONS

To accomplish a job that involves thinking, it is often necessary to isolate yourself from the many daily distractions you face as a front-line supervisor. These distractions include interruptions from employees,

PERFORMANCE COMPETENCIES

After you have finished reading this chapter, you should be able to:

- List and describe ten barriers to concentration

- Describe eight steps to improve your concentration

- Describe twelve ways to make your meetings more productive and worthwhile

- Eliminate time wasters

customers, superiors, emergency problems, repair tasks, filling in for an absent employee, and, of course, e-mail and the telephone.

Freida makes it a practice to arrive at her desk thirty minutes ahead of her team of employees each morning. "I need to get away from telephone calls, employee interruptions, and normal noise to improve my concentration. Thirty minutes before the gang arrives is worth an hour when the shift is under way."

Greg, foreman of a construction crew, stays on site for an hour or so after everyone else has left. "I need some quiet time to plan for the next day. I concentrate on having all the supplies ready for the crew when they arrive so that we can get off to a fast start. And, of course, it is a mistake to read blueprints unless you have 100 percent concentration."

Hank has found a park bench near his noisy office where only the birds and the breeze can be heard. "When I have a knotty problem or need to concentrate on a report that is due, I often take my briefcase and head for my second office. On rainy days, I simply wait until I get home that night."

Isabelle divides her job as a supervisor into two categories. "First, I have my work time, which is devoted to tasks, counseling employees, keeping everyone informed, and making routine decisions. Then I have my mind-time responsibilities, which include doing work schedules, setting goals, making big decisions, and doing some creative thinking. Work time (90 percent) occurs under all kinds of conditions; mind time occurs when I step back to a quiet place where I can view the operation from a distance."

CONCENTRATING TO LEARN VERSUS CONCENTRATING TO MANAGE

Anyone can improve his or her power of concentration. Those with college degrees have obviously had opportunities to increase this power by mastering study habits and techniques. This practice gives them a slight advantage. But a big difference distinguishes concentrating to learn from concentrating to solve real work problems.

For example, supervisors have so many immediate tasks to perform that when they concentrate on a major problem they must walk away, quickly concentrate, and then return to the remaining tasks. They do not have the luxury of sitting in a library where the environment is conducive to concentration.

People who have trained their minds to do analytical thinking—especially when numbers and formulas are involved—seem to have the edge when deep concentration is required. These same people are often good at goal setting and planning because they like to figure things out. This ability does not mean, however, that those with a different background cannot learn to concentrate at a level sufficiently high to be effective. All it takes is practice and a few simple rules.

When Martin accepted the position of manager with a chain restaurant, he didn't fully realize how much planning would be involved. A high school dropout, Martin never focused his mind on anything for more than a few moments. How did he survive? His superior told him to always isolate himself for thirty minutes each workday and do nothing but develop a written priority list of duties to perform that day. Slowly, through mental discipline, Martin learned to plan ahead. Along the way, he also learned to concentrate in other areas.

BARRIERS TO CONCENTRATION

In the busy, sometimes hectic, field of work, it is never easy to take time away from other responsibilities in order to concentrate on a special project. Many barriers keep supervisors from what we might term *pure thinking*. Some of these barriers are physical; others are psychological. Check the items in the following list that frequently keep you from concentrating.

- Telephone calls
- Interruptions by employees or co-workers
- Noise
- Preoccupation on another matter
- Lack of training in how to concentrate
- Low tolerance of frustration
- Lack of motivation
- Procrastination
- Fatigue or stress
- A "to-heck-with-it" attitude
- Problems and demands at home
- E-mails

THE EFFECT OF PERSONALITY

Due to many factors, including the influence of personality and personal work preferences, some people find it easier to concentrate on certain types of mental activities than others. Some actually enjoy the process. Bill and Hazel provide us with an excellent example.

Bill and Hazel operate a successful quick-stop reproduction and printing operation. You seldom see Bill because he is in the back office, thinking through problems and planning ahead. His training as an engineer and computer programmer has given him unusual powers of concentration that fit his quiet personality. Hazel, in contrast, works out front, doing a superior job with customers. She loves people and makes the most of her outgoing personality. Obviously, the division of work between Hazel and Bill is ideal. But last year, Bill had open-heart surgery, and Hazel found it necessary to take over his work in addition to doing her own. By the time Bill returned, things were a mess. "What did you expect?" said Hazel. "I can't deal effectively with demanding customers and concentrate at the same time."

WEARING TWO HATS

Does the foregoing example mean Hazel lacks the powers of concentration that Bill possesses? To the contrary, she has selected the type of work activity that she prefers and is more suited to her personality. Further, her activities in working with customers do require a form of mental focus. Were the situation reversed, and Hazel were absent for a period of time, Bill would likely struggle in that form of mental activity.

To some extent, managers like Hazel develop compensating measures to balance with their natural preferences and strengths. Yet no supervisor is fortunate enough to have another person to do her concentrating all the time. Most supervisors must wear at least two hats. One is used to deal with daily operational tasks (working with customers, dealing with production factors, etc.), and the other (a concentration hat) is used for planning purposes. If your strengths and inclinations are more in line with Hazel rather than Bill, you can nonetheless, with desire and training, hone your concentration skills.

TIPS ON HOW TO CONCENTRATE

In assuming your responsibilities as a new supervisor, learning to wear both hats effectively is important. Here are a few tips that will assist you in wearing your concentration hat.

Limit your time.   It is not how much time you spend concentrating that is important, but rather how intensely your mind is focused while you are at it. Experience shows that when you limit yourself to a certain amount of time for concentration purposes (say, thirty minutes instead of an hour), you accomplish more.

Matt, a supervisor in a machine shop, has a difficult report due each Friday morning. For years, he has devoted a full afternoon on Thursday to completing the report. Then he discovered that if he allocated only two hours each Thursday afternoon (always in a quiet front office where no one could reach him), he could complete the report in half the time with fewer mistakes. In discussing this change with his superior, Matt said, "Apparently, when I limit my time, I concentrate better."

Set a firm line with others during times needed for concentration.   In the time you have planned to concentrate, make it known that it is time in which you do not wish to be interrupted, except in emergencies. Make it known that you

are available at any time before or after that time. Develop an understanding with your team regarding when to anticipate this time or how you will signal them that this time is needed.

Russ found that every other Tuesday morning worked well for him to devote to planning time. He shared his schedule in advance with staff and also posted it on his electronic calendar which was accessible to others. On occasion, he needed concentration time outside this regular time, so he put a hotel-style "Do Not Disturb" sign on his door handle, with a note indicating when he would be available again.

Divide and conquer big projects.   When facing a major project like preparing an annual report or budget, it is often a good idea to divide the work into smaller parts. Short, intense periods of concentration make more sense than trying to concentrate for an extended period of time when mental fatigue can set in.

Sylvia wanted to write an orientation manual for her corporation, but every time she sat down to put her thoughts in order, an interruption occurred and she would become frustrated and give up. Then, with permission from her superior, she tried a different approach. She left work early each Friday afternoon and went straight home, where she devoted two solid hours of concentration to the project. By spreading out the work, Sylvia was able to complete the work in six weeks. Her superior was most complimentary when she turned in the finished project.

Visualize the benefits.   Concentration is aided when the rewards that come from a completed project are pictured in advance. Such visualization (imagery) can provide more motivation than was previously present.

When Polly's divorce was final, she had to decide whether to do her own income tax or pay a professional. To keep expenses down, Polly decided to do it herself. To provide motivation, she pictured herself on a skiing trip with the money she would save. Always good with figures, she discovered she enjoyed the process because it gave her a better view of where her limited income was going. It also gave her an annual ski trip.

Project a professional image.   Managers who learn to concentrate on setting goals, establishing priorities, and completing special projects communicate a more professional image to upper management. They demonstrate they can come through when clear thinking and decisive decisions are necessary.

Roberto had the reputation of being a happy-go-lucky supervisor who got the job done, but was not interested in a higher position. When he turned thirty, Roberto decided to go back to finish his college degree so that he could give his career a boost. In doing so, he learned how to concentrate, and after he submitted a few new projects, management took a second look at Roberto as middle-management material.

Getting it done.   Procrastination is the postponement of an important project without a good reason. It is, in effect, backing away from the periods of high concentration necessary to get something accomplished.

Raymond discovered that self-talk was his best method to get into a mood in which he could concentrate. He would say to himself: "Here you go again, backing away because you are too lazy to concentrate. Get it done now so that you will feel better this weekend."

EIGHT STEPS TO SUCCESS

The next time you need to concentrate on a major problem or project, follow these simple steps:

1. *Isolate yourself.*   Find a location where you are free from interruptions and excessive noise. Once you arrive, make yourself comfortable. Relax enough so that other matters leave your mind. You are then ready to concentrate.

2. *Review the situation.*   Be open to new information. Research the situation, gather data, and ask questions. Probe others for their advice. Study the data you have collected.

3. *Give yourself a time limit.*   With full concentration, fifteen minutes is a long time. Attempt to beat the time allotments you have used in similar situations in the past.

4. *Outline what you intend to do and get started.*   Most people think better with a pencil in their hand.

5. *List all options.*   Review the various possibilities and strategies that might improve the situation or solve the problem.

6. *Weigh and decide.*   Thinking means tossing possibilities back and forth in your mind until you come up with the best approach or solution.

7. *Make a decision or complete the project.*   Whatever has required your concentration now needs to be stored in your memory bank for present implementation and future use. Concentration almost always produces something of value.

8. *When you find yourself procrastinating on an important project, take action.*   Organize your day to allow some period of time for the project and

work on it for the entire time allotted. Just do it! Remember the adage, "The job never started takes the longest to finish."

MANAGING YOUR TIME

When you establish sound goals for your department and yourself and learn to set priorities on a daily basis, will you automatically become more effective at managing your time? Not necessarily. You still need to deal with the basic problem of time allocation itself.

Why should you make a special effort to manage your time? You will get employees off to a better start. Some managers believe that when they arrive at work twenty to thirty minutes ahead of their staff they can:

1. Improve productivity attitudes when they greet staff arrivals with an upbeat message or compliment to start the day.
2. Do a better job of organizing their day.
3. Set a better example for their employees.

When you learn to manage your time well, you will realize these benefits:

1. *You will be less frustrated.* A well-organized supervisor senses and handles problems before they get out of hand. You can prevent fires rather than spending more time putting them out. Because you are on top of your job—not always catching up—productivity is more even, fewer emergencies and unpleasant surprises emerge, and you have fewer problems to handle. In short, you can create the extra time you need to be a manager.
2. *You will have the time you need to prepare for the future.* Until you learn to organize and manage your time well enough to take on additional responsibilities, you are not promotable. You cannot prepare for the next position if you are bogged down in your present job. You cannot do a good job of personal career development if you habitually operate on a crisis basis. You must make more time now through better time management to prepare for a bigger role in the future.
3. *You will achieve a better work-life balance.* Consider Frank's experience:

Despite his young age and modest formal education, Frank is a successful, highly respected executive in a demanding field. He has time to play racquetball each day, never neglects his family, devotes time to his church, takes care of personal business matters, and still has time left over for social and personal leisure activities.

The need for effective time management and allocation is a matter of simple math. Each day we are given 24 hours. Each week contains 168 hours—no more, no less. We all have the same amount of time. We may know people who get a lot more done in those hours than we do. We may wish to better manage our time. Of course, we really don't have the entire 168 hours to manage. We need to sleep, for instance. If we sleep 8 hours a day, that amounts to 56 hours per week. Subtracting out the 56 hours from the 168 hours in a week leaves us with only 112 hours to manage. This number is further reduced if we subtract out the time it takes to do things that cannot be avoided or done while working. For instance, your personal hygiene takes time, as do eating and traveling to work. Then, once we get to work, the precious time we need to plan and handle those higher-priority items is eaten up by the constant operational pressures we face. Clearly, if you are going to be successful in the long run as a manager, it is imperative that you get a handle on managing your time.

HOW TO MANAGE YOUR TIME

Change your attitude toward time. Learn to value your on-the-job time more fully. Take notice of how long it takes to do things, and you will likely realize that you are spending more hours than necessary on certain assignments. When you spend more time than is necessary on job tasks, that time will encroach on your leisure time and influence your lifestyle. To the extent possible, take the attitude that you must complete your work in the standard eight-hour day. The only alternative to better time management is to dip into your personal time. If you learn to manage your working hours, you will enjoy your nonworking hours more.

Delegate more. The best way to save your own time is to let somebody else do the task. Many managers could save far more time than they think if they delegated more effectively. Nothing is more revealing than to see a manager who is overworked while his people are underworked. Yet it happens frequently.

Look for and take shortcuts. There is usually more than one way to complete a task. Try to find the single best way and the one that takes the least amount of time. Could you get people to come to see you instead of taking the extra time to go to see them? Would a written note to a superior in advance of a meeting help you accomplish more in less time when you arrive? Could you set up a luncheon meeting to accomplish a business goal and still enjoy it? Could you save time by discussing the problem with an expert instead of struggling with it too long yourself? You will manage your time better if you use a little more of it to figure out the fastest route to get where you are going.

Group tasks together. If you watch a supervisor who has learned to manage time well, you will discover that little jobs and tasks are grouped together so that they can be accomplished at the same time. A trip or meeting might be delayed until it can accomplish more than one thing; a trip to the executive offices in the same building can be planned so that the mail can be picked up, a report dropped off, and an executive seen all in one trip instead of three; five or six people can be brought together to save time on communication; a list can be made in advance so that a counseling session will cover everything and make a follow-up unnecessary. Sometimes a manager has developed the skill to do more than one thing at the same time without offending others. When stalled on the telephone, the supervisor might read some official publications; a business matter might be introduced while walking to another meeting; when a dull staff meeting is tied up on a problem that does not involve the supervisor, he or she might plan a priority list for the next day.

Cut down on interruptions. To manage your time effectively, it is often necessary to keep others from using up time that is critical to your performance. Consider the following suggestions.

Keep Others from Using Up Your Time

1. Respect other people's time. When you do, you send an unspoken message that you prefer not to interrupt others and would appreciate the same treatment in return.

2. Indicate availability. Let people know when interruptions are okay. Schedule blocks of time when you are free for visits.

3. Decline to be interrupted. When someone asks, "Have you got a minute?" say, "Not at this time, because I'm in a deadline situation. I'll get back to you when time permits." If you do it in a pleasant voice, no one should be offended. Be sure to get back to them as you said you would.

Make Meetings More Efficient

Most supervisors find that it is important to have short staff meetings on a regular basis. Such meetings provide an excellent opportunity to introduce changes, solicit input, explain, and ask questions. Staff meetings can dissipate tensions, improve relationships, communicate an important message quickly, and result in increased productivity. But if not conducted properly, staff meetings can waste time and thus do more harm than good. Here are some simple tips to organize your meeting to reduce wasted time and increase the chances for a productive meeting:

1. Do not call a staff meeting unless it is necessary.

2. Have a specific goal or purpose to accomplish, and announce it before you begin the meeting. It might be helpful to prepare an agenda and submit it to attendees in advance.

3. Ensure that attendees know their roles in the meeting and how to participate and that they arrive prepared.

4. Do not include any item that can be covered more efficiently outside meeting time or that only requires a few to address rather than the whole group.

5. Keep the meeting as short as possible. Set a firm but realistic timeframe to cover each agenda item. Hold to it and then go on to the next item.

6. Use care in selecting the location of the meeting to avoid distractions and interruptions.

7. If a group decision is involved, get as much participation as possible.

8. Seek alternatives to any decision proposed so that the final decision is the best one.

9. Keep the meeting upbeat and energetic.

10. Enjoy a little laughter.

11. Use the meeting to demonstrate your leadership.

12. Conduct a personal evaluation so that you can do even better the next time.

Eliminate Time Wasters

Eliminate the little time wasters. Some manufacturing plants do micro-time and motion studies on their production employees. Employees are filmed doing their work, and then they carefully view their motions in an attempt to eliminate unnecessary activities. Perhaps this technique would be good to use with supervisors. A film would probably show you many ways to save time through elimination of needless motions or activities.

Do not waste time looking for things that you use often. Put things back in their proper places. Organize your office so you can find what you need, whether a file or a piece of equipment. Searching for a misplaced item eats up time.

After sorting your mail, handle a piece of paper only once. It sounds easy, but it is often difficult. If a request for a report comes across your desk, do it. Don't sort it and place it back on your pile to only re-sort later. If it is a lengthy report or assignment, see if all or part of it can be delegated. Much correspondence can be completed in a few minutes once you sort it. Take a close look at your present habits through the "Supervisor's Time-Waster Assessment Scale" that follows. As you complete it, keep in mind that in controlling your time more effectively, you do not want to squeeze all the joy out of your job. Your goal is to use your time wisely so that you will enjoy your job more, not less.

SUPERVISOR'S TIME-WASTER ASSESSMENT SCALE

Circle the number that best indicates where you lie between the two extremes.

Total your score at the end of the exercise.

When I arrive at work in the morning, I get started immediately.	5 4 3 2 1	It takes me at least thirty minutes to get started in the morning.
I do not procrastinate; my priority list prevents delay.	5 4 3 2 1	I procrastinate because I never know what to do next.
I keep personal activities to an absolute minimum.	5 4 3 2 1	I let personal activities eat away my on-the-job time.
My schedule is rigid; I never overextend a coffee or lunch break.	5 4 3 2 1	Two-hour non-business lunches and forty-minute coffee breaks are common with me.
I'm an extremely fast reader and I waste no time on trash mail.	5 4 3 2 1	I need a reading-improvement course; I waste too much time reading.
My telephone conversations are to the point and deal only with business matters.	5 4 3 2 1	I socialize on the telephone —my number one time waster.
I delegate as many tasks as possible.	5 4 3 2 1	Failure to delegate is a serious problem with me.
I refuse to let others waste my time in pointless conversations.	5 4 3 2 1	When people use up my time just chatting, I can't seem to break away.
I don't waste a single minute oversupervising.	5 4 3 2 1	Oversupervising is killing my time-management plan.

I schedule my time between appointments.	5 4 3 2 1	I often keep either myself or others waiting.
I stay motivated until I go home.	5 4 3 2 1	"Afternoon drag" slows me down to a crawl.
My objectives are clear; I know where I am going.	5 4 3 2 1	My objectives are fuzzy; I often go in the wrong direction.
I socialize on the job only after the day's objectives have been reached.	5 4 3 2 1	I look for opportunities to socialize to escape from work.
I have no pet projects; I stick to my priority list.	5 4 3 2 1	I can't stay away from some time-wasting pet projects.
I counsel my employees but never become overinvolved.	5 4 3 2 1	Every time I counsel an employee, I become overinvolved.
I avoid mistakes by working steadily at an even tempo.	5 4 3 2 1	I make foolish mistakes by hurrying to catch up.
My priority list and general attitude eliminate crisis management.	5 4 3 2 1	I am always putting out fires and operating in a crisis.
I maintain a highly efficient personal filing system.	5 4 3 2 1	My personal filing system is a time-wasting mess.
I ask for help with tough problems that consume time.	5 4 3 2 1	I would rather solve my own problem no matter how long it takes.
I make maximum use of time-saving equipment such as computers.	5 4 3 2 1	Doing things the old-fashioned way gives me more personal satisfaction.

Total Points _____

If you scored more than 90, you are a highly organized supervisor and you waste almost no time. If you scored between 70 and 90, you need a slight improvement. If, however, you scored less than 70, you would probably enjoy work more and improve your future by eliminating some needless, perhaps frustrating, time wasters. If you scored a 3 or lower on any one area, you should look for ways to improve your time management skills in that area.

Learn techniques for managing your e-mail. For example, identify select times to check and respond to your e-mail throughout the day rather than become a slave to the little "ding" that tells you that e-mail has arrived and compels you to respond immediately. Don't write lengthy e-mails. E-mails are best for operational and directive types of communication; if the matter requires a longer conversation, have it in person rather than through e-mail. Also, if there are specific individuals with whom you regularly communicate through e-mail, or a sub-group of individuals with whom you correspond on specific matters, create special sub-folders and set automatic preferences so that these e-mails are directed to the sub-folders and get your priority attention. Finally, if you get routine e-mails from list servers and vendors you don't want, hit the "Unsubscribe" link that some senders provide out of courtesy, or simply reply with a short message such as "Unsubscribe" or "Please remove me from your list." If that doesn't work, you can also set an automatic preference that directs such e-mails to your Delete Folder that you can then delete at a later time.

INVENTORY ANALYSIS CHART

Now that you have completed the "Supervisor's Time-Waster Assessment Scale," you may wish to log your time among various activities for a typical day. This approach using the "Eight-Hour Day Inventory Analysis Chart" will help you compare the actual time you spend with the time you should spend.

EIGHT-HOUR DAY INVENTORY ANALYSIS CHART		
Activity	**Time Spent in Minutes**	**Optimum Time in Minutes (your opinion)**
Paperwork (reports, correspondence)		
Checking other's work or close supervision of others		
Communication (counseling)		
Telephone calls and e-mails		
Command meetings (imposed by management)		
Problem solving (putting out fires)		
Planning		
Other_____		
Other_____		
Other_____		
Total		

1. Add both columns.
2. Subtract "Time Spent" from "Optimum Time."
The difference is time wasted.

PERFORMANCE **CHECKLIST**

1. Concentration is being able to focus your mental attention on a chosen project while you temporarily set aside matters of less importance. To accomplish a job that involves thinking, it is often necessary to isolate yourself from the many daily distractions that you face as a front-line supervisor.

2. Concentrating to learn is different from concentrating to solve real work problems. For example, supervisors have so many immediate tasks to perform that when they concentrate on a major problem they must walk away, quickly concentrate, and then return to the remaining tasks.

3. Many barriers keep supervisors from being able to fully concentrate. Many of these barriers are physical; others are psychological. These barriers include telephone calls, interruptions, noise, preoccupation with other matters, low tolerance for frustration, procrastination, fatigue, stress, e-mails, and distractions from home.

4. To improve your concentration, consider these tips: (1) Limit the time you devote to a specific task; (2) set a firm line with others during times needed for concentration; (3) divide and conquer big projects; (4) visualize the benefits of the completed task; and (5) don't procrastinate.

5. To concentrate on a major problem or project, (1) isolate yourself; (2) review the situation; (3) set yourself a time limit; (4) outline what you intend to do and get started; (5) list all options; (6) weigh and decide; (7) make a decision or complete the project; and (8) when you find yourself procrastinating on an important project, take action.

6. When you learn to manage your time, you will be less frustrated, have more time to prepare for the future, and achieve a better work–life balance.

7. To manage your time more effectively, change your attitude about time, delegate more, look for and take shortcuts, group tasks together, and cut down on interruptions. You must also keep others from using up your time, make meetings more efficient, and eliminate time wasters.

8. To identify where and how you need to better manage your time, use assessment tools like the "Supervisor's Time-Waster Assessment Scale" and the "Eight-Hour Day Inventory Analysis Chart."

TEST **YOURSELF**

For each of the following statements, check true or false.

True   False

1. Concentration is nothing more than being able to focus your mind on one subject to the exclusion of others.

2. Without a college education, it is impossible to master the skills of concentration.

3. Lack of motivation is not a barrier to concentration.

4. Most supervisors wear two hats: one for work time on operational tasks, and one for concentration.

5. Some supervisors are capable of thinking things through but fail because they do not know the techniques of concentration.

6. The more time you give yourself to complete a project, the better your concentration will be.

7. Visualizing a reward you intend to give yourself when a project is finished is an aid to concentration.

8. Do not delegate as a way to manage time.

9. Using a computer makes concentration more difficult.

10. When you find yourself procrastinating on an important project, the best advice is to take action by organizing your time to work on part of the project each day.

Turn to the back of the book to check your answers.

Total Correct ＿＿＿

DISCUSSION **QUESTIONS**

1. How can you improve your power of concentration? Discuss a personal plan for doing so.
2. Do you agree or disagree with the concept that you have to invest a little time to save a lot of time? Explain.
3. What signals might a supervisor receive when his or her time is managed poorly? What signals might be received when activities are overorganized?
4. Do you support the idea of taking a daily time inventory to improve time management? Is logging time for only one day sufficient? Should time be logged during or at the end of the day?

HYPOTHETICAL **PROJECT**

Imagine that, for whatever reasons, you have been putting a task off for weeks. You just can't seem to motivate yourself to start on it. Implement the "Eight Steps to Success" on this task. Once completed, ask yourself the following questions:

Was the chapter helpful?   Yes ☐   No ☐   Not much ☐

Which tip helped the most?   _____

Do you feel you will be able to do better the next time?   Yes ☐   No ☐   Not much ☐

What would you do next time to improve your concentration?   _____

Will learning to concentrate better keep you from
procrastinating so much in the future?   Yes ☐   No ☐   Not much ☐

List and describe four ways to improve your time management.

1. _____   2. _____
3. _____   4. _____

CASE 1: **THINKING**

Lisa and Lester are discussing how some students get better grades than others even though they spend less time preparing for examinations. Lisa states: "I think it is simply a matter of concentration. Many bright students do poorly because they never learn to concentrate. Of course, there is a big difference between learning to concentrate to retain information and solving problems out in the real world."

"Here on campus, we concentrate to learn, pass tests, and earn a degree," replies Lester. "Students who never learn to concentrate are disadvantaged in real life because they don't focus their minds on problems and create plans for the future. The purpose of a college education is to teach you to think and concentrate. Nothing more, nothing less."

"I'm not so sure," replies Lisa. "Concentrating on campus is simply learning to store knowledge so that we can pass exams and move on to something else. In the real world, you deal with tough problems and difficult decisions in a work environment that is hectic. To be honest with you, I think a non-college person can learn to concentrate on the job as well as a college grad. I agree that college teaches one to think, but as far as concentration is concerned, I don't believe there is much carryover from campus to the work place. Concentration comes first, thinking next."

Do you agree with Lisa or Lester? Defend your answer.

CASE 2: ANALYSIS

Ricardo has been working extra hours to catch up on everything he needs to do in his department. No matter how he tries to save time, he never catches up. As a result, Ricardo has become increasingly irritable, haggard, and ineffective. Unable to solve the problem, Ricardo makes an appointment with Bill and then makes a big pitch for an assistant to help release the pressure. But Bill replies that better time management would solve Ricardo's problem. He asks Ricardo to log how he spent his time yesterday. Ricardo turns in the following table:

Based on this time inventory, do you agree or disagree with Bill? Support your answer. How might Ricardo improve his time management?

SAMPLE OF RICARDO'S TIME INVENTORY FOR ONE DAY

Activity	Time	Activity	Time
Preparing written request to Bill attempting to justify a 20 percent increase in budget next year.	60 min.	Typed up five extra copies of a productivity report so that all five employees would be informed.	30 min.
Discussing next month's production schedule with Marty; will do same with Renee, Karl, and Giselle later.	15 min.	Struggled again with a new layout plan that would free about forty square feet for a new piece of equipment on order. Got disgusted and tore up new and previous plans. Impossible.	50 min.
Handling thirteen telephone calls, only three of which were personal.	50 min.	Trip to union hall to talk to our agent about a grievance that had been continuing too long. Meeting took 30 minutes. Transportation time: 20 minutes each way.	70 min.
Worked in stockroom alone doing a reorganizing job. Left note so that Julie would understand	50 min.	Waited 20 minutes to see Bill to discuss time-management problem. Conversation lasted 10 minutes.	30 min.
Interviewing woman sent by Personnel as a possible replacement for Giselle, who is leaving in two weeks. Decided that individual is not suitable.	50 min.		
Repairing broken equipment that only I could fix. I asked Karl and Marty to take an early lunch while I repaired it so that they could continue working when they returned.	60 min.		

PERSONAL GROWTH EXERCISE

Think of something job related that you have been putting off. Go right now, or as soon as possible, and work on it for no more than 15 minutes. Write down your reaction. How did it feel to focus your concentration this way?

TO LEARN **MORE**

The following references provide guidance on planning and running effective meetings:

Mina, Eli. *The Complete Handbook of Business Meetings.* New York: AMACOM, 2000.

Mosvick, Roger K., and Robert B. Nelson. *We've Got to Start Meeting Like This! A Guide to Successful Meeting Management*, rev. ed. Indianapolis: Park Avenue Productions, 1996.

Streibel, Barbara J. *The Manager's Guide to Effective Meetings.* New York: McGraw-Hill, 2003.

The following references provide practical guidance and tips on time management:

Mayer, Jeffrey S. *If You Haven't Got the Time to Do It Right, When Will You Find the Time to Do It Over?* New York: Simon and Schuster, 1990.

Morgenstern, Julie. *Time Management from Inside Out.* New York: Henry Holt and Company, 2000.

Smith, Hyrum W. *The 10 Natural Laws of Successful Time and Life Management.* New York: Warren Books, 1994.

chapter **sixteen**

ESTABLISHING GOALS AND PLANNING

"People are more motivated to change when they have participated in planning the change."

Cliff Goodwin

"It's great to be a lowly employee instead of a supervisor because you can report to work without thinking. You know, just stumble in and let the job grab you instead of you grabbing the job. Let the supervisor do the planning, scheduling, and thinking. After all, she's getting paid for it. Let her see to it that you have a productive day."

This quotation may not express the best possible employee attitude, but it contains enough truth to cause the supervisor to ask some pointed questions. If the supervisor doesn't give the department direction, who will? If she or he doesn't organize, plan, schedule, and pick up the loose ends, where will such leadership come from? If the supervisor doesn't provide the employee with a good day, who is to blame?

Some fairly basic differences separate the positions of employee and supervisor. Generally, the employee can become involved in the activities of the department without worrying too much about the overall direction of the department. The employee can relax without having to fit what he or she does into a total plan.

The worker can achieve job satisfaction without sweating out reports, plans, figures, purchases, statistics, comparisons, and other matters relating to these planning issues. The supervisor, however, must constantly look at the overall picture. Are all employees properly assigned and fully productive? How is the department doing in comparison with others? How much increase in productivity might be expected in the next six months? What cost factors can be eliminated or reduced?

PERFORMANCE COMPETENCIES

After you have finished reading this chapter, you should be able to:

- Explain the use of a Gantt bar chart
- Explain the formula for successful planning
- Tie department goals to organization-wide plans

THE IMPORTANCE OF PLANNING

The role of a supervisor is a far cry from that of an employee. You cannot just let things happen but must make them happen. You must control a multitude of factors, deal with countless emergencies, and pick up a variety of loose ends, constantly directing and guiding the activities of others. No matter how many details must be faced, no matter how frantic the pace, you must stay on top of the situation and in control. How can you do all these things? By being an organized person with a definite plan.

Managers must occasionally pull themselves away from the trees so that they can see the forest. They must learn to concentrate (see Chapter 15) so that they can develop significant, appropriate, and practical goals. The degree to which a manager is successful in seeing the big picture will determine the long-range success that he or she will enjoy.

The Gantt Bar Chart

Henry L. Gantt, an early management consultant, recognized that any sound plan is made up of a number of interlocking projects (smaller plans) that are dependent on each other and must be molded together under a time limitation. He designed a bar chart showing the relationship of time to various subprojects in a master plan. Assume that you are the owner of a restaurant that needs remodeling, but you do not wish to close down. You might construct a Gantt-type chart like the following one to show how the restaurant could be remodeled one section at a time.

Network Analysis Plan

Production engineers often design highly sophisticated plans when a new product is to be manufactured. A plan that stresses an awareness of each step in a

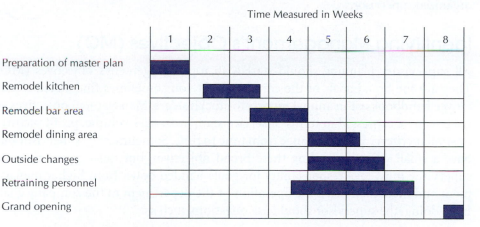

Restaurant Remodeling Chart

Time Measured in Weeks

	1	2	3	4	5	6	7	8
Preparation of master plan	■							
Remodel kitchen		■						
Remodel bar area			■					
Remodel dining area					■			
Outside changes					■			
Retraining personnel				■				
Grand opening								■

production path is called *network analysis*. A chart clearly identifies each step (some operating simultaneously) in an entire project—one that might take months or years to complete. For example, Program Evaluation Review Technique (PERT) is a well-known system that the U.S. Navy used to save almost two years on a missile project.

Master Calendar

Effective managers who set project deadlines for themselves frequently use calendars. Such deadlines act as reminders and facilitate productivity. Calendars can also be used for pending business appointments, staff meetings, conventions, and so on. Some managers prefer large calendars that can be displayed in their office as a reminder to all staff members. Others prefer pocket varieties that can be used both at home and on the job. More frequently anymore in today's technology age, managers and their staff use electronic calendars that can be made accessible to all, including remotely through Internet access, and provide convenient access to project completion dates, appointments, and other matters, and also allow individuals to schedule meetings on each other's calendars. Managers use their individual preferences depending on their needs and the sophistication of the projects they must manage.

FORMULA FOR SUCCESSFUL PLANNING

Beginning supervisors do not need highly complex systems to handle their responsibilities, but they can benefit from a simplified one. The following formula serves this purpose:

$$MO + DP + SP = DS$$

Put into words, it means the following: MO (management objectives) plus DP (department plan) plus SP (small plans) equal DS (department success). Each symbol in this formula will take on a special meaning as you continue toward becoming a more organized supervisor.

Identifying Management's Objectives (MO)

All supervisory planning should start with top management's objectives (MO). They are the broad goals of the company that you sometimes find stated in employee handbooks or in annual reports to stockholders. Management objectives, or goals, can be expressed in terms of service standards, sales volume, profit pictures, or similar criteria and will change from time to time. Sometimes the supervisor may have a small voice in forming these broad objectives, but most of the time the supervisor must take responsibility for goals handed down from higher management and must then relate the operation of the department to the company goals. In so doing, the supervisor should ask questions such as:

1. What are the current objectives of my company?
2. What are my department's responsibilities in helping management achieve these objectives?
3. How might my department contribute more to reaching these objectives?
4. Is my department doing anything not in conformity with these goals?
5. Is my department doing anything that is superfluous or redundant that, if eliminated, would help management better reach these objectives?

Departmental Plans (DP)

Obviously, management objectives are never reached unless they are implemented with actual productivity within reach of the smaller divisions making up the organization. So, DP is added to the formula because a department cannot contribute significantly to management objectives without a plan of its own. This is the point where you come into the picture. With the assistance of your employees, you should develop the departmental plan and gear it to broad management objectives.

Departmental plans can take many forms, so you may receive considerable help from your manager in building your plan. She or he may ask you for a monthly, semi-annual, or yearly written plan; provide the necessary forms; and give you a model to work from. However, if your manager does not ask you for a plan, you may prepare one exclusively for your own purposes. In either case, you should do the following:

1. Make your plan workable because an impossible goal does not motivate.
2. Identify fewer (three or four) vitally important achievable goals that contribute most to achieving management objectives. (Note: Many less-important goals may in fact be tasks necessary for the fulfillment of these more important goals.)
3. Make your plan flexible so that you can adjust to changes beyond your control.
4. Include all elements or factors over which you have control.
5. State the expected increase in productivity (tangible, sales, or service) in clear terms. Always include previous figures for comparison.
6. Tie your plan to management objectives.

A workable departmental plan is not easy to develop. It will take time, effort, and some communication on your part, but without it, you have no direction. The kind of plan you develop will depend on many variables that cannot be discussed here. Your employees should be involved in the formulation of the plan because they will be expected to help accomplish it.

Let's assume that you now have a developed departmental plan. It contains the broad objectives you hope to reach in your department in the next six months or year. It states the things you hope to achieve so that your department will show growth and improvement and will make its maximum contribution to the company as a whole. If you can accomplish these goals or come close to them, your reputation as a manager will be greatly enhanced. Once you set these goals, you have committed yourself. Management may not hold you firmly to them, but managers will probably refer to them from time to time.

DEPARTMENTAL PLAN (EXAMPLE)

Six-Month Plan

- ☐ Develop a more effective orientation program for new employees.
- ☐ Make better use of FAX equipment. Delegate responsibility to an assistant.
- ☐ Institute a weekly staff meeting to improve communications and morale.
- ☐ Achieve a 5 percent increase in productivity with one less employee.
- ☐ Establish a computer bulletin board communications network.
- ☐ Initiate individual communication sessions for each employee to enhance motivation.
- ☐ Coordinate this plan with a formal performance evaluation process.
- ☐ Update computer software to enhance the tracking of in-process inventory.

Small Plans (SP)

We now come to the next part of the formula, the SP, or small plans. You cannot, of course, reach the goals of your overall plan unless you make it work by dividing it into little plans that are achievable on a daily or weekly basis. In short, you need a continuous supply of small plans or goals to augment your major departmental plan. Many experienced supervisors develop a daily checklist (tied to departmental plans), which they follow as closely as the situation permits.

> "While driving to work in the morning, I organize my day by making up a list of things to do. When I get to my desk, I write this list on my calendar pad and assign priorities. I then spend the rest of the day trying to check them off. It works for me."

> "I never leave work, even if I'm late, until I have a priority list of things to do when I show up the next day. This list makes it easier for me to leave my problems at work and gives me a good starting point the next day. I'd recommend it to the beginning supervisor."

"For the last twenty years, I've made it a practice to show up fifteen minutes early every morning so that I can organize my daily plan. I find I can sort things out more clearly this time of day."

Small daily plans eventually add up to the successful completion of overall departmental plans. The daily checklist is an excellent practice and is strongly recommended for both the new and the experienced supervisor. The key to such a list is setting up the right priorities and following certain rules. (Setting priorities will be discussed in Chapter 17.) It must be emphasized, however, that the only worthwhile goals are reachable goals. For that reason, small, short, and immediate goals make sense. Some supervisors divide their small plans into daily and weekly classifications. A weekly goal might include something that takes more than one day to accomplish, such as changing a basic procedure, training a new employee, or contacting a series of customers. A daily goal might include taking someone to lunch, counseling with an employee who seems unhappy, finishing a report, or similar activities. As noted in the discussion of Department Plans (DP), whether you call them goals or tasks, these are all the things you must do on a daily or weekly basis that contribute in some way to accomplishing the larger goals defined within the Department Plan.

DAILY PLAN (EXAMPLE)

Today's Checklist

- ☐ Clean and reorganize supply room.
- ☐ Write complaint letter to supplier.
- ☐ Compliment Gregg (new employee) on his progress toward his personal productivity potential.
- ☐ Get monthly report on quality control to boss.
- ☐ Counsel Mary on absenteeism.
- ☐ Handle late delivery complaint from key customer.
- ☐ Have slow leak in front tire checked.
- ☐ Meet with computer software consultant at 10:30 A.M.

Department Success (DS)

Department Success (DS) is a combination of many factors and personal characteristics, but being an organized person is certainly one of them. It is especially true of supervisors because only those who can organize a small department can organize a larger operation. The sooner you demonstrate to your superiors that you have the ability to organize yourself and your department, the sooner you will start your climb up the organizational ladder.

As a way to review, let's now apply the formula to a single case involving JoAnn, a young bank manager. She has been a manager for only a short time and has been charged with the responsibility of opening up a branch in an enclosed shopping center. How might the formula apply to her?

Management objectives (MO).   JoAnn works for a statewide banking operation that has four basic goals at this point: (1) to trim overhead expenses; (2) to maintain profits; (3) to improve the image of the bank through a higher quality of service; and (4) to improve the cultural mix of employees and bring more women into top management. JoAnn feels strongly that her small branch (only nine employees) can contribute to these companywide objectives.

Departmental plans (DP).   A few weeks before she opened her branch, JoAnn was required to submit a plan for the first six months of operation. It was based to some extent on what other new branches of the same size and in similar situations had experienced. It included the following key goals for the period: (1) the operation would become profitable by a specified date; (2) the department would achieve specific deposit and loan figures, stated monthly; and (3) the operation would meet specific customer relations targets that would satisfy all clients, especially those business organizations in the shopping center that would depend heavily on her bank.

Small plans (SP).   JoAnn has her own system when it comes to small-action plans or goals. Each weekend (usually at home), she develops a few weekly goals. She writes them in her appointment notebook. They include goals such as (1) special public relations efforts through calling on a few key clients, (2) getting reports to the head office in better shape and before deadlines, (3) planning a short staff meeting, and (4) performing a training job that needs to be done. But JoAnn does not let it go at that; she also uses a daily goal or task system. Every morning when she arrives and opens the bank (she tries to beat everyone else by twenty minutes), she sits down and writes on her desk calendar the smaller things she wants to accomplish before she goes home. Often there are deadlines or time orders for these priorities. Some of these tasks she has thought about en route to work, so it takes only a few minutes to write them down. She may add one or two during the day, but she makes an effort to check them off as she goes. Again, this activity is a private matter. On days when she completes all her small goals, she has a great sense of satisfaction. Sometimes, of course, she must postpone a few goals until the next day because a hectic pace prevented her from attending to them.

Implementation of the formula, simple as it may be, can convert a disorganized, unsuccessful supervisor into an organized, successful one. If JoAnn desires to move into a higher position at a later date, she is smart to adapt the formula to her own style. Here are some final tips that will help you put it into operation:

1. *Keep your departmental plans simple.*   A departmental plan is simply a proposed blueprint, or map, for the future. An ultra-sophisticated plan may look pretty, but it may not be workable. Keep it simple and attainable.

2. *Organize yourself on a daily basis.*   Most supervisors need a simple procedure to follow each day in order to accomplish first things first and follow through on other activities. The daily checklist is a worthwhile tool.

3. *Achieve results through people.*   Your departmental plan and your daily checklist are useless unless you put them into action through people. You must develop your human relations skills to make your plan work.

4. *Be a do-it-yourself goal setter.*   Create a sense of urgency. Assert yourself by creating objectives for your unit. Do not wait for your superior to encourage

you. Communicate that you are already an organized person with an upper-management future.

USING COMPUTERS

Today, the front-line supervisor needs to be computer literate in almost all supervisory roles. Would-be supervisors who fail to learn computer systems or take advantage of management information systems (MIS) may find themselves on the outside looking in.

Supervisors must rely on instant information to make decisions. Sophisticated MIS changes occur regularly. The quantity and quality of data, as well as the speed at which it can be obtained, must be used to advance productivity. In short, supervisors must utilize computers to stay in the information and communications "game."

Computerized information systems are reshaping many organizations. Traditional departmental boundaries are giving way to information networks available to all; even more important, the computer facilitates decentralization in organizations with little or no loss of control. The pace of business leaves no room for debate. The supervisor who does not play the computer game with enthusiasm is heavily handicapped and will eventually lose out to those who do. Fortunately, most future supervisors are already computer literate. Later, as they move into higher management, they are likely to find themselves traveling on an airplane using a laptop computer with access to messages and information anytime, anywhere—an indispensable part of their effectiveness.

Software

To illustrate how the supervisor of the future can make maximum use of the computer, all we need do is review the basic software packages currently available.

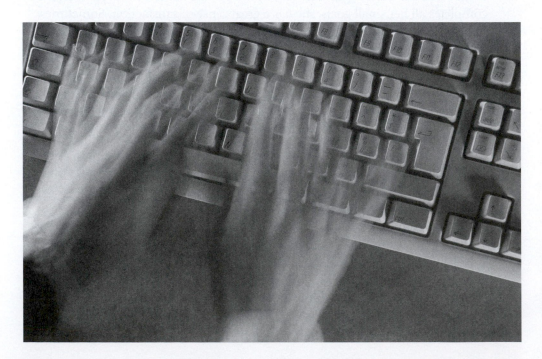

Word Processing. Word processing allows a busy supervisor to be his or her own secretary. For example, a bulletin may need to be written (with graphics), edited, and posted in a hurry. This is no problem with a word processor.

Spreadsheets. This software allows the supervisor to turn the computer's memory into a large worksheet in which data formulas can be tested. For example, a supervisor might want to discover what hiring a new employee might do to profitability. A few moments on the computer and the answer is on the screen.

Database Management. These programs make it possible to obtain and review information from a larger base to make comparisons.

Graphics. This capability allows a supervisor to display information in the form of charts or graphs that can be used in short departmental meetings and other forms of communication.

Presentations. Some programs allow the supervisor to create slide presentations that incorporate graphics, charts, pictures, embedded videos, and other features to provide visual information to accompany presentations at meetings, conferences, and so forth. Other programs allow users to create high-quality brochures, pamphlets, binders, portfolios, proposals, and reports that may be especially important when seeking to impress clients or superiors.

Networking. Programs that interface permit the transfer of data to and from other supervisors and managers. The impact of networking on interorganizational communications is already being felt.

Project Management. This software allows the manager and his team to scale large projects and break them into smaller projects and provides mechanisms for establishing and scheduling tasks and deadlines, tracking progress, and ensuring that steps necessary for completing elements of a large project that are assigned to multiple team members are completed in sequence and on time.

Calendaring. This software allows managers to not only place calendar entries, but to also list and prioritize daily tasks and set up automatic reminders. It also includes tools for scheduling meetings. Others can also be granted access to view co-workers' and the manager's calendars to check availability and schedule meetings.

PERSONAL PERFORMANCE CONTRACTS

Your superior may wish to work out a personal performance contract (PPC) with you, or you may wish to work out one for yourself and submit it to your superior. You may also wish to develop a PPC for each employee you supervise. A PPC establishes future goals for which an individual becomes accountable.

In simple terms, a contract is a written agreement between an employee and his or her manager that forecasts accomplishments to be achieved within a specific time period. Where possible, benefits should be tied to accomplishments.

Here are the normal steps taken in the development of a PPC:

1. Write out the specific needs or goals to be accomplished.
2. List the top three objectives that become the essence of the contract.

3. Gain supervisor approval.

4. Develop an action plan so that both parties will know what the employee will be doing over a given time frame.

5. Emphasize the self-development aspects of any contract.

6. Conduct reviews to ensure steady progress.

7. Remember that any contract is a two-way street. Whether the employee reaches her or his goals may depend on the supervisor's contribution to the contract.

PERFORMANCE **CHECKLIST**

1. Managers must spend time planning. They must occasionally pull themselves away from the trees so that they can see the forest. They must learn to concentrate so that they can develop significant, appropriate, and practical goals. The degree to which a manager is successful in seeing the big picture will determine the long-range success that he or she will enjoy.

2. Among the tools managers use to engage in long-range planning are the Gantt Bar Chart, Network Analysis Plans such as PERT (Program Evaluation Review Technique) diagrams, and master calendars that allow managers to oversee overall team efforts, set deadlines and reminders, and facilitate productivity.

3. A basic formula that managers can use to plan is $MO + DP + SP = DS$, which means management objectives (MO) plus department plan (PD) plus small plans (SP) equal department success (DS).

   • Supervisory planning begins with top-management's objectives (MO), which are the broad goals of the company. These can be expressed in terms of service standards, sales volume, profit pictures, or similar criteria and will change from time to time. The supervisor must take responsibility for goals handed down from higher management and must then relate the operation of the department to the company goals.

   • DP (department plans) is added to the formula because a department cannot contribute significantly to management objectives without a plan of its own. With the help of employees, the supervisor should develop a departmental plan and gear it to broad management objectives. Employees should be involved in the formulation of the plan because they will be expected to help accomplish it.

   • You cannot reach the goals of your overall plan unless you make it work by dividing it into small plans (SP) that are achievable on a daily or weekly basis. In short, you need a continuous supply of small plans or goals to augment your major departmental plan.

4. To realize department success (DS) using this formula, consider these additional tips: (1) Keep your departmental plans simple, (2) organize yourself on a daily basis, (3) achieve results through people, and (4) be a do-it-yourself go-getter.

5. Computers and associated software provide supervisors significant support in their planning efforts. These software packages assist supervisors with the following support: word processing, spreadsheets, database management, networking, graphics, presentations, project management, and calendaring.

6. Your superior may wish to work out a personal performance contract (PPC) with you, or you may wish to work out one for yourself and submit it to your superior. You may also wish to develop a PPC for each employee you supervise. A PPC establishes future goals for which an individual becomes accountable. It is a written agreement between an employee and his or her manager that forecasts accomplishments to be achieved within a specific time period.

TEST **YOURSELF**

For each of the following statements, check true or false.

True   False

____   ____   1. A PPC (personal performance contract) establishes future goals for which an individual becomes accountable.

True	False	
____	____	2. Supervisors are more motivated to reach objectives handed down from above.
____	____	3. A supervisor seeking promotion should prepare a departmental plan whether requested by management or not.
____	____	4. PERT is a form of analysis identifying each step in a plan.
____	____	5. In the supervisor's planning formula, DS stands for "declared solution."
____	____	6. Small plans (daily) should augment and correlate with departmental plans but not organizational plans.
____	____	7. Supervisory plans should start with top-down objectives in most cases.
____	____	8. Most supervisors keep a written copy of their specific long- and short-term goals in case their superiors ask to see them.
____	____	9. The Gantt bar chart is designed to interlock various interdependent projects under a time limitation.
____	____	10. Employees should be involved in the formulation of the proposed project or plan because they will be expected to help accomplish it.

Turn to the back of the book to check your answers.
Total Correct ____

DISCUSSION **QUESTIONS**

1. Do you agree that when supervisors prepare their own written plans (with little or no pressure from management), they are more likely to translate the plan into motivating goals?

2. In what ways will an organized plan affect the productivity of your employees?

3. How might you involve your employees in the planning and organization of a department plan? What effect does participation in planning have on motivation?

4. Could a supervisor "overplan"? That is, be too concerned about what is to be done when, by whom, and completed on a certain date? What effect could overplanning have on employees' productivity? Why?

CASE: **PLANNING**

Gerald is a strong, almost obsessed proponent of personal planning and organization. He uses an elaborate system of daily, weekly, and long-term goals for himself. He uses a personal computer at home for both personal and business purposes. He believes that organization is the best form of personal discipline and that goal setting is the most motivating thing a person can do. Each night, before he leaves work, he writes all of his goals for the following day on a desk pad. He spends some time each weekend at home setting goals. He always submits a complex plan to his superiors, and it is always on time. He gets satisfaction from checking off a written goal when it has been accomplished.

Yolanda is also a strong believer in goal setting and good organization, but her approach is flexible and unstructured. She does not follow any specific formula, and she never writes anything down. Rather, she keeps a changing master plan in her mind. She constantly revises it when driving on the freeway or while relaxing at home. She claims that it takes too much time to prepare a written plan, that upper-management ignores most of the plans submitted, and that changes make them obsolete almost immediately. She also believes that too much structure keeps one from being creative and flexible.

Do you support Gerald or Yolanda? Defend your position. Would you recommend a compromise? Explain.

PLANNING EXERCISE

As you have learned, large organizations usually require their managers to submit detailed plans every six months or every year. Such plans act as goal statements for the manager, and the manager's appraisal usually reflects the progress that has been made toward the goal. Both corporate and self-accountability are involved.

Some superiors believe in Personal Performance Contracts and ask those under them to submit such contracts for their signature. Some submit them to their superiors on a volunteer basis.

Assume that you have started a business of your own. Do you believe in the value of making plans enough to make one for yourself? Or would you play it by ear as you go along so you would have more flexibility? Write out your decision and explain your stand.

PERSONAL GROWTH EXERCISE

Write a personal performance contract for yourself. Use the steps outlined in this chapter. Share it with your supervisor and ask him or her to comment on it and suggest any revisions. Then, commit to fulfilling the contract with your supervisor's support. Do this for six months and evaluate the results. Has the process helped you become more effective in planning and organizing and to be more productive? What other benefits have you derived from this process?

chapter **seventeen**

SETTING PRIORITIES

"It's the job never started that takes the longest to complete."

J. R. R. Tolkien

Improving Productivity
Leading Teams
Communicating Effectively
Managing Conflict
Improving Performance
Managing Time
Benefiting from Change

P riorities are a vital part of any plan. In one respect, they are the plan. They indicate what you feel is most important and what can be ignored temporarily. Obviously, people who are good at setting priorities accomplish their plans or goals more easily and efficiently than those who are not.

In putting a plan into operation, you need to concentrate on doing the most important tasks first. Just because a particular task is assigned to you first does not mean it should be handled ahead of other things; just because you didn't have time to do something yesterday does not mean it should have top priority today.

GOALS, OBJECTIVES, AND PLANS

A wise person once said, "A goal is a dream with a deadline." So true! Setting a goal is the first step in achieving the goal. To illustrate, let us say that you are at point A. Point A is the actual state of affairs where you are at present. Let us say that you decide point A is no longer satisfactory and you wish to make changes. Think of the changes as a journey from point A to point B. Point B is the desired state of affairs, how you want things to be. Point B becomes your Goal. The actions you take to move to point B become your Objectives. Getting to a goal may take many objectives. Those things that impede your progress to the goal are called Obstacles.

Reaching goals often involves overcoming tough obstacles. It certainly includes planning. Planning is essential to reaching almost every goal. Few people would go on a vacation without planning it in advance. Decisions about where to go, how to get there, how long to stay, how much money to take, and what clothing to pack are but a few of the important objectives to plan before going. Taking that first step on

PERFORMANCE COMPETENCIES

After you have finished reading this chapter, you should be able to:

- Explain the importance of setting priorities

- Explain three benefits to setting goals

- Explain the ABC method for setting priorities

a 1,000-mile journey is an objective; so is taking the last step. The better the planning, the more likely the goal will be achieved.

As a supervisor, you may need to make changes to point A, the actual state. If the changes you make are likely to affect the work or routine of your employees, you should involve them in the planning stage of the change, not just in the implementation stage. Often, employees resist change because they were not involved in the planning. If you desire to move your employees to point B, to the desired state, you will need their motivation and cooperation to move, to change. An effective way to encourage this motivation is through involvement.

Setting goals can lead to the following benefits:

Achieving more. You become more organized in your work. By prioritizing your activities, you can give more attention to getting the important things done first. You have more energy to devote to your work because your efforts are focused. Goal setting is synonymous with change. One sets a goal because the current state of affairs needs to change. If current productivity levels need to improve, specific productivity goals need to be set. The goal becomes the target for all activity.

Improving self-confidence. Reaching goals builds self-confidence. Self-confidence promotes growth and personal development. As one achieves goals, one also becomes less fearful of risk taking. Resistance to change may be a by-product of fear. Setting goals and formulating a plan help to overcome fears. The confidence your employees have in you as their leader will improve also as your goals become reality, especially when they benefit directly from the goal.

Communicating more clearly. An effective goal is precise, has set priorities, and is documented. It communicates to everyone where they are headed.

Meeting deadlines. Deadlines or due dates cause things to happen; they are control measures. Procrastination may result from unspecified due dates rather than lack of motivation on the part of those the changes affect. Target dates for things help to move activity toward goal accomplishment.

CRITERIA FOR SETTING PRIORITIES

There are two basic yardsticks to follow in setting priorities. The first yardstick involves the measure of relevance and value and can best be determined by asking the question, "What is the best use of my time right now?" The second yardstick involves the measure of timeliness and immediacy. Deadlines often dictate priorities, and immediate needs and emergencies are your first priority. This measure, therefore, can best be determined by asking the question, "What commands my attention right now?"

In the absence of matters that command your immediate attention—looming deadlines, immediate needs, and emergencies—the best use of your time will normally be those planning issues that will better ensure your department will be successful in the long term and will meet its goals. The best use of your time would also include spending time coaching and developing staff and managing their performance, because such matters contribute to your department's long-term success. Focusing on

matters that are of higher importance or value to the organization and its long-term success also constitutes the best use of your time, particularly when circumstances allow for sufficient time to concentrate and handle them well rather than under the constant pressure of unreasonable or sudden deadlines. These matters are also important because when managed well they will contribute to your career success. Finally, in the absence of pressing demands, deadlines, and emergencies, taking time to develop your skills through training, professional development, and to further your educational goals constitute the best use of your time.

Of course, your ability to address many matters that are most relevant and valuable to the organization, to your team, and to you will often be impacted by matters that you must handle because they are timely and immediate. When there are immediate deadlines, needs, and emergencies, regardless of their long-term value and relevance, you must nonetheless attend to them. Naturally, many of these matters, such as daily operational matters, customer-service needs, and legitimate requests from employees and superiors, all command your attention *right now* and constitute the best use of your time *right now*, because they involve the normal expectations of doing business.

On the other hand, many matters should neither command your attention nor be viewed as the best use of your time, regardless whether others say they should. For example, we receive all kinds of e-mails from all manner of senders who do not warrant our attention and could waste our time if we allowed them to. Employees may want our time, but if their needs are groundless and they simply want to vent excessively without constructively looking for solutions, the energy devoted to this may not be the best use of our time and attention. Pointless projects that are on your "To Do" list or in your job description, but that do not contribute to organizational goals and are essentially ignored or forgotten by superiors anyway, also fall into this category. Finally, frivolous activities like non-business-related Internet surfing, entertaining gossip from employees, and excessive discussions about your personal life that impact work also belong in this category.

There is a third yardstick of sorts that involves your personal measure of judgment. You are the best judge of your time and priorities. The challenge is using your best judgment to manage the natural tension between what commands attention and what constitutes the best use of your time, while reducing or eliminating what does neither.

THE ABC METHOD OF SORTING THINGS OUT

Some managers use a simple ABC system to help them prioritize tasks. Priority A includes "Must-do" items that are critical. Priority B is "Should-do" items but without critical deadlines involved. Priority C constitutes "Fun to do" or "When I have time" tasks that can usually be saved for slack periods.

A supervisor's priority list should be made up and constantly revised according to sound principles and sound thinking. Setting priorities is a decision-making process whereby you rank order the tasks that need to be done by you and the people who work for you—first, second, third, and so on down the line. Following such an order in taking care of tasks and problems will help you reach your goals. It is not as easy as it sounds, however. Listed here are eight questions to ask yourself when setting priorities.

1. If I deal with this problem first, will it automatically solve others later?
2. If I deal with this problem first, will it delay the solution of another that will eventually cause severe damage to productivity or my career?
3. If I delay action on this problem, will it solve itself?
4. What can I delegate on my list so that I can get to more serious problems sooner?
5. Will taking care of this small problem first free my mind to take care of my number one problem later?
6. What tasks must I complete quickly so that I will not hold up the schedule of other people or other departments?
7. Can I group a few things together and save time by solving them all at once?
8. Is the time psychologically right to take a problem up with my boss, or should I wait for a more appropriate time?

You can see that setting priorities is a complex, demanding process that you can never perfect. Yet the more effective you become at it, the more success you can anticipate. Many managers have learned that keeping a written list of priorities is best for them; others prefer to carry a list around in their minds, a list that constantly changes as changes occur in the work environment.

ADVANTAGES OF A WRITTEN LIST

You may have the aptitude to keep a running priority list in your mind, but most beginning supervisors find it advantageous to write out a list on a desk pad for the following reasons:

1. Writing the list is a form of self-discipline. When you know what needs to be done next, you are better organized and less likely to waste time.
2. The list frequently eliminates forgetting, which can get one into trouble with superiors. Some supervisors simply prefer to trust visible lists instead of their memories.

3. Completing a list and checking off items is satisfying and motivating. A priority list is, in effect, a personal reward system.

Return to the Departmental plan (Example) (Six-Month Plan) in Chapter 16, page 239 and prioritize the activities. List them from highest priority (A) to lowest priority (C). By prioritizing, you will readily recognize how it affects the completion of objectives.

KEEPING PRIORITY LISTS FLEXIBLE

The first thing you learn about setting priorities is that the order may not last long. All it takes is a call from your manager, an emergency situation, an unexpected human relations problem, or a mechanical breakdown to force you to make up a new list. A priority list is not a static thing and may need revision many times a day. In fact, many supervisors automatically reevaluate their priorities every time they move from one completed task to another. Then, you may ask, why make a list in the first place? The primary reason is to keep all responsibilities, tasks, and problems in view. A priority list should include all tasks that need to be done to reach your goals as soon as possible. Obviously, a cardinal mistake would be to leave something off the list that should be on it. But even if your list is complete, you can still make mistakes by putting one task or problem ahead of another. For example, if you spend your time on what should be a lower-priority matter, you are neglecting something more crucial, resulting in more harm than benefit. To illustrate the importance of this concept, look at the following examples:

Sid was a department manager for a major retail chain. Last week, it was announced that his store would have its annual inspection by a team of top officials. Sid wanted a good report so badly that he gave top priority to cleaning up and rearranging the department, and everything else was neglected. Predictably, Sid and the department received a 100 percent rating. But what happened to the other priorities? For one thing, Sid neglected to turn in a non-computerized merchandise reorder list on time and the department was out of stock for two weeks. Sid—and his company—paid a high price for a poor priority decision.

Gayle was so fed up with the poorly organized files in her department that she finally decided to reorganize them herself, making it her top priority. Once she got into the task, she discovered that things were worse and took much longer than she anticipated. As a result, she neglected other important matters, including annual reviews of the six people in her department. Her superior was upset about it. Later, as Gayle thought it over, she realized that if she had taken care of the reviews first, she could have used them to motivate her employees to clean up the files themselves. She permitted her frustration to overemphasize one problem at the expense of another that should have been first priority.

Duke was chief of a repair crew that had been working long hours due to heavy storm conditions. No sooner did they make one repair than they were sent to do another. Each day, Duke was supposed to turn in written reports on finished projects, but last Tuesday he wasn't organized, failed to set any priorities, and forgot to turn in the report. As a result, another repair crew was sent 100 miles away to do a job that Duke's crew had already completed. It was an embarrassing situation.

EFFECTIVE PRIORITY SETTING

How can you set priorities that will make it easier for you to reach your goals and keep you out of trouble? Here are some suggestions.

- Give priority to any problem that is rendering you ineffective as a supervisor. Sometimes an upsetting human relations problem might be bothering you, such as a conflict with one of your employees or a serious communications conflict with your superior. Such situations can disturb you emotionally and make you ineffective, or at least not up to standard in the rest of your work.

- Do not focus only on your top-priority task. Frequently supervisors become so involved in reaching one goal that they neglect others, resulting in more harm in the long run. Keep all your priorities in mind and balance them to prevent shortsightedness.

- Sometimes it is good to delay a problem or task, giving it a lower priority. Some problems become so complicated that an immediate solution is impossible. More time is needed to evaluate the facts and measure the total impact. In such instances, you might wish to drop the problem to the bottom of your list, where you can watch it but not forget it.

- Sometimes you can group goals into a meaningful sequence. Many supervisors are good at putting their daily goals into a priority pattern that saves time and effort. Into this category fall such things as making one trip accomplish three goals or arranging tasks in sequence so that they are easier to accomplish.

- If something has been on your list for a long time, either do it or forget it. An item that keeps showing up on a priority list soon becomes an irritant. Do not give it that power.

- Do not push what should be a high-priority item to the bottom of your list because of fear. Some managers keep what should be top-priority items undercover because they are afraid to face them. This kind of denial is a serious mistake because time solves very few problems.

- Oscillating back and forth from one priority to another is unwise. Once you put a task near the top of your list, try to complete it within a reasonable period of time. If you start something and then keep switching to another priority, you will lose all motivation to complete the project.

HOW TO GET STARTED

If setting up a priority list is a new experience for you, the following tips will help you get started. Later, after you have had additional experience, you can adapt the process to your own style. If you are not currently a supervisor, you may wish to set up a personal priority list.

1. Select the task or project that will, in your opinion, advance the productivity of your department the most, and put it at the top of your list. Leave it there until it is completed or a more important task surfaces.

2. List two additional tasks or projects that are less important, but should still be numbers 2 and 3 on your pad. Frequently these tasks present less time pressure.

3. List, in succession, any tasks (reports, appointments, telephone calls, counseling, etc.) that either must or should be accomplished before you leave work.

4. Select and list a "fun" project—something you can look forward to doing as an end-of-day personal reward—near or at the bottom of your list.

5. Try to restrict the number of tasks on your list to about seven. Too many priority projects can lead to confusion and demotivation. Even though it may be your goal to accomplish as much as possible in a single day, some tasks will wait until tomorrow. Those who overschedule themselves take the risk of turning out poor-quality work with higher levels of frustration.

DAILY PRIORITIZED PLAN (EXAMPLE)*

1. Meet with computer software consultant at 10:30 A.M.

2. Handle late delivery complaint from key customer.

3. Get monthly quality-control report to boss on time.

4. Write complaint letter to supplier.

5. Clean and reorganize supply room.

6. Counsel Mary on absenteeism.

7. Compliment Gregg on his progress in reaching the personal productivity potential.

* (Compare to example in Chapter 16, page 240)

Check off the items on your priority list and prepare a new one at the end of the day. You will transfer some unfinished tasks to the new list, realign them, and add new ones. This process accomplishes two psychological goals. First, it helps you leave your responsibilities at work so you will be free to enjoy your leisure time. Second, arriving at work the following day with a list prepared saves time and can be self-motivating.

Setting priorities for personal tasks off the job can be as important as those at work. If you use what you have learned in this chapter in both environments, you will automatically do a better job of balancing home and career.

PERFORMANCE **CHECKLIST**

1. For a supervisor, setting goals and establishing priorities can lead to achieving more, builds self-confidence, allows the supervisor to communicate more clearly the direction the department is headed, and helps the supervisor meet deadlines.

2. The two yardsticks for determining priorities are (1) relevance and value, and (2) timeliness and immediacy. When determining relevance and value, ask, "What is the best use of my time right now?" When determining timeliness and immediacy, ask, "What commands my attention right now?" Higher-priority items such as long-range planning and developing yourself and staff in order to achieve greater success generally constitute the best use of your time. However, these matters must be deferred whenever items like daily operational matters, needs, and demands of customers, employees, and superiors and emergencies arise because these items command your attention right now. Frivolous matters such as non-work-related Internet use, gossip, and excessive discussions about your personal life must be set aside altogether.

3. A practical method for prioritizing numerous items is through the ABC method, in which you prioritize A items as "Must do," B items as "Should do," and C items as "Fun to do" or "When I have time."

4. Using a written list to prioritize items is helpful because it supports self-discipline, it frequently eliminates the concern about forgetting your priorities, and the process of checking items off the list is motivating.

5. Because needs and demands change, you must be flexible about listing priorities and willing to adjust as needed.

6. Additional suggestions for prioritizing include: Give priority to correcting any problem that renders you ineffective; do not become shortsighted by focusing only on top-priority tasks and ignoring all other tasks; delay some tasks to give yourself time to evaluate them before addressing them; sequence goals whenever possible to be more efficient and save time; either complete items that have been on your list a long time or remove them; do not push a higher-priority item down the list because of fear; and focus on an item and get it done rather than oscillate between items and get nothing done.

7. When prioritizing each day: (1) select first the task or project that will best advance productivity; (2) list two additional tasks or projects that are less important but also involve less time pressure; (3) list all tasks that must be done before you leave work; (4) select a "fun," personally rewarding end-of-day project and put it toward the bottom of your list; and (5) try to limit your total list to no more than seven.

TEST **YOURSELF**

For each of the following statements, check true or false.

True   False

_____ _____ 1. Your most urgent task should be given a priority level of A.

_____ _____ 2. Doing the most urgent task first can head off potential problems.

_____ _____ 3. Priorities in most jobs change so fast it is foolish to write them down.

_____ _____ 4. Sometimes, but not often, delaying a task or responsibility is smart.

_____ _____ 5. Sometimes priorities can be clustered and then accomplished together.

_____ _____ 6. Setting goals and formulating a plan helps overcome fears.

_____ _____ 7. Priorities should be coordinated with departmental and organizational goals.

_____ _____ 8. A priority list of about twenty items is ideal.

True   False

____   ____   9. A task that keeps showing up at the top of a list should be taken care of quickly or forgotten.

____   ____   10. Setting priorities effectively is an excellent manifestation of self-discipline.

Turn to the back of the book to check your answers.

Total Correct ____

DISCUSSION **QUESTIONS**

1. Do you agree with the belief that those who do not keep a written priority list needlessly burden their minds?

2. What advantages might come from keeping a priority list on a computer instead of a personal notebook?

3. What is the relationship between setting long-term goals and setting daily priorities?

4. When you are confronted with a seemingly endless list of priorities that command your immediate attention, how do you manage to find time to accomplish those higher-level priority items that contribute to long-term organizational success for you, your team, and the organization? Discuss your ideas with classmates. What will be the consequences to you, your team, and your organization if you don't manage this balance?

CASE: **PRIORITIES**

Note: Do not turn the page 256 until told to do so.

OBJECTIVE

To provide simulated experience in setting priorities under pressure.

PROBLEM

You (as Ricardo) left Monday morning for a one-day company-sponsored training program in supervisory leadership. Your department was turned over to Renee, but she became ill and went home. You were called to return on an emergency basis and arrived five minutes ago. The time is 1:00 P.M. on Monday. As you walk into your workstation, you face ten critical problems.

PROCEDURE

A priority list of problems are listed below. Please read, evaluate, and assign a priority number to each problem. In other words, decide which problem you would handle first, second, third, and so forth. You will have five minutes to prioritize the tasks.

Turn the page and read all ten problems. You are now ready to assign the priority numbers in the appropriate squares in the left-hand column. While participants are making their priority choices, the instructor or trainer should list the choices in abbreviated form on a blackboard so that the results can be compared. When the time is up, the instructor should invite one individual at a time to put her or his priority list on the board and explain it in front of the group.

CASE DISCUSSION AND QUESTIONS

Discussion should center on the differences between the priority patterns put on the blackboard. Why might one be better than another? Should the broken equipment have received priority on all lists? Did anyone save time by grouping? Are some people intimidated by a telephone or their boss?

PRIORITY **EXERCISE**

PART I

Assign priorities to the following list of tasks. Write the number 1 in front of the first task you would do, and so on throughout the list.

____   Complete an overdue written report to your superior.

____   Have a private communication session with an employee on a discipline problem you have put off dealing with for days.

____   Return a call to the Human Resource department that you sense will mean trouble.

____   Complete a nasty filing job that you cannot delegate.

PRIORITY LIST

☐ A formal grievance from Renee is on your desk. To read and digest it would take fifteen minutes.

☐ Bill has left word that he wants to see you in his office immediately upon your return. Anticipated time: sixty minutes.

☐ You have some very important-looking unopened mail (both company and personal) on your desk. Time: ten minutes.

☐ Your telephone is ringing.

☐ A piece of equipment has broken down, halting all production in your department. You are the only one who can fix it. Anticipated time: thirty minutes.

☐ Someone is seated outside your office waiting to see you. Time: ten minutes.

☐ You have an urgent electronic mail notice to call a Los Angeles operator. Both your mother and the company headquarters are located in Los Angeles. Time: ten minutes.

☐ Gerald has sent word that he wants to see you and has asked that you return his call as soon as possible. Time: ten minutes.

☐ Giselle is in the women's lounge and claims to be sick. She wants your permission to go home. It would take about five minutes to get the facts and make a decision.

☐ In order to get to your office by 1:00 you had to miss lunch. You are very hungry, but you figure it will take thirty minutes to get something substantial to eat.

PRIORITY EXERCISE *continued*

_____ Complete airline arrangements for a trip to Chicago to a professional convention—already approved by management.

_____ Handle a computer malfunction.

_____ Do a therapeutic fun job to relieve the inner tensions you feel.

PART II

Using the tips from the text, list your actual priorities for tomorrow. (If you are not currently a supervisor, list your personal priorities.) List no more than seven. See the authors' comments in the back of the book.

PERSONAL GROWTH EXERCISE

Take out five pieces of paper and on each one write down something that you value doing very much. After doing this, crumple them, scramble them, and place them in front of you. Now throw one away. Now throw another one away. Open up and look at the remaining three items. Assume now that you were required to eliminate the two items because you have no time to do them. Write down your reaction. What did you learn? What does this tell you about the importance of setting priorities?

TO LEARN MORE

For more resources on how to prioritize refer to the following reference:

Merrill, A. Roger, and Rebecca R. Merrill. *First Things First: To Live, to Love, to Learn, to Leave a Legacy.* New York: Fireside, 1995.

chapter **eighteen**

MAKE DECISIVE DECISIONS

"Delay is preferable to error."

Thomas Jefferson

Improving Productivity
Leading Teams
Communicating Effectively
Managing Conflict
Improving Performance
Managing Time
Benefiting from Change

Ｈow would you react to the following advertisement if you found it in your favorite newspaper?

FOR SALE

SUPERVISOR's PROBLEM-SOLVING MACHINE

Guarantees Better Decisions with Less Worry

Easy to Use!   No Tricks!

Write Scientific Systems for Further Details

You would probably be highly skeptical and quickly pass it off as an unethical come-on or a joke. And you would be right because no such thing as a sure-fire decision-making device could replace the judgment of supervisors. The great majority of decisions you are paid to make as a supervisor must be made in your mind and not by gadgets, gimmicks, or even sophisticated computers. You can, however, do certain things to improve your decisions.

You can learn how to make decisions more systematically and train yourself to think through problems more logically. You can remember to take into consideration all factors that should influence the decision. In other words, you can become methodical. An example of how you can be methodical in dealing with paperwork is to choose quickly one of the following options:

Act on it now.

File for future reference.

PERFORMANCE COMPETENCIES

After you have finished reading this chapter, you should be able to:

- Describe three approaches to problem solving

- Describe three kinds of decisions that often face the supervisor

- Use the Group Decision Making Through Needs Clarification model to make decisions

- Define high- and low-consequence work and people problems

Refer it to someone else.

Trash it.

Do not leave correspondence of any kind in your in-basket. Decide what to do with it the first time you touch it. If the task requires a large time commitment to accomplish, put it in a designated place marked for things to act on at your next opportunity. Making decisions (problem solving) is no job for a scatterbrained amateur, an impulsive individual who overreacts to every problem, or a person who sees only the surface of the problem. It takes emotional stability, a logical mind, and deep thinking to come up with sound answers to tough problems. This point is illustrated by some sample management comments.

"I'd make Helen a supervisor tomorrow if she could only learn to make clear-cut decisions instead of being so wishy-washy about every little problem."

"We finally had to transfer Drew back to his old job. He had great potential as a supervisor, but when it came to making even simple decisions, he fell apart. Fear and frustration took over, and everyone lost confidence in him."

"Gregg keeps getting into hot water because he makes impulsive decisions instead of using his head. His career is grounded until he puts more thought into his decision making."

THREE APPROACHES TO PROBLEM SOLVING

As a supervisor, you will find that each day a constant variety of large and small problems will come to you from all directions. You can use one of the following three approaches in dealing with them:

1. You can stall or delay action through any number of often-used ploys. For example, you can bury the problem in red tape, shuffle it in a circle until it disappears, overconsult with your boss until he tells you to forget it, or simply procrastinate until (you hope) a decision is no longer necessary. Using this wishy-washy approach will doom you to failure. Not only will you lose the respect of your superiors, but you will kill the productivity of your employees. The very nature of your job forces you to become a decision maker, and there is no escape from the responsibility. You will be expected to make good decisions, but good or bad, they must be made. Except in unusual cases, stalling or delaying will only compound the original problem.

2. You can temporarily dispose of your problems by making quick, superficial decisions with little or no thinking and even less logic. If you adopt this approach, you will do the following:

    a. Use your hunches instead of your rational powers.

    b. Refuse to consider side effects.

    c. Give each problem (large or small) the same off-the-cuff treatment.

    d. Violate the concentration techniques you learned in Chapter 15.

    If you take this road, you will create more problems than you solve. You will survive for a while, but in the end, you will drown in your own confusion.

3. You can be professional in your approach and learn to solve your many problems through sound decision-making practices. It means following a system, using logical steps, and thinking. It is not easy, but it is the only way you can make decisions that will contribute to greater departmental productivity, that will be enthusiastically accepted by the people who work for you, and that will build a good reputation for you with management.

THREE KINDS OF DECISIONS

Supervisors make three kinds of decisions. The **autocratic** decision is one that you make by yourself. You do not consult anyone, and you accept full responsibility for the consequences of your decision. Your second choice is talking over the problem with another person, perhaps a more experienced superior. The result is called a **consultative** decision. Two heads are frequently better than one when a serious decision must be made. It is foolish to make a poor decision on your own if an expert is available to help you make a better one. The **group** decision is a third possibility. When a problem involves the entire staff, they should participate in the decision, especially if their own decision will satisfy them better and motivate them more. This approach would be the only acceptable process in a true team operation.

For autocratic and consultative decisions, you may find that the following "Seven-Step Decision-Making Model" will fit into your personal comfort zone. If so, embrace it and use it whenever appropriate. Its use can measurably improve your decision-making track record.

SEVEN-STEP DECISION-MAKING MODEL

Assume that you have accepted a new position with an organization located several miles away in an unfamiliar urban area. While studying a map at your kitchen table, you decide to experiment with the seven-step method. Here's what might happen.

Steps	Example
1. Define the desired outcome.	You see at least three different routes you might take. You want the best one.
2. Establish decision criteria.	You want the shortest, fastest, safest route, the one that will cause the least wear and tear on your car and use the least gas.
3. Define alternatives.	Mark off what appear to be the three best routes on your map.
4. Get all the facts.	You will measure the time, number of stops, gas usage, traffic density, and other factors on each route. You will drive a different route each day for three successive days.
5. Weigh and compare.	Compare all facts and opinions to decide which route is best under all conditions.
6. Opt for the best alternative.	Once you have *thought it through,* you can make the decision with confidence.
7. Follow-up.	After implementing a decision, evaluate its effectiveness against desired outcomes.

Often it is best to take a few seconds to decide what is involved in a decision before you start applying any logical procedure. As in taking a trip, you need to stop and figure out how to proceed. Consider this step the "decision before making the decision." For example, for many supervisors it is helpful to divide problems into those that are job oriented and those that are people oriented. Once they make this preliminary decision, they can apply the seven-step procedure.

For decisions that directly affect your employees' work or routine, it is wise to involve them in decision making, especially when decisions bring change. Any time you need the motivation of your employees to carry out a decision, it is a good idea to involve them; participation is a motivator for many employees.

GROUP DECISION-MAKING MODEL

The following Group Decision Making Through Needs Clarification model is an effective model for group decision making. The supervisor, acting as facilitator, with an appointed recorder from the group, follows the model. The model is ideal for fostering group consensus.

1. *Communicate the situation to the group.*   Identify the issue and openly discuss the need for a group decision. Decisions are often needed when changes are being considered. It is a good time to differentiate the "Actual State of Affairs" from the "Desired State of Affairs." Maintain an open atmosphere where questions, concerns, and perceptions about the situation can be explored. In this step, it is important that everyone understand why a decision is being considered.

2. *Brainstorm all possible decisions.*   As a group, with the recorder writing on a flip chart or white board, generate as many ideas as possible. Be creative. Do not evaluate or choose any one decision at this time. Let the ideas flow. The selection process comes next.

3. *Evaluate the list of possible decisions.*   Examine the idea list generated and begin to evaluate the pros and cons of each item. Evaluate the alternatives by considering at least three areas of inquiry. The answers to these questions are the criteria for the selection and become the justification for your choice.

   Inquiry 1:   Will the choice improve the situation? Will it solve the problem? What is the probability that we will achieve our desired state or goal?

   Inquiry 2:   Will the choice meet the needs of those involved in carrying out the decision? Will those involved in implementing the decision be motivated to carry it through to completion?

   Inquiry 3:   Do we, as a group, have the resources, such as time, money, and expertise, to carry out the decision? How much help will we require from others not in our group?

   Asking these questions for each alternative will eliminate some ideas immediately. Others look good and are put on a short list of possibilities to be evaluated again.

4. *Choose the best alternative.*   Do not rush to a decision. It is best to postpone a decision when more discussion is needed. Be sure everyone buys into the decision. It is useful to ask everyone whether they are motivated to carry out the decision. If the answer is no, start over.

5. *Develop an implementation strategy.*   The decision of the group must be put into action. Clarify and organize the timed, sequenced series of steps (objectives) needed for implementing the decision. This process should clarify the precise steps that must be taken, who is responsible for each step, when each step should be completed, and how the team will follow up to check progress. Complete discussion about this may be best left for another meeting. Allowing your group time to think about how they will implement the decision will help in the long run, but schedule an implementation meeting soon. Group decision making should be used during the implementation meeting.

6. *Follow-up.*   Evaluate the effects of the decision. Has the situation changed in the desired way? If so, celebrate. The supervisor must personally thank everyone involved. If change hasn't occurred as desired, follow up allows the team to reevaluate and use the same decision-making process to implement new strategies.

Some may think that this level of participation in decision making takes too much time. It does take time, but consider it an investment. People are more motivated to carry out a decision if they have had a part in making it. Overcoming resistance to unilateral decisions takes a great deal more time in the long run. This Group Decision Making Through Needs Clarification model works in family situations as well as it does at work.

JOB-ORIENTED PROBLEMS

The two basic kinds of job-oriented problems are minor problems that require quick answers but have little permanent influence on department operations, and major problems that have deep and lasting influence. Most of your decision making will deal with minor job problems that you should be able to handle on the spot.

Where should this new item be stored? Which report should be completed first? Should I delegate this task or do it myself? Which color would be best? Should I write or telephone my answer?

LOW-CONSEQUENCE WORK-ORIENTED DECISIONS

Most job-oriented decisions the front-line supervisor makes are low on the consequence scale. Even a bad decision will have little impact on productivity or the image of the supervisor. Faulty low-consequence decisions are usually easy to correct. Generally speaking, minor problems can be solved immediately and then forgotten. They should be disposed of in an orderly and efficient manner without consuming too much time. The major threat with these problems is that they may become psychological hang-ups for the supervisor when a clear-cut decision is not obvious and, through indecision, the supervisor permits the problem to become a major source of frustration. This kind of distortion is a luxury the supervisor cannot afford. The following half-minute procedure will help you make quick, frustration-free, low-consequence decisions.

1. Take time to restate the problem and review the facts in your mind (about ten seconds).
2. Compare the first answer you think of with at least one other possibility. Weigh one against the other and try to come up with the best choice. If a decision is not obvious, make one anyway (about fifteen seconds).
3. With confidence that you have made the right decision, announce it to those involved and move on to something else (about five seconds).

It is a serious mistake to make a big thing out of a low-consequence decision. You will lose the respect of your supervisors and the confidence of your employees. Recognize a small problem for what it is, give it the treatment recommended here, trust your judgment, and then move on to something more important.

HIGH-CONSEQUENCE WORK-ORIENTED DECISIONS

Major job-oriented problems that will have a permanent influence on the operation of your department, however, must be given more serious treatment and more time. These problems probably challenge existing policies or procedures or involve changes in technology, layout, design, reporting methods, procedural patterns, control systems, safety rules, or basic production methods. They are major because they touch on something basic in the department and because they probably have complicating side effects. Job-connected problems of this nature and scope deserve careful attention and your best logical thinking. When they occur, lean heavily on the seven-step procedure and these additional suggestions:

- Avoid the temptation to make a quick decision. Gather all the available facts even if it means making a major project out of it. Ask yourself these questions: What has been done in the past? Why isn't it working today? Will a new system or approach work better? What is the real source of the problem? What are the other factors? Write down all these facts so that you clearly see the detailed overall picture.

- If you decide to make an autocratic decision, write down and study each possible solution. Slowly eliminate those that do not conform to company policy or have side effects that might do more damage than good. Reduce the list to the two or three possibilities that offer the best permanent solution.

- If a clear choice is not evident, use the consultative-decision approach. Ask your superior or a key employee to talk over the remaining solutions. Sometimes possibilities need to be talked over so that the person making the decision can compare one solution with another.

- If the decision you need to make will have significant impacts on your employees and you risk losing their trust and goodwill if you make decisions without their input (and you have time to deliberate) use the group decision-making model.

- After some careful weighing, choose the solution you feel is best and take it to your immediate superior for his or her reaction and approval. Tell why you made the decision and what results you expect. If approved, take the time to communicate the decision to all the people involved.

- Follow-up. To make sure the decision is implemented properly and that misunderstandings are eliminated you need to check back with those involved.

Major job-connected problems should not be solved in haste or under pressure. When they occur, slow down and follow the logical steps outlined here.

LOW-CONSEQUENCE PEOPLE PROBLEMS

The most important thing you can learn about decision making is that people problems are quite different from job problems and demand special treatment. Job-connected problems deal with tangibles or procedures that influence people; people-connected problems deal with the people themselves—their disappointments, frustrations, hostilities, and personality conflicts. People problems may stem from job problems but they exist primarily inside the employee. Approaching people problems requires your most sensitive handling. Success with these problems depends both on making a fair decision and on the way you work with the people involved.

People problems fall into two categories: simple employee requests that require only limited decision making, and deep-seated, complicated problems that require considerable time and all the skill you can muster.

Supervisors often receive special requests from employees concerning work schedules, procedures, breaks, and personal matters that are important to the individual but relatively insignificant in the total operation of the department. In most cases, you can listen carefully and give an on-the-spot yes or no answer within a few seconds without spending a great deal of time and effort. To play it safe, however, ask yourself these three questions before answering such requests:

1. Is there a written policy that governs such requests? If so, it should be applied (except in unusual cases) and should be explained carefully to the employee.

2. Will granting the request damage relationships with other employees in your department? If so, it should be refused (except in unusual cases) and the reasons made clear to the person making the request.

3. Will granting the request seriously endanger the health and safety of others? If so, it should be refused and the reasons should be given.

When evaluating these questions, consider whether the decision to grant or deny the request is fair and consistent with similar decisions you've made, whether you've made the same decision for others under similar circumstances in the past, and whether you would make the same decisions for others under similar circumstances in the future. When a special request does not violate any company policy, will not damage the supervisor's relationship with others, and will not endanger the safety of others, it should be granted graciously and quickly.

HIGH-CONSEQUENCE PEOPLE PROBLEMS

Any people problems other than simple requests should be considered potentially high-consequence problems. They fall into two classifications: (1) those pertaining to one individual only—these problems are usually highly personal and psychological and should concern the supervisor only because they influence productivity; (2) those that involve two or more employees—these often involve friction in the relationship between two or more departmental employees and usually affect productivity. Supplement your seven-step procedure with the following suggestions:

- Listen carefully to all problems or complaints. If something is important to one of your employees, it is also important to you. Do not ignore or belittle any problem, no matter how trivial it may seem at the beginning.
- People problems usually involve two or more people, so always make an effort to gather information from all sides. Do not take sides while you are gathering the facts.
- Weigh all the facts carefully before you make a decision. Ask yourself these questions: Will the decision be fair to all concerned? Will it violate any company personnel policies? Do any potential serious side effects need consideration? Will the decision violate any human relations principles? Write down two or three possible decisions for careful evaluation before you choose one.
- Using good counseling techniques, openly communicate to all parties involved your decision and why you made it. Take time. Encourage a two-way conversation. Listen to any negative reactions, but stand firm on your decision.
- Follow up by working to restore or rebuild any relationships that may have been temporarily injured because of your decision.

THE GROUP DECISION

The group-decision approach can accomplish a great deal if the supervisor uses it skillfully. It should be used when (1) the decision will have an influence on employees; (2) the decision requires no urgency; (3) departmental priorities permit;

(4) you are willing to abide by the decisions the group makes; and (5) you have created and maintained a team approach.

Leadership and decision making are inseparable. As you start out, you may not always choose the correct decision-making process (autocratic, consultative, group) that is most compatible with the type of decision to be made. Do not expect to bat a thousand, but be satisfied with the best average you can achieve, learning as you go. If you make a mistake, do not hesitate to make a second decision to correct it. Nothing will affect more forcefully your upward mobility than your willingness to improve your decision-making style.

Once the decision is ready to be announced, do it in a decisive manner. The more confidently you communicate that you have made the right decision, the more acceptance it will receive—and the more leadership you will have demonstrated.

PERFORMANCE **CHECKLIST**

1. There are three basic approaches you can take to problem solving:
   a. Stall or delay action until (you hope) a decision is no longer necessary, which will likely result in a loss of respect from superiors and will kill productivity in your team.
   b. Temporarily dispose of problems by making quick, superficial decisions, which are generally done with little or no thinking or logic and lead to confusion.
   c. Engage in sound decision-making practices that will lead to greater productivity, decisions that your team will accept, and a good reputation with management.

2. There are three kinds of decisions that supervisors can use:
   a. The autocratic decision is one you make yourself without consultation and for which you accept full responsibility for the consequences.
   b. The consultative decision is one you make after consultation with superiors or experts who can provide insight that will help you.

c. The group decision involves participation of your team and is preferable if it will motivate the team and would more likely be accepted by them if they have input in making it.

3. The seven-step decision-making model is useful for making autocratic and consultative decisions. The steps are: (1) Define the desired outcome; (2) establish decision criteria; (3) define alternatives; (4) get all the facts; (5) weigh and compare; (6) opt for the best alternative; and (7) follow-up.

4. The group decision-making model involves the following steps: (1) Communicate the situation to the group; (2) brainstorm all possible decisions; (3) evaluate the list of possible decisions; (4) choose the best alternative; (5) develop an implementation plan; and (6) follow-up.

5. In general, there are two kinds of problems you must tackle as a supervisor: (1) work-oriented problems, and (2) people problems.

a. Low-consequence work-oriented problems are generally easy to correct and should be resolved quickly without excessive deliberation.

b. High-consequence work-oriented problems generally challenge existing policies or procedures or involve changes in technology, layout, design, reporting methods, procedural patterns, control systems, basic rules, or basic production methods. They require the proper decision-making process, examination and weighing of alternatives, and follow-up to ensure the decision made is properly implemented.

c. Low-consequence people problems generally involve simple employee requests that require limited decision making. Provided the request does not violate any company policy, will not damage the supervisor's relationship with others, and will not endanger the safety of others, it should be granted.

d. High-consequence people problems generally involve either (1) those pertaining to one individual that are highly personal and psychological and can impact productivity, or (2) those involving two or more employees and generally involve friction that affects productivity. They generally require effective listening, careful gathering and weighing of facts, effective counseling techniques to communicate and manage decisions made affecting the parties, and follow up to restore relationships.

TEST **YOURSELF**

For each of the following statements, check true or false.

True   False

1. Bad decisions usually come about because supervisors spend too much time getting the facts.

2. Deciding first whether a problem is minor or major can make your second decision a better one.

3. Delaying a decision usually compounds the problem.

4. Never make on-the-spot decisions.

5. In making quick job-oriented decisions, there is no time to compare alternatives.

6. Supervisors show a weakness when they consult others on a major decision.

7. Fear of making a wrong decision can result in a poor decision.

8. The six-step decision-making process is good for job-connected problems only.

9. Good people decisions require taking sides.

10. Even if a major decision is a bad one, it is usually better than no decision at all.

11. An individual decision is called an *autocratic decision.*

12. After implementing a decision, evaluate its effectiveness against the desired outcome.

Turn to the back of the book to check your answers.

Total Correct _____

DISCUSSION **QUESTIONS**

1. Why do some beginning supervisors find it so difficult to make even minor low-consequence decisions?

2. Challenge or defend the practice of dividing decisions into two categories: job oriented and people oriented.

3. Do most supervisors involve their employees in the decision-making process as much as they should? If not, why don't they?

CASE: **TERMINATION**

OBJECTIVE

To provide a simulated experience in evaluating the causes for and potential dangers in termination.

PROBLEM

Ricardo has made up his mind that he wants to give Giselle the required two-week termination notice. He bases his case on the following: (1) Her productivity dropped about six weeks ago and has never come back up to previous levels. (2) She has been absent twice during this six-week period and late several times. (3) She has, despite suggestions from Ricardo, consistently overextended her coffee breaks. (4) Renee has threatened to quit if Giselle is not transferred out of the department. (5) At 3:30 yesterday afternoon, Giselle walked off the job crying. (6) Under a staff reduction policy, should Giselle be terminated, her position might be eliminated.

Bill claims that Ricardo does not have sufficient cause for termination. (1) He has not formally "written

up" Giselle twice previously about violations, as required by company policy. (2) Ricardo has not had a heart-to-heart talk with Giselle for two weeks. (3) Although walking off the job is technically a cause for dismissal, Bill feels the case has not been fully investigated. (4) He fears that Giselle might appeal her case to the local civil rights commission. (5) If the case is not investigated, Giselle could draw unemployment insurance by contesting the termination procedure, which would cost the company money.

CASE DISCUSSION AND QUESTIONS

Students should vote independently for either Bill or Ricardo. Discussion should then center on causes for termination and why business organizations must protect themselves against unfair practices in this area. Which position is more sound, Bill's or Ricardo's? Defend your view.

DECISION-MAKING **EXERCISE**

Write out a brief description of the number-one on-the-job problem you currently face:

Using the six-step decision-making model, complete the following:

Define desired outcome

Write out decision criteria

List alternatives

Discover and list all possible facts

Weigh and compare alternatives. (This is a purely mental process.)

Write out your decision

How do you intend to announce and implement your decision? See comments from the authors in the back of this book.

PERSONAL GROWTH **EXERCISE**

If you are completely honest with yourself, what would you say is your preferred decision-making style? Is it autocratic or consultative, or are you most comfortable with facilitating group decision-making processes?

Given your preferred style, when is this style most effective in the work you do (or plan to do) as a supervisor? When is it a hindrance to your effectiveness as a supervisor?

WHERE DO I GO FROM HERE?

"There go my people. I must find out where they are going so I can lead them."

ALEXANDRE LEDRU-ROLLING

chapter nineteen

COMMON MISTAKES YOU DON'T WANT TO MAKE

Improving Productivity
Leading Teams
Communicating Effectively
Managing Conflict
Improving Performance
Managing Time
Benefiting from Change

"We cannot afford to forget any experiences, even the most painful."
Dag Hammarskjold

"I've been in upper management for twelve years and, in my opinion, the greatest mistake most supervisors make is to back away from and be too soft with the employees in their departments. Sometimes you'd think the supervisor is working for the employee and not the other way around."

"I can't help but think that for many supervisors their biggest mistake is old-fashioned stubbornness. They appear to listen to their employees and superiors, but they go right ahead and do it their own way. They lock themselves in with their closed minds."

"I've been supervising supervisors for more than twenty years with the same company and, in my opinion, their biggest mistake is underestimating the true potential of the people they supervise. They write off people before giving them a chance. This one failure has cost my company millions."

"Most managers multiply their problems because they think they communicate with their people when, in fact, they do not. It's their biggest mistake."

I f you were to do a survey asking fifty different management people to name the biggest mistake made by front-line supervisors, you could easily receive twenty or so different answers. But if you examined the essentials of all those responses, they would probably all fit into one of the following categories.

PERFORMANCE COMPETENCIES

After you have finished reading this chapter, you should be able to:

- Explain three behaviors to avoid doing as a supervisor

- Describe how a supervisor might "straitjacket" his employees

- Explain the importance of finding potential first in employees

FAILURE TO COMMUNICATE

All work is a process that is accomplished by communicating. Whether they will admit it or not, many supervisors fail to establish and maintain a good communications system within their department and their company. If the people around you are to become sufficiently informed, you must set up a system to ensure that it happens. You will have to weave it into your departmental plan and put it on your priority list. You must make time to communicate. If you don't, you'll be faced with a constant flow of human relations problems from your employees because they will feel left out, neglected, unappreciated, and frustrated. Serious misinterpretations will occur between you and others both inside and outside your department. Morale will eventually drop, and so will productivity.

How can you set up a communications system to prevent this deterioration from happening? Here are some suggestions.

Create daily two-way conversations.   Consider taking ten, twenty, or thirty minutes each day to talk things over with your employees. If you supervise many people, you might rotate among them so that you will have some personal communication at least every week or so. Keep in mind that it is sometimes more important to listen than to talk.

Set up a bulletin board as a communications headquarters.   When the proper physical facilities are available, a bulletin board can be a valuable tool. Let's look at how it is used by one supervisor.

Linda has trained her nine employees to check the bulletin board the first thing in the morning and two or three times during the day. Sometimes she leaves messages for the whole group and sometimes for individuals. Employees are, of course, encouraged to leave messages for others, including Linda. Here is how she puts it: "My little bulletin board is an integral part of my system. I just don't have time to contact everyone personally all the time, so I write a lot of bulletins and notes. It really works."

An "electronic bulletin board" can be accomplished on a network of computers to replace or supplement the traditional kind.

Hold group meetings.   Try to hold short group meetings from time to time for communication purposes. Nothing can substitute for the interplay of group communications if such meetings do not take too long, are not overstructured, and are held when necessary. Group meetings are extremely useful when major changes in procedure are necessary.

Send interoffice communications.   Most organizations have a voice mail or e-mail system to keep upper management, supervisors, and other staff informed. This written form of communication should be used to (1) keep others informed, (2) initiate requests, and (3) reply to inquiries, whether written or by telephone.

Use other communication techniques.   In addition to the frequent use of the telephone, the supervisor can arrange formal two-way meetings in the office, arrange for luncheon communication sessions, and sometimes take advantage of coffee breaks and trips outside the plant or office for communication purposes. Conversations between supervisors of different work units promote teamwork. Look for ways to help peers. Regular informal communication helps you learn about the business and how you can make a greater contribution.

You will, of course, have to develop your own system based on your particular situation and needs. The most important factor, however, is to maintain the system on a daily basis. It is a difficult responsibility and no one has created a perfect system, but everyone seems to agree that unless you keep people informed, they can and will misinterpret you, resulting in problems for everyone involved. Constant and effective communication with your employees sends the message that you value them as people.

FAILURE TO EXERCISE STRONG LEADERSHIP

A shocking number of both new and old supervisors seem reluctant to exercise the forceful leadership management wants, employees respect, and the job requires. Too many supervisors back away from an aggressive employee or avoid any confrontation with those who work for them.

Why? Several reasons seem to explain such behavior. Some supervisors would rather be popular than effective. In other words, they are simply too sensitive to the possibility of receiving a negative reaction from an employee if a firm stand is taken. In other cases, the manager is intimidated by those he or she is supposed to lead. Both responses may stem from a fear of people that needs to be dissipated. Leo is a good example.

Most of the employees in Leo's department loved him. Some said he was the finest supervisor they had ever known. He was kind, sensitive, and calm in all situations. There was a very harmonious climate inside the department most of the time. It naturally came as a shock to the employees when Leo was given a non-supervisory job and replaced by another supervisor. Why did management take this step? They removed Leo because he was permitting a few employees to take advantage of him. Rules were being broken, and production was down. Leo had been counseled on the problem, but he couldn't face taking the necessary disciplinary action to correct the situation. As a result, management had no choice but to transfer Leo to a nonsupervisory job.

Some supervisors mistakenly believe that time solves all problems. The people who perpetuate this myth fail to see that one unsolved problem often sets up a chain reaction that creates others. They also fail to recognize that a problem left unsolved can fester and damage a relationship beyond repair. Marge was naive in this respect.

Marge grew up in a home where problems were never dealt with openly. Communication was restricted to pleasant subjects. As a result, she formed the habit of keeping most of her personal problems inside. The habit had become so much a part of her that when she became a supervisor she followed the same pattern. What happened? She soon had so many unsolved problems that her boss had to come to her rescue.

Solving problems too quickly (without getting the facts) can be a serious mistake, but expecting time to solve them for you is simply going to the opposite extreme.

These reasons, among others, are why many supervisors fail to provide the strong leadership needed. Some people are much too introverted to communicate their feelings to others. Others have more faith in the behavior of their employees than is justified. A few simply refuse to recognize that the supervisor must be a leader to survive. The precautionary measures suggested here will help you avoid such traps.

Talk about it when it first affects you.   Learn to say what is on your mind when you first have a reaction. At least two good reasons make this step an important one: (1) If you don't discuss something that is troubling you as soon as it begins to affect you, it will bother you until it emerges too harshly. The pressure caused by holding it back may make you hostile, leading to misinterpretation. (2) When your employees are permitted some small infraction a few times, they begin to build a defense against the time when you reprimand them for it. The defense makes them less communicative and sometimes adds an explosive element that would not exist if you had corrected the infraction at the beginning.

Say what is on your mind, and say it often.   Don't bury your thoughts until they become distorted. Open and frequent communication is an effective way to demonstrate strong leadership.

Tell it the way it is.   It is a mistake to cushion your verbal communication in soft words and tones so that what you say is taken too lightly or disregarded. Be firm, be clear, and let people know you mean it. Employees can take more frank talk and constructive criticism than you think. Be specific and focus on the behavior or situation that bothers you. Stick to the facts and never insult an employee by calling him or her a name, such as lazy or incompetent. Also, remember that there is a vast difference between directness and crassness. When you "tell it like it is," find ways to convey your message to minimize defensiveness and show you are supportive.

Let your employees feel that you are leading them.   Most employees like the security of strong leadership from their supervisor. Be considerate, sensitive, and fair—but above all, be decisive. If you are, you will dissipate a great deal of apprehension and confusion among your employees.

Seek respect rather than popularity.   You are ill-advised to run a popularity contest in competition with other supervisors. Be content to build honest working relationships based on the integrity of doing a good job and not on personal favors that bring immediate gratification but destroy respect. Recognize the difference and you will be a more successful leader.

As a supervisor, you may need to take a firm position with a problem employee, with a fellow supervisor, or during a management meeting. But how firm? How assertive need you become to be effective as a supervisor? What kind of balance between passiveness and counterproductive aggressiveness should you strike? Here are some tips:

- Keep in mind that strong leadership is as important with teams as under the traditional approach.
- Becoming more assertive may be uncomfortable for you at the beginning. If so, it may take time to establish the balance you seek. Be patient with yourself, but don't err on the side of weakness.
- In general, you want to show strength without aggressive behavior that will injure relationships. It means being firm but understanding, taking a position but also being open to compromise, and maintaining respect for others and the position they take.
- To protect the productivity of your department (and the firm's profit), you have the right to speak up and take a stand. Your challenge is to do so and, at the same time, build good human relationships in all directions.
- As you make your moves, assume a "win–win" attitude. Be assertive to the point where you, your colleagues, and your company come out ahead. But no further! Keep in mind that you can show strength in your eyes, posture, and demeanor, as well as your voice. Choose your words carefully.

You know you are showing the right degree of assertiveness when others are equally open, direct, and forceful with you.

MAKING AND BREAKING PROMISES

A promise can be exciting and ego building to make, but sometimes a distressing impossibility to keep. A promise kept may bring a great deal of inner satisfaction, but a promise broken can be embarrassing and humiliating beyond expectation. Unnecessary promises are too easy to make. The supervisor with a great desire to build good relationships and to increase productivity is prone to make unnecessary promises.

John, a successful supervisor, was so impressed with one of his new employees during the first-month review that he promised the new employee all his support when the time came to appoint a new assistant. Two weeks later (much sooner than John expected), he was forced to appoint someone else as his assistant because the new employee had not served the ninety-day probation period necessary for eligibility. Having to go back on his promise put John in an awkward position. He paid a high price for breaking a promise he didn't need to make in the first place.

A promise is emotionally accepted. Promises made in a climate of excitement may appear different to you in the cold light of reality, but the changed perspective may not have reached your employees. They fail to understand that busy supervisors with many responsibilities can easily forget a promise, even though it was sincerely made. In other words, the receiver sees and feels a promise differently from the giver. The supervisor who ignores this difference is asking for trouble.

Promises easy to keep are also easily forgotten. It is easy to convert a request into a promise and then promptly forget it. For example, an employee might ask you for a special favor such as requisitioning a new, inexpensive tool. If you don't do it immediately or write it down to remind yourself to do it later, you may forget it. The world won't end because of your neglect, but sooner or later, your poor memory will cause you embarrassment and make it necessary to rebuild a relationship. Even small promises must be kept, and only the organized person who can follow through should make them. A broken promise may be labeled a lie.

How can you guard against making foolish promises you may not be able to keep? Tell the employee making the request that you can't promise, but you'll do everything in your power to make it come about. Such an approach helps you avoid making a promise, but it still enables you to support the employee. Don't permit yourself to be carried away by your own enthusiasm so that you make promises to create or maintain good relationships with employees.

Of course, you are not expected to avoid completely making promises. Sometimes you must and should make them. Try the following suggestions to help you keep them.

Write them down.   You will have a much better chance of keeping promises if you write them in your notebook or on your desk calendar.

Admit you might forget.   Tell the employee you intend to keep the promise but you would appreciate a reminder at the appropriate time. It puts some of the responsibility on the employee and helps ensure that you will keep the promise.

If possible, keep it now.   If you can fulfill a promise before the day is over, do it. It is a mistake to postpone a promise that can be kept immediately.

"Under promise and over deliver."   This is the advice that Rudy Guiliani, former Mayor of New York, gives in his book *Leadership*.[1] What does it mean? Whether you are a politician or a manager, you want to be able to make promises because they can provide hope, expectation, and motivation, but you know that any promise not delivered will lead to disappointment and distrust in your leadership. Therefore, if you do make promises, promise only what you know you can realistically deliver—or a little less. Then, work hard to deliver at least what you promised and then some. When you do, you will delight your employees or whomever else you have promised because they will receive more than what they expected.

If, in your role as a supervisor, you can learn to make few promises but keep those important ones you do make, you will avoid a common and costly mistake.

STRAITJACKETING EMPLOYEES

Call it prejudging, underestimating, downgrading, or prejudice. Whatever the name, many supervisors put their employees in a psychological straitjacket, preventing them from growing into the kind of workers they could become. This problem

usually arises because supervisors are unaware of the restrictive climate or barriers they build. They may think they are communicating with the employees, but they aren't. At least three kinds of supervisors restrict their employees in this way.

The typecaster.   This supervisor wants to classify and pigeonhole all employees. Rather than accepting and treating everyone as a separate, unique individual, this manager insists on putting people into groups. For example, a male manager may think that all women who work are first and foremost housewives, so he overlooks the professional career woman. A mature manager may think that all young people prefer not to have early responsibility and ignores those who do. The manager may think that all employees work primarily for money and thus pays little attention to psychological needs that are often more important than money. A manager who has had a bad experience with one employee from a different culture may assume that all future employees from the same background will behave in the same manner. Such managers refuse to be convinced that typing people automatically sets the stage for getting exactly what they expect, no matter how things could have been.

The snuff-out artist.   This supervisor squelches the ambition and creativity of employees without knowing it by having an overpowering demeanor, which may include speaking in a gruff voice, using a bulldozer approach, or adhering to a stiff, militaristic style. This supervisor's personality is so powerful that he or she snuffs out the sparks of creativity in employees.

The poor perceiver.   This supervisor is not sensitive enough to see the potential abilities of employees. He or she doesn't see hidden talent and therefore fails to recognize a special contribution that deserves a compliment, or doesn't recognize improvement in a new employee and thereby fails to reinforce it. The poor perceiver does not recognize and treat employees as separate individuals because he or she does not see their differences. Employees recognize this behavior and may give up.

How can you guard against putting your employees in straitjackets? How can you train yourself to bring out the potential of your employees instead of restrict it? Here are three suggestions that may help.

Take time to know your employees. Occasionally relax for a few moments with each employee during coffee breaks or other informal sessions so that you can better perceive and understand their special needs and individual personalities. What are their interests and ambitions? Are they going to school part-time? Gaining insight into individuals as people instead of as employees will help you avoid putting anyone in a psychological straitjacket.

Look for potential first and performance second. Although all employees must be judged on their performance, it is a mistake to evaluate performance without first looking at the individual's potential. Most employees have an undiscovered skill, talent, or aptitude that could be used in their work if they were encouraged to use it. Discover and encourage the use of hidden abilities in those who work for you. This same philosophy applies to the hiring process as well. It is often said that you can always teach someone the skills they lack when you hire her or him, but you cannot teach intangibles like work ethic, the eagerness or ability to learn, and openness and flexibility to take on new tasks and challenges. In other words, you can't teach potential. So look for such traits when you hire employees and you will have an easier time getting them to an acceptable level of performance once you hire them.

Give employees the reassurance they need to take advantage of the opportunities you provide. To realize their potential, some employees need large doses of encouragement that you can provide. Sometimes it means giving people something to do on the spur of the moment so that they won't have time to worry about it or helping them forget a mistake and letting them try again. It is amazing how many people will grow and bloom under the supervision of a person who provides both reassurance and opportunity—these build confidence.

FAILURE TO ENJOY YOUR ROLE AS A MANAGER

Many psychological rewards and "perks" come with a supervisory position. If you don't step back occasionally and enjoy them, you will render yourself less effective. For example, one of your rewards is more freedom. Enjoy this freedom by giving yourself workdays filled with variety and special challenges to eliminate boredom. Remind yourself that your employees can afford to be negative or have occasional down days, but you can't. If you appear overburdened, washed out, haggard, and down, those who work for you will pick it up and the entire department will reflect your negative attitude. No matter how effective you are in other ways, if you don't stay positive and upbeat, the productivity of your department can drop and your own career will be damaged.

The very nature of the supervisor's job involves making minor mistakes. You will be no exception. With so many responsibilities, you can't avoid it. It is important, then, to avoid making the serious mistakes, the costly ones that damage both the department and your future as a supervisor. Reflect on your mistakes and learn from them—doing so is the cornerstone of personal growth and development.

PERFORMANCE **CHECKLIST**

1. One mistake you don't want to make as a supervisor is to fail to communicate. To prevent this, create daily two-way conversations; set up a bulletin board as a communications headquarters; hold group meetings; send interoffice communications; and use other communication techniques such as hold formal meetings in your office, arrange luncheon communication sessions, and take advantage of coffee breaks and trips outside the office or plant for communication purposes.

2. A second mistake you don't want to make is to fail to exercise strong leadership. To ensure you do take a firm leadership stance: talk about important issues when they first affect you; say what is on your mind and say it often; tell it the way it is; let employees feel that you are leading them; and seek respect rather than popularity. When exercising strong leadership, do not use aggressive behavior that will hurt relationships. Be firm but understanding, taking a position but also remaining open to compromise and maintaining respect for others and their positions. While you have the right to take a stand, the challenge is to build good human relationships at the same time.

3. A third mistake you don't want to make is to make and break promises. When an employee makes a request you can't promise you will be able to meet, let the employee know you will do everything in your power to make it come about. When you do make promises, write them down so you won't forget them. Admit to the employee that you might forget so you would appreciate a reminder. If possible, honor the promise right away. Finally, "Under promise and over deliver," so that you do not promise more than is realistic and will delight others when you deliver that and perhaps a little more.

4. A fourth mistake you don't want to make is to straitjacket employees. The three most common ways supervisors straitjacket employees is to (1) pigeonhole employees and view them incapable of more than what is minimally expected, given the typecast assigned them; (2) squelch their ambition and creativity by engaging in overbearing, gruff behaviors; and (3) fail to perceive their unique contributions and abilities. To ensure you don't do this, take time to know your employees, look for potential first and performance second, and give employees the reassurance they need to take advantage of the opportunities you provide.

5. The fifth mistake you don't want to make is to fail to enjoy your role as a manager. No matter how effective you are in other ways, if you don't stay positive and upbeat, the productivity of your department can drop and your own career will be damaged.

TEST **YOURSELF**

For each of the following statements, check true or false.

True   False

____ ____   1. The typecaster is effective as a supervisor because he or she treats different employees differently.

____ ____   2. The autocratic leader may, without knowing it, be a "snuff-out artist."

____ ____   3. Look for performance first, potential second.

____ ____   4. The best advice is to promise what you can and be sure you deliver exactly that.

____ ____   5. Seek popularity, and respect will automatically follow.

____ ____   6. It is less dangerous to become assertive when one has a "win–win" attitude.

True   False

____   ____   7. Failure to establish and maintain a good communication system is the mistake supervisors most frequently make.

____   ____   8. Silence can lead to misinterpretation.

____   ____   9. An "electronic bulletin board" can replace or supplement the traditional kind.

____   ____   10. Constant and effective communication with your employees sends the message that you value them as people.

____   ____   11. Focus on the behavior or situation, not the employee, when discussing habits that bother you.

____   ____   12. Reflect on your mistakes and learn from them; this is the cornerstone of personal growth and development.

Turn to the back of the book to check your answers.

Total Correct ____

DISCUSSION QUESTIONS

1. Why do many managers fail to receive the obvious signals (low productivity, complaints, etc.) that they are not communicating with their employees?

2. Which supervisor would you prefer to work with? Supervisor A is a visible leader who knows when to get tough and can be curt at times when giving directions, but at least you always know where you stand. Supervisor B is a quieter, easy-going leader who is consistent and easy to work with but doesn't always push you or others on performance issues when you think perhaps he should. Explain your point of view.

3. What can be done to help a manager who consistently stereotypes employees and thereby fails to encourage the development of their potential abilities to contribute?

CASE: INTIMIDATION

Since he took over the department, Ricardo has been under subtle pressure to grant Karl a series of special favors. Most of the pressure has come from Karl himself, who let Ricardo know from the beginning that he would support Ricardo in turn for certain freedoms to which he was entitled anyway because of his seniority and special knowledge. Some of the pressure, however, has come from outside sources in the form of warnings. For example, one supervisor told Ricardo, "Treat Karl with kid gloves because he has powerful connections upstairs." The supervisor did not specify who these "powerful connections" were. So far, Ricardo has gone along with the requests, although with growing resentment. It all came to a climax yesterday, however, when Karl asked if he could leave early Friday for personal reasons that he did not explain. Ricardo came back with a fast and emphatic no and walked away. Since then, the following has happened: (1) Karl has been silent and sulky; (2) Renee came to Ricardo and complimented him on his stand in behalf of the other departmental employees; (3) the supervisor who warned him initially about Karl has reminded Ricardo that a previous supervisor resigned because Karl initiated a campaign to get rid of him.

Ricardo discusses the following options with you in confidence:

1. Stand pat and do nothing.

2. Protect your flanks by going to Bill and explaining the history of the problem and why you feel you must stand pat or lose the respect of the other employees. Tell him you want his complete support, or you may seriously consider resigning.

3. Back down by calling Karl into your office and telling him he is free to leave early Friday, but must keep his special favor requests to an absolute minimum in the future.

4. Call Karl into your office and tell him firmly that you resent his going over your head and talking outside the department, and that you intend to stand by your decision and defend it all the way to the top.

Which option would you support? Why? What changes would you suggest to Ricardo in using it? What other option (not on this list) might you propose?

MISTAKE ELIMINATION **EXERCISE**

The text refers to five common mistakes supervisors don't want to make. This exercise is designed to help you identify and eliminate other mistakes that can impede your career progress. These potential mistakes could stem from your own personality. For example, perhaps you have a compulsion to talk too much and not listen enough, or you have trouble managing your time. Other mistakes you wish to avoid are those you have noticed and resented from supervisors you have worked under. Try to sense the pitfalls that are apt to trap you in the future and do something about them so that your career will not suffer. List ten of your high-probability mistakes. Feel free to include those listed in this chapter.

See remarks from the authors in the back of this book.

PERSONAL GROWTH **EXERCISE**

Think of a success you have had recently. Analyze it by doing the following:

- Identify specifically what happened.
- Analyze why these things happened.

- List at least three things that you learned from this experience that you will generalize to your life and your future work as a supervisor.

NOTE

1. Rudolph W. Giuliani and Ken Kurson, *Leadership*. New York: Hyperion, 2002.

chapter **twenty**

CONVERTING CHANGE INTO OPPORTUNITY

"To improve is to change; to be perfect is to change often."

Winston Churchill

PERFORMANCE COMPETENCIES

After you have finished reading this chapter, you should be able to:

- Explain how to become visible in the organization

- Explain the effects that change has on stress

- Explain the straight-line and zigzag patterns used for moving up in management

- Describe the seven steps to follow for making a Plan B

- Explain three reasons for having a Plan B for your career

When you hear the words *downsizing, outsourcing, layoffs, lean and mean, restructuring, relocating, decentralizing, new information technology,* and *retraining,* you know that change is around the corner. Change is anything that happens in our environment that requires a human adjustment. The dramatic tempo of change continues to accelerate, and the impact falls more on the supervisor than on staff employees. As a beginning manager, the way you accept and interpret changes to your staff and how you cope personally will have a measurable effect on departmental productivity and your future success.

Many times an individual hears about a pending change and promptly converts it into a dragon instead of an opportunity. You hear comments like these:

"There is no security in a big company anymore."

"These constant changes are giving me a nervous breakdown."

"I'm not hanging around for this; early retirement may be my solution."

How you cope with change as a supervisor will depend on your attitude. Some people have the capacity to view change as opportunity; others reject even good changes with hostility. What is your attitude toward change? The "Attitude-Toward-Change Scale" has been prepared to provide a few clues. Please rate yourself on all factors and compute your total score.

ATTITUDE-TOWARD-CHANGE SCALE

	4	3	2	1	0	
I view any change as an opportunity, not a threat.	4	3	2	1	0	I reject all change as a personal threat.
If my organization should introduce new equipment for me to use, I would be delighted.	4	3	2	1	0	If forced to learn how to use new equipment, I would be openly hostile.
A reorganization of my firm would be welcome; my flexibility would give me an advantage.	4	3	2	1	0	I would hate any form of reorganization; I like things stable and totally predictable.
I have an excellent superior, but a change would not bother me.	4	3	2	1	0	I have an excellent superior; a change would devastate me.
New work assignments and responsibilities motivate me.	4	3	2	1	0	New work assignments and responsibilities demotivate me.
All the social and political changes taking place today are exciting to me.	4	3	2	1	0	I wish I had lived 100 years ago.
Predictability is dull.	4	3	2	1	0	Predictability is beautiful.
The possibility of a career change intrigues me.	4	3	2	1	0	The possibility of a career change deflates me.
I have confidence that I can quickly change my behavioral patterns to fit any contingency.	4	3	2	1	0	In all honesty, it is almost impossible for me to change my behavioral patterns.
I can change my career and lifestyle goals quickly.	4	3	2	1	0	My career goals and values are bedded in cement.

TOTAL [   ]

If you scored greater than 25, you appear to have a positive, flexible attitude toward change. You should be able to handle future changes effectively. If you scored less than 25, you have less flexibility than you may need to cope well with future changes.

Not all changes are good or necessary. Resisting an ill-advised change can be a worthy mission that will protect and benefit your firm and your employees. But most changes are inevitable, and the sooner they are accepted by you as a supervisor, the better it will be for your employees. In spite of short-term adjustment disadvantages, many changes have long-term advantages that make the adjustment worthwhile. It will be your responsibility to communicate this situation to your employees when it occurs.

A TIME OF RAPID CHANGE

Alvin Toffler, in his 1990 book *The Third Wave*,[1] develops the concept of the electronic cottage. At some distant time, he predicted, most employees will work in their own homes, where electronic equipment will permit instant communication with and directions from a central management source. Teachers will teach from their homes. Production workers will use sophisticated equipment to produce parts for a company miles away. Commuting to factories, skyscrapers, and other work places will be a thing of the past for many. People who live together will work together.

Now, well into the first decade of the twenty-first century, an argument can be made that forms of the electronic cottage have arrived. For example, when you call a customer service support line for assistance with a technology issue, such as a glitch in a software program or problems with your personal computer, you don't know whether the person answering the phone is working in your hometown, across the country, or halfway around the world, or whether he or she is wearing business clothing and sitting behind a desk in a cubicle, or sitting behind a personal computer at home wearing pajamas.

In *The World Is Flat: A Brief History of the Twenty-first Century*, Thomas Friedman writes about the convergence of a number of circumstances, such as the fall of Communism, the growth and universally accessible nature of the web, outsourcing and off-shoring, and the creation of a global fiber-optic network and other technologies, that have dramatically changed the way corporations and countries interact and compete in the global marketplace, and provide unprecedented opportunities for individuals to participate:

> Clearly, it is now possible for more people than ever to collaborate and compete in real time with more other people on more different kinds of work from more different corners of the planet and on a more equal footing than at any previous time in the history of the world—using computers, e-mail, networks, teleconferencing, and dynamic new software.[2]

Management expert Peter Drucker discusses these issues in the context of radical changes in the work we do, the way organizations must rethink their contract with workers and how they manage them, and the expectations workers have in this new society. Specifically, a significant transformation is occurring as the economy and business shifts from an Industrial-Age Model, in which management operates on a top-down, command and control philosophy, to the Information or Knowledge-Worker Age Model, where management and workers must operate more as partners:

> Increasingly, performance in these new knowledge-based industries will come to depend on running the institution so as to attract, hold, and motivate knowledge workers. [This] will have to be done by satisfying their values, and by giving them social recognition and social power. It will have to be done by turning them from subordinates into fellow executives, and from employees, however well paid, into partners.[3]

There is no question that business and industry, including transportation, manufacturing, banking, finance, law, medicine, healthcare, retailing, education, and government, are feeling the impact of these changes and must adapt new management and organizational models if they are going to survive. As a management person, you will be caught in the middle as your organization struggles with these challenges and implements sweeping changes in response. As it does so, it will be your responsibility to see that these changes are accepted by those you lead. Even more critical, so that change can take place, you will need to teach employees new techniques and procedures, new technologies, and new mind sets in the way work is done. Although this won't make your job as a supervisor any easier, you can view these changes as either opportunities to prepare yourself for future opportunities, or you can take a negative view and eliminate yourself from the race. Better to take May's viewpoint:

When May heard that her firm would adopt yet another update to the new financial data management system, her first reaction was negative. As an operations officer, she knew the change would involve substantial new responsibility for her. She would have to undergo additional training that would be difficult. Besides learning new skills and processes, she would have to spend many hours of additional time helping her nine employees adjust. At first, she even considered changing her career. But after talking things over with a close friend, she decided to turn the announcement into an opportunity. She was among the first to enroll in her company's in-house training on the new system. She also enrolled in an advanced-level course in financial data management processing at a local college to update her skills and enhance her knowledge. May was determined to take advantage of change to improve her own future. Her superiors were quick to recognize her positive attitude toward changes over which they, too, had little control. She was pleasantly surprised to be selected as one of a small group of managers to lead the implementation of the new system, which she gladly accepted because it was a positive step toward being considered for advancement later on.

ORGANIZATIONS CHANGE TO SURVIVE

At one time in the United States, a supervisor felt lucky to work for a stable, predictable corporation. The supervisor could anticipate security and upward mobility within the framework of a single large organization. The corporate womb was a safe, comfortable place to be. A front-line supervisor could blueprint a career path to the top with confidence. The supervisor knew, at least to some extent, what was ahead.

Today, the supervisor should feel lucky if he or she works for an organization that is sufficiently flexible to adjust to changes and survive. Organizations that are too slow to adjust will be left behind. Supervisors and employees who belong to such organizations will find themselves unemployed.

Changes are hitting firms of all sizes with increasing magnitude. Mergers, takeovers, and staff reductions are in the headlines. You should not infer that the organization you are currently working for is so vulnerable to change that it may turn belly-up. But if your organization is not adaptable enough to survive, your job may disappear. Your attitude should not be, "I hope my organization can resist change and stay the way it is." That's how Doug responded:

Doug couldn't understand why his firm needed to make changes. As a result, he resisted what few changes were made and refused to learn new techniques that were revolutionizing his particular career area. Because of inflexible, shortsighted management, his firm went into bankruptcy, and Doug was left out on a limb. His failure to learn new techniques left him unprepared for a similar job with another firm. He had contributed to the demise of his organization and permitted himself to become obsolete in his career specialty.

Instead, your attitude should be, "I'm lucky that the management of my organization is flexible enough to keep the organization alive and changing." As a supervisor, you are in a key role to help your organization survive and prosper. You will need to be flexible enough to reorganize your department, accept new technology and assignments, and, most of all, assist your employees in making necessary adjustments.

THE WORKFORCE CHANGES

Along with society and the economy, the U.S. workforce has changed rapidly. It is becoming multicultural and multilingual. Women are moving into all occupations and making faster progress up executive ladders. African-, Latino-, Asian-, and other Americans with strong ethnic ties, as well as a growing number of people who identify themselves as biracial and multi-ethnic, are achieving greater and greater upward mobility. First-generation workers from other countries are arriving and making adjustments to the workforce. We are also experiencing a time when workers continue to produce and make viable contributions at later stages of life, resulting in an unprecedented period in which four generations (Traditionalists, Baby Boomers, Generation Xers, and Millennials) are working together in the workplace. At the same time, companies are experiencing increasing pressure to manage issues like immigration; the pending retirement of the largest generational cohort (Baby Boomers); the demands of workers for greater flexibility and choice regarding work–life options; and the need to recruit, develop, reward, and retain talent in various fields in order to remain competitive in a global economy where giants like India and China are gaining advantage. Needless to say, the new workforce is a challenge to the front-line supervisor, because it is he or she who must work with all individuals on a personal, one-on-one basis, and ensure employees are engaged, work effectively together in team environments, and remain committed to the organization.

Ten years ago, Herbert had twenty employees in his department: seventeen white males, two white females, and one African-American male. Today, thanks to his human relations skills, productivity is higher with only sixteen employees. The composition is as follows: five white females, three white males, two African-American males, two Asian females, one African-American female, one Hispanic male, one female who identifies herself as biracially African-American and Latino, and one Arab male who emigrated from Kuwait. The age mix ranges from 22 to 63. Whereas all employees had been full-time, one is a student working part-time, two employees (one male and one female) are on extended family leave to care for newborns, and one older worker has negotiated a part-time schedule in order to begin a phased retirement, because he volunteers twice a week to teach reading skills for a community literacy program. Herbert takes pride in the multi-cultural, dual-gender, and multi-generational mix of his department. From the start, he accepted the change as a personal challenge and enjoyed helping the few remaining senior, traditionally majority culture employees in his department to adjust to the opportunities presented by the influx of new talent.

MANAGEMENT BURNOUT

This *Supervisor's Survival Kit* is designed to prevent burnout. The chapters on managing yourself have been written to help you do the best possible job and still protect your emotional health. Supervisors who establish realistic goals, maintain comfortable priorities, and manage their time are in a position to balance their careers with their personal lives. This balance helps prevent burnout when things are stable. When major changes occur, they always introduce stress; the perceptive supervisor is prepared for temporary adjustments until career and home are again properly balanced. A balanced, happy, activity-centered, relaxing home life is one of the best insurances against stress generated in the workplace.

CHANGE AS A SOURCE OF STRESS

Employee stress comes from many sources: work overload, role conflicts, oversupervision, ambiguity, insecurity, and change. Although you want to protect your employees from such pressures, you cannot provide a 100 percent stress-free work environment. In fact, mild positive stress (eustress) stimulates greater productivity. Some work environments such as the media, advertising, and political activity have built-in eustress. The way you handle change in your department, however, can eliminate a great deal of harmful stress (distress) that might injure employees and eat away at productivity standards.

To convert dragons into caterpillars, you should portray changes as opportunities for growth instead of problems to overcome. You should communicate such changes in a non-threatening way as far in advance as possible so that employees have time to adjust. You should also explain why such changes are necessary. Employees who participate in the planning of change experience a reduction in the stress that change can bring.

As you accomplish these goals, consider the following suggestions:

Turn change into an opportunity for yourself.   When it comes to change, it doesn't hurt to think of yourself first, because if you don't succeed, those

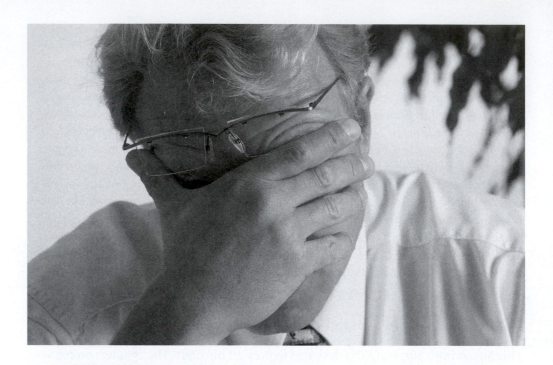

working for you will be left unprepared. It is bad enough to work for a supervisor who is negative about change; it is even worse to work for one who neglects to prepare you for the future.

Communicate the advantages of change.   Tell your staff that changing now may save their jobs later. State that the way to protect their retirement pensions in the future is to change to greater profitability now. Communicate this message individually, in staff meetings, and during formal appraisal periods. Prepare your people to anticipate change and learn to roll with the punches. You will be doing them an immense favor.

Help them through the natural transition from letting go of old ways to accepting new opportunities.   In *Managing Transitions: Making the Most of Change*, William Bridges discusses the three phases of this necessary change process: (1) Letting go of old ways and old identities; (2) working through the "neutral zone," which is the natural but often awkward and uncertain period where the "new" is still ambiguous and the individual needs time to accept new patterns and ways of thinking; and (3) making a new beginning where the person develops new identities, finds new energy, and sees new possibilities. Through this transition, it is important to recognize that while organizational change may come quickly, individuals' psychological acceptance of change does not. As a supervisor, you must patiently help them move to accept the change and the new future it presents while allowing them to grieve the loss of the old without criticism or minimizing their feelings.[4]

Follow up with advanced, hands-on training.   Frequently, highly capable people take their skills with them to a new company or community, only to discover that their competencies are obsolete. Do not let obsolescence happen to your staff. Provide them with the kind of training they need to stay up-to-date with career demands where they are or where they move in the future. Allowing your staff to rest on their career laurels is doing them a disservice.

Help employees balance stress with rest and relaxation. As noted, not all forms of stress are bad. A healthy level of stress is an essential component of work as employees engage in the energy, focus, and effort needed to produce their best results. However, at some point, a limit is reached when productivity declines if the stress needed to produce becomes too great without the opportunity for rest. Obviously, in the midst of significant change and the constant demand to produce, burnout will occur if we are not attentive to this need for balance. Herbert Benson, a mind/body researcher, identifies four steps to help individuals achieve this balance. The first step is to engage in intense, focused attention of the issue or problem at hand to the point where maximum productivity is achieved. When this point is reached and the person begins to have stressful feelings (fear, anxiety, boredom, etc.), the second step is to step away from the problem and do something completely different that produces a relaxation response. This can include any number of activities, such as deep-breathing exercises, short walks, sleeping on it and returning to the problem the next day, enjoying pleasant conversation with a colleague, and so forth. The third step occurs when the individual experiences a "breakout" and becomes completely immersed in the issue or problem with new energy and insight that was made possible through engaging in the relaxation response. The fourth step is a return to the "new-normal state" in which the individual is able to perform the work or handle the problem or issue with renewed self-confidence. While you as a supervisor cannot control the outcomes suggested through each of these steps, nor provide expansive opportunities for rest for employees in certain positions, you should always understand how periods of rest and "walking away" from work will facilitate greater productivity and then strive to provide such opportunities.[5]

When one accepts the premise that change is inevitable, it is possible to take pride in being able to cope with change effectively. Anything you can do to help your employees experience this pride will make you a superior supervisor.

HAVING A PERSONAL PLAN B

If you are happy and effective as a front-line supervisor, chances are excellent that you will eventually aspire to further upward mobility. Success at one level has a way of pushing an individual toward a higher level for many reasons, including the prospect of additional financial rewards, greater ego satisfaction, and the opportunity to test one's leadership ability in more demanding situations.

What about you? Would you like to use your first supervisory position as a springboard? Do you have ambitions to climb the management ladder? If so, this chapter will have special meaning for you because it is designed to take you above and beyond the realm of operating a successful department. You, too, can reach the upper levels of management by building strong working relationships with other supervisors and executives; you can play the management game with experienced professionals in a way that will help you contribute to the growth of both the organization and yourself. Sound interesting? Here is how Bob, a supervisor, sizes up the situation:

Even with a four-year degree in business administration, it took me more than two years to become the kind of front-line supervisor I wanted to be. I had more to learn than I suspected when I started out. Once I had everything under control, however, I became intrigued with taking the next step. I then discovered a whole new dimension of communications, human relations, decision making, and management know-how. The first-line supervisor is a babe in the woods compared to the experienced middle manager. I suddenly realized I had just started to learn what I would eventually need to know to move up to more competitive middle management positions. It appeared far more demanding than I had expected, but I decided to start preparing myself. I had taken the first step successfully, so why stop? Besides, I had a feeling that if I didn't keep preparing for something bigger, I might lose interest in what I already had. I work for a rather high-powered organization and if you stand still too long, others often pass you by.

Do you agree with Bob? Do you feel it might be wise to prepare for a more demanding role in management? If so, most executives would agree that you must start playing the management game from your present position as a front-line supervisor. Consider making the following moves now.

Making Yourself Visible

Make yourself visible. To make yourself visible, you must be seen and talked about by management people above you. You must be noticed, which you can accomplish in a number of ways.

Speak up in staff meetings.

Turn in written suggestions for improvement and change through channels.

Make appointments through appropriate channels with upper-management people to ask questions about the company, business objectives, or to receive job or career advice.

Be seen around the facility.

Lead a cross-functional team.

Participate in organizational events or recreational activities.

Take advantage of lunch to meet other people.

Take a special assignment with a higher profile or that is especially valued by upper management.

Of course, the best way to be visible is to do a quality job and get recognition from doing it. In fact, it may be more important to be visible silently rather than physically or verbally. You need to avoid being visible in a negative way. Some supervisors become too aggressive and play the management game too forcefully, hurting instead of helping their personal progress.

Show strength from your present position. If you are to move up toward executive management, you must occasionally stand pat and refuse to be pushed around. It may mean quietly standing up to your own superior and other management people when you know you are right and have all the facts to document your case. It may mean holding your own in a controversy over the role of your department or fighting back in an acceptable way when someone tries to invade your area of responsibility. You cannot build a reputation as a strong leader if you always back down under pressure. When you know you are right, stand up for your ideas. It is the best way to win the respect of some top managers.

Always defend and protect your employees to outsiders. You cannot move up the executive ladder without the enthusiastic support and loyalty of the employees in your department. You earn some of this loyalty when you go to bat for them with outsiders. This way you keep departmental problems inside the department, where they belong. The easiest way to destroy a good departmental image is to air dirty laundry with outsiders, which your employees are free to do any time they wish. However, if you defend and protect them, they will probably do the same for you.

Do your homework. If you keep your department in top shape at all times, you will not be vulnerable to those who may wish to stop your personal progress. Some extremely ambitious supervisors spend so much time playing management politics that they neglect their department and defeat themselves. You can afford to work on outside communications only when your department is completely under control. You can make outside moves only when you yourself are safe from attack.

Stand firm with other supervisors. You will need the support of other supervisors if you hope to join middle management, because in many cases you will be supervising them following your promotion.

Sound, healthy relationships with other supervisors can be developed, but it is naive to expect them all to be open and supportive. You are their competitor, so some may use devious tactics to undermine you, try to outmaneuver you to gain something you both want, or even try to trick you into making a poor move that will give them an advantage. Of course, most will be aboveboard and easy to work with. Even when other competitors use unfair tactics, your best move is to win their respect without resorting to the same methods. Protect yourself and your department while maintaining your personal standards and your belief in human relations principles. Be tough in defending what you feel is right, but avoid revenge or vindictiveness. Such conduct will only destroy the reputation you are attempting to build.

Be a team player in staff meetings. The staff meeting is the perfect setting to make either good or bad impressions, so it will be a challenge to get the right kinds of reactions from other management people in this environment. Here are some suggestions that might help:

1. Don't hesitate to speak up when you have something to say, but don't overdo it. Too much talking and not enough listening are serious problems.
2. Make a critical contribution now and then, even if it is something your own manager doesn't want to hear. In short, say what you really believe; don't just accommodate the group.
3. When you do say something, be brief and stick to the topic at hand.
4. Support others enthusiastically if you agree with them. It is a sound way to build relationships with other supervisors.
5. If you lose interest in a staff meeting that is dragging, try not to show it. Sometimes you can tolerate it by arranging your priorities, thinking about a problem, or engaging in some other mental activity, so long as you don't miss anything vital.
6. Never show personal hostility in a staff meeting.

Read and study. The supervisor who stops reading is locking the doors to opportunity and throwing the key away. Required reading includes company brochures, bulletins, reports, and research papers, as well as outside articles and books on management techniques. The ambitious supervisor must keep informed on company matters and prevailing management practices or, sooner or later, he or she will be passed by.

Look as though you are ready. It should go without saying that a junior manager on the way up must look ready. You should project an image of confidence, demonstrate leadership, stay constantly organized, and handle problems with finesse. In short, you should communicate upward—through your leadership style—a readiness factor that shows you are stronger than your competition.

Two different routes can take you to the top: On the straight-line route, you climb the ladder of your present organization; on the zigzag route, you change employers. The choice you make is critical and should involve a careful study of your own personality, values, and lifestyles.

The Straight Line to the Top

If you are currently a supervisor for a sizable organization you respect, you may prefer to work your way to the top within this firm. You might say to yourself, "This strong organization has a bright future, and I prefer to settle in and build my career without looking outside for better opportunities." The straight line is a comfortable pattern to take. It permits you to enjoy your work, build long-term working relationships, and feel secure without constantly working to build outside contacts. It also permits you to stay in one geographic location without making frequent moves. You can enjoy staying in the same home, permitting your children to mature in the same school system, and generally establishing your roots in the community of your choice. In the past, most top executives followed this pattern to the top.

You should, however, take the following three precautions. First, you must make certain that the organization you select has growth potential and can survive under changing conditions. Second, you must stay motivated. When ambitious supervisors who accept this strategy become complacent, management is forced to go outside to fill top leadership roles. Third, you must assertively communicate to management that you are capable, loyal, creative, and dependable, and because of these characteristics, you deserve the next promotion available. You cannot assume that management will recognize your accomplishments. This is the approach used by **stabilizers**.

The Zigzag Pattern

The alternative to the straight-line approach is zigzagging your way to the top by moving from one organization to another, always making a major contribution as you go. The zigzag pattern takes more energy, involves more risk, and requires greater flexibility. Those who make this pattern work (**scramblers**) usually stay with one firm for a minimum of two years. They are highly motivated and constantly learn new ideas to take with them as they travel on. They spend a great deal of time making contacts. These individuals talk about their "Plan Bs." A Plan B is a well-devised strategy that permits the individual to move quickly to a new firm if promotional opportunities begin to fade. While most supervisors spend all their energy on their jobs, scramblers work hard to contribute where they are but exert extra energy to locate better opportunities elsewhere; they put their personal careers ahead of the organization. Being more assertive in promoting themselves, they do not always play by traditional rules.

One precaution that a scrambler should take, however, is not to move too quickly or too aggressively from position to position. While companies value ambition and appreciate employees who make no apologies for seeking advancement opportunities, if they perceive you as a "job hopper" who switches to a different company at every possible opportunity, they will likely also perceive that you lack true commitment to anything but yourself and your single-minded ambitions.

Are you a scrambler or a stabilizer? To gain some indication of the approach with which you are most comfortable, complete the following scale.

SCRAMBLER-STABILIZER SCALE

Please circle one number to rate yourself honestly on a scale from 0 to 4.

I will always welcome any geographic move that enhances my career.	4 3 2 1 0	I would turn down any job opportunity that involves moving.
Zigzagging from one firm to another would be intriguing to me.	4 3 2 1 0	I hate the process of adjusting to new work environments.
My career is first; my personal life is second.	4 3 2 1 0	My personal life is first; my career is second.
Getting to the top through zigzagging is more of a challenge.	4 3 2 1 0	Getting to the top in one organization is more of a challenge.
I am willing to take risks even though I might lose my job.	4 3 2 1 0	I will not take any risks that put my job in jeopardy.
My ultimate loyalty is only to myself and my career.	4 3 2 1 0	I am 100 percent loyal to my organization.
I do not intend to follow traditional rules in order to get to the top.	4 3 2 1 0	I intend to follow traditional rules to the fullest extent.
I enjoy the job-seeking process, especially interviews.	4 3 2 1 0	I hate the job-seeking process, especially interviews.
I am willing to spend the extra energy to have a Plan B ready and waiting.	4 3 2 1 0	I do not bother with a Plan B. I devote my energy to my firm and my job.
It would not bother me in the least if I lost my job tomorrow.	4 3 2 1 0	I would be devastated if I lost my job tomorrow.

TOTAL [   ]

If you scored 25 or higher, you should give the zigzagging pattern (scrambling) careful consideration. If you scored lower than 25, the straight-line pattern appears to be a better choice for you.

Developing Plan B

Seven steps are involved in the preparation of a Plan B.

Step 1: Revise and keep up-to-date a superior résumé.

Step 2: Streamline and become more effective in your Plan A (your current job situation) so that you will have more free time to design an excellent Plan B.

Step 3: As difficult as it may seem, start learning more from your present job.

Step 4: Verify your competencies to make sure you are up-to-date in your professional arena.

Step 5: If necessary, return to college for additional training or engage in a do-it-yourself upgrading project.

Step 6: Do some creative networking from your present position. Make it a major effort!

Step 7: Use your Plan B to gain a promotion where you are, or use it to win a better position outside. Include it in your résumé and refer to it during interviews.

As you can see, an effective Plan B is much more than something you devise in the back of your mind. Rather, it is a sophisticated strategy that usually takes a minimum of six months to complete. A Plan B is equally effective for both stabilizers and scramblers.

It's Okay to Play Both Ends Against the Middle

Nothing unethical is involved in preparing a Plan B while you continue to operate effectively in the job you were hired to perform. You have the right to improve your competencies whether you eventually wind up using them where you are or in a new role. In most cases, people engaged in preparing a Plan B start doing a better job with their Plan A, and everyone winds up ahead.

Most observers agree that the zigzag route will take a person to the top faster, but it has its disadvantages. First, the individual must occasionally uproot his or her family to make a geographic move. Second, the person needs more talent and energy to make it work. Third, if not careful, the individual may create resentment among fellow workers—which can, in turn, force the person to make a move more quickly.

Although the zigzag route is attractive in many respects, not everyone can make it work. The scrambler is a person with high intelligence, great energy, and a willingness to take risks. Although moving from one work environment to another is demanding, some evidence indicates that it builds better leadership. The individual has to make more adjustments and decisions. The very act of moving seems to enhance the individual's personal growth.

If you want upward mobility, your master plan should take into consideration the advantages and disadvantages of both patterns. The "Scrambler–Stabilizer Scale" will assist you in this undertaking. Assume that you are highly ambitious and capable of excelling in higher leadership roles. Which pattern fits your personality and values?

The Importance of a Plan B

Although scramblers must design and implement a Plan B if they intend to zigzag their way to the top, stabilizers can also benefit from a Plan B for the following reasons:

1. Mergers, takeovers, and highly volatile market conditions may render your position (or even your employer) obsolete. Without a Plan B, you can, through no fault of your own, be unemployed.

2. Having a Plan B will help keep you informed about what is going on in the marketplace and thus contribute to your professional growth where you are now employed. For example, in forming a Plan B, you may discover that you need to return to school to upgrade your competencies. The new skills will help your present firm.

3. A Plan B can help keep you motivated. Knowing you are capable of building a career elsewhere can make you feel better where you are currently employed. You will feel more secure. You will be more inclined to speak up and contribute more without fear. If you are doing an excellent job and your superior discovers you have a Plan B, she or he may appreciate you more.

Stabilizers can benefit from a Plan B without ever exercising it.

NETWORKING

All scramblers and most stabilizers believe in some form of networking. Networking is the practice of actively seeking out and building relationships with colleagues inside and outside your firm—significant people who can keep you informed and, if necessary, come to your aid at a later date. If sound, mutually rewarding relationships are built, such networks can provide you with a career support system, an inner circle of colleagues who can help you professionally.

Network inner circles can include co-workers and superiors in the same company, counterparts in competitive organizations, trade association friends you may see only at conventions, college professors you have maintained relationships with, and many others.

PROTECTING THE CAREERS OF YOUR STAFF FROM THE WINDS OF CHANGE

Just as you will want to protect your career from the winds of change, you will want to be concerned with the future of your staff. You will want to help them keep their skills upgraded by providing as much on-the-job training as possible. The more you enhance their careers (whether they stay with your firm or eventually move on), the more productive they will be now and the more they will respect you as a supervisor.

PERFORMANCE **CHECKLIST**

1. We are experiencing a time of rapid change in our society, economy, workforce demographics, and the way we work and employees are managed. Supervisors will be challenged more than ever before as their organizations respond to these challenges and implement change in order to survive. Supervisors will need to be prepared to educate their employees on new techniques, procedures, and technologies, as well as new mind sets on the way work is done. They must also see these challenges as opportunities and be supportive of change rather than take a negative view.

2. Supervisors must help employees manage stress, both positive stress (eustress) to maximize productivity and harmful stress (distress) that will adversely impact employee well being and productivity. Some suggestions for doing this include turn change into an opportunity for yourself; help employees through the natural transition from letting go of old ways to accepting new opportunities; communicate the advantages of change; follow up with advanced, hands-on training; and help employees balance stress with rest and relaxation.

3. Regardless of the relative stability (or lack thereof) of your current work situation as a result of the impacts of change in your organization or industry, it is important to have a personal Plan B so that you will be prepared for your next career opportunity, whether that is within your current organization or elsewhere.

4. As part of your personal Plan B, it is important to make yourself visible within the company so that you might be more readily considered for advancement opportunities. You can do this through participating in meetings, supporting team efforts, and leading cross-functional teams, remaining positive and supportive of organizational goals and initiatives, accepting special assignments of particular importance to upper management, and seeking ways through appropriate channels to communicate with upper management regarding the company's long-term goals and business objectives or to seek career advice.

5. In developing your personal Plan B, you must evaluate your preferences between moving from company to company in order to advance or to remain within the same company. Stabilizers prefer to remain long-term in their current company. To be successful, they must ensure they work hard to stay current on their skills and find ways to remain engaged in order to be considered for advancement opportunities. Scramblers prefer the "zigzag" approach and move from company to company to advance. While this can often lead to quicker advancement, there is a cost in terms of constantly moving, uprooting family, and not establishing firm roots within the organization or community. Scramblers must be careful not to move too quickly or risk being perceived as a "job hopper."

6. The seven steps to developing a Plan B are: (1) Keep your resume up to date; (2) become more effective in your current situation (Plan A) in order to have more time in developing your Plan B; (3) learn more from your current job; (4) ensure your competencies are up to date; (5) seek more education or training, if necessary; (6) do more creative networking while in your current position; and (7) use your Plan B to gain a promotion within your current organization or to win a better position outside.

TEST **YOURSELF**

For each of the following statements, check true or false.

True   False

____ ____ 1. Companies generally value scramblers over stabilizers because moving from job to job and organization to organization demonstrates the kind of leadership potential they are looking for.

____ ____ 2. Most people have more trouble adjusting to change than they anticipate.

____ ____ 3. When other options exist, it is sometimes good to resist an ill-advised change.

____ ____ 4. One is fortunate to belong to a conservative organization that knows how to insulate employees from change.

____ ____ 5. Many departments will become multicultural, but none will become multilingual.

____ ____ 6. Change is a primary source of stress for workers.

True   False

____   ____   7. Organizations slow in adjusting to change do their employees a favor.

____   ____   8. The impact of change falls more on employees than supervisors.

____   ____   9. It is reasonable to expect employees to adjust quickly to organizational change.

____   ____   10. Employees who participate in the planning of change experience a decrease in the stress that change can bring.

Turn to the back of the book to check your answers.

Total Correct ____

DISCUSSION **QUESTIONS**

1. Can all changes be converted into opportunities? Defend your answer through examples.

2. What can supervisors do to minimize stress within themselves? For the employees? Evaluate such possibilities as physical exercise and meditation.

3. Would you agree that change is the primary source of stress in our society?

4. Think of your own situation. How much change is in your life? How do you react to change, and how might your reaction be modified to reduce stress?

5. How, in your opinion, can ambitious stabilizers compete more successfully with talented scramblers within the same organization?

6. Do you agree that moving from one organization (environment) to another is a good way to improve one's leadership ability?

7. Should stabilizers develop a Plan B even if they have no intention of leaving their firms?

8. What are some benefits of joining a trade or professional organization associated with your profession?

CASE 1: **CHANGE**

OBJECTIVE

To provide the supervisor with insights and techniques to help a negative mature worker accept change.

PROBLEM

Yolanda is concerned about Brenda. During more than twenty years with the organization, Brenda was highly productive. For the past year, however, she has been negative to both co-workers and customers. Every time a change is mandated by top management, Brenda becomes more vocal and more negative. Now, co-workers are complaining and customers are turning to competitors. In addition, Brenda's inflexible attitude toward change is hurting the productivity of everyone who works with her. Yolanda agrees that something must be done. The organization has a non-termination policy for employees in Brenda's category.

PROCEDURE

Divide the class into small groups of four or five. Each group selects its own chairperson. The group then develops a counseling strategy that will help Brenda cope with change and restore her previous positive attitude and high productivity.

The strategy should include (1) counseling techniques, either directive or nondirective; (2) a decision on whether Mutual Reward Theory (MRT) would be effective; (3) the number of sessions recommended; and (4) the choice of superiors who will be involved.

Give each group at least twenty minutes to develop a strategy, followed by an opportunity to present its conclusions to the class or seminar.

CASE DISCUSSION

Compare the strategies presented and evaluate their probable effectiveness in improving Brenda's attitude.

CASE 2: **DECISION**

Eric is thirty years old and an engineer for a giant utility. Commuting daily from the suburbs to a central city headquarters, he arrives early but refuses to work beyond 4:30 P.M. except in emergencies. Eric puts his personal life first and clearly separates work from his private life. He is highly family and church oriented.

Management believes that Eric is talented, ethical, and patient enough to play the corporate game. Eric's co-workers know he is extremely ambitious and is growing increasingly impatient. Eric is usually motivated, but now his ambition is beginning to flag. He has the impression management is keeping him in an unnecessary holding pattern, possibly because of a prior image resulting from some unfortunate experiences early in his career. The solution is aggravated now because management is heaping responsibility on Eric without giving him additional recognition. He senses that they view him as "good old dependable Eric."

Eric prefers the straight-line pattern to the top because it gives his family stability and permits him to maintain his present church connections. He is, however, considering the zigzag pattern. Other firms would recognize his skills and experience, and a new job in a new environment would provide greater personal growth. Eric freely admits that he is in conflict between the two upward mobility patterns.

What advice would you give Eric? On what values should he base his decision? Can Eric take the zigzag path without sacrificing family values? What impact could adverse economic conditions have on such a decision?

CHANGE IMPLEMENTATION **EXERCISE**

Assume that you are in a state of semi-shock. You have just attended a top-level meeting where your superiors announced a major change. It could be a technological change (transition to a new computerized system) or an organizational change (moving a facility to a new location some miles away). You anticipate substantial resistance from a majority of the ten employees in your department. If you can help your department make a better adjustment than the other four departments similar to yours, it will be a feather in your cap, because your productivity will go up while theirs will drop. Your goal, therefore, is to set up a plan to help your employees adjust quickly with little impact on productivity.

Listed next are ten possible steps you can take. First, cross out those that in your judgment will do more harm than good. Second, assign priorities to those that remain by placing the number 1 on the blank opposite the action you would take first, and so on down the line. When you have finished, turn to the back of this book to compare your answers with those of the author.

1. _____ Wait a full day to make certain my own attitude is positive toward the change—even if rumors spread throughout the department.

2. _____ Adjust my own attitude immediately (take a positive view) and announce the change in a department meeting before employees hear about it from another source. Encourage group participation.

3. _____ Follow up this meeting the next day with a detailed plan that will make the change easy on everyone and enhance the careers of those who take a positive view.

4. _____ Have private communication sessions with those whom you think will show the most resistance.

5. _____ Announce a "change adjustment" party at your home for Saturday night.

6. _____ Using the "Attitude-Toward-Change Scale" in the chapter as a model, prepare a new scale, administer it on your employees, and follow up with one-to-one communication.

7. _____ Prepare and announce six training sessions for all department personnel to help implement the change.

8. _____ Check out your transition plan with a superior to make certain you have not left out an important step.

9. _____ Announce you will be available for some career counseling for those who prefer to resign rather than adjust.

10. _____ Invite all employees to submit (verbally or in writing) any suggestions they have that will facilitate the change. Set up individual communication sessions with those having the most trouble adjusting.

TO LEARN **MORE**

To learn more about the generational mix in today's workforce, refer to the following references:
Lancaster, Lynne C., and David Stillman. *When Generations Collide: Who They Are, Why They Clash, How to Solve the Generational Puzzle at Work.* New York: HarperCollins Publishers, 2002.
Martin, Carolyn A., and Bruce Tulgan. *Managing the Generation Mix: From Collision to Collaboration.* Amherst, MA: HRD Press, 2002.

To learn more about managing stress, refer to the following resource:

Loehr, Jim, and Tony Schwartz. *The Power of Full Engagement: Managing Energy, Not Time, Is the Key to High Performance and Personal Renewal.* New York: Free Press, 2003.

NOTES

1. Alvin Toffler, *The Third Wave.* New York: Bantam, 1991.

2. Thomas L. Friedman, *The World Is Flat: A Brief History of the Twenty-first Century.* New York: Farrar, Straus and Giroux, 2005, p. 8.

3. Peter F. Drucker, *Managing in the Next Society.* New York: St. Martin's Press, 2002, p. 24.

4. William Bridges, *Managing Transitions: Making the Most of Change*, 2nd ed. Cambridge, MA: Perseus Publishing, 2003, pp. 4–5.

5. "Are You Working Too Hard? A Conversation with Mind/Body Researcher Herbert Benson," *Harvard Business Review* 83, no. 11 (November 2005): 53–58.

Special Final Exercise: Leadership Potential Scale

Rank yourself on the Leadership Potential Scale one more time. When you are finished, compute your score. Compare it with your earlier score. The comparison measures the progress you have made (in increased self-knowledge and self-confidence) since you first completed the exercise in this guide.

Circle the number that indicates where you fall in the scale from 1 to 10. After you have finished, total your scores in the space provided.

I can develop the talent and confidence to be an excellent speaker in front of groups.	10 9 8 7 6 5 4 3 2 1	I could never develop the confidence to speak in front of groups.
I have the capacity to build and maintain productive relationships with workers under my supervision.	10 9 8 7 6 5 4 3 2 1	I'm a loner. I do not want the responsibility of building relationships with others.
I intend to take full advantage of all opportunities to develop my leadership qualities.	10 9 8 7 6 5 4 3 2 1	I do not intend to seek a leadership role or to develop my leadership skills.
I can develop the skill of motivating others. I would provide an outstanding example.	10 9 8 7 6 5 4 3 2 1	I could never develop the skill of motivating others. I would be a poor example to follow.
I can be patient and understanding with others.	10 9 8 7 6 5 4 3 2 1	I have no patience with others and could not develop it.
I could learn to be good at disciplining those under me—even to the point of terminating a worker after repeated violations.	10 9 8 7 6 5 4 3 2 1	It would tear me up to discipline a worker under my supervision; I'm much too kind and sensitive.
I can make tough decisions.	10 9 8 7 6 5 4 3 2 1	I do not want decision-making responsibilities.
It would not bother me to isolate myself and maintain a strong discipline line between workers and me.	10 9 8 7 6 5 4 3 2 1	I have a great need to be liked; I want to be one of the gang.
I would make an outstanding member of a "management team."	10 9 8 7 6 5 4 3 2 1	I would be a weak member of a "management team."
In time, I would be a superior leader—better than anyone I have known.	10 9 8 7 6 5 4 3 2 1	My leadership potential is so low it is not worth developing.

Total Score_____

Answers to True and False Questions

CHAPTER 1

1. T (Those who have not developed specific skills often are generalists with broad backgrounds and make outstanding managers.)
2. F (Supervisors are usually expected to survive without the kind of frequent support they are asked to provide their own employees.)
3. T
4. F (Many changes may be needed.)
5. F (Supervisors should maintain a discrete distance from those they supervise.)
6. F (Managing diversity often requires the supervisor to accept the challenges that differences among people and their perspectives bring and find ways to utilize both differences and similarities to create synergy and achieve better results.)
7. F (Many people without any previous exposure to leadership roles become excellent first-time supervisors.)
8. T (While the need to develop conceptual competence increases as you advance to higher levels in the organization and the need to develop technical competence decreases as you advance, the need to develop interpersonal competence remains constant regardless of your level of responsibility within the organization.)
9. F
10. F

CHAPTER 2

1. F
2. F
3. T (This means keeping pressure from superiors (upstairs) from reaching employees and hurting productivity.)
4. F
5. F (Try to learn as much as possible from your predecessor.)
6. F (Supervisors should make the initial contact in most cases.)
7. F (As long as you don't overtax yourself, the more you study about your new role, the better. That is the purpose of *Supervisor's Survival Kit*.)
8. T
9. F
10. T

CHAPTER 3

1. F
2. F
3. T
4. F (More decisions as well as more important ones.)
5. T
6. F (Supervisors will also receive more power.)
7. F (Fewer)
8. F
9. T
10. T (Money is an extrinsic motivator or, as Frederick Herzberg defines it, a "hygiene factor" that does not contribute to increasing motivation.)

CHAPTER 4

1. T
2. T
3. F (In most cases, there is an established procedure or accounting method to measure departmental productivity.)
4. T
5. F (Physiological needs must be met first.)
6. F (Management appraises the supervisor as an individual and measures departmental productivity, for which it holds the supervisor responsible.)
7. F (Generally, 80 percent of performance barriers are external to the performer, so focusing more attention on those issues will often lead more quickly to improved performance.)
8. T
9. T
10. F (Job aids and other documentation on how to perform tasks are external factors that the organization must provide the employee to assist him or her to perform.)

CHAPTER 5

1. T
2. T
3. F (The supervisor has a responsibility to mend them quickly.)
4. T (Some workers are so insecure that daily support is necessary to get maximum productivity.)
5. T (Cries of "Unfair!" will be heard immediately.)
6. F (It is best to see the relationship first to gain greater objectivity.)
7. F
8. T

9. T

10. T

CHAPTER 6

1. F

2. F (Some work environments require a firmer discipline line—for example, a plant in which dangerous equipment could injure workers.)

3. F (Busy employees are more positive because they don't have time to become bored and negative.)

4. F (Some slight adjustment is frequently necessary.)

5. F

6. T

7. T

8. F

9. T

10. T

CHAPTER 7

1. F (Opposite)

2. F (Also applies to customer satisfaction, etc.)

3. T

4. T

5. T

6. F

7. T

8. T

9. F (The tool is the Plan-Do-Check-Act model.)

10. F (It takes only one negating sign.)

CHAPTER 8

1. T

2. F (Some supervisors often perform better under a more traditional structure.)

3. T

4. T

5. F (Under the "team" approach.)

6. F (This is an example of accommodating employees from different cultures.)

7. T

8. T

9. T

10. T

CHAPTER 9

1. T
2. T
3. T
4. F
5. F (End of the day is not a good time, because the employee may be anxious and ready to go home for the day.)
6. T
7. T
8. T
9. T
10. F (Everyone will have bad days; wait longer to see a trend.)

CHAPTER 10

1. T
2. F (The downfall of most supervisors is delaying PC sessions that would make both parties feel better.)
3. T
4. F (Normally three corrective interviews are required.)
5. F
6. T (Employees resent carrying an extra load or seeing co-workers get by with unacceptable behavior.)
7. F (These individuals do not always cause disturbances. They often do the best they can, but have lower potential to produce.)
8. T
9. F (Other employees are resentful when the supervisor adjusts a discipline line for one individual, even if it gives everyone more freedom.)
10. T

CHAPTER 11

1. T
2. F
3. T
4. F
5. T
6. F
7. F (More valuable when not motivated.)
8. T
9. T (This is a form of behavioral interviewing which asks open-ended questions. Close-ended questions, to which answers like "yes" or "no" are called

for, do not elicit meaningful information as effectively as open-ended questions do.)

10. T

11. T (Because of breaks and other needs that full-time workers have in contrast to part-time workers, more time actually devoted to work per hour can often result with part-time workers.)

12. F

13. T

14. T

15. T

CHAPTER 12

1. F (The opposite is correct. Final responsibility for ensuring the task is completed remains with the supervisor.)

2. T

3. T (Favoritism exists when new assignments are always given to the same people, leaving others out.)

4. T

5. F (Other employees will eventually discover that a task has been delegated. Communicating the delegation is also important so that others will know who is now responsible for the task in the event they are required to assist this individual with the task.)

6. T (Successful supervisors delegate.)

7. T

8. T

9. F (If you are bored with them, others will also be bored. While delegating some boring tasks may be necessary, you should also find tasks to delegate that the person will find interesting or challenging.)

10. T

CHAPTER 13

1. T

2. F (Many workers retain negative images of classroom teaching techniques employed by former teachers.)

3. T

4. F (Most supervisors are too hasty in giving instructions.)

5. F

6. F

7. T

8. T

9. F

10. T

CHAPTER 14

1. T (Management is always trying to improve them.)
2. F
3. F (Most supervisors are too lenient.)
4. F (The worker's personality should not be involved in an evaluation.)
5. F (Base the evaluation on the employee's productivity.)
6. T
7. F (Only good performance in one area influences all other areas. The horn effect does the opposite.)
8. F (It gives the same average rating to all characteristics.)
9. F (They should always be discussed.)
10. F (Future goals should be discussed before the process is completed.)

CHAPTER 15

1. T
2. F
3. F
4. T
5. T
6. F (The opposite is generally true.)
7. T
8. F (Do delegate!)
9. F
10. T

CHAPTER 16

1. T
2. F (They are motivated when they are involved.)
3. T
4. T
5. F
6. F (Daily plans should correlate with organization plans also.)
7. T
8. F
9. T
10. T

CHAPTER 17

1. T
2. T

3. F (They change, but writing them down is still a good idea for most managers.)
4. T
5. T
6. T
7. T
8. F (A priority list should include about seven tasks.)
9. T (If not, it becomes a source of irritation.)
10. T

CHAPTER 18

1. F (Supervisors spend too little time getting the facts.)
2. T
3. T
4. F (Minor decisions should be made on the spot.)
5. F (Alternatives can be compared in a few seconds.)
6. F (It is wise to consult others on complex problems.)
7. T
8. F (The process can be used in making people-oriented or personal decisions also.)
9. F
10. T (Not making a decision can often lower productivity more than making a bad one that can be changed later.)
11. T
12. T

CHAPTER 19

1. F (He is guilty of stereotyping.)
2. T
3. F (Look for the traits, characteristics, and potential that an individual has to perform and you can train and develop him or her to perform at the expected level later.)
4. F (The best advice is "Underpromise and overdeliver.")
5. F (One can respect a person who is not popular.)
6. T
7. T
8. T
9. T
10. T
11. T
12. T

CHAPTER 20

1. F (Both scramblers and stabilizers are valued. Scramblers must not move too quickly between opportunities or they will risk being perceived as "job hoppers" rather than leaders with advancement potential.)
2. T
3. T (Resist only when changes are not necessary.)
4. F (One is fortunate when management can adjust to change and keep the organization alive.)
5. F
6. T
7. F
8. T
9. F (While employees may need to adapt quickly, supervisors must understand the psychological component of change in which people need time to let go of old ways and struggle through until they will be able to fully accept new opportunities.)
10. T

The Authors' Responses to Exercises

CHAPTER 1: LEADERSHIP POTENTIAL SCALE

Please consider this scale a pretest of your leadership potential. When you have completed this guide, you will be invited to take it again (as a post-test) so that you can measure the progress you have made.

CHAPTER 2: TAKE-OVER EXERCISE

The authors believe that it is normally a better strategy to move into a new department as a supervisor with a somewhat low, firm discipline line. Moving in too high (being overly friendly) and then lowering the line later can cause resentment and lower productivity. Moving in at a lower (more distant) level and then becoming more permissive later can increase employees' self-motivation and productivity. It is natural for employees to regard a new supervisor with some anxiety. To dissipate this anxiety too soon to gain immediate popularity can cause problems later. The authors, therefore, support Strategy 2 over Strategy 1 as more effective when starting out as a manager.

CHAPTER 4: PRODUCTIVITY EXERCISE

Employees are motivated by different factors so there can be no preferred list that applies to all individuals. Experience shows that the real benefit of this exercise comes from the dialogue that occurs when two people compare their responses. Do not hesitate to invite people to participate in this exercise. It is a learning opportunity for them, too.

CHAPTER 5: COMMUNICATION EXERCISE

In teaching certain fundamentals to others, putting definitions in "your own words" or giving specific examples of how the fundamentals can be applied are necessary if learning is to take place. If you are currently a supervisor, the purpose of this exercise is to get you to apply each of the irreplaceable foundations to a specific individual under your supervision. If you are preparing to be a supervisor, the idea is to do the same hypothetically.

CHAPTER 6: RESTORING MORALE EXERCISE

A number of "action packages" might get the morale (and the productivity) of the department back up, but *it is unlikely*. One possible combination is: (1) a group meeting with a soft approach followed by individual sessions, (2) greater involvement in decisions, and (3) spending more time with employees. The truth is that any combination of actions decided on (and implemented properly) by anyone is probably the best combination for that individual.

Based on experience in the field, the most common single word that explains why the morale of the department has deteriorated is *communication*—the lack of it. Once morale has dropped to a low level, it is very difficult for the same supervisor to raise it again. That is why management often decides to transfer the supervisor to another role and bring in a replacement.

CHAPTER 7: IMPLEMENTATION EXERCISE

This exercise is designed to illustrate the "gaps" that can exist and what can be accomplished to improve quality. It is anticipated that students will have to dig deeply to come up with improvement measures in each category.

CHAPTER 8: MULTICULTURAL EXERCISE

Here are some suggested responses:

1. Take time to introduce the individual to all team members. Do not rush the process as it builds confidence in the newcomer.
2. Encourage the individual to enroll in an English as a Second Language (ESL) course.
3. Have a short daily meeting to answer questions the new employee may have.
4. Encourage the new employee to discuss informally her or his background in a staff meeting where refreshments are served.
5. Do a weekly review on progress being made for one month and continue on a monthly basis.

CHAPTER 9: TECHNIQUE ANALYSIS EXERCISE

The authors would use the *directive technique* on situations 1, 2, 4, 6, 8, and 10 for impact purposes. But remember that the direct approach is not a chew-out session; the supervisor simply lays the cards on the table to save time and get an immediate response from the individual being counseled. Non-directive counseling is more relaxed and is designed to help the worker see a situation in a better light and readjust or set new goals. The employee does most of the talking. Directive counseling is designed to get the facts and strengthen the discipline line with the individual. The choice of technique depends on the relationship the supervisor has with the employee and the results of any previous sessions between the two. Knowing these two approaches gives the supervisor confidence to initiate the interview in the first place—and that is their purpose.

CHAPTER 10: MRT COUNSELING EXERCISE

The authors would agree to provide all three rewards, although we would first want to discuss openly what constitutes "getting off a worker's back." We would also insist on a fair reward exchange that includes higher productivity, reduction of hostility on the part of the employee, and greater cooperation with co-workers. If a reasonable reward exchange was negotiated, we would want to review the outcome within thirty days. We would give the technique an excellent chance of success. (In our view, mutual reward is the best technique available.) We also believe that the supervisor does have the right to initiate a reward exchange session with his or her superior. Results can be as good in an upward approach as a downward one.

CHAPTER 11: JOB QUALIFICATION CHECK LIST EXERCISE

The idea here is to encourage you to come up with your own qualification list to fit your own work environment. If you design your own pattern, it will mean more to you.

CHAPTER 12: DELEGATION EXERCISE

The authors favor delegating (1) the weekly stock count, (2) the weekly report, (3) the e-mail message, and (4) the routine routing meeting, in that order. Depending on other responsibilities, Ricardo may want to keep the weekly fun job and daily delivery job because a supervisor needs some therapeutic tasks, and communication with superiors is vital for upward mobility. Obviously, the quality of training that takes place in the preparation of subordinates to take over responsibilities is the key to successful delegation. Additional thoughts regarding this scenario are provided in the "Suggested Answers to Case Problems" in response to the case "To Delegate or Not to Delegate."

CHAPTER 13: KNOWLEDGE TRANSFER EXERCISE

When you have actually practiced the four-step teaching method on another person, you will have convinced yourself of its value. It is best, of course, to practice teaching a skill to someone you supervise. If you are not in supervision, select a skill you can teach a friend or a child. Don't pass up this opportunity. It will improve your management skills.

CHAPTER 14: RATE YOURSELF EXERCISE

This exercise introduces you to the "sensitivity factor" involved in all performance evaluation systems. If you have a superior who will take time to rate you, use this matching experience to build a better relationship with this person. To be a success, a formal evaluation should leave the person evaluated more highly motivated.

CHAPTER 15: HYPOTHETICAL PROJECT

Many individuals procrastinate writing a letter or thinking through a problem because they have more trouble getting into the "mood" to concentrate than actually performing well after they get started. Once these people build confidence in their ability to concentrate, they procrastinate less.

CHAPTER 16: PLANNING EXERCISE

If you built a strong case for a written plan, you have made a good decision. Such a plan could include the net profit you hope to achieve for the period involved and how you intend to achieve it. Such plans, if they are reasonable and flexible, can be self-motivating. If you opted for a non-written plan for greater flexibility, don't lose track of the goals involved. Keep in mind that you are accountable to yourself, and only through reaching your own goals will you achieve a sense of fulfillment.

CHAPTER 17: PRIORITY EXERCISE

This exercise has only one purpose: to start the habit of setting your priorities each day. It is a habit you should acquire as soon as possible. There is no substitute.

CHAPTER 18: DECISION-MAKING EXERCISE

Don't avoid or give up on this exercise. Until you have actually used the process several times, you stand little chance of weaving it into your behavioral pattern. If the process becomes a habit, however, you will be able to make better decisions faster.

CHAPTER 19: MISTAKE ELIMINATION EXERCISE

Believe it or not, it is possible to anticipate mistakes you are likely to make and avoid making them. You will not eliminate all mistakes, but you will make fewer. The effort is worthwhile.

CHAPTER 20: CHANGE IMPLEMENTATION EXERCISE

The authors would eliminate 1, 5, 6, and 9, and then assign priorities as follows: 2, 3, 8, 7, 4, and 10. The important thing, of course, is to make an analysis that meets your own special needs and then come up with a plan. You should not expect your employees to adjust to change without some help from you.

Role Profiles for Cases

Identifying with the nine profiles that follow will help make the cases in *Supervisor's Survival Kit* more realistic and enjoyable. Some of these cases are presented as case studies involving class discussion while others are presented as role-plays requiring student participation. If you have the opportunity to play a role, you will be expected to make decisions from the viewpoint of the character you portray. For example, if you are given the role of Bill, the General Manager, you will attempt to act in a way you feel a person in that position and with his personality would act. The more you study and identify with these roles, the more intriguing you will find the cases.

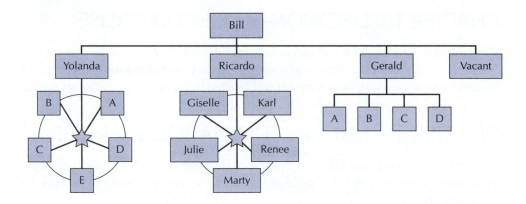

The chart provides reporting relationships of each individual in our hypothetical organization. The differences between the organizational structure for Ricardo's and Yolanda's groups in contrast to Gerald's group reflect how these supervisors manage their employees conceptually. Ricardo and Yolanda conceive their groups as more team-focused and themselves as team facilitators, whereas Gerald conceives his group and his responsibilities in more of a traditional, hierarchical manner. These differences do not necessarily reflect the management structure as would appear on a formal organization chart.

(Note: For readers unfamiliar with characters from prior editions of *Supervisor's Survival Kit*, references to "Mr. Big," "Supervisor Joe," and "Mr. X" refer to characters that appeared in those editions, but who are not part of the profiles in this edition.)

BILL, GENERAL MANAGER

As Bill, you have overall responsibility for the operations of the organization and management of staff. You have been in your position for a little over a year, having joined the organization after holding progressively responsible management positions in similar organizations over the past fifteen years. You replaced Mr. Big, who retired to join a small management consultant firm. At the time, the organization was undergoing significant change, including fluctuating economic conditions that adversely impacted profits, competition from similar businesses (foreign and domestic), and difficulties with employee turnover and morale. Although Mr. Big was an effective, trusted manager, it became evident that different leadership was needed to set a new course.

You have big shoes to fill, but feel you are up to the task. Like Mr. Big, you are recognized by your superiors and staff as ambitious, efficient, and a good listener. You recognize the importance of achieving maximum productivity from people and evaluating them accordingly rather than based on personality. You are also good at setting priorities and managing your own time and expect the same efficiency from others.

Where you differ from Mr. Big is that you support more of a team-based management approach rather than a hierarchical, pyramid structure. You also understand that each of the front-line supervisors you manage has his or her unique management preferences that you want to support, so long as their methods are consistent with effective management practices. While you would like each to embrace a team concept, you recognize that you cannot rush change. This is why two of your supervisors, Yolanda and Ricardo, are modeling the team-based approach, while Gerald continues to function more in a hierarchical framework. You are patient.

You are forty-three years old. You have a four-year college degree in business administration. You credit your career advancement to this education, your leadership qualities, and a strong work ethic. You are a bit of a scrambler, though lately have needed to be more stable to support your family. Your pre-teen daughter is very active in sports and drama. Your younger son is developmentally disabled and requires your and your wife's constant attention.

You never gave much thought to the discipline line you maintain, though you suppose it is more permissive than firm. Yet you don't tolerate repeated, uncorrected poor performance and bad behavior. Yolanda was in her role when you came on board and you promoted Gerald and Ricardo to their roles. Gerald replaced the ubiquitous Mr. X, who you would have terminated had he not seen "the writing on the wall" and sought employment elsewhere. Mr. X supported a very autocratic style of management that you do not embrace. Ricardo is very new to his role and has made a number of mistakes to show it. You believe in his ultimate success and view yourself as a teacher for him.

RICARDO, SUPERVISOR

As Ricardo, you were recently promoted to your role as supervisor, replacing Supervisor Joe, your former boss, who took a job elsewhere. You have worked for the organization for four years, half of that time as a part-time employee while taking courses at a local college, another year and a half as a full-time employee, and the past half-year as a supervisor. When you worked part time, you had some reservations about the organization, particularly because of a pervasive attitude among full-time employees that you don't count as a part-timer and should just be thankful to have a job. Consequently, most of the dirty jobs were dumped on you.

How times change. When Bill came on board, you began to feel increased acceptance for your work and your ambition to pursue a college education. Then, when Joe left, Bill asked whether you ever considered taking on a supervisory role with the organization. You were floored by this because you assumed others on your team would be considered for such opportunities because of their seniority. At the time, you were nearing completion of a two-year associate's degree. When Bill offered the supervisor role a few months later, he was very supportive of your plans to continue pursuing a bachelor's degree in business by taking night courses.

Bill has been accessible to you as you learn your position. He has encouraged you to set your own course with respect to your management style, but has clearly demonstrated a preference for team-based approaches and collaborating with all supervisors when significant organizational and operational decisions are involved. He also encourages you to consult with Yolanda and Gerald as much as with him. Yolanda seems confident and also adopts a team-based approach, though you feel at times she works more independently than Bill would prefer. You appreciate Gerald's firmness and sense of order and decorum with his staff, while maintaining their respect, though you sometimes wonder if he is too rigid.

You consider yourself a scrambler and will probably look for another supervisory position eventually. But you have a lot to learn at this point so you don't envision moving on too soon. You are twenty-four, single, and come from a large family. You are considered handsome and people think you are a sharp dresser. You are personable and people generally feel at ease around you. You also have no problem offering your opinion, occasionally to your detriment.

YOLANDA, SUPERVISOR

As Yolanda, you are a college graduate who believes in participative and team-based approaches to management. You involve your employees in departmental decisions when possible and pride yourself on your sensitivity to individual needs. You have developed your own informal communications system. You are assertive in manner and consider yourself a scrambler rather than a stabilizer.

Although you did not intend to stay in the organization more than two years, you were persuaded by Bill to stick around to support the changes he was seeking to implement. Beyond the natural confidence you felt in Bill as an effective leader, there were three other considerations that persuaded you to stay on longer: (1) You were offered a reasonably generous and competitive pay increase; (2) you were recognized as the senior supervisor within the organization; and (3) Mr. X has moved on. When you worked with Mr. X, you sensed a deep conflict between your management style and his. You operate on a low-key and somewhat permissive basis but nevertheless, often achieve high productivity. In contrast, Mr. X was authoritarian and used strict controls to manage staff. You are glad he is gone.

You are not sure about the management styles and skills of your colleagues, Ricardo and Gerald, but are willing to trust Bill and his reasons for selecting them as supervisors. Because Ricardo is new to supervision, he seems awkward, uninformed, and perhaps a little too happy-go-lucky for your tastes. Though you at times feel that Gerald exhibits some of the same traits as Mr. X, his approach is much more respectful toward his staff. He clearly believes in developing his staff and demonstrates clear leadership ability as the result of his Marine training.

You are twenty-six, recently married, and enjoy skiing with your husband. You like the idea of becoming a top executive and will seize the next step up the corporate ladder whenever the right job with competitive pay comes along.

GERALD, SUPERVISOR

You are forty-two years of age. You were raised in the inner-city neighborhood, but you seldom think about it anymore because you have worked hard and now have a nice home and most things you need to achieve the lifestyle you desire. Your wife works in a government job, and you have two teenage children.

You completed a four-year hitch in the Marines. Because of your advancement in the Marines, you feel certain of your leadership abilities and are glad to have the chance to utilize them in your new role as supervisor. You recently completed some continuing education evening classes to improve your English and Math skills and are now returning to the continuing education program to take classes in management.

You have worked as a supervisor for about a year. You were promoted shortly after Bill came on board and Mr. X left. You understand Bill and Yolanda's concerns about Mr. X, but don't necessarily agree with them. You can appreciate the need for a management style that is more directive and controlling and less participative. Sometimes that's the only way to get things done. This does not mean that such a manager is uncaring or unable to garner and maintain the support and trust of his staff. At the same time, you realize that Bill promoted you in part because you are more sensitive to people and their needs than others who were considered for the position and, therefore, could act as more of a stabilizing influence for your staff and for the organization overall. These are traits that Mr. X appeared to lack. In fact, your tendency to be a stabilizer is something you offer that Yolanda and Ricardo do not.

Your level of productivity is generally on par with Yolanda. You realize that Bill promotes more of a team-based approach to management. You aren't averse to team-based approaches, but it just isn't your style. Bill doesn't push you more on this issue because your team remains productive, you are comfortable with yourself and your management style, and your employees are generally supportive and willing to follow your direction. You worry that this may change if productivity declines.

KARL

As Karl, you have seniority over all the other employees in Joe's department. In fact, you have served under six different supervisors. You are married and have five children. Two are outstanding students in the local high school and your oldest is a sophomore at the state's flagship university.

You feel you are a loyal, friendly, helpful employee, but you see no reason to extend yourself. You manage to keep your productivity at a safe average, and that is about as far as you intend to go. Compared to the other supervisors you've had, you feel Ricardo is about average. He's no better or worse than some of the other young supervisors you've adjusted to. And, like the others, he won't last long. He'll probably move on in a year or two. So, why worry? After all, you taught him most of what he knows about the job, and he still comes to you for advice. You figure you're safe.

You could have become department supervisor some years ago, but you turned it down because you didn't want the people problems involved. You feel the pay is fairly good and the benefits are great, so you coast along. You are tired and you feel old. It struck you recently that your oldest child in now almost as old as most of the supervisors you've had. You wonder how many more of these young, upstart supervisors you can take.

Your main interest is fishing, and the more time you spend in your camper, the better life is for you. If it weren't for that, you would hate your job more than you do.

RENEE

As Renee, you are thirty-six years of age but entered the labor market only two years ago, after your divorce. You have a sizeable mortgage and two children to raise. Everyone can see that you are socially active, but you never talk about your private life. You are well groomed and able to communicate in a persuasive manner. People in management respect your assertiveness.

Although you had only two semesters of college years ago, you know you are above average in intelligence. You learn quickly and are currently taking a course at your local community college in supervision. The course is interesting, but you aren't sure it is that beneficial. You are taking it more to demonstrate to management your interest in advancement rather than to learn anything. Though your work experience is not extensive, you do have leadership experience you can put on your resume, such as leading your kids' PTA and scout groups, and volunteering with various community and charity organizations.

Because of your innate sense for leadership, you become impatient with Ricardo and his limited experience as a supervisor. But then, you are impatient with most of the other employees as well. On the other hand, you respect Bill and the other supervisors, especially Yolanda, and your goal is to impress them so that you'll be considered for the next supervisory position when it becomes available. Or perhaps you'll be considered for Ricardo's job after he moves on or slips up. Meanwhile, you sense some hostility from your co-workers because you exhibit such confidence, but you pass this off as unimportant.

Ricardo and Bill know that your personal productivity is substantially higher than that of others in the department, but you are not going to sit around and wait for further management recognition. You intend to promote yourself. Although you have been with the organization for little more than two years, if an advancement opportunity doesn't open up soon, you will exercise your Plan B and move to a competitive organization at a higher salary and, hopefully, in a leadership role. You are a scrambler.

MARTY

As Marty, you are thirty-nine years of age. You were raised in a rural setting and graduated from a small high school where you met and later married your high-school sweetheart. You lived in the same small town for most of your life, but moved about five years ago to a larger community where the organization is located because there were better job opportunities for both you and your wife. Your wife also works full-time. You have one child, a daughter, who is in second grade.

You and your wife agree that life is better than where you lived before because job opportunities are better and there are more social activities in the community. You also like the church you attend. Your struggle is with trying to understand all the talk about diversity and inclusion that occurs within the workplace these days. You don't always understand how or why differences in culture between co-workers really matter. Yet, you try hard to interact with all your co-workers and live by a personal mantra to "simply treat people as people." It's served you well so far.

In previous jobs, you feel you demonstrated good judgment and leadership skills. You worked effectively as a team leader in these settings, though primarily with men who had similar backgrounds as you. You never held the job title of supervisor or similar management rank. Nonetheless, you have good references from former bosses who can speak to your leadership qualities. You have considered taking a course or two in supervision at the local community college, but so far have not looked into it.

You have earned the respect of Ricardo, Bill, and (you feel) all your fellow employees except Renee. You hope to become a supervisor in a few months and perhaps qualify for Bill's job a few years from now. You feel you are better qualified than Renee for promotion because you are more sensitive to people and therefore have a stabilizing influence on the department. Although you recognize that your personal productivity is not as high as Renee's, you feel you contribute more than she does to the productivity of others.

GISELLE

As Giselle, you are twenty-five years old and have two years of college behind you. Everyone agrees that you are good at your job. You like your position, but it would not upset you should you not come back to work tomorrow. You somehow feel you could get a better job if you really tried. You are seldom absent from work and never late. You know your productivity is above average, but you also know it could be higher if you felt there was someplace to go in the organization. If a promotion came along now, either Renee or Marty would get it, so why push? You recognize that you are not highly motivated and believe nothing management can do will change you. You felt that way when Mr. Big was in charge and don't feel any differently now that Bill is in charge.

Ricardo isn't the kind of guy you'd go all out for anyway. You think he is doing his best, but as far as you're concerned, he doesn't understand people well enough to get them to work together as a team. You think he is too easygoing. It's not the worst place in the world to work, though. The physical facilities are excellent, and the pay is okay. At this point, you are making slightly more money than your husband.

JULIE

As Julie, you are the only part-time employee in the department. You work twenty hours a week while taking a full program at a local college. You are nineteen. You are outgoing, trendy in dress, and have lots of friends. You are the first member of your family to go to college, for which your parents are very proud.

You like Ricardo, Bill, and the company, but do not intend to stay there after you finish school. Your job is simply a means for income to support your education, not a life ambition. You are grateful that Ricardo has been flexible with your schedule so that you can come and go as necessary to concentrate on your studies. In exchange, you understand that you are expected to work hard and not engage in socializing while at work. You generally achieve this, but slip occasionally.

You don't mind the work you are assigned, but often feel you get the thankless work that others don't want to do. You seldom get assignments that challenge you and engage your mind and interests. There's no way you would tolerate this if you were a full-time employee, and would become bored and find employment elsewhere—fast! For now, you bide your time. At times, to cope, you engage in quiet rebellion by surfing the Internet and texting friends. You are careful to do this at times when no one notices or when work is light. Who should mind?

You are what is known as a "digital native" because you grew up with technology and never knew life without it. You are constantly on your cell phone and the Internet and engage in electronic social networking activities. Most of your co-workers lack your savvy and ease with technology. Some, like Karl, appear not to know what a computer is. Perhaps that's an exaggeration, but it frustrates you when your co-workers look at you as though you are the odd one.

Suggested Answers to Case Problems

The typical supervisory problems presented in this book were designed as springboards for individual thinking and discussion. None of the problems have exact answers because only the essential facts of each problem are outlined. It is therefore impossible to give definitive or complete answers to any problem. The following answers, then, are nothing more than an account of how the authors would approach the problem with the available facts. Each suggested answer should serve only as a guide to the independent thinking of the reader and the discussion leader.

CHAPTER 1

CASE: CHOICE

Both Renee and Gerald should make good supervisors. The authors favour Gerald because his greater sensitivity to the needs of the employees could lead to greater productivity. Renee has a more authoritative rather than permissive style, and because she has neglected to build strong relationships with co-workers, they may resent her being promoted over them. Resentment plus a heavy-handed attitude could make productivity increases difficult. Gerald's sensitivity (and the fact that he has built better relationships with co-workers) makes him more acceptable to the employees, which could be converted into higher productivity.

CHAPTER 2

CASE: STRATEGY

The authors support Strategy 2 over Strategy 1 because it is better to begin a little more firmly and become more permissive later than be overly friendly upfront and tighten the discipline line later. (Refer to the response to the Take-Over Exercise in the Author's Responses to Exercises for further explanation.) However, a blend of these two strategies or a third strategy is also possible. When starting out as a manager, it is important to remember that you must establish your authority early while also demonstrating that you are supportive and want employees to trust and feel comfortable with your leadership. Based on your personal leadership style and the character, competence, and maturity of the employees whom you manage, being both friendly and firm are important. You must manage this blend in a way that is suitable to both you and the situation.

CHAPTER 3

CASE 1: WHAT DO EMPLOYEES WANT?

The authors presume that class discussion of employee needs will result in close agreement to what Frederick Herzberg suggests regarding hygiene and motivator factors, as well as what studies suggest regarding what employees say are their most important needs. These relate to appreciation and feeling "in" on things while needs like good wages, though not unimportant, contribute less to their true motivation. At the same time, it is important to recognize that no two employees (and no two students in class) will share the same opinion on what they consider to be true motivators. For example, some will adamantly insistent good wages are their primary motivation and will provide very rational reasons for believing so. So, care must be taken not to generalize.

CHAPTER 4

CASE 1: APPROACH

Marty's approach could fail because of the following pitfalls: (1) Overemphasis on being a good model could be so time-consuming that Marty might neglect other important duties. (2) Those inexperienced at professional customer relations often need to learn skills and techniques that are best communicated through training. Being a good model is important, as long as Marty does not devote too much time to it, but it does not replace individual or group training. (3) "Good guys" do not always make the best supervisors. Some discipline is usually necessary. Marty needs to come up with the right combination of being a good model, providing the right kind and amount of training, and maintaining discipline.

CASE 2: PEFORMANCE BARRIERS AND SOLUTIONS

It is clear from the way the role profiles are structured that a lot of the performance issues relate to the 20 percent of performance barriers that involve matters internal to the employees that are within their direct control. Karl, Renee, Giselle, and Julie, in particular, each have unique attitude issues that may affect performance. The scenario does not clearly identify many external performance barriers, which serves only to support the authors' statement that care must be taken to ensure these barriers are identified before putting the entire burden on the employees for performance problems. For example, although Karl has become quite complacent, are there organizational issues relating to motivation and incentives that have led to this complacency? Julie appears very technology savvy and could perhaps contribute in more meaningful ways, but do structures and systems, and simply the inherent bias against "part timers," result in an underutilization of her skills and a decrease in her motivation and productivity? There is also a question about whether most of these employees, other than Julie, have appropriate skills and knowledge relating to technology and computers and whether such skills are relevant to their work. Could the lack of training and experience in these areas affect their productivity? Finally, does the recent transition in leadership from Mr. Big to Bill cause any concern among employees about the direction and financial viability of the company that affects morale? What other questions might you ask to identify possible external barriers to performance?

CHAPTER 5

CASE 1: INTERVENTION

It's a toss up between immediate intervention or wait for two or three days. The great majority of employees faced with severe personal problems appreciate their supervisor's support. If the problem has rendered the employee ineffective, the supervisor can suggest taking a day off. The supervisor should act before the individual influences the productivity (and perhaps the safety) of others. Under modern competitive conditions, productivity cannot be permitted to drop for long. A good supervisor talks with the employee in a sensitive way without prying or attempting to invade the privacy of the individual.

CASE 2: REQUEST

The following three steps are recommended for Gerald:

Step 1: Bill needs to show and discuss the letter openly with Gerald so that he can verify the contents of the letter and Jane's productivity contribution. In doing this, Bill needs to be extremely careful to protect Gerald's ego.

Step 2: The termination procedure of the firm needs to be reviewed carefully so that Gerald does not make a decision too soon. Also, such a discussion should (hopefully) lead to a solution whereby Jane can be retained.

Step 3: The possibility of working out a flexible schedule should be explored. Mrs. Pitts appears to be a most valuable employee. If this fact is substantiated, adjusting to her needs might be in the best interest of the company and of all individuals concerned; however, no company rules or procedures should be violated.

CHAPTER 6

CASE: CLIMATE

Class discussion will likely reveal a wide variance in opinion on how this list should be prioritized. With a few notable exceptions, many of these choices have merit. The choice a manager would ultimately take will depend on how firm a discipline line he or she feels is needed. A manager with a more firm line might take a more direct approach, being clear in the need for immediate performance improvement. A manager who takes a more relaxed line might demonstrate the need for change through taking action first to set an example for the team, as well as engaging in supportive conversations to help employees improve. Of the choices that would be ineffective, withdrawing and acting hurt (#5) seems manipulative and dysfunctional. Also, having a party at home (#7) might help build the team somewhat, but doesn't get directly at the problem of low productivity; it could also be perceived as a reward when one is not warranted. Finally, going to Bill and asking for suggestions (#9) might be helpful, but Ricardo would need to approach Bill carefully or he may come across as an ineffective and indecisive leader unable to manage productivity problems through working directly with his team.

CHAPTER 7

CASE: PHILOSOPHY

The scenario suggests that the organization's stated commitment to quality is incongruent with its behaviors. The organization should examine the negating and confirming signs of its commitment to quality and address the negating signs before it moves too quickly to training. Without examining their commitment to quality, reaffirming that they are committed, and seriously looking at correcting past behaviors and quality defects, employees will not accept the quality program. Because Bill is relatively new to the organization, replacing Mr. Big, he may be able to achieve this turnaround more effectively than Mr. Big might have because Bill may be perceived as a new face with a renewed commitment to quality that may serve to energize supervisors and employees to make needed changes. However, he must be made aware of employees' attitudes about his alleged commitment to profits at the expense of quality and work so that he can change these perceptions through his actions.

CHAPTER 8

CASE 1: PYRAMID VS. CIRCLE

The authors believe that in most instances in today's work culture the team or circle style of supervision is most appropriate and effective to support employee motivation and empowerment, quality, employee involvement in decision making, and development of a culturally diverse work team. This is not to say, however, that there are not situations where the pyramid structure makes more sense. For example, highly regulated work environments where workers must perform repetitive tasks and where safety concerns are paramount may lend themselves more to a pyramid structure. Further, when employees within a work group are ineffective in working as a team or lack the maturity to do so, the supervisor or his or her organization may have to maintain or re-introduce more of a pyramid structure to give management more direct control in how employees function. Finally, some supervisors may simply not be completely comfortable with the team approach, and their leadership style may lend itself more to using a pyramid structure of management.

CASE 2: ACCULTURATE VS. ACCOMMODATE

Ricardo should learn more from Julie about how she can help with automating the inventory control records and, if her ideas make sense, begin to incorporate her in the process that Karl has started. In doing this, he may need to realign her other duties so that she'll have time to assist with this effort, particularly since her time is limited as a part-time employee. At the same time, Ricardo will need to work with Julie to make her understand that the ways in which she communicates with Karl may need to change. She cannot be curt and must learn to be more cooperative. Ricardo may need to also work with Karl to gain more acceptance of Julie's assistance without feeling threatened. For both employees, Ricardo will need to find ways to help them understand the very different ways in which they work, think, and communicate and learn to adapt so they can understand each other better and work cooperatively. He may need to work with them for awhile to help them through these initial difficulties. He will need to help each learn to respect the other's contribution to the effort.

CHAPTER 9

CASE: TECHNIQUE

In this situation, the authors recommend technique 2 (non-directive) because the facts have not been verified. Ricardo needs to know Julie's side of the story. It is possible that Julie has a good explanation for both irregularities reported. If a violation has occurred, Ricardo should check with Bill to determine whether a written warning should be issued first to Julie. The nondirective technique could save Ricardo from an embarrassing mistake if he were to come down hard on Julie, only to find out that the night watchman reported unverifiable facts.

CHAPTER 10

CASE: CONFRONTATION

An employee who is assertive is not generally a problem employee. This is the situation with Renee. Although she may not have the best attitude about the situation or toward Ricardo, and is taking a firm position, she is simply seeking to get what she wants in a more direct way than is warranted or that will likely achieve her desired outcome. The most obvious problem with this scenario is that although Ricardo and Renee both tell themselves that they will listen to the other, they both essentially have made up their mind about the others' attitude and what outcome should result. This situation calls for more of a non-corrective interview than a corrective one. It should be used as an opportunity for Ricardo to address concerns about Renee's behaviors, which are hurting her chances for promotion, while also seeking to listen to her point of view. Ricardo will need to change his attitude, though, if such a meeting is to be successful. He must return to a more objective framework, check any negative emotions he has about Renee, and be sure he conducts his meeting with Renee in the same way as he would for any other employee, notwithstanding Renee's assertive approach.

CHAPTER 11

CASE 1: STAFFING, PART 1

Complete a job analysis to determine the required skills needed to do the job. Construct a questionnaire to be used during the interviews that explores the applicants' abilities and experiences. Contact your local EEOC office for pamphlets on conducting interviews. Ask for information and guidance about interviewing from your Human Resources office.

CASE 1: STAFFING, PART 2

A key consideration will be the specific skill sets and expertise needed for the work. Typically, independent contractors are retained because they offer unique skills that may be difficult to find among full- or part-time workers, particularly for the kind of compensation required. Retaining an independent contractor will at least save on payroll and social security taxes. On the other hand, for more routine work functions, a part-time worker might be best and compensation will be less. Another consideration is how long a worker is needed and how important it is to have someone who can commit longer term to the organization's goals, mission, and business objectives. A part-timer would be best if a longer-term commitment is needed.

CHAPTER 12

CASE: TO DELEGATE OR NOT TO DELEGATE

All these tasks can be delegated. Individual choice and preferences may dictate the order in which they should be delegated, so each group in the class may report different results. There is no right or wrong method for prioritizing these tasks. However, for each task, Ricardo should keep the following considerations in mind when deciding when, how, and to whom to delegate:

Task 1: If there is nothing truly confidential about the information, then this task can be delegated. If Renee is trustworthy, then she would be a good candidate for this task. Ricardo must let go of the notion of losing control. The more information staff can have about the operation, including these departmental figures, the better. Ricardo should take the stance that there is nothing to hide. On the other hand, any task that truly does involve confidential information should remain in the hands of the supervisor.

Task 2: This is an ideal task for delegation because Ricardo has found an employee (Giselle) who would love doing it and would do it better than Ricardo could. A supervisor should embrace rather than shy away from opportunities that allow an employee to shine and demonstrate superior knowledge and ability. This should not be seen as a diminishment of the supervisor's abilities or role. Ricardo should also find other ways to connect with employees and facilitate communication.

Task 3: Ricardo should manage the employees who grumble about this task rather than allow this circumstance to be an excuse for not delegating it to them. They may grumble because they are not sufficiently trained to do it and end up producing a count that is wrong. Ricardo will need to provide thorough training on the task, perform the task with them initially, and monitor their work for awhile until they do the task correctly.

Task 4: Ricardo should first address his concerns about this task with Bill. He should verify whether it will be okay with Bill to assign this task to Karl. If Bill is adamant that Ricardo should do this task, even if it is menial and could be easily delegated to Karl, Ricardo may nonetheless need to retain this task. Otherwise, he should assign the task to Karl but monitor it closely, particularly because it seems to be a task that Ricardo's superior is also keeping an eye on.

Task 5: Of all the tasks on this list, Ricardo may especially want to keep this one if it is his only chance to connect with upper management on a weekly basis. The "task" in this case is actually something much larger and more important than making a delivery; it is maintaining visibility and connection with upper management. This redefined task can have benefits both to Ricardo's career and to his team as a way to keep the team visible to upper management and to inform the team of information he receives about the company from upper management. On the other hand, if Ricardo has other ways to connect with upper management, he should assign the delivery task to someone else.

Task 6: Meetings are an ideal way to get other employees involved and provide them exposure. Ricardo must instill more trust in Marty regarding this task and ensure that Marty reports back to him regarding what he learned and decisions that were made during the meeting.

CHAPTER 13

CASE: TRAINING

The authors believe that orientation training for new employees should be tied to personnel turnover and productivity, both of which are already measured by most firms. Superimposing Bill's complex system on these instruments could be interpreted as duplication and somewhat heavy-handed. The proposal also violates sound principles of delegation, in that the supervisors should be given authority to orient employees in their own style. If turnover and productivity results do not come up to standard, then supervisors should be held accountable. In addition, the plan appears to be overly ambitious. It is doubtful whether Bill will be able to follow through with so many evaluation meetings.

CHAPTER 14

CASE: OPTION

The authors support Yolanda's technique over Gerald's technique in most cases. Gerald's technique has elements that provide for employee voice and objectivity and, therefore, is not completely form- or process-driven. Nonetheless, Yolanda's technique comes closer to the relationship- and communication-driven approach that the authors suggest is more effective. Employees will generally feel more supported and that the process is more fair and objective through approaches that are closer to Yolanda's technique.

CHAPTER 15

CASE 1: THINKING

The authors agree with both Lisa and Lester. Lisa has a point when she says that concentration comes first and thinking comes next. Until supervisors focus their attention on a problem or project, it is impossible for them to get their thinking "gears" in motion. Lester makes a good point, however, when he states that learning to concentrate for study purposes prepares people to concentrate in the workplace.

CASE 2: ANALYSIS

The authors believe there are significant time management issues presented by Ricardo's time inventory:

Preparing request to Bill: Ricardo's time might have been better spent discussing the issue before spending time preparing the report, particularly because the issue concerns Ricardo's time-management skills, which, if corrected, would likely eliminate the need for an assistant.

Discussing production schedule with Marty: Ricardo would be more efficient if he discussed this with the whole team at the same time instead of with one employee at a time.

Thirteen phone calls, of which three are personal: The question is how much time he spent on these calls and whether all these calls were necessary, personal or otherwise.

Reorganizing stock room: This is Julie's job; let her do it.

Interviewing woman who is ultimately determined to be unsuitable: The question is whether prescreening might have determined that the woman was unsuitable or if Ricardo could have determined this more quickly than 50 minutes.

Repairing broken equipment: Instead of taking lunch, perhaps Marty and Karl could learn how Ricardo fixes the equipment and fix the problem themselves next time. This is a responsibility that should be delegated.

Typed up extra copies: Has Ricardo never heard of a copy machine?

Struggles with layout plan, ultimately pitching it: As described in the chapter, Ricardo needs to find a time to concentrate, focus his full energy on the project, and get the task completed. He will waste time if he continues to be frustrated and throws out each attempt, requiring him to start from scratch each time.

Trip to union hall to discuss grievance: Ricardo could have saved 20 minutes by making a phone call instead of traveling to the union hall.

Waiting for Bill to discuss time-management problem: The question is whether Bill or Ricardo was responsible for this wait. Did Ricardo arrive early? Did he make an appointment in advance or just show up, hoping to see Bill? Even if there is a wait, perhaps there is paperwork Ricardo could take with him and complete while waiting.

CHAPTER 16

CASE: PLANNING

It would appear that Gerald may be guilty of overdoing a good thing and stifling the creativity of his staff. Few people enjoy doing things "by the numbers." Yolanda, however, may be going too far in the other direction. The majority of high-level managers feel it is helpful and motivating to have written goals submitted by those in lower positions. Perhaps a blend of both planning patterns would be best, giving some autonomy to supervisors so that they express their management/leadership styles.

CHAPTER 17

CASE: PRIORITIES

As noted in the text, the two questions to ask when deciding this priority list are, "What is the best use of my time right now?" and "What commands my attention right now?" Clearly, matters that involve emergencies or that are urgent for other reasons should command your immediate attention. Family emergencies, such as the potential emergency represented by the electronic mail notice from Los Angeles, would fall within this category. Beyond that, matters that are of prime importance to your supervisor or the organization should command your attention next and should probably take precedence over the needs of peers, the employees you manage, or strangers (such as the person waiting outside Ricardo's office). If productivity would be affected if the matter is not addressed, such as the broken equipment, it is important to the organization and should be dealt with immediately. Many of the items on the list do not necessarily provide sufficient information to determine how urgent or important they are, so Ricardo will have to use his best judgment regarding how to align them.

CHAPTER 18

CASE: TERMINATION

Ricardo should probably heed Bill's advice and follow the steps Bill suggests to ensure that termination, if still warranted once the steps are implemented, is legally sufficient. This case illustrates the difficulties and challenges of making tough decisions and ensuring the decision is based on the best information available.

CHAPTER 19

CASE: INTIMIDATION

The authors favor parts of Option 2, with some important variations. First, Ricardo should counsel with Karl, at which time he should take a pleasant but firm position. Second, Karl should communicate the results to Bill, and during this meeting he should also take a strong stand. He should not, however, threaten to resign because he would be using the same intimidation technique on Bill that Karl is using on him. Such emotionally charged actions often backfire.

Supervisors who permit an employee to intimidate them lose some of their position power and effectiveness in dealing with others, thus undermining their own chances of success.

CHAPTER 20

CASE 1: CHANGE

The authors recommend a non-directive intervention for Brenda, particularly since she is a long-standing employee whose behavior change is relatively recent. Yolanda should engage in conversation with Brenda to explore the reasons for her negative attitude and inflexibility. Perhaps once Brenda feels she is being listened to, Yolanda can identify concrete steps she can take that will help Brenda feel more comfortable with the changes that are occurring. There may be other personal issues that have developed recently that are affecting Brenda's behavior. She is entitled to the benefit of the doubt at this point. Engaging in an MRT discussion may also be beneficial. Perhaps there is a different exchange that Yolanda and Brenda can discuss that would better meet Brenda's needs now in light of recent changes and the fact that Brenda is a longer-term employee. If a meaningful MRT conversation hasn't occurred lately, such a discussion may reveal new opportunities that will satisfy both Brenda and the company. Because individuals typically need time to deal with change, it will require patience on Yolanda's part to work with Brenda, which also means that a number of meetings may be involved. Yolanda is probably the best superior to assist in this process, though perhaps Yolanda can get advice from Bill and others regarding how to counsel Brenda, if she needs it. The directive approach should be avoided unless nondirective attempts prove unsuccessful and deeper performance issues are involved requiring correction.

CASE 2: DECISION

Eric is in a perfect position to prepare a Plan B. In fact, he should have started one some months ago. Apparently, he does not sense that it is ethical in this situation to play both ends against the middle. A true Plan B would prepare him for upward mobility in his present firm, but if things don't work out, he will be ready to accept excellent outside opportunities. Chances are good that by the time Eric has a Plan B ready, he will have solved the problem. One reason a resolution is likely is that in doing his Plan B, Eric will have restored his positive attitude.

Special Cases

The following eight cases have been designed to supplement the text. They may be used for classroom discussion, outside assignments, or for examination purposes. They are especially appropriate for those preparing to be office supervisors.

Students are encouraged to write out their answers out and match them with those of the authors found at the end of this section.

CASE 1: MATURITY

Before Barbara was promoted to office manager, she, Sophie, and Daisy had all sorts of fun during and after work. The threesome, all computer operators in the same department, frequently enjoyed going to the theater. Last summer they became even closer when they took a one-week cruise together.

Barbara was recently promoted and now supervises both Sophie and Daisy.

Although Barbara now sees less of Sophie (Barbara's new position is demanding of her time), the two remain good friends. Sophie has been willing to redefine their relationship. She understands Barbara must be more distant and structured on the job—she must live up to her own new standards as management—and cannot discuss confidential management matters after work. They enjoy each other as much as ever.

Not so with Daisy. Daisy resents the fact that she does not receive favored treatment on the job and that things are not totally the way they were before Barbara's promotion. Daisy does not seem mature enough to accept the change. As a result, Barbara is taking Daisy out to lunch tomorrow to discuss the problem. Barbara wants to keep the friendship and still play out her role as her supervisor. How should she approach the problem? Will she succeed?

CASE 2: IMBALANCE

Five of the six employees in Julia's department are frequently absent or late, receive too many personal telephone calls, and overstay their breaks to discuss family-oriented problems. Julia has come to the conclusion she could achieve a 10 percent increase in productivity if she could teach them how to achieve a better balance between home and career. Freda, a single parent with three children, is the only employee who maintains a good balance. Her productivity is measurably higher.

Yesterday, Julia took a plan to her boss who gave her permission to implement it. She will schedule a one-hour meeting each Friday afternoon (the hour prior to departure) for the six employees. The topic? How to balance home and career to increase productivity. Julia intends to rely heavily on Freda, who, despite her many responsibilities, has apparently achieved an excellent balance.

Will Julia's plan succeed? Can Julia anticipate improvements if open discussion of the problem takes place?

CASE 3: UPDATE

Yesterday, Jason discovered that the local community college would offer a one-time-only update course for professionals working with computers. He called the instructor and discovered that it was an eight-week program (three hours each Tuesday night), and that through individual instruction, each student could make substantial progress, regardless of his or her current level of competency. Classroom equipment is either comparable to or more advanced than that in Jason's office.

Jason has already decided to enroll himself, but he knows his six-member staff needs the training also, especially Marcy and Delphine. This morning, Jason asked his superior if the firm would pay the modest tuition fee for each member and, also, finance a "graduation dinner" for those who complete the course. He received an affirmative answer.

Jason is elated because he feels it will bring new efficiency to his office as well as make it a more cohesive, friendly group. His strategy to get 100 percent enrollment—which he will present at a staff meeting tomorrow—is to make it all sound like fun. He will also make a serious comment similar to this: "If nothing else, enroll for your own future. If you should leave our firm, you will need to update yourself on automated equipment to qualify for a job elsewhere."

Will Jason's plan work? Will he get 100 percent participation?

CASE 4: BURNOUT

Mr. Fisk, executive vice president of a large credit union, has received numerous complaints regarding the negative behavior of Reggie Davis, his office manager. Summarized, the complaints say that Reggie has become irritable, distant, and is unable to make decisions—all characteristics he has not displayed in the past.

Having attended a company-sponsored seminar on Stress Management, Mr. Fisk discusses the problem with Reggie in two different private communication sessions. At the end of the second session, Mr. Fisk says to Reggie: "The workload in your office is not greater today than it was a year ago, when you were in complete control. In my opinion, you are creating your own stress by not organizing your work. All you need to do is to have a daily and weekly priority plan, delegate more, and manage your time better; then the stress you feel will dissipate into thin air. You have permitted your job to get the upper hand on you. With self-discipline, you will be back on top where you belong and where we need you."

Is Mr. Fisk's solution simplistic? What other factors might be involved? How would you work with Reggie?

CASE 5: STAFFING

Jackie is in a quandary. Mrs. Q, whom she has trained as her replacement, has turned in her resignation at the worst possible time. Yesterday, Jackie got a strong signal from her boss that she was up for a big promotion if she had a replacement trained. Her fear is that management will now pass her over when they discover Mrs. Q is leaving and a strong replacement is not available. If you were Jackie, which of the following actions would you endorse? If you prefer a different action, write it out.

1. Through some strong private counseling, persuade Mrs. Q that your job is hers if she will just stick it out a little longer.
2. Accept Mrs. Q's resignation gracefully and start a crash program training a replacement. Tell your boss about your plan.
3. Ask the human resource department to recruit a replacement for you with Mrs. Q's qualifications.

CASE 6: TERMINATIONS

Your name is Stella, and you consider yourself a humanist. A highly competent and respected office manager, you always place people ahead of equipment, profit, and other business concerns. You are extremely proud of your staff and their high productivity.

Your company—currently going through a profit squeeze due to a decrease in sales—recently employed a systems analyst to make a log study of your office. The final report—discussed yesterday with your boss and his superior—recommends the elimination of three positions. An implementation plan is due from you tomorrow.

In thinking it over, you have decided to accept the recommendation on an "attrition basis" only. With a staff of 22, and based on personnel turnover figures in your office from the past, you calculate it will take only six months for you to receive three voluntary resignations. This approach will eliminate the ugly problem of terminations. If your plan is not accepted, you intend to stick with your humanistic values and resign.

Are you being realistic?

Will management accept your plan?

CASE 7: CHANGE

When Malcolm, manager of the eight-employee automated payroll department, returned from his vacation, he found his staff confused and upset. Apparently, a top-level management decision had been made to move the payroll department to an undesirable location in an old annex. In talking with the general office manager, the move was verified. Malcolm also discovered that an equipment supplier had been authorized to design a new, open-office layout for the annex. This, also, would be a major psychological change for his staff.

In explaining why Malcolm or his assistant had not been involved, the office manager said that his superior wanted to move fast and that the other departments involved wanted fast action.

Although Malcolm is distraught over the way things have been handled, he decides to turn the change into opportunity. As a result, he devises a four-step plan to take to the office manager next Monday.

Step 1:   Malcolm will request the opportunity to review the floor plan under preparation. If changes are necessary to maintain high morale and productivity, he will ask authority to make them.

Step 2:   Malcolm will ask permission to schedule two after-work meetings with his staff to prepare for the change. Each meeting will last one hour in the annex and discussions will center on enhancing the work environment. Through attendance at the meetings, each employee will earn a three-day weekend in the future.

Step 3:   Malcolm will attempt to use the poor way the situation has been handled to get some badly needed new office equipment for the payroll department.

Step 4:   To build a stronger company-wide identification for the payroll department and for him, Malcolm will ask for funds to hold an open house, with refreshments, once everything is in place in the new location.

How, in your opinion, is Malcolm going about turning change into opportunity? If you were his superior, would you accept the plan? Will the plan help Malcolm build stronger relationships with his staff and others in the organization?

CASE 8: TAKEOVER

Martha is pleased with herself, but she is also worried. The good news is that she has accepted a job as manager with a different firm at a sharp increase in pay and better benefits. The bad news is that yesterday, her first day in her new job, she discovered her department is a mess. Most equipment is at least a generation behind, there is a massive backlog of correspondence, there is no apparent work-flow pattern or schedule, and employee morale is at rock bottom. Can she pull things together?

In analyzing the severity of the situation, Martha feels she must exert strong, dynamic leadership. This had not been her style in the past, but she thinks she can do it. Starting tomorrow, she intends to stir things up, make decisive decisions, show a strong sense of humor, and generally create a new kind of working environment. Her approach will be, "A new broom can sweep clean if everything is upbeat." She intends to weave other skills, such as delegating, training, and so forth into her style at a later date. She believes the office needs an immediate and positive force to effect change. Nothing else will work.

Do you agree with Martha's strategy?

What are the flaws?

What are the dangers?

The Authors' Responses to Special Case Problems

The special cases presented were designed to be springboards for individual thinking and discussion purposes. There are no exact answers. Those that follow are nothing more than an account of how the authors would approach the problem with the limited facts presented. They should serve only as a guide to the independent thinking of the reader and discussion leader.

CASE 1: MATURITY

Barbara should be as relaxed, friendly, and non-directive as possible in her approach. She should state how important their non-working relationship is to her, and then give Daisy every opportunity to discuss why she finds it difficult to redefine their relationship under the new circumstances. If Daisy opens up on all aspects of the problem, there is a reasonable chance that she will learn how to accept Barbara as a strong manager during the day and a close friend after work. Either way, Barbara must communicate to Daisy that as her manager, no on-the-job favors can be granted.

CASE 2: IMBALANCE

Julia's plan is risky and will succeed only if her employees become convinced that by changing their habits both their careers and their home life will improve. To accomplish this, Julia must be highly skillful as a seminar leader and do some deep research so that she can make some suggestions based on facts. For example, a discussion on food-preparation strategies (especially where children are involved) could be helpful. Freda's ideas should be welcome, but relying too heavily on her, especially if she is held up as a model, could be counterproductive. If all goes well, Julia should be able to see some improvement in behavior and productivity within a period of thirty days.

CASE 3: UPDATE

Jason's plan may work, but only if he does not apply pressure of any kind to attend. Getting 100 percent participation is unlikely. Under no circumstances should those who volunteer be favored in any way over those who do not. It is possible that an employee who does not volunteer at first may seek to enroll later. If this happens, Jason's plan is working.

CASE 4: BURNOUT

Mr. Fisk may have discovered during the communication sessions that Reggie's problem is personal and not stress-related—at least as far as his job is concerned. If so, his firm stand may be defensible. Mr. Fisk may be getting tough in an attempt to save Reggie's career. If the problem is related to stress on the job, Reggie deserves a more sensitive approach. Perhaps attending a stress-management seminar would do more for Reggie than it did for Mr. Fisk.

CASE 5: STAFFING

The author favors solution two because it is possible more training time exists than Jackie realizes. Jackie is playing it smart to involve her boss immediately, and she should communicate that the new person already under training is a stable employee with long-term potential.

CASE 6: TERMINATIONS

Stella should be encouraged to recommend her "attrition" plan to management, but she is unrealistic when she places her humanistic values against the firm's attempts to survive financially. If Stella documents her plan effectively, chances are good management will accept her proposal. Terminations are difficult and usually costly.

CASE 7: CHANGE

Malcolm is making an excellent attempt to turn a disturbing change into an opportunity. If even part of his plan succeeds, Malcolm stands to come out ahead with both his employees and his superiors. Malcolm should prepare himself to "give" a little on some of his ideas. Step 3 should be eliminated from the plan.

CASE 8: TAKEOVER

Within bounds, the authors like Martha's strategy. To turn the department around, she must demonstrate leadership. To postpone or neglect the utilization of good management techniques is a mistake. Martha needs all of her management abilities plus her leadership skills to succeed. One big danger is that Martha will expect too much too soon from her staff. She should communicate to her superiors that steady improvement will occur.

Photo Credits

p. 4, goodshoot.com® ; p. 9, goodshoot.com®; p. 19, goodshoot.com® ; p. 37, Pearson Education/PH College; p. 43, Michal Heron/Pearson Education/PH College; p. 52, goodshoot.com® ; p. 56, goodshoot.com® ; p. 24, goodshoot.com® ; p. 70, Brady/Pearson Education/PH College; p. 74, goodshoot.com®; p. 85, good-shoot.com®; p. 89, goodshoot.com®; p. 99, goodshoot.com®; p. 105, © Dorling Kindersley; p. 106, © BananaStock Ltd; p. 113, goodshoot.com®; p. 117, © Dorling Kindersley; p. 129, goodshoot.com®; p. 131, goodshoot.com®; p. 145, © Dorling Kindersley; p. 149, goodshoot.com®; p. 156, © Dorling Kindersley; p. 161, good-shoot.com®; p. 176, goodshoot.com®; p. 180, goodshoot.com®; p. 186, Vincent P Walter/Pearson Education/PH College; p.188, Vincent P Walter/Pearson Education/PH College; p. 196, goodshoot.com®; p. 210, © Dorling Kindersley; p. 220, Steve Gorton © Dorling Kindersley; p. 223, goodshoot.com®; p. 236, © Dorling Kindersley; p. 242, goodshoot.com®; p. 249, goodshoot.com®; p. 252, goodshoot.com®; p. 260, goodshoot.com®; p. 265, goodshoot.com®; p. 272, goodshoot.com®; p. 277, goodshoot.com®; p. 284, Dave King © Dorling Kindersley, Courtesy of The Science Museum, London; p.288, goodshoot.com®.

Index